D1522922

THE BOYS OF MILO

Michael Williams

ISBN 978-1-6381-4431-1 (Paperback)
ISBN 978-1-6381-4432-8 (Hardcover)
ISBN 978-1-6381-4433-5 (Digital)

Copyright © 2021 Michael Williams
All rights reserved
First Edition

All rights reserved. No part of this publication may be reproduced, distributed, or transmitted in any form or by any means, including photocopying, recording, or other electronic or mechanical methods without the prior written permission of the publisher. For permission requests, solicit the publisher via the address below.

Covenant Books, Inc.
11661 Hwy 707
Murrells Inlet, SC 29576
www.covenantbooks.com

Sixty percent of the Milo boys of the Southeast Warren High School graduating class of 1967 served in one capacity or another during the Vietnam era. That high percentage was the norm rather than the exception for previous and subsequent years. Some were fortunate and embraced the military experience. Some were lucky and returned home unharmed. Some were unlucky and brought home the scars of war, both physical and mental. For others, the memories of war strongly remain some fifty years later, to the point of not wanting to talk about their experiences. Two paid the ultimate sacrifice. Regardless of which branch of the military they served, army, air force, navy, marines, or national guard, I salute you all. This is a brief tribute to some of the boys of Milo.

* ⭐ *

CONTENTS

INTRODUCTION

I have seen something else under the sun: The race is not to the swift
or the battle to the strong, nor does food come to the wise or wealth
to the brilliant or favor to the learned; but time and chance happen
to them all. Moreover, no man knows when his hour will come:
As fish are caught in a cruel net, or birds are taken in a snare, so
men are trapped by evil times that fall unexpectedly upon them.
—Ecclesiastes 9:11–12

L ike a pot of slow-brewing campfire coffee that has perked unattended for hours and hours, to the point it makes me ask the question, should I toss it or should I drink it? I've got to do something. I've elected to drink and stiffen my soul with its stoutness and remember a time that made me smile but, at the same time, brought tears. We are trapped by unforeseen events in our lives. Embrace them, discard them, remember them, or forget them. To each his own. It can be our rugged path of self-destruction or our paved highway to understanding. Drink with me, boys of Milo, and all who have known us.

* ⭐ *

I LIKE IKE

My childhood years were spent growing up in the small Iowa town of Milo. It had a meager population back in the early 1950s, just under five hundred residents. Not much has changed in the past sixty years, including the population. Life moved pretty darn slow for most folks in the community, and that was a good thing as I see it now. There was no racial diversity in Milo. Gee whiz, I never met a black person until later in life as an adult when I signed up for a hitch in the military. The same is true for Hispanics and Asians. I didn't know any rich people from Milo either. I dare say there were more working outhouses in Milo located some forty paces from the backdoor of many homes (including mine) than any of the newfangled Jacuzzi bathtubs. We all existed together in a safe and isolated bubble of tranquility.

It was easy to tell when someone was either coming or going to Milo. Roads in all directions were rock gravel, and cars left a huge gray rooster-tail cloud of dust as they buzzed into town. To the astute observer, the size of the plume that followed those cars served to gauge its speed more so than the speedometer itself.

And then things changed. The year was 1957, and Highway 205 was paved leading into town from the west and connected Milo to Highway 65 and, for the most part, the rest of the world. I'm not sure if funds for that four-mile strip of pavement came from Eisenhower's Federal-aid Highway Program of 1956 or whether it had been in the hopper for some time. Certainly eight-year-old boys weren't privy to that information anyway.

On a sidenote, in that same year, 1957, President Dwight D. Eisenhower welcomed President Ngo Dinh Diem of Vietnam to the United States for a visit. Ike personally met Diem at the airport in

Washington DC, a gesture only made twice in his presidency to any foreign dignitary.

If only the boys of Milo knew then how busy the traffic on newly paved Highway 205 would become, which took them out of their isolated bubble of tranquility and on a fateful trip that changed the lives of 60 percent of the young men who called Milo their home.

IS THIS HEAVEN? NO, IT'S MILO

T hinking back, what a charmed life all the people in Milo lived. As a young kid, I had it all, or so I thought. A gouge in the perfection of Milo's purity came on Monday, June 11, 1956. A lone gunman from Chicago, toting a sawed-off shotgun in broad daylight, robbed the local branch of the People's Trust and Savings Bank of $1,400. It didn't take long to catch the criminal. The Nebraska Highway Patrol arrested thirty-five-year-old James Kehler in Harrington, Nebraska, the following Sunday driving a stolen car. Warren County sheriff C. J. Richards assured the community, they had their man as Kehler signed a written confession. Everyone I knew called Sheriff Richards by the nickname "Skinny." Nothing could have been further from the truth.

Another terrible, terrible crime in Milo occurred forty-seven years later, long after I had left the community. On January 13, 2003, farmer Rodney Heemstra shot and killed his neighbor Tom Lyon over a land dispute. That shook the Milo community to the core. No out-of-town criminal committed the dastardly deed. It was one of our own who shot and killed another in cold blood.

You will find no statistics on the crime rate in Milo. Other than the two previous incidents mentioned, growing up there was literally a walk in the park. In 1516, Sir Thomas Moore wrote a book entitled *Utopia*. In it he described an ideal place, an imaginary society free of poverty and suffering. A place where everything seemed perfect. What a place to grow up, and I experienced all that in Milo. Even the 1989 Kevin Costner movie *Field of Dreams* touched on the wonderment of that ideal setting. In the movie, Shoeless Joe Jackson emerged from the tall cornfield, as earlier described by Oscar Hammerstein in 1943, as "high as an elephant's eye." Then Joe asked, "Is this heaven?" To which Ray Kinsella, the character portrayed by Costner answered, "No, it's Iowa." Call it what you like, but for me, Milo was Utopia or heaven on earth or Shangri-la. It was all the goodness gathered in one place, and it was called Milo. Even the German meaning behind the name Milo inferred mildness, peace, and calm.

Truly the entire town of Milo resembled a huge parklike setting where young kids roamed without any fear of danger. Milo employed no policemen that patrolled the streets. The biggest fear was some lady who witnessed any wrongdoing and called your mother. That's who dealt out the punishment, our parents. We had just one phone in the house, and our connection was a party line. I remember our phone number had just three digits, 6, 1, J. No dial, no push buttons, and certainly no voice-activated calls. To make a call, I simply picked up the phone and told the operator to whom I wanted to speak. My most frequent calls were to Grandma's house. As I said, it was as simple as picking up the phone and telling the operator I wanted to call Grandma. She knew and made the connection. There were no street signs or house numbers. Everyone knew everyone, and that was good. Keys were left in the car ignition overnight, residents didn't lock their doors—heck, dogs didn't even bark because they knew your scent and would just wag their tails, awaiting a scratch of their ears. Life was good.

I had a paper route and delivered the *Des Moines Register & Tribune* to about sixty residents on the south side of town. My uncle Dan, who was more like a brother than an uncle, as he was less than a year older than me, delivered to the north side of town. If my memory is correct, I earned about three cents for each delivered newspaper. In a week's time, I made ten dollars, and it was all profit. I was rich, or so I thought.

It was in 1960 that I reached the minimum age necessary to join the Boy Scouts of America. Man, oh man, that was such a huge social event. Milo Troop 136 had about thirty boys, and we had stuff going on all the time. Hiking, camping, knot-tying contests, gun-safety training, swimming, foot races, outdoor cooking, and about every other fun thing you could think of under the sun. I could hardly wait between the Tuesday night weekly meetings. Looking back, I must pay tribute to the adults in the community who made those days such a wonderful moment in the Milo boys' lives. Kudos to our leaders Bob Christianson, Jack Weaklend, Charley Rodgers, Dean Vander Linden, Joe Biddle, Eldon Nutting, and Merrill Mosher.

Nearly every weekend, a hunting or fishing trip became part of the agenda, depending on the season. My dad, myself, Grandpa Jack, and Uncle Dan packed our guns in the trunk of our 1956 Buick Special and headed off to some nearby timber or grassy slough in search of wild game. Squirrel, rabbit, pheasant, and quail were regular menu items at the dinner table. In the spring, the morel mushrooms garnished our meals, along with fresh catfish, bullheads, crappie, or bass. Looking back, we didn't hunt or fish for sport. We hunted because we needed the meat. In the fall, coon hunting season arrived. I didn't own a coon dog but had some relatives who did. Unless you have experienced an all-night coon hunt chasing the hounds through the darkness of night, with only the light of a cheap flashlight, listening to the varying tones of the dog's howls and using that as your directional compass, a void exists in your life. Basically I lived a life written about in some outdoor magazine. I wonder how many of today's teenagers have tasted squirrel or rabbit. I dare say not many. Skinning a squirrel was an art but didn't compare to the skill it took to carefully peel the hide of a coon so as not to damage the pelt.

Now let me fast-forward fifty years to the time I took my eleven-year-old grandson target shooting to teach him the skills I honed as a youngster hunting wild game, just outside the city limits of Milo. I shot hundreds of boxes of shells over the years and considered myself a pretty darn good marksman, both with the .22 rifle and the shotgun. Add to that my twenty-five-year stint in the military and firing the M16 carbine gave me a sense of expertise with just about any weapon. I can confess now that when I was just twelve years old, I illegally bagged my first pheasant, shot on the fly, with my .22 rifle. No, it wasn't a headshot, but it was an awfully good shot. Alvin York would have been proud.

Each summer, my church hosted an annual gun night where the guys gather to burn off some testosterone, shoot some guns, and afterward, incorporate some spiritual conversation into the evening around a huge campfire and then gorged themselves with hot dogs. My grandson, Tyler, helped me as we took our guns to the shooting range nearby. Already set up was a shooting table with multiple boxes of shells, clay pigeons, and a catapult. I made a second trip to the car and retrieved some lawn chairs. Upon my return, I saw that Tyler already had my twenty-gauge shotgun loaded and was in a shooting position. Before I could utter a word and say, "Wait a minute, let me show you how—" and then he shouted, "Pull." One of the guys from the church had previously loaded the catapult with the orange clay pigeons, and it was in flight within a second. *Boom!* He destroyed it with a direct hit. Then—"Pull!"—a second clay pigeon went airborne. *Boom!* Another hit.

I shook my head as I looked him in the eye and asked the obvious question, "Where in the heck did you learn to shoot like that?" It took me a couple of years to be that good of a deadeye shooter back when I was his age and many, many, many missed shots.

His reply was, "Oh, Grandpa, I have this as one of my video games at home, I'm pretty good at it, don't you think?" I had to agree but thought to myself, *I bet he can't skin a squirrel.* Oh, how times have changed.

In 1961, my dad, Curt Williams, organized and then coached the first Little League team for the town of Milo. Kids literally came out of the cornfields, much like Shoeless Joe Jackson in the Iowa-produced movie *Field of Dreams*, and played on Milo's Little League team. There were so many kids like myself who were starved to play on an organized team. I vividly remember the day my dad brought home for me a very expensive baseball glove he purchased. He paid $60 for the Rawlings ball glove, with Bob Skinner's autograph burned into the leather thumb. Bob Skinner played first base and outfield for the Pittsburg Pirates from 1954 to 1963 and then finished his twelve-year career with the St. Louis Cardinals. My mom absolutely hit the ceiling when he told her the price. He earned $80 per week as a furniture upholsterer at Ginsberg's furniture store in Des Moines. One can never truly understand the love of a father for their son and the sacrifices they made on their behalf. I used that ball glove through my freshman year on the baseball team at Simpson College. I only wish I still had the glove today. Great memories, great friendships, great kids, and the team was pretty darn good too. Yes, indeed, life growing up in Milo was like heaven on earth.

> *I must go on boasting. Though there is nothing to be gained by it, I will go on to visions and revelations of the Lord. 12:5–7. I will boast about a man like that, but not about myself, except for my weaknesses. Should I choose to boast, I would not be a fool, because I would be speaking the truth. To keep me from being conceited I was given a thorn in my flesh, a messenger from Satan, to torment me.* (**2 Corinthians 12:1**)

If the boys of Milo, who lived those utopian days, could have only known in advance the thorns that awaited them.

PLAY BALL

I started my freshman year of high school in the fall of 1963 at age fourteen. For me, it was all about sports. I loved playing sports. As an eighth-grade graduate, I was allowed to play for the high school baseball team the summer before school began. Football soon followed, then on to basketball and track in the spring. Sports was a great avenue of escape, not just for me but all the boys of Milo. I dare say, every one of the Milo boys participated in one or more sporting activities. We were teammates, we were comrades through the summer, winter, spring, and fall.

Our fantasy dreams continued, spurred on by the euphoria of small-town meaningless athletic victories on dusty ball fields surrounded by cornfields and grazing cattle, sprinkled with a spattering of fans in the bleachers. Sports tricked us then, much as it does the multimillion dollar professional athletes who perform in today's televised mega events. Our games played out weekly on the diamond, the gridiron, the court, or the cinder track. No, we didn't *play-for-pay* back then; in fact we would likely have paid to play. I had visions of becoming a professional baseball player and follow the footsteps of my idol, the Brookfield Bomber, Eddie Mathews of the Milwaukee Braves. Oh, the thought of being on the field with the likes of Albert "Red" Schoendeinst, Selve "Figedity-Lew" Burdette, "Hammerin Hank" Aaron, and the unflappable Joe Torre was beyond comprehension.

That same year, 1963, the Los Angeles Dodgers, behind Sandy Koufax, clobbered the New York Yankees in a four-game sweep to win the World Series. Koufax became the series MVP and, shortly thereafter, the Cy Young Award winner. Playing against that Yankees team, which included Whitey Ford, Mickey Mantle, Roger Maris,

Bobby Richardson, Jim Bouton, Clete Boyer, and Yogi Berra, became a mesmerizing event that kept this fourteen-year-old spellbound to the black-and-white television screen. If I could just throw a curveball like Koufax, my dream had a chance to become reality.

Perhaps because of my childhood naivety or the illusive dreams of a young teenager, it became so, so easy to feel impervious to the events of the world that would soon impact my life and those of my teammates. Sooner rather than later, our games ended, and real life greeted us cold and hard. It came at us, not as a soft lollipop curveball that broke away from the plate but instead a chin-high fastball that knocked us backward into a stumbling fall.

HISTORY 101

I sat in freshman government class, watching the clock on the wall, awaiting the bell to ring for dismissal. It was early afternoon on a Friday, November 22, 1963, only a handful of days before Thanksgiving. Our teacher, Mable Cole, stepped out of the room for a moment but returned within a few minutes. She had a very somber look about her, then addressed the class in a very matter-of-fact voice. "I would like to tell you that the president of the United States has been shot and killed."

As if on cue, the dismissal bell rang, which normally signaled a mad and noisy exit into the hallway. Nobody moved. Nobody said a word. Everyone looked at one another in disbelief. Finally someone said, "What?"

She repeated, "The president of the United States, John Kennedy, has been assassinated. Class dismissed."

What we didn't know at the time was the decision made by President Kennedy just twenty-four hours earlier that could have made a huge, huge difference in the lives of the Milo boys. On November 21, 1963 a draft, NSAM (National Security Action Memorandum) 273, endorsed by President Kennedy (but not yet signed), encouraged the United States to establish goals to phase out US military activities in Vietnam by the end of fiscal year 1965.

Dallas, Texas police captured Lee Harvey Oswald, the accused assassin of President Kennedy, within forty-five minutes of the shooting. A whirlwind of bizarre events followed. On November 24, 1963, while authorities transported prisoner Oswald to another facility, Jack Ruby, a Dallas strip club owner, approached the human barricade that escorted Oswald to a security van. He broke through the line and shot Oswald with a pistol below his left rib cage. An ambulance rushed Oswald to Parkview Hospital, the same hospital that treated President Kennedy. Exactly two days and seven minutes after Kennedy died, so did Oswald.

Two more days passed. Lyndon B. Johnson, the newly appointed president of the United States, endorsed NSAM 273. However, the Johnson draft of NSAM 273 differed from the intent of the document Kennedy endorsed. It stated:

> (1) It remains the central object of the United States in South Vietnam to assist the people and government of that country to win their contest against the externally directed and supported communist conspiracy. A test of U.S. decisions in this area should be the effectiveness of their contribution to this purpose.
>
> (2) The objectives of the U.S. with respect to withdrawal of U.S. military personnel remain as stated in the White House Directive dated October 2, 1963.
>
> (3) It is in the major interest of the U.S. government that the present provisional government of South Vietnam should be assisted in consolidating itself and holding and developing increased public support.

In a nutshell, President Johnson declared the United States all in in support of the government of South Vietnam. In 1963, the US had slightly over sixteen thousand troops in country.

Out of chronological order in the chain of events already mentioned was the overthrow and assassination on November 1, 1963, of the South Vietnamese leader, Ngo Dinh Diem—the very same man who President Eisenhower welcomed with open arms in Washington DC, in 1957.

The US denied any prior knowledge or participation of the coup against Diem. However, years later, released documents revealed that

US officials actually encouraged the South Vietnamese generals to follow through with their plot to eliminate him. Diem was deemed a roadblock for US goals in the region due to his dictatorial rule and disliked by the South Vietnamese people.

Webster's dictionary defines the word *quagmire* as a soft murky land that shakes or yields under the foot. Something that is difficult or precarious that may cause entrapment. Yes, indeed, that perfectly defined Vietnam in the years that followed.

* ★ *

SCOOTER HOCKEY

It was the fall of 1966, a crazy one indeed. I was a senior in high school and had the world by the tail, or so I thought. I even had my own car, a 1962 seafoam-green Chevy Impala. It had the standard column shift or "three on the tree," as it was called. Pretty cool, I thought.

Things happened rapid fire that year, which now seem like such a faint memory. Isn't it silly how nonsensical events stick in one's mind? The UCLA Bruins basketball team won their third NCAA basketball tournament behind Lew Alcindor, coached by John Wooden and Assistant Coach Denny Crum. The miniskirt became the current rage, uh-huh. The Beatles performed their last live concert on August 1966, in San Francisco at Candlestick Park. These events had no significant impact on anything important, but the thoughts of those events burrowed into my brain and just wouldn't leave.

That year in high school, one of the new rages during physical education class was the scooter hockey game implemented by Coach Dick Forinash. I had never heard of the game before nor have I ever seen it played since leaving Southeast Warren High School.

The objective of the game was similar to ice hockey and included a very short hockey stick and a plastic puck. However, rather than playing on ice skates, each player sat on a wooden scooter with swiveled wheels and pushed themselves in duck-walk fashion around on the gym floor, jostling with other players, attempting to get the puck through the goal. It served as a great aerobic workout and specifically focused on the leg muscles.

It was one such afternoon in the gym when the game was going hot and heavy and, to be frank, tempers flared just like typical ice hockey games, with elbows and hockey sticks swinging just a little too aggressively. Coach Forinash blew his whistle that marked the end of the second period of play and for player substitutions.

As I stood up from my scooter and headed to the bleachers for a much needed rest, I saw someone enter the gym from the vestibule doorway located at the southwestern corner of the building. The guy struggled as he made his way through the double doors, and it was glaringly obvious his crutches made the task a difficult maneuver as he approached our group. As he entered the gym, everyone focused on his presence. I saw a full-length cast on one of his legs that went completely up to his hip as he peg-legged his way closer. A few more seconds, and I thought, *Holy cow! That's Mike Crabb*. He graduated just two years prior. He was a senior on the Warhawk basketball team then, and I was an upstart underclassman. Mike lived just two blocks from me in Milo.

"My god, Mike," Coach Forinash asked? "What happened, were you in a car wreck?"

Mike never was one quick to talk, and his response took a while. "No, I'm home on convalescent leave from the army," he answered.

About three or four of the scooter hockey players all asked in unison, "So what happened to you, man?"

Again a slow response, as if thinking about what to say, Mike began, "I was on patrol while in Vietnam and tripped a booby trap along a trail in the jungle. Nearly near blew my leg off. Lucky I'm alive." Mike had been in Vietnam just two short months.

I noticed a Plexiglas window implanted in the upper thigh of the cast. I couldn't understand the reasoning for that but later found that it allowed the medical professionals to access the specific site of his wound so it could be periodically cleaned.

Needless to say, the third period of the scooter hockey game didn't happen. Everyone crowded around Mike and asked questions for the rest of the school period. Not many answers came forth. Mike was pretty tight-lipped about his war experience.

I reached out to Mike nearly fifty years later and asked if he could share his military experience with me. He was as tight-lipped then as he was back in 1966. Understandably so, the scars of war go much deeper than the superficial wounds of the flesh. I had the opportunity to meet Mike's son, Alex, who is an attorney in the area. It took just one glance when I first met him to know, beyond any shadow of doubt, that he was Mike's son. He certainly represented the spitting image of Mike as a younger man. Alex told me he knew I had reached out to his dad about his Vietnam experience. He also told me that what little I knew was way more than anything his father had shared with him. Mike remained tight-lipped about his days in the US Army when he served in Vietnam. There are many brave men, just like Mike, with their past buried deep within.

> *Are not two sparrows sold for a penny. And not one of them will fall to the ground apart from your Father. But even the hairs of your head are all numbered. Fear not, therefore; you are of more value than many sparrows.* (__Matthew 10:29–31__)

God infuses every moment and every event with a defined meaning and gives all the assurance that He understands what we are going through. I often wondered just why Mike visited his old high school back in 1966, while recovering from his injury. It certainly wasn't for sympathy. Even more certain, it wasn't for any type of bravado. I would guess it momentarily transported him back to a tranquil time, to a place he felt safe, to his roots, and to the quiet community in which he grew up. However, Mike's appearance that day at the scooter hockey game was a stark reminder, not just for me but also for many other classmates, that the door swings both ways. I and many other Milo boys would soon depart from our utopian life in Milo and take that trip down Highway 205, headed for points unknown, all the while dressed in fatigues, flight suits, dungaree jeans, 1505s, and class-A dress uniforms, ever conscious of our gig line, should anyone notice.

COLLEGE LIFE

I n the fall of 1967, I enrolled at Simpson College, located in nearby Indianola, Iowa. It was a small private college with about six hundred students at the time. Since my hometown of Milo was a mere fifteen miles away, I commuted to class each day. I carried a full academic load of twelve-semester hours. Tuition at the time was just over $600 per semester. I can't say I had a real goal in mind when I entered college. College simply seemed like the thing to do.

I plugged away attending class through my freshman year and academically received acceptable grades. That next spring, I went out for the baseball team but never had so much as a single plate appearance and only a brief relief pitching performance against Grinnell College. That was a tough pill to swallow. I had been the "big cheese"—or so I thought—with my high school team but got a rude awakening that gauged my skill level when competing against other college athletes. It was one and done for me. A good life lesson learned.

Pride goes before destruction, and a haughty spirit before a fall. (***Proverbs 16:18***)

Getting some quality playing time wasn't that big a deal, I reasoned to myself. Besides I had a part-time job at the local car dealership (Guy Hornaday Buick/Oldsmobile) where I shuffled cars on the lot, ran errands for parts, and cleaned used cars that were taken in trade. I attended class each weekday until 2:00 p.m. and then headed to my job for a four-hour shift.

I turned eighteen in August of 1967 and gained the opportunity to play the lottery. No, not the lottery to win big money but the draft lottery. It was my lucky day, you could say, or maybe not? My birthday of August 8 was drawn as number 48 on the list. What did that mean for me? It meant that if there weren't a sufficient number of other lucky guys from Warren County like me, whose birthdays were drawn before mine, I moved up in selection order real quick. One of my best Milo buddies, Ed Mosher, drew number 363. He was born on February 21. Ed all but pretty much had a free pass. He would not see military service unless he voluntarily signed up. I didn't worry too much about my induction status into the military at the time. Gee whiz, I held a (2-S) draft classification as a full-time college student. The classification to avoid was (1-A). That meant you were ready and capable of duty immediately.

A huge event in 1969 dramatically changed my life. No, it wasn't Neil Armstrong's space shot that put the first man on the moon on July 20, 1969. To me, it was something way bigger than the moon shot. My high school sweetheart, Judi Bishop, accepted my marriage proposal, and we tied the knot on August 24, 1969. She graduated from high school in May 1969, and just turned eighteen the month before. I had my twentieth birthday a few weeks before the wedding. What a wonderful decision that turned out to be. As Ralph Kramden of the *Honeymooner's* fame said, "Alice, how would you like a trip to the moon?" Together we took that trip and landed in the Sea of Tranquility. After fifty years of marital bliss, our rocket boosters are still a go. "Do you copy that, Houston control?" I definitely won the lottery with her, but I often said, being so young and dumb certainly had its advantages.

We lived in a small furnished apartment on the town square of Indianola, located on the second floor above a shoe store. I switched part-time jobs to earn another dime per hour, pumping gas at a local service station. I did minor automotive repairs, fixed flat tires, and changed oil. Judi got a decent job with Northwestern Bell telephone company in Des Moines. We were in love, and things seemed perfect, or so we thought.

Just a month or two into our marriage, reality set in. It took money to survive. My part-time job at $1.40 per hour turned into a full-time job to make ends meet. Subsequently I skipped several college classes, and my grades plummeted. I worked forty hours per week and only brought home a measly $50.

It was a Sunday afternoon, and I worked a twelve-hour shift at the service station (Lee's Rapid Service) when my buddy Ed Mosher pulled in for gas. He was driving a 1963 split-window burgundy-colored Chevrolet Corvette. "Holy crap, Ed! Where did you get the moolah to buy this thing?" I asked him.

"Willie," he replied, as he always had a nickname for everyone. Quite frankly, most were not as flattering as mine. He often called me "Worm," short for Willy Worm (a 1950s television character), which then morphed into Willie Worm, and then into Willie Williams. "You need to get a real job instead of this," he told me.

I mumbled back, "Well, maybe so, but I'm going to school, and this is just a part-time thing till I graduate." I didn't really want to tell him that I hugged this gas pump forty hours per week and had been missing class to work extra hours.

"I might be able to get you on where I work," he told me as if he read my mind about my cellar-dweller job as a grease monkey with dirty fingernails and a grubby oil-stained shirt. "I work at the packing house in Des Moines, lugging beef onto semitrailers. The starting pay is over $3 per hour," he fired back.

My jaw dropped. "How much per hour?"

"You heard me right," he said. "Over $3 per hour. Go apply. Feel free to use my name as a reference." And then he drove off.

I spent the rest of the day with thoughts whirling within my head. *Driving a Corvette and making three dollars per hour, wow! That is more than double what I make.* When I got home that night, I relayed my encounter with Ed to my wife, Judi. Grades for the first semester of my junior year at Simpson College were released just the week before. I was embarrassed at the results. I received an F, two Ds, and an incomplete. The high point was a lone C in English literature.

The time came for me to make a career decision. I wanted a piece of that pie. I liked Ed's Corvette, I certainly wanted to double my wages, and I wasn't all that fond of school work either. Easy choice, or so I reasoned.

But the cares of the world and the deceitfulness
of riches and the desires for other things enter in and

*choke the word, and it proves unfruitful. (**Mark 4:19**)*

Within a week, I had a job with Bookey Packing Company located on Maury Street in Des Moines. Ed proved to be correct. My starting pay was $3.15 per hour. I worked alongside Ed and a couple of other guys I knew from Simpson College, both were linemen on the football team. The beef quarter carcasses weighed about 150 pounds each, and the work pace was nonstop. It reminded me of a strenuous workout in the weight room at the college gym. Added to the rigors of lugging the beef into semitrailers, there was a crazy initiation implemented by the rough, tough, muscle-bound workers. I'd get tripped or bumped into with the quarter of beef balanced on my shoulders and fall to the ground or drop the beef. It seemed funny to everyone but me. I sat down to rest, my back and shoulders ached.

The foreman came up to me and said, "Are they too heavy for you?"

"Oh no," I answered. "I can carry them okay. It's just carrying so many so fast that wears me down."

"Well, I've got an easier job for you until you get used to the pace," the foreman barked.

My answer was, "Great! What is it?"

I followed him into the cooler where dozens upon dozens of sides of beef hung on hooks attached to rollers. The rollers were on a track that allowed the beef to be pushed instead of physically lugged to the doorway, then to the refrigerated semitrailers park outside. I thought to myself, *Oh, I can do this, a piece of cake.* The foreman, in his bloodstained white trench coat, brought me a short ladder upon which to stand. I wasn't quite sure what he had in mind, but anything had to be easier than lugging those huge sides of beef. He shouted to me, "The guys will be taking the beef off these hooks and into the trailers. The rollers need to be switched to the set of tracks that leads the other direction back into the cooler. Here, stand on this ladder so you can easily reach the rails."

I looked up, and it appeared the rails were maybe eight feet in the air. It only took two or three steps up the ladder to reach the rollers. The luggers came into the cooler, almost running. The first guy balanced the beef on his shoulder, I reached down and removed the hook, then lifted the hook and roller onto the return rail. It wasn't too bad, maybe the weight of a heavy bowling ball. Then the next guy quickly moved into position, and I repeated the switch of the rollers to the return rail. Then another, then another, then another. I could see I was smack-dab in the middle of another initiation prank. The line moved quicker, and the crew actually ran back from the trailers to grab another side of beef. I had no rest. After a dozen or so switches of the roller, my right arm gave out. I switched to my left arm to keep pace with the luggers. I switched another dozen rollers, and my left arm weakened. The line moved even faster, or so it seemed. I repositioned myself on the ladder and began to use both arms at once to switch the rollers. Suddenly as if shot with a gun, both my arms dropped to my side. I couldn't even lift my arms above my head, let alone pick up a roller and transfer it to another rail. The sweat poured off my forehead despite the chilly temperature of the cooled meat storage room. Everybody had a big laugh, except me. Again I sat down to rest. The day was nearly over, and I could not have been happier.

Day two for me at the packing house was very enlightening. Again I was positioned on the ladder, switching the rollers to another track. My arms and shoulders were absolutely killing me from the labors of the previous day. They were so weak I could hardly reach up and scratch my head. What kept running through my mind that morning was, *Three dollars per hour…three dollars per hour.* By lunch break, I was finished. I told the foreman if he didn't have anything physically easier than this, I quit. I lasted a mere two days. That was the only job in my entire life I walked away from, failing in the task. But it certainly opened up my mind. Maybe a college education wasn't such a bad idea after all? A job like this would make an old man out of anybody by the time they were in their thirties.

I went back to see my former employer, Paul Lee, of Lee's Rapid Service. He was thrilled to have me back. What got lost in my thought process was my status as a full-time student and my (2-S) classification with the Selective Service. All of a sudden, I became

(1-A) since I dropped out of school, and I was positive I had jumped to the top of the list for induction into the military. My game plan became simple. I would plug away working until I heard from the draft board. Also I thought if I was committed to work forty hours per week, surely I could find something better than the $1.40 at the service station. Boy, oh boy, what a naive thought that became. I submitted dozens of job applications, and the moment any potential employer realized my draft status, the response was, "I'm sorry, you're not what we are looking for."

My choices narrowed. It was too late to jump back into college since the second semester already began. My choices became army, navy, air force, or marines. I chose the United States Air Force (USAF) with an enlistment date of February 10, 1970.

Little did my high school buddy Ed know the role he played in my decision to join the military. I often wondered exactly why guys raised their right hand and swore to defend and protect this country. Mine was like so many others. Not much of a choice.

HISTORY 102

B etween 1964 and 1975, Iowa sent 115,000 men and women to Vietnam. Some were patriotic and dreamed of wearing the uniform of a US soldier. Some, like me, made a conscious choice—the lesser of evils—and chose the USAF over other branches. Others readily volunteered and signed up for a hitch in hopes of getting some training that easily transferred to a civilian job once discharged from active duty. Others were forced to join because of the draft, and then some became "ground pounders," carried rifles, and slept in foxholes. A few joined the National Guard or reserves in hopes of staying home, but those ranks filled rapidly, and the door of opportunity within those organizations quickly closed.

During WWII, the average infantryman in the South Pacific saw forty days of combat in four years. There is no doubt, beyond any question, that those soldiers were true war heroes. In the words of Tom Brokaw, a well-known journalist and former nightly news TV anchorman, they were the "greatest generation." In Vietnam, because of the mobility of the helicopter, the average infantryman saw 240 days of combat in just one year. It's unfathomable why the soldiers of the 1960s and 1970s are not held with the same high regard.

During WWII, two-thirds of all inductees were drafted into military service. During the Vietnam War, two-thirds of all inductees volunteered for military service. Just stop and think about that for a minute. Our country was not under direct attack in the 1960s and 1970s like the day which lives in infamy—December 7, 1941. The Vietnam-era American soldier stood as tall as any generation that ever wore the uniform of the United States of America.

Statistics revealed that 63.3 percent of all enlisted causalities in Vietnam volunteered for the military. When officer ranks were incorporated with enlisted numbers, the percentage of volunteer casualities jumped to 70 percent. Of the 2.59 million soldiers that served in Southeast Asia, 304,000 earned the Purple Heart for combat injuries. Iowa lost 869 brave soldiers during the Vietnam conflict. The average age was just twenty-three years old. Five Iowans received the Congressional Medal of Honor. There were a few draft dodgers, a phrase attached to those who avoided the military at all costs. Some even surrendered their citizenship and headed to Canada. I knew no one like that and certainly no one from Milo.

To date, there are 2,200 cases of missing in action (MIA) since the end of the Vietnam War on April 30, 1975. In contrast, there are still 78,000 MIAs or unaccounted for from WWII, and 8,100 MIAs from the Korean conflict.

In the 1994 book written by former president Richard Nixon, *No More Vietnams*, he stated, "No event in American history is more misunderstood than the Vietnam War. It was misreported then, and it is misremembered now. Rarely have so many people been so wrong about so much. Never have the consequences of their misunderstanding been so tragic."

OFF I GO INTO THE
WILD BLUE YONDER

It was a Sunday, February 9, 1970. I signed my enlistment papers and completed my physical exam a few weeks earlier. I had one stinking day left as a civilian. That morning, I walked from our apartment, located on the town square, to the nearby grocery store. There I encountered Art Wright and his wife, Carol. Art was a Milo boy too. He was a year behind me in school, and his wife, Carol, graduated in the same high school class as my wife in 1969. After a brief hello, how are you, we discovered that both of us were shipping out very soon. Art was home on leave after his initial infantry training and headed to Vietnam for his next duty assignment. I told him I was shipping out the next day but headed to Lackland Air Force Base (AFB) in San Antonio, Texas, for basic training. I suggested to him, "We ought to celebrate, don't you think? How about going out for pizza tonight?"

We all agreed to meet that night at the Pizza Hut restaurant on Highway 65 in Indianola. We were all just kids. Not old enough to even buy a beer. Art and Carol had been married just a short time, just like Judi and I, but Carol was already pregnant. We laughed and talked about the good times growing up in Milo.

Art was one cool dude. I guess television producer Gary Marshall possibly knew Art. I say that based on the fact that Art was the spitting image of Arthur Fozarelli, affectionately known as Fonzie, from the *Happy Days* TV series. Certainly Art was the template Gary Marshall had in mind for the character Fonzie that first aired on television four years later in 1974. Yes, both even shared the same name, Arthur. Art smoked cigarettes, wore the collar of his jacket turned up, and absolutely everyone—simply everyone—liked him, especially the girls.

After pizza that evening, we shook hands and wished each other well for the military adventure that awaited us. We both had no clue what fate had in store for us. I never saw Art again.

Monday morning, February 10, 1970, at O-dark ridiculous, I went outside and started my car, a 1968 red Opal Kadet, and warmed it up for the short drive to the military entrance processing station (MEPS) located at Fort Des Moines on Army Post Road. The German-made Opal Kadet groaned as I cranked the ignition switch. I thought to myself, *Not today, baby, please start.* After several attempts and the thought of a dead battery, it popped off. Maybe I'll make it on time. I had been instructed to report to the MEPS at 5:00 a.m.

It was bone-chillingly cold that morning. The manual transmission of my car refused to shift into neutral. The gear grease was so cold it had the consistency of peanut butter. I pushed in the clutch and waited several minutes until the transmission gear oil warmed up enough and allowed me to shift to neutral. As I waited in the car as the transmission warmed up, I blew two or three warm breaths of air into my hands, cupped over my mouth, that allowed my numb fingers to get a feel for the radio's knob. I turned to the early morning farm news on WHO radio, 1040 on the dial, and listened for the weather report. I found the station just in time. The morning grain report first, however, corn was $1.06 per bushel, soybeans sold for $2.35 per bushel. Beef cattle sold for $28.40 per hundred-pound carcass. "Holy cow, the weather, I want the weather," I shouted to the radio. "I'm no farmer." The announcer Herb Plambeck, soon came on the air and reported the windchill factor that morning at -50 degrees. I set the blower fan on the car heater on high, then headed back inside to warm up. I spit before I reached the doorway to our apartment. It froze solid in midair before hitting the ground. Yep, it was cold that day.

That very same day, Secretary of Defense Melvin Laird arrived in South Vietnam on a fact-finding mission for recently elected President Nixon who had been in office less than a month. The purpose of the trip encompassed a progress report for the Vietnamization of that country. Laird stated, "The policy of turning over greater responsibility to Southeast Asian (SEA) nations is a policy that will be steadfastly adhered to and could be called irreversible." He continued, "The accelerated withdrawal of US combat troops depended on three things, (1) progress in the Paris Peace Talks, (2) the level of North Viet Cong military activities in South Viet Nam, and (3) the moves of Vietnamization for the South to take over the major burden of the war against the Communist."

In 1970, the United States had 234,600 troops in Vietnam. That number was down by half from the high of 536,100 troops in 1968. US combat deaths in Vietnam tallied 4,221 in 1970. That number declined significantly from a high of 14,589 in 1968. It appeared I was going in on the tail end of the war. Thank God! The question then became, just how would I and the boys of Milo figure into the statistical data of the war?

I finally arrived at the Des Moines airport midmorning actually in great anticipation of my trip to Texas. A military bus shuttled me and about thirty other recruits from the MEPS the few short blocks to the Fleur Drive location of the airport. That day marked the first time I flew in an airplane. As I walked through the terminal, I saw high school classmate Roger Hasting. We talked briefly. He was home on emergency leave from Vietnam. His father had died. We wished each other well, then headed in opposite directions. There were no transportation security agents (TSA), there was no screening area with X-ray machines that checked the contents of my single bag, there was no concourse or Jetway either. With just a handwritten paper ticket clutched in my fist, I walked out onto the tarmac and up the rear airstairs of a United Airlines 727. First stop was Dallas, Texas, and then on to San Antonio. Hello, USAF, here I come.

BASIC TRAINING

I arrived in San Antonio late in the afternoon of February 10. Just as soon as I exited the airplane, two training instructors (TIs) greeted me and the others destined for barracks life the next six weeks. They seemed somewhat cordial, until we left the public area of the terminal and onto a military shuttle to the base. That's when the courtesies stopped. I can assure you, I never heard so many profane cuss words come forth in one sentence in such rapid-fire sequence since the time a cow knocked a gate off its hinges on my uncle Jim's farm that nearly crushed his hips. The cow nearly paralyzed my uncle Jim. Gee whizz, I did nothing to bring forth such scorn from the TI. I was just there.

After six weeks of marching and singing cadence, running in combat boots, push-ups, "yes, sirs," "no, sirs," memorization of military jargon, understanding rank structure, saluting protocol, multiple M16 firing-range visits, making a bunk with tight hospital corners that allowed the TI to bounce a quarter off the blue wool blanket as a means of testing the quality of my work, a couple of trips in the field and exposure to tear gas, stand-up in rank inspections where the TIs' eyes peered right through your person and looked for the slightest faults in dress or personal appearance, and of course, a quick course on spit-shined boots, I finally, finally made it through basic training.

We stood in tight formation as our TI called out our names and dispensed my first set of permanent change of station (PCS) orders. Technical Sergeant Hart barked out, "Williams, you're headed to New Jersey, and it looks like you are going on a direct duty assignment (DDA). Congratulations, soldier, you'll make a good fireman."

I didn't understand a DDA, so cautiously, I approached him after all the orders were handed out. He told me DDA meant a direct duty assignment, that I would not be going to a technical school but instead sent directly to my duty station, McGuire AFB, New Jersey. There I would be enrolled in an on-the-job training program (OJT). I had exactly ten days to report. I later discovered that the training school for firefighters was located in Rantoul, Illinois, more specifically Chanute AFB, located a mere four-hour drive from Milo. Why the heck did I have to go to New Jersey? I filled out what the USAF called a "dream sheet" that listed places I dreamed for an assignment. My mother lived in Washington State, so of course, I wrote down McChord AFB, Seattle, Washington. I got orders to the complete opposite end of the country. Go figure that one. I assumed that's why it was called a dream sheet. Nobody ever got what they wanted. I had never before traveled east of the Mississippi River, but that was about to change.

I made a quick sprint to the nearest pay phone on base. There was a huge line, and I waited my turn as hundreds of other new basic graduates phoned home and told their families their destination. Of the entire sixty troops in my basic training squadron (3703), I was the only married guy. I didn't want to call just anybody, I wanted to call my wife to tell her I'll be home to give her a huge, huge kiss in two days! Then I told her, "We're going to New Jersey."

As a reward, we were given a day pass to visit the historic downtown San Antonio that afternoon. Where do you go when you have $10 in your pocket, you're underage for drinking, and worried sick that you may be held back another week if you are late reporting back to the barracks on time? Yes, of course, one choice. We went to the Alamo. And this I can affirm, I truly understood the phrase, "Remember the Alamo." The same phrase shouted when Texans fought to gain their independence from Mexico in 1836. We all remembered the Alamo, but more vivid in our minds, we remembered our six weeks of boot camp.

I made it back to Milo in April 1970, for a short visit home, right after basic training. To my surprise, my uncle Dan Reeves, just arrived home from Vietnam after a one year tour of duty there. I was leaving, and in a sense, he was coming home. It was the only time we saw each other when we both wore the uniform. I wore the USAF blue, he wore the US Army green. We had always, always been pretty tight not just as relatives—being almost the same age—but as super good buddies. Dan was glad to be home. However, Dan was a changed man. I didn't totally realize just how much his demeanor changed at first. It was, perhaps, forty years later, when we rode together to the Milo American Legion Post 263 meetings and talked about our military past: where we went, who we met, what we  did, what we saw, what we hated about it, and what we liked about it, and, almost as important, what we would like to forget, if we could. Herein lies the story, *The Boys of Milo*. Please join me in this journey of great Milo boys who turned into great men.

HORSE MANURE

enny and Lucille Crabb of Milo had five children, four were boys: Jim, Jerry, Sam, and Mike. Their only daughter, Sandy, was Sam's twin sister. Mike was the Purple Heart soldier who interrupted the game of scooter hockey a few years earlier. Kenny was a proud man and well known as a hardworking fella. He lived in town yet farmed 160 acres southwest of Milo near the old Greenwood racetrack where he kept a herd of about one hundred head of Angus cattle and hauled rock, lime, and sand with one of his huge trucks in his spare time. When I think of him, I always see a strong guy that wore striped Oshkosh bib overalls and enjoyed every opportunity for a good laugh.

As a young teenager, I remember an encounter with him as I helped his neighbor, Loyicene Mosher. I cleaned out the horse manure from a small barn that housed her ponies. Kenny arrived with a fresh load a straw for bedding. After we unloaded the bales, the sweat profusely dripped from our foreheads. A nearby garden hose provided instant relief as all three of us took a drink of cool water. Suddenly Kenny put his finger on the tip of the hose and gave me a squirt of cold water right in the face. I jumped back, and he immediately turned the hose on Loyicene. She too got a cold squirt. I laughed it off, but apparently that was not the end of it. She picked up the hose and returned the favor to Kenny. I watched from a distance as the water fight took on a new dimension. There I was, a youngster about to enter high school as a freshman and found myself entertained by two adults in their fifties as they sprayed water at each other like little kids who laughed and screamed in the park. When it finally ended, all three of us were soaked through and through. Such were the encounters of fun and frolic in Milo. Good entertainment was cheap.

I know now what I didn't know back then. Kenny also served in the military. He was a hardened combat soldier who fought in the US Army against the Japanese during WWII, in the jungles of the Philippines. The fighting in the Philippines cost the lives of 13,884 US soldiers, with another 48,541 wounded of the 300,000 Americans who fought in the archipelago, comprised of 7,641 islands. My respect for Kenny increased tenfold when I learned of his past. How could someone flip a switch and forget about the war? How could someone be so fun-loving and enjoy life when they had a front-row seat to some of the darkest times in the history of the world? An even greater respect surfaced when the father watched as all four of his sons enlisted in the military, two of which would see combat in Vietnam with one seriously injured.

Behold, children are a heritage from the Lord, the fruit of the womb a reward. Like arrows in the hand of a warrior are the children of one's youth. Blessed is the man who fills his quiver with them. He will not be put to shame when he speaks with his enemies in the gate.
—Psalm 127:3–5

JAMES K. CRABB, SPECIALIST FOURTH CLASS, E-4

United States Army
January 5, 1960–December 15, 1962

Jim Crabb, the oldest son of Kenny Crabb, joined the US Army on January 5, 1960, at the tender age of eighteen. After he completed his basic training at Fort Leonard Wood, Missouri, the army sent him to an eleven-week advanced school where he earned the MOS of 631.10, a wheeled vehicle mechanic.

In April 1960, Jim's first duty assignment sent him to Schoffield Barracks, Hawaii, an army installation comprised of eighteen thousand acres on the island of Oahu. There he was assigned to the Second Brigade, Twenty-First Infantry Division. Nobody argued that his duty was a bad assignment, nobody.

Jim served two years and five months in Hawaii. He received an honorable discharge and returned to Milo on December 15, 1962. Jim died in January of 1998.

JERRY C. CRABB, SPECIALIST FIFTH CLASS, E-5

United States Army
June 8, 1960–June 7, 1963

Jerry was the second oldest of the Crabb boys. He enlisted in the army just five days prior to his eighteenth birthday and only six months after his older brother, Jim, stepped forward and raised his right hand. Jerry completed basic training at Fort Leonard Wood, Missouri. Upon completion of boot camp, he took an advanced course and earned the MOS of 632.20, a track vehicle mechanic. Track mechanics maintained vehicles such as tanks and armored personnel carriers (APCs).

Jerry spoke little about his military experience, much like that of his youngest brother, Mike. He too was very private about his time in the army and very tight-lipped. Even close family members knew little about where he went and what he did.

His military records revealed that he spent time at Fort Carson, Colorado, and then was deployed to Korea about February 1962, where he served for one year and four months. During Jerry's time in Korea, an event that gained national attention in the United States was the defection of Army Private First Class Allen Abshier to North Korea on May 29, 1962. He had been caught multiple times for the use of marijuana while on duty. He was slated for a court martial, but rather than face the charges, he opted to cross the demilitarized zone and defected to North Korea. Then just three months later, another US soldier, Private James Dresnok, defected to North Korea. He claimed the reason for defection was his fear of being sent to Vietnam. Fortunately for Jerry, his small-town upbringing in Iowa implanted enough sense that such bizarre actions never entered his mind. Jerry returned to Fort Carson and was honorably discharged from active duty on June 7, 1963, after exactly three years with the US Army. Sometime after that, in the early 1970s, he joined the US Naval Reserve unit located at Fort Des Moines and spent a few years with them.

I once again encountered Jerry about that time. I myself had just discharged from active duty and lived for a short time in an apartment complex located just down the street a few blocks from a television repair shop Jerry owned and operated in Des Moines. On more than one occasion, Jerry came by to fine-tune my color-tube television. For those who remember Jerry, one of the first things that comes to mind was his love for motorcycle racing. Jerry raced two wheelers, three wheelers, and go-carts well into his senior years. A vivid memory of mine as a preteen was the wheelie Jerry popped on his dirt bike as he roared past my house in Milo. He rode on that back tire for well over a block. That was Jerry, no fear, no cheer. Unfortunately Jerry died on January 6, 2018, at age seventy-four.

SAM CRABB, WARRANT OFFICER 4, RETIRED

United States Army
May 28, 1962–May 27, 1965
US Army Reserve
November 1, 1971–May 3, 2003

S am Crabb, the third son of Kenny Crabb and brother to Jim, Jerry, and Mike, became the first of the Milo boys that marched off to war and ended up in Vietnam.

Sam graduated from Southeast Warren High School on May 22, 1962. On May 28, 1962, Sam enlisted in the US Army and left for basic training at Fort Leonard Wood, Missouri, at the tender age of seventeen.

He completed the eight-week basic training, and after a two-week furlough to visit family back in Milo, headed to Fort Rucker, Alabama, where he entered the basic aircraft maintenance course. His MOS (military occupational specialty) with the army would be 670.0, 676.40, 675.10, 675.20, 151A, 160A, and 256A.

Just a month or so after entering advanced helicopter training, things changed dramatically. The date was October 22, 1962. What came to be known as the Cuban Missile Crisis changed things for

Sam and a whole lot of other soldiers. A U-2 spy plane spotted the construction of missile sites in Cuba with medium-range capability that directly threatened the United States. President Kennedy placed a quarantine blockade around the island nation as Russian ships approached Cuba. On October 25, a Soviet ship, the *Bucharest*, crossed the quarantine line. An aircraft carrier, the USS *Essex* as well as a destroyer, the USS *Gearing*, intercepted the Soviet vessel as it refused to cooperate. The US Joint Chiefs of Staff placed the entire United States military on DEFCON 2 (defense condition), the highest alert ever issued by the US military since the end of World War II.

Sam's maintenance school for helicopter repair stopped. The army issued him a weapon and placed him on guard duty at Fort Rucker. He patrolled the base guarding POL dumps (petroleum, oil, and lubricants), the commissary, and airfields. Guard duty was grueling and consisted of eight hours on duty and four hours off, twenty-four hours a day for more than thirty days. Others within the school at Fort Rucker were sent to Key West Florida in anticipation of military action.

On October 28, the Soviets began the dismantling of the Cuban missile sites, and the world stepped back from the brink of war. In return, the United States removed antiquated Jupiter missiles from Turkey. Sam and the entire world breathed a sigh of relief.

The army placed Sam in a holdover company. After more than a month in this company, he departed for a two-week furlough in Milo. In the middle of December 1962, he departed his home and headed to the Oakland Army Terminal located near the San Francisco Bay. His single mission there was simple—wait for his passport to arrive. He waited there for two weeks before it arrived. Yes, back in 1962, US military personnel were required passports when they traveled to Vietnam. At that time, soldiers were considered Military Assistance Command Vietnam (MACV) advisers that provided assistance to the South Vietnamese. Once his passport arrived, Sam departed Oakland Army Terminal for Vietnam on December 29, 1962. Travel to Vietnam was by air in a Pan Am Boeing 707 passenger aircraft. He arrived at Tan Son Nhut Air Base, located near Saigon, on New Year's Eve day, 1962.

As he exited the plane, he heard his name shouted aloud. "Crabb, Crabb." Captain Robert Lawrence, the commanding officer of the 339th Transportation Company personally greeted him to Vietnam. Together he and one other soldier walked across the tarmac and boarded a U-6 de Havilland Beaver, flown by Captain Lawrence. Within minutes, they were airborne and headed to Nha Trang, home base for the 339th. As they flew low and slow, Sam noticed holes in the floor of the aircraft. The Beaver was a single-engine aircraft that accommodated up to six passengers. Captain Lawrence observed Sam repeatedly glance at the holes in the floor and the ceiling of the aircraft. No questions came forth, and with nothing more than eye contact, the captain spoke out, "Bullet holes, ground fire."

Sam's thoughts wondered, *Why am I getting this special treatment? Why the fanfare greeting at Tan Son Nhut? Why the special flight to Nha Trang?* Maximum speed for the Beaver was 158 knots. The distance between Tan Son Nhut and Nha Trang measured 193 miles. The trip took slightly over an hour before it touched down to a crowd of cheering soldiers. Sam knew it was New Year's Eve day and, no doubt, a cause for celebration. He was wrong. Captain Lawrence told him that he was the very first replacement for the 339th Transportation Company in the last fourteen months. His arrival and that of the other soldier meant that two GIs would be going home. It was a joyous day as Sam's arrival was the ticket home for another soldier.

At Nha Trang, Sam became a member of the aircraft recovery team. His first duty with the 339th became a gruesome eye-opener to the situation at hand. He was assigned cleaning of the cockpit of a recovered helicopter previously shot down. The pilot had been shot and killed. Splattered blood covered the windshield, flight controls, and floor. Dutifully, and with reverence, Sam performed the menial but necessary task of cleaning the cockpit. The H-21 Shawnee tandem rotor helicopter would fly again with no evidence as to the fate of its previous crew.

The recovery team mission was to recover damaged helicopters that were either shot down or went down due to mechanical failure. As part of a nine-member team, Sam soon found himself in the jungle of the Central Highlands. On such excursions, a security team of ten to twelve Republic of Vietnam (RVN) soldiers escorted them and gave some sense of protection while the recovery team, armed with weapons and wrenches, made the necessary repairs.

On his first recovery mission, he responded to a H-21 Shawnee helicopter crash. The H-21 garnered the nickname the "flying banana" because of its shape. After traveling up a seven-thousand-foot mountain in the Central Highlands, the recovery team arrived on site. Lying on its side was the Shawnee near the edge of a deep cliff. Immediately they dug foxholes, set up a perimeter defense, and began the task of evaluating and repair of the aircraft. Each night, Sam crawled into his foxhole with his M14 carbine by his side, in hopes that the next day would be the last day before the job was finished. After five days of evaluation and limited repair, it was determined the aircraft could not be salvaged in its condition and location. During the next seven to eight days, the team cleared an area of the bamboo forest large enough to allow for a sling-load aircraft to hoist the downed chopper to a military airfield for repair. The military also brought in chemical defoliants at this time to open up the jungle area.

With a sling load, the damaged aircraft was lifted with another helicopter and flown to a secure location. Sam's team used machetes and removed bamboo trees and brush and provided a safe area for another aircraft to be brought in. During this period, they lost one or two RVN soldiers per night. RVN reinforcements continued to arrive. The Vietcong (VC) repeatedly captured them at night and carried them off. Their mutilated bodies were found the next morning. They knew the VC was all around them and watched their every move. Occasionally Sam would get a glimpse of movement in the jungle, but the bamboo was so dense he could only see a few feet in any direction.

A couple of days into the recovery mission, the VC assaulted their positon. The recovery team had no artillery support. Their only weapons were M14s, hand grenades, and a BAR (Browning automatic rifle). That first battle lasted approximately three hours. Gunfire, adrenaline, the smell of gun powder in the air, and sheer fear and terror was unrelenting. The firefight seemed as though it lasted the entire day.

The VC set the jungle undergrowth on fire in an attempt to push the recovery team into the open and away from the aircraft. The VC attempted to recover the remains of the crashed aircraft and use the components and parts from the aircraft to create explosive devices to be used against South Vietnam and American soldiers. When bamboo burns, no other sound compared to the *pop, pop* of the bamboo shoots as the hollow stems exploded and echoed like rifle shots through the jungle. With a twist of fate, the wind direction changed, and Sam's team set a back fire. This temporarily put the VC on the run.

During the mission, a sniper appeared from across the mountain ridge. He shot at their heads instead of their bodies. He was a pretty good shot as a lot of his shots came close! SSG Patterson, a Special Forces NCO assigned to their team, ordered them to the secured area of their compound. He came up with a plan. PVT Blackstone and Sam were ordered to climb down a side of the mountain to draw the attention of the sniper. SSG Patterson found a spot where he could get a shot at the sniper. Luckily Sam and Blackstone were able to create a diversion, and SSG Patterson eliminated the problem.

A few days later, Sam's recovery team captured a Vietcong scout. They turned him over to the RVN security force for interrogation. Sam stated, "I don't recall whatever happened to him."

The team ran low on C rations due to the duration of the mission. They radioed to command headquarters of their shortage, and C rations were scheduled to be dropped from an L-19 fixed-wing aircraft. CPT Montoyer flew the aircraft and received very heavy small arms ground fire. He gave the plane a lot of RPMs to increase his speed and possibly red-lined the aircraft engine before releasing the C rations. The C rations bounced in the clearing and tumbled down a very steep embankment. CWO James, the officer in charge of the mission, tried to send the remaining Vietnamese security group after the rations. They refused!

CPT Montoyer made another attempt at a C ration drop. This time, he approached at a higher speed and received much heavier small-arms ground fire from the Vietcong. He released the rations earlier than he wanted. CWO James had told the Vietnamese that if they didn't stop the rations from rolling down into the ravine, they would have to go after them. The C ration cartons weighed between sixty to seventy pounds each.

They fell from the aircraft at speeds in excess of 100 mph. Some Vietnamese ran out to catch the rations in midair. Sam ran toward the Vietnamese, dove through the falling cartons of rations onto the bamboo, and shoved the Vietnamese out of the way. A carton of C rations hit the back of Sam's legs and spun him around 180 degrees. Initially he didn't know if he had been injured since his legs were numb.

All UH1 medical evacuation helicopters were deployed to the southern part of Vietnam in support of operations in that area. There were very few medivac helicopters in country at that time. Medical care would have to wait for the trip down the mountain.

The H-21 Shawnee helicopter was a piston-engine driven aircraft. It had a reciprocating engine rather than a turbine engine and thus had a carburetor. Once the team stabilized the exterior damage, the task of getting it upright began. To sling load the H-21 out of the jungle the marines were called upon to assist. The marines performed the sling loading with an H-34 helicopter. The marine aircrew performed an aerial evaluation of the site. They determined the area was too hot, and they declined to assist in the evacuation of the disabled helicopter. The decision was then made to destroy the aircraft where it lay. The recovery team filled the damaged helicopter with as much explosives as they could spare and then called in the air force which later fired rockets into the helicopter to complete the destruction.

Once the helicopter was prepared for destruction, the recovery team prepared to depart the area. The trip down the mountain area was difficult and long due to the injuries sustained during the dropping of the cartons of C rations.

As they slowly traveled downward, the recovery team encountered the Viet Cong, and a heavy firefight ensued. After thirty to forty-five minutes and the loss of three RVN soldiers, the action ended. There was no count of enemy casualties due to the dense jungle area. Sam and the recovery team continued down the mountain and reached their vehicle transportation prior to the arrival of darkness. They observed as the air force destroyed the H-21 from the LZ with bombs. Sam's team then traveled approximately forty-five minutes to a fire base used by a RVN artillery unit for firing on Vietcong and NVA positions.

When they arrived at the fire base, there were two US soldiers and a contingent of RVN troops atop the hill. These army soldiers were assigned to assist and train the RVN soldiers on the use of the positioned 105 howitzer weapon. Sam remembered the sergeant as a burly red-headed guy whose character reminded him of Ernest Borgnine, the Hollywood movie star who, earlier, served in the US Navy during World War II aboard the USS *Slyph* and performed antisubmarine duty off the East Coast of the United States.

Sam spent the night on the hill and attempted to sleep on a bamboo pad in a small hut that had been used for a chicken coop. Sleep did not come that night. The 105 howitzers, with an effective range of five miles, fired all night long. The howitzer fired with the rhythm of a metronome, every five minutes.

Once back at Na Trang, word filtered down that the artillery encampment they had left a few days earlier had been overrun by the VC. Both US soldiers were killed and their bodies mutilated. The RVN atop the mountain also perished.

Major Miller, commander of the special forces headquarters at Nha Trang, nominated Sam and each member of the recovery team for the Silver Star. The Silver Star is given to those who show gallantry with their actions against the enemy forces during combat operations. The Silver Star ranks third in military awards, only behind the Medal of Honor and the Distinguished Service Cross.

It wasn't long before the recovery team received another call. In April 1963, another H-21 Sikorsky had gone down, and the extent of damage was unknown. The helicopter was intact with the exception of numerous holes caused by small arms fire. The helicopter could not be started, and the six-rotor blades had received damage. The blades could be repaired with tape (tape the army calls one-hundred-mile tape) and flown to a secure site for blade replacement. After troubleshooting the engine, it was determined the carburetor had to be replaced. The carburetor mounted on the forward side of the engine next to the firewall and in a very difficult area to reach. Since Sam was one of the smaller-sized mechanics among the group, he squeezed inside the cowling and reached through a maze of hydraulic and fuel lines and removed the carburetor for repairs. Alas, the job was completed.

The day after returning to Na Trang from this mission, Sam noticed his forearm began to swell. It became infected from the exposure to the hydraulic and fuel lines that dripped onto his chaffed and scratched skin when he reached through the small opening to remove the carburetor. Exposure to petroleum products, especially when absorbed through the skin, are extremely harmful and, if left untreated, can cause nervous system damage and tumors in the liver and kidneys. After a trip to the medics, some medication, and a few days in a sling, the swelling in his arm diminished, and Sam was good to go again.

As a helicopter mechanic on a recovery team, Sam made the rounds at various bases in Vietnam. During his time there, he completed ten aircraft recovery missions. Each and every mission resulted in encounters with the enemy. He spent most of his time in the jungles surrounding the communities of Soc Trang, Pleiku, Da Nang, Da Lat, Qui Nhon, Vung Tau, and Bam Me Thout. Despite his MOS as a helicopter mechanic, by his mere presence, he experienced many dreadful encounters with the enemy.

In 1963, the United States had just 16,300 troops in Vietnam. That year, 118 US troops were killed in action in the jungles of Vietnam. Those numbers soared dramatically over subsequent years and peaked at 536,100 US troops in Vietnam and 16,899 killed in 1968. Just as Sam had dodged the hazards of numerous firefights and falling ammo boxes in the jungles of Vietnam, his good fortune continued. In September 1963, just nine months after he arrived in Vietnam and three months prior to his scheduled rotation date, Sam received military orders that sent him back to the States where he reported to a newly formed division, the Eleventh Air Assault Division (test) at Fort Benning, Georgia. This new division was created to explore the theory and practicality of helicopter assault tactics. In the words of one of his fellow comrades in Nha Trang, "Crabb, you're one lucky son of a b—." After a two-week furlough back in Milo, Sam headed to Fort Benning where he joined headquarters, First Brigade, Eleventh Assault Division as a mechanic on the UH-1D (Huey) helicopters.

It was at Fort Benning, on January 3, 1964, that Sam received a knock on his door in the barracks. New aircraft were scheduled for pickup at Fort Hood, Texas. The original crew chief assigned to this mission lived off base in a mobile home. That day, his furnace quit working, and he had no heat. He requested relief from the mission of aircraft pickup and was allowed to stay home and make necessary repairs to his furnace. The knock at his barracks door meant Sam was assigned this mission as his replacement. A C-7 Caribou aircraft flew Sam and three aviators to Fort Hood that day in hopes of completing the UH-1D helicopter pickup and return to Fort Benning in a few days.

The following day, an infantry unit of the Eleventh Air Assault Division planned a static display for inspection of assorted armament and field equipment. It was no big deal as Sam relayed the story. The nine aircraft on the flight line (helipad) needed to be flown a quarter of a mile from the helipad to another helipad. The infantry unit could then prepare for their static display inspection. The crew chief, who remained home to repair his furnace, was assigned to fly in one of the helicopters for the short trip from one helipad to the other. When he and the pilot lifted off that morning, dense fog surrounded the airfield. The pilot easily spotted the helipad, visible below the fog, as he stood next to the chopper before liftoff. As the Huey increased pitch and hovered toward the pad, it rose above the fog level. The young aviator was a recent graduate of the Army Aviation Flight School and was not Instrument Flight Rated (IFR). The pilot missed the landing and attempted what is known as a "go-around." As he attempted this go-around and circled left over a four-lane highway, he did not have enough altitude and the helicopter skids caught the top of evergreen trees, went inverted, and the Huey crashed. Both the pilot and the crewmember were killed.

Still in Texas, Sam quickly got word of the accident and fatalities. *Holy cow*, he thought to himself. *If that guy's furnace had not been on the blink, he would have flown to Texas, not me, and I would have been the crew chief on that Huey.* He remembered back to the time in Vietnam where the falling crate nearly crushed him. Again he pondered, *We don't know why things happened the way they do, but they will be with you* for your remaining years?

On June 29, 1965, the Eleventh Air Assault Division (test) was inactivated to the newly raised First Cavalry Division (airmobile).

Sam discharged from active duty with the US Army on May 27, 1965. He returned to Iowa where he found employment with Brady Manufacturing, a company that made farm equipment. He worked there five years, and then the military knocked at his door again.

In November 1971, he accepted a position as an army reserve technician for the US Army Reserve. He once again became reunited with his favorite helicopter, the UH-1H (Huey). To gain full-time employment, the army reserve position mandated membership in the US Army Reserves. Once again, Sam was in uniform. He maintained that position until his retirement on May 3, 2003, retiring at the rank of chief warrant officer 4.

MAX L ROBINSON, SPECIALIST FOURTH CLASS, E-4

United States Army
June 8, 1960–June 7, 1963

In 1960, Max became part of the first graduation class of the newly consolidated school district of Southeast Warren comprised of students from Milo, Lacona, and Liberty Center. He graduated in May, and in June, he voluntarily enlisted as an eighteen-year-old recruit into the US Army.

Max went to Fort Bliss, Texas, for basic training. Upon completion of boot camp and advanced infantry training (AIT), he attended a course and acquired the designation as military occupational specialist (MOS) 716.10, a personnel specialist.

His first permanent duty assignment sent him to Fort Myer, located in Arlington, Virginia, where he was assigned to 1st Battalion, 3rd US Infantry Division, commonly referred to as the Old Guard. The Old Guard is the oldest active duty infantry unit in the history of the US Army and dates back to 1784.

The 3rd US Infantry is the official ceremonial unit that provided, and still does, specialty services for a number of time-honored duties. Included are the prestigious honor guards that escort the president of the United States, Sentinels at the Tomb of the Unknown Soldier that provide a twenty-four-hour watch over one of the most sacred sites in America, and military escorts for funeral processions at Arlington National Cemetery where horse-drawn caissons pull burial caskets of fallen military heroes. They are present at the arrival of senior dignitaries and march in parades as the only authorized unit that display fixed bayonets. The organization is the epitome of spit and polish and only the very elite soldiers—the best of the best—are selected as unit members. Its regiment motto is *"Noli me tangere,"* taken from Latin which means "touch me not."

While stationed at Fort Myer, Max met his future wife, Dorothea, an attractive Ohio girl who worked at the Pentagon in the office of the Joint Chiefs of Staff (JCS). The JCS provides the Secretary of Defense of the United States as well as the president with vital information about security and defense issues pertinent to the country. Dorothea mentioned to me in conversation about her and Max's time in the Washington DC area. "He was such a handsome soldier in uniform. I watched from a distance as he participated in burial ceremonies at Arlington Cemetery. It was a sight to see. All the pomp and circumstance were amazing." She went on to say that Max never marched at the Tomb of the Unknown Soldier but interacted with them daily. Most of his time during the weekday was spent in the office as a clerk where he handled correspondence within his unit as well as outside agencies that requested their services.

Max discharged on June 7, 1963, and returned to Iowa after exactly three years of active duty with the US Army. For a number of years until his retirement, Max managed the Sears store at Merle Hay Mall in Des Moines. He dabbled in real estate investments and became quite adept at flipping properties for a profit. Max and Dorothea had three children and were married for fifty years. Unfortunately, Max died of cancer in 2014.

* ☆ *

LARRY DEAN BENEDICT, PRIVATE, E-1

United States Marine Corps
October 2, 1961–October 1, 1964

Orville Kennedy lived on the south end of Milo and was a well-respected member of the community. I knew Orval pretty well. He was the Milo postmaster as well as owner and operator of the Milo Meat Locker. He was also a good friend of my father.

One thing I noticed about Orval as a youngster, when I accompanied my dad into the freezer section of the Milo Meat Locker, was the huge scar on the upper part of his left arm. For the longest time, I assumed he accidentally cut himself while working at the locker. Only years later did I learn that was not the case. He was severely injured in World War II during the Battle of the Bulge as a member of Company B, 51st Armored Infantry when a piece of shrapnel cut across his chest and into his arm. He came within inches of death. Orval spent thirty days in a London hospital before he recovered. His son still has the shrapnel as a keepsake and reminder of the sacrifices made not just by his father but by all the veterans.

One would think that Orval would be opposed to the military after he himself endured the horrors of WWII. Even though he rarely spoke of his time in the army, he certainly was not opposed to his sons serving, despite potential dangers. He was a proud patriot and, in fact, encouraged his sons to join the military.

Orval had three sons: Ron (known as Butch), Tom, and stepson, Larry Benedict. Within one year, all three volunteered for the military. Tom enlisted in the air force, Butch in the army, and Larry in the US Marines. I asked Larry what prompted him to join the military. His answer was simple. "My dad told me I *had* to join." I then asked him why he chose the marines. Again his answer was simple. "I had never been to California, and I knew that if I joined the marines, I'd be going to boot camp at the Marine Corps Recruiting Depot (MSRD) located in San Diego. It was an easy choice for me."

Larry left for basic training and reported to Camp Pendleton for basic training on October 1, 1961. Once finished with all the rigors of boot camp, Larry stayed in the San Diego area and was assigned to the S-1 Battalion at nearby Camp Talaga where he earned the MOS of 0141, office administrator. Larry spent his entire three-year enlistment at Camp Talaga. In his own words, "It was easy duty, I only worked perhaps three or four days per week and was given frequent liberty. I think I spent more time goofing off while outside the San Clemente gate than I did in uniform."

The most memorable event during his time in the USMC was his work on the military instruction manual, *How to De-Arm a Nuclear Bomb.* Larry, along with a senior noncommissioned officer (NCO) and a lieutenant, put together the lengthy instruction manual. None of the three authored the manual but became responsible for editing, formatting, and typing the document.

In 1960, the United States' inventory of nuclear weapons amounted to 18,638. In just five years, that total increased to 31,149 warheads. During the height of the Cold War, over 70,000 nuclear weapons existed throughout the world, primarily in the custody of Russia and the United States. Dearming and dismantling nuclear weapons, a most sobering task, encompassed not just the physical aspect of avoiding a nuclear incident but the global political impact and legislative actions required to curtail nuclear proliferation throughout the world. Larry played a small part as a marine to eliminate the nuclear threat to the world.

Larry discharged from active duty with the USMC on October 1, 1964, and returned to Milo. When he met his stepdad, Orval, he presented him with a gift he had picked up at the post exchange (PX). It was a book entitled *The Battle of the Bulge*. Orval looked at it, handed it back, and then said, "I don't want to read this. I've already lived it."

THOMAS D. KENNEDY, AIRMAN SECOND CLASS, E-3

United States Air Force
March 9, 1961–March 5, 1965

Of all the kids I knew in Milo that were older than me, I looked up to Tom Kennedy perhaps more than any other. Probably because he was a good athlete in every sport. Tom was a tall guy, six feet and two inches, and a physical specimen of strength. He also was the pitcher on the high school baseball team, and as an eleven-year-old, I attended every home game. As Reggie Jackson said many years later, "I'm the straw that stirs the drink." Tom was that guy in Milo. I recall the time when he hit a baseball that in today's jargon would be called a moon shot. As I watched from the bleachers, the ball hit the brick schoolhouse in deep center field. There was no home run fence at the Milo ball diamond, but if there had been, his blast would have easily cleared not just a high school home run fence but any Major League fence. Gee whiz, even when I played on the high school team a few years later, I never once came close to hitting the schoolhouse during a game. During practice, I'd stand on second base and hit fly balls to the outfielders and still couldn't get close to hitting the schoolhouse. Tom was a stud on the baseball team and pretty darn good on the basketball team as well.

Tom told me that a few colleges coaches had contacted Coach Lister about his ability on the ball diamond and the basketball court, but college was not in the cards for him. He confessed that he missed the second semester of his senior year on the basketball team because of poor grades. He went on to say that studying wasn't his cup of tea, and that the rigors of academia at a higher level likely would have not been very fruitful. Once he again, he confessed, "What was I to do beyond high school?" He wasn't sure which direction he would be headed.

His dad, Orval, strongly suggested, "Join the military and go find yourself."

Tom's sense of direction changed on March 9, 1961, when he enlisted in the air force and headed to Lackland Air Force Base (AFB) in San Antonio, Texas, for basic training. It became a stark wake-up call for him in many ways. Tom reflected, "Back in Milo, I had a lot of self-confidence about my own abilities. I was pretty good in sports, and those who competed against me knew it too." All that changed within the first twenty-four hours of basic training. Tom went on to say, "We didn't get to bed in boot camp till very late that first night, then early the next morning, about 0400. The training instructor barged in the barracks, turned on the bright fluorescent lights, and started yelling and screaming. He threw trash cans and banged on the legs of our bunks and rousted everyone out of bed. I thought to myself, 'What in the dickens did I get myself into?' Suddenly I was no longer a big fish in a small Iowa farm pond. I became just a tiny minnow in a huge ocean. The military didn't give a hoot or holler who I had been prior to enlistment. They became focused on who I would become."

Tom wasn't 100 percent certain he made the right decision to join the military, but he fell in line, marched to the beat of the air force cadence, and managed to finish basic training without too much disruption.

His advanced technical schooling sent him to Sheppard AFB, in Wichita Falls, Texas, where he studied the skills of a data processing machine operator, an air force specialty code (AFSC) of 68530. Tom explained that the data processing operator predated today's computer skills. "We entered information on punch cards, then inserted them into an IBM 407 data processor that totaled numbers with simple statistical tabulations."

Once his advanced training at Sheppard AFB ended, the USAF sent him to his first duty assignment to March AFB, located near Riverside, California. It was there that Tom found his niche and actually enjoyed the business office atmosphere and duty hours of 0800h to 1600h.

On October 14, 1962, the Cuban Missile Crisis, a major confrontation between the United States and Russia during the height of the Cold War, changed the routine for Tom. The USAF pulled Tom from his job as a data processor at March AFB, handed him an M16 rifle, and placed him on guard duty on the tarmac where he protected assigned aircraft from any potential unknown threats. In a nutshell, Tom wasn't too happy with the new duties. His eight-hour-a-day job in an air-conditioned office became twelve hours on duty, twelve hours off duty. The mundane march up and down the flight line while he endured the hot sun of Southern California dampened his love for the USAF. In Tom's own words, "What griped me most about the duty was the inequity of the assignment. The security police normally assigned guard duty were given a shift of eight hours on duty and sixteen hours off duty. I and others augmented to help out actually carried the bulk of work." Tom grumbled but did the job.

One particular day, during the fourteen days of the crisis, Tom found himself off base where he lost track of time. He knew he would be late for his assigned guard duty but hurried as much as possible. As Tom told the story, "When I arrived at the main gate, the security police awaited me. I couldn't have been more than half an hour or so late, but I was taken into custody and incarcerated in the base stockade for thirty days as punishment. Additionally the air force busted me in rank and took away a stripe. During that time in custody,

I performed work details where I cut grass, pulled weeds, and, on one instance, waxed the floor of the base gym. It wasn't fun by any stretch of the imagination. I got the message." Tom was released early from the stockade after serving twenty-five of the thirty-day sentence based on his good behavior. Shakespeare's quote, "It's better to be three hours early rather than one minute late," certainly rang true to Tom's ears henceforth.

Tom returned to Milo on military leave on August 2, 1963, and married his high school sweetheart, Judy Jones. After a month-long honeymoon, Tom returned to California and reported in at Travis AFB, on September 9, where he boarded a chartered flight for his first overseas duty assignment to the island of Guam. His wife remained in Milo.

Guam, the largest of the Mariana Islands, is located 5,800 miles west of California and comprises just 210 square miles. It was the home of Andersen AFB as well as Naval Base Guam, both strategic military locations in the Pacific Ocean where hard-fought battles in World War II took place as well as on adjacent islands of Saipan and Tinian.

Once at Andersen AFB, Tom was assigned to headquarters, 3960th Combat Support Group, under the Strategic Air Command (SAC). Upon his arrival, Tom experienced climatic shock. "I sweat not stop for the first three days in the tropical heat and humidity. It took a while to adjust to the tropical temperatures. Our barracks had no air-conditioning, just louvered windows and a ceiling fan. It drained the sap right out of me."

Once he settled in at his office job, he continued the task of feeding punch cards into the data processing machine, mostly with the production of paychecks for those assigned duty at Andersen AFB. Tom described his time there. "It was good duty, I couldn't complain too much, but I never truly adjusted to the rigors of the military."

Tom hadn't been on the island very long before he experienced his first typhoon. Thunderstorms and hurricanes back in Iowa never phased Tom too much, but typhoon Elaine, which hit the island on August 23, lasted nearly four days and pummeled the base with

115-mile-per-hour (mph) winds. Tom heard stories of past typhoons and one in particular that sucked a refrigerator right out of a soldier's barracks. Tom reflected, "We hunkered down and watched while it rained sideways for a few days. I won't forget Elaine."

While at Guam, Tom took his skills as a pretty good high school round baller and joined the base basketball team. There he competed against others within SAC as well as the swabbies on the far end of the island. He even took a trip with the basketball team and traveled to Japan and played games against the Yakota Air Base team.

In November 1963, South Vietnamese president Ngô Đình Diệm was killed by a group of his own army officers who disagreed with his handling of Vietcong threat to the regime. In Vietnam, the coup was referred to as *Cách mạng*. The United States knew of the planned coup yet did nothing to intervene. Back home, American citizens paid little attention to that event, but it marked an uptick for the US military in the Vietnam quagmire. Tom became acutely aware that things changed on the island of Guam. He said, "I woke up one morning and looked out onto the tarmac. It was filled with B-52 bombers, I guess something was going on?" As Walter Cronkite would say each night, back in the States, as he signed off from his evening news broadcast, "And that's the way it is."

Tom finished his overseas tour. He spent one year, five months, and twenty-five days in Guam. He returned to Travis AFB where he was honorably discharged from active duty on March 5, 1965, and returned to Milo.

In subsequent years, Tom owned and operated a small-town grocery store in Pleasantville, Iowa. Today he is retired and lives in Des Moines.

RONALD J. KENNEDY, PRIVATE, E-1

United States Army
August 1, 1961–September 12, 1962

Ron Kennedy was Tom Kennedy's older brother. Nobody called him Ron. He went by the nickname Butch. At one time, he dated my next-door neighbor, Shirley Burson. I frequently saw him when I attended the high school baseball games where he played first base or pitched on the same team as his brother Tom. Butch was a left-hander, except for one interesting ambidextrous quality. He wrote with his right hand, but other than that, he was a southpaw all the way. He batted left-handed, he threw a ball left-handed, and he shot pool left-handed.

I viewed Butch as a rough-and-tumble guy, and if ever I found myself in a pinch, I wanted him on my side. Some characterized him as stubborn, if not bull-headed, but well liked by those who knew him. I likened him to Popeye the sailor with a pair of strong forearms, who told it like it was, "I yam what I yam and that's all that I yam."

Butch joined the US Army on August 1, 1961, and headed to Fort Leonard Wood, Missouri, for his basic training. Shortly after he finished his advanced infantry training (AIT), he attained the MOS of 112.0, a heavy weapons infantryman.

In November 1961, Butch found himself at Wilkins Barracks, Kornwestheim, Germany, with the Seventh Army as a member of the 385th Military Police (MP) Battalion. The 385th MP provided law enforcement throughout the Stuttgart area. Additionally his unit manned Checkpoint Charlie at the Brandenburg Gate in Berlin which separated East and West Germany.

Butch discharged from the army at Fort Hamilton, New York, on September 12, 1962. He returned to the Milo area where he worked construction jobs in the concrete business for years. He died of a heart attack on October 19, 1999.

RONALD P. HENSEL, SPECIALIST FOURTH CLASS, E-4

United States Army
June 23, 1965–June 22, 1967

On June 18, 1965, Nguyen Cao Ky took power in South Vietnam as the new prime minister. He represented the tenth South Vietnamese government leader in the previous twenty months that led the woefully struggling country. That same week, General Westmoreland advised Washington that he needed more American soldiers than previously approved and proposed that the US bomb the railroad from North Vietnam to China, mine Haiphong harbor, and carry out B-52 strikes.

Milo boy Ron Hensel graduated from high school in May 1962 and soon enrolled in the Iowa Barber College. He began a lifelong career as a barber in Indianola in 1963. Less than two years into his profession, Uncle Sam called for his services. Ron began his military tour of duty on June 23, 1965, when drafted into the US Army. He became one of the "additional" soldiers General Westmoreland requested. Ron represented the Milo boy persona perhaps as much as anyone could imagine. His father, Don, served as the Milo mayor, and his mother, Betty, at one time worked as the Milo postmaster.

The draft board informed Ron that a taxicab would pick him up at the Warren Hotel, located just off the southeast corner of the Indianola town square on Wednesday, June 23. He would then be transported to the MEPS center at Fort Des Moines for processing. As Ron arrived a few minutes late to the hotel, he noticed the taxicab as it pulled away with no passengers onboard.

As the army phrase went, "If you're early, you're on time, if you're on time, you're late." Ron was late and then some. Ron had his mother drive him to Fort Des Moines in his recently purchased 1965 green Chevrolet Impala.

Ron attended basic training at Fort Leonard Wood, Missouri, slightly more than three hundred miles south of Milo, and just a short five-hour drive into the "Show Me" State. Oh no, Ron didn't make the drive South; he, too, took his first airplane ride to Kansas City and then bussed to Fort Leonard Wood.

On August 2, 1965, Ron turned age twenty-one. Already several weeks into his basic training indoctrination, his blistered heels reminded him that army life was not a bed of roses. His parents knew the significance of that day as well and planned an unannounced trip to visit their only son. Ron reflected on that moment some fifty years later. "Mom and Dad drove down to visit me on my birthday. They brought along a small sack of Iowa homegrown tomatoes. They knew I loved tomato sandwiches with mayonnaise. They thought I'd get to spend the day with them, a Monday. The army allowed us to see one another for perhaps fifteen minutes. I never got to eat the tomato sandwiches. Perhaps the drill instructor thought I had not yet earned my pound of salt."

> *You are the salt of the earth, but if salt has lost its taste, how shall its saltiness be restored? It is no longer good for anything except to be thrown out and trampled under people's feet.* (**Matthew 5:13**)

"Whatever the case," he continued, "it became the first of many military lessons learned during my time in the army." *You're in the army now, you're not behind a plow, you'll never get rich, you son of a b%#&h, you're in the army now.*

September 1965, saw Ron report to his advanced training school at Fort Gordon, Georgia, the 504th Military Police Company, located just a few miles southwest of Augusta, Georgia. His MOS became 95 Bravo. The US Army molded him into a military police-man, better known as an MP.

In November 1965, Ron finished his initial MP training and received his first duty assignment. A very high percentage of MPs during that time were destined for duty in Vietnam. As luck would have it, Ron's assignment sent him to Europe. There he was assigned to a Cold War missile site, Rheinbollen, located in Dichtelbach, Germany. He served there just six months before new marching orders sent him in another direction.

In April 1966, the US Army selected MP Hensel for mandatory cross-training to a new MOS, as an 88H, stevedore. Stevedores are the military version of a longshoreman that handle cargo on ships, onloading and offloading material. His new duty assignment sent him to Fort Eustis, Virginia. Fort Eustis was located adjacent to Langley AFB, near Newport News.

There Ron spent time in the Chesapeake Bay, aboard a LARC (light amphibious resupply cargo) ship honing the skills of maneuvering cargo from one LARC to another or from dockside to a LARC. The initial training period consisted of eight weeks of classroom as well as field training. Just prior to completion of the 88H stevedore school, Ron received orders to Vietnam. As he figured, it was just a matter of time anyway before he would be headed to Southeast Asia (SEA).

A twelfth-century French theologian, Alain de Lille, wrote, *"Mille viae ducunt homines per saecula Romam,"* (a thousand roads lead men forever to Rome). Back in 1966, however, especially if you were in the US military, all roads didn't lead to Rome, but instead, they led directly to Vietnam. Just like the unlucky draw card in the board game of Monopoly which read, "Go directly to jail, do not go past 'GO,' and do not collect $200." Ron wasn't headed to jail; he was headed to Vietnam. Like so many soldiers, it was pure luck, and he drew the short straw.

Ron became resigned to his fate. He was reluctant to tell his parents of his new assignment in the army. Then there came a moment of divine intervention. A surprise out of nowhere that so impacted Ron, there were no words to describe his emotions.

> The anger of the Lord will not turn back until He has executed and accomplished the intents of His heart. In the later days you will understand it clearly. **(Jeremiah 23:20)**

Just two weeks before his scheduled departure to Vietnam, word came that Fort Eustis would be receiving a large influx of troops slated for training. Things began to ramp up for the US Army's continued involvement in Vietnam. As a result of the pending increased troop presence at Fort Eustis, the need for additional MPs became a priority. For Ron, it became a simple matter of being in the right place at the right time. He was already a qualified and trained MP. He was already assigned to Fort Eustis. His orders to Vietnam were cancelled. Yes, indeed, this time, he exchanged his short straw for one of the longest in the bundle.

Ron finished his two-year enlistment in the army as an MP at Fort Eustis, not a stevedore in Vietnam, but an MP assigned Stateside. Ron fulfilled his military obligation as a draftee and was honorably discharged from active duty on June 22, 1967. Today Ron resides in Montezuma, Iowa. There he maintains his small-town barbershop located on the west side of the town square. Ron is active in the Montezuma American Legion Post 169.

RONALD BURSON, SENIOR MASTER SERGEANT, RETIRED

United States Air Force
August 16, 1965–March 15, 1999

R on Burson was the kid next-door when I grew up in Milo. He was three years older than me. I never once called him by his given name, Ron. I always knew him as Rusty. His parents, George and Mable, always called him Rusty, as well as his older sisters, Coleen, Connie, and Shirley. It was some time later in life for me that I became aware of his real name, Ronald. The nickname Rusty is usually given to someone with red hair or a ruddy complexion. Neither was the case for Rusty. He had dark hair and fair skin. I would guess the nickname likely came from somewhere else. Wikipedia explained that those with the nickname Rusty tend to be a powerful force to all whose lives they touched. They are capable charismatic leaders who often undertake large endeavors with great success. They value truth, justice, and discipline, and may be quick-tempered with those who do not. That's the Rusty Burson I knew for the last sixty years, a real stand-up guy and a straight shooter.

Rusty joined the USAF on August 16, 1965, just one year after he graduated from high school. He did basic training at Lackland AFB, Texas. After six quick weeks of boot camp, he too received a direct duty assignment (DDA) to Edwards AFB, California, where he began his military career as an air operations specialist. His air force specialty code (AFSC) was 271X0.

The duties of an air operations specialist included flight planning guidance, flight records and data coordination, standard evaluation, and airfield operational management. In a nutshell, Rusty kept his finger on virtually every aspect of aircraft movements generated from Edwards AFB. That was a huge task since Edwards AFB was the hub of activity for the majority of experimental aircraft in the USAF inventory. Rusty had a bird's-eye view of unique and cutting-edge aircraft most aviators only saw in photographs and read about in magazines.

The X-15 flew at Edwards AFB during Rusty's time at the base. The X-15 was a hypersonic-rocket-powered aircraft that set the airspeed record of Mach 6.72 (4,520 mph) at an altitude of 102,100 feet. Because of its high-fuel consumption, the USAF launched the X-15 from the underbelly of a B-52 mothership at 45,000 feet, usually at a speed of 500 mph. Its rocket engine only provided thrust for up to 120 seconds, and its flight lasted only 12–15 minutes, and landed in a controlled 200-mph glide onto a dry lake bed. During the X-15 program, thirteen flights exceeded the 50-mile-altitude threshold, and the eight pilots immediately received astronaut wings. Neil Armstrong and Robert White were two of fifteen pilots that flew the X-15 at Edwards AFB and later became icons in spacecraft history.

Another cutting-edge aircraft that flew out of Edwards was the XB-70A Valkyrie, a six-engine bomber that flew at speeds of Mach 3 with an altitude of seventy thousand feet. Only two prototype Valkyries ever flew. During Rusty's time at Edwards, one crashed in 1966 while in formation flight when it clipped wings with a smaller aircraft. The only other surviving XB-70A can be found at the Wright-Patterson AFB museum in Dayton, Ohio. Rusty commented that the XB-70 crash began a bad week of flying at Edwards AFB when seven aircraft crashed in seven days.

The YF-12, a twin-seat version of the SR-71 Blackbird, a secret reconnaissance aircraft, also flew during Rusty's stint as an air operations specialist at Edwards AFB. It once held the speed record of 2,000 mph and eighty-thousand-feet altitude.

Another unique aircraft stationed there was the M-2F1 lift body. This aircraft had a wingless lifting body airframe and was referred to as the flying bathtub. The wingless design concept was conceived as a horizontal means of landing a spacecraft. Airman Burson had a front-row seat to some amazing aeronautical history, and for anyone who was an aviation fanatic, the diversity of aircraft that passed through Edwards encompassed about every imaginable fixed-wing aircraft in the USAF inventory.

On June 1, 1967, Rusty received permanent change of station (PCS) orders to Stuttgart, Germany. After some time off to visit family in Milo, he arrived in Germany on July 1, 1967. There he provided operational support for aircraft assigned to SHAPE (Supreme Headquarters Allied Powers Europe). Stuttgart was best known as the manufacturing location of the German cars, Mercedes-Benz and Porsche, and an ideal tourism location.

His time in Europe wasn't without some excitement. In 1968, Rusty caught a military hop on a T-39 Saberliner from Stuttgart to Torrejon Air Base, Spain. The T-39 was a military jet passenger aircraft that primarily shuttled dignitaries on short-range travels. Rusty was lucky enough to find an empty seat among the four available. The distance between Stuttgart and Torrejon measured just 613 miles. Shortly after takeoff, the aircrew announced an in-flight emergency. The aircraft lost power on one of the two engines. The Extended Twin Engine Operations (ETOPS) rating for the T-39 was about 120 minutes, more than adequate time to stay airborne at a lower altitude and airspeed to accommodate an uneventful landing. Rusty didn't know that, so he cinched his seat belt tighter. Thoughts of his time at Edwards AFB raced through his mind as he remembered all aircraft crashes there which were a common thing. He glaringly knew that. He personally witnessed numerous aircrafts that dropped unexpectedly from the sky with disastrous results that had problems less significant than the T-39 he was aboard. He just hoped and prayed to

God that the Saberliner would land without incident. It finally made a successful landing, and Rusty couldn't get off the aircraft soon enough. *Wow! A close call*, he thought. *Perhaps taking the Eurorail train back to Germany might be a strong possibility.*

The year 1968 proved to be a bad one for Rusty. In addition to his near disaster (in his mindset) on the T-39, he got word that a dear friend of his, Gene Hendricks from Plainfield, New Jersey, had been killed on October 21, 1968, when the C-47 aircraft he was aboard crashed in Darlak, South Vietnam. Gene and Rusty went through basic training together. Both were later stationed together at Edwards AFB and worked at base operations. Rusty got PCS orders to Germany on June 1, 1967, his good buddy Gene got orders to Vietnam in October that same year.

Many a soldier wrestled with the question, "Why him and not me?" Life and death should be more than a flip of a coin. That question still lingers in Rusty's mind today.

> *And they said to one another, "Come, let us cast lots, that we may know on whose account this evil has come upon us." So they cast lots, and the lot fell on Jonah.* (**Jonah 1:7**)

Rusty's tour of duty at Stuttgart lasted twenty-five months. He then returned to McGuire AFB, New Jersey, on August 9, 1969, where he discharged from active duty as a staff sergeant.

In March of 1973, Rusty joined the Iowa Air National Guard (IANG) at its Des Moines location. With his initial enlistment with the IANG, he again worked in the base operations section with the 132nd Tactical Fighter Wing. In December that year, he accepted a job with the IANG as an air technician. The air technician status provided civilian Department of Defense (DOD) employment contingent with his status as a traditional guardsman. That same year, he cross-trained to an administrative position in the publishing and distribution office (PDO) where he worked as an offset press operator. He served in that capacity for four years.

In 1978, at the personal request of Colonel Jerry Swartzbaugh, commander of the 124th Tactical Fighter Squadron, Rusty transferred back into base operations. With the unit's conversion to the A-7 Corsair aircraft in 1976 and an increased operational tempo, Rusty's active duty experience and expertise in the area of flight operations facilitated a smooth transition for the unit's new aircraft, affectionately called the SLUF (slow ugly *fellow*), from the unit's previous aircraft, the F-100 Super Sabre. The pilot slang for the outgoing F-100 characterized the aircraft with two simple words: *lead sled*. The air operational tempo at Des Moines upticked significantly with the A-7 but was mild compared to flight activity Rusty experienced during his tour of duty at Edwards AFB.

An advancement opportunity surfaced in 1986. Rusty assumed the position of the base training NCO and held that position until his retirement in March of 1999 with the rank of senior master sergeant. That thirteen-year stint in the training office proved to be a challenging one. During that period, the IANG, as well as the USAF, saw tremendous changes regarding upgrade training and professional military education (PME). There were times when advancement through the rank structure hinged on correspondence courses for technical knowledge in any given career field. Those career-development courses (CDCs) included study manuals and monitored classroom testing. During Rusty's time as the base training NCO, the computer age within the military burst upon the scene and dramatically changed the educational atmosphere. Word processing capabilities and online testing facilitated a new era for military training. PME already existed, but a new awareness of its impact on leadership within the military became the key criteria for promotion, coupled with high test scores in technical job skills. Airman leadership school (ALS) as well as the NCO academy, the Senior NCO Academy, and the CMSgt Leardership course became the avenue for advancement. That, combined with the Community College of the Air Force (CCAF) program, which offered associate college degrees for specific careers within the USAF, elevated the quality of individuals with the IANG and the USAF. Gone were the days of the "good old boy" promotions.

Added to the hectic pace of routine training requirements, the 132rd Fighter Wing underwent an aircraft conversion between 1989 and 1990. The 1965 vintage A-7 Corsair aircraft the unit flew since 1976 departed and headed to the boneyard located at Davis-Monthan AFB, Arizona. The new F-16 Falcon became the unit's primary aircraft. Lieutenant Colonel Al Reeve flew the first F-16 sortie for the 132rd Fight Wing in December 1990. That conversion of aircraft required hundreds of maintenance personnel to cross-train to the F-16. Of the one thousand members of the unit, about half were in the maintenance squadron and required some form of retraining. Those maintenance personnel attended lengthy in-residence schooling at various locations across the country. As the training NCO, Rusty coordinated and oversaw all the educational adjustments required to put the F-16 in the air. That was no small task by any stretch of the imagination.

Since his retirement from the military in March 1999, Rusty continued his relationship with the military. He is currently the director of the Warren County Veterans Affairs.

JAMES FRANKLIN SPENCER, SPECIALIST FOURTH CLASS, E-4

United States Army
September 13, 1965–September 12, 1967

Jim was four years older than me. He lived in the country a few miles southwest of town and the third oldest of eleven kids. We first met on the high school baseball team in the summer of 1962. Jim was headed for his senior year in high school. I had just finished seventh grade and about to turn thirteen. Unfortunately I was too old for Little League and too young for high school ball. However, I made every home high school game and always sat on the bench, as if a member of the team. I became the official bat boy, and Coach Gerald Lister rewarded my loyalty with a uniform. The community schools of Milo, Lacona, and Liberty Center reorganized in 1959, and some of the uniforms still worn by sports team reflected those individual communities. That was the case for the baseball team, no doubt due to school finances. My hot itchy wool gray uniform proudly revealed the Milo Mustangs name.

There was a huge difference between me and Jim. He outweighed me by about thirty pounds and several inches taller. He was a pretty darn good ball player. I was just out of Little League with a skill level that matched. Jim was a gamer, a player who stood out among the others on the ball team. He was a man among boys. He often showed up at games, just minutes before the first pitch, sporting a five-o'clock shadow. No razor had yet touched my face. At age thirteen, I didn't even have a learner's permit, let alone a bona fide driver's license. I rode my bicycle to the home games and arrived hours early to help Coach Lister chalk the diamond

I vividly remember the occasion I was nearly called into action as a thirteen-year-old for the high school team. The opposing team had arrived, played catch to warm up, and had already taken their infield practice of ground balls, throwing it around the horn and fly balls to the outfield. It became time for the Warhawks to take the field for their round of practice grounders. Coach Lister stalled as much as possible. We only had nine players in uniform and that included me. Jim was not there! Coach Lister told me to grab my glove and head to second base. Gee whiz, I didn't even have a ball glove with me, so the coach asked the opposing team if they would loan me a glove. I could not have been more elated than if called up to the Major Leagues. I took ground balls and turned two in a practice double play as efficiently as Frank Bolling of the Milwaukee Braves. It had all the makings of a great day. Just as the first batter for the opposing team stepped into the batter's box, I saw Jim out of the corner of my eye as his car pulled behind the fence of the dugout. He hurriedly put on the wool Milo jersey, and without a word ever said, the coach pointed to me at second base and motioned me to the bench. My heart sank, but the spirit of the team rose when Jim stepped onto the field. I don't even remember if our team won that game. I held no animosity. Jim was hands down the better ball player. He would come to the rescue many times again in the years to come. Not just for the baseball team but for the US Army.

When the summer of baseball in 1962 ended, over fifty years passed before Jim and I would meet again. Time has a cruel way of playing jokes on people. This time when we met, we both were old men, gray-haired, slower in step but with our memories still intact. Then Jim spoke as he reflected on his military experience as we drank coffee at Smokey Row Coffee House in Pleasantville, Iowa.

Jim attended Drake University and played on the baseball team when he received his draft notice in the fall of 1965. He didn't carry the minimum twelve-semester hours of classes, so he didn't

qualify for a student deferment from the military. On September 13, 1965, he departed for basic training at Fort Leonard Wood, Missouri. The month before, August 18–24, the United States began its first major ground operation against the Vietcong in a preemptive strike (Operation Starlite) against 1,500 VC forces located at Chu Lai. It didn't take much baseball savvy, or a sophisticated score card, for Jim to figure out he'd soon be in the game.

When at basic training, Jim scored well on the physical fitness testing as well as aptitude and IQ scores. So high, in fact, that, coupled with some college credits, the US Army offered him an officer's commission if he would sign up for a longer hitch. "No thanks," he told them, "not interested." They again approached him and offered him enrollment to flight school as a helicopter pilot. "No thanks," he again told them.

Still the army pursued him. "You'd be an excellent special forces soldier," they told him. "You should consider that as a viable option." Jim again declined the offer.

The army became somewhat relentless in their pursuit of recruiting Jim to something beyond an infantryman. He told the story of a particular special forces sergeant that confronted him daily about joining the elite group. One day, as his outfit marched the two and a half miles to the firing range, the special forces sergeant again approached Jim. This time, the sergeant engaged in a tactic that belittled Jim, that he probably wasn't good enough anyway to cut the mustard. Jim finally had enough of the baloney. The special forces sergeant challenged Jim to a footrace. If he won, Jim had to sign up. If Jim won the race, the sergeant agreed to leave him alone for the rest of his training. Wearing combat boots, both took off from the firing range for the lengthy two-and-a-half-mile jaunt back to the barracks. As the sergeant approached the designated finish line, Jim just sat on the steps and smiled. He won the race by a huge margin and handed one of the army's elite special forces soldier a huge piece of humble pie. Just as in high school, Jim was a man among boys.

After basic training, the army sent Jim to Fort Sill, Oklahoma, for advanced infantry training. There he acquired a MOS of 1120B, weapons expert.

In January 1966, Jim found himself en route to Vietnam. He flew out of Travis AFB, California, located just north of San Francisco, and island-hopped to Saigon with stops in Hawaii, Wake Island, and the Philippines.

As we sipped coffee, Jim continued his story. He looked me in the eye and said, "That first twenty-four hours in Vietnam was my worst. I was scared stiff. I was ticked off, and an entire gauntlet of emotions wrapped me into a ball. I didn't know what to think. I filled out paperwork to document my arrival that night with a pen-light so as not to reveal my location. I became a member of the First Infantry Division, the 'Big Red One.'

"That next morning, about twenty of us climbed into the back of a duce and a half truck and left Saigon, headed to Phouc Vinh, about ninety-five miles north of Saigon. In my recollection, it was more of a cattle truck than a transport vehicle. As we drove through the streets of Saigon, a single shot rang out. One of guys with me in the truck was hit and killed."

For Jim, his Vietnam experience was simply surreal. There are no words in the English language to adequately describe the madness that existed in Vietnam. It was as if he left the light and walked into total darkness, an abyss of hell. The five senses deceived each of those who served there. What they did, what they saw, could not be reality, yet it was. The young American soldier saw death and destruction never before imaginable. Their ears became accustomed to the bark of gunfire, the explosions of mortars, the screams of dying soldiers, the *whop whop* of helicopter blades, and the roar of howitzer cannons. The distinctive smell of burned human flesh, the repugnant odor of diesel fuel that cooked off human waste, the aroma of hot jet exhaust filled their nostrils and lungs to the point it made them puke.

There was no kindness or softness to be found in Vietnam. Visually expended brass artillery shells were scattered about, smoking hot gun barrels were common, soggy boots, blood and sweat-stained fatigue shirts were common to many. Bullet-riddled aircraft, no longer airworthy, could be found piled together awaiting salvage or scrap. C rations tasted like cardboard and desensitized the palate with a bland nothingness that only a dash of Tabasco sauce could revive.

Strangely enough, the Vietnam soldier accepted all this as normal, the stuff of war. If he couldn't deal with it, he simply had to man up. There were many who couldn't deal with it, or even carry on with a stiff upper lip. During WWI, it was called shell shock. During WWII, it became combat stress reaction (CSR) or battle fatigue. In Vietnam, it became post-traumatic stress disorder (PTSD). Any normal person under those circumstances would go insane. Many soldiers resorted to alcohol or drugs to dull the pain. Too many brought the war home with them and are still fighting battles fifty years later. As the saying goes, you can leave Vietnam, but Vietnam will never leave you.

> *If we say we have fellowship with Him while*
> *we walk in darkness, we lie and do not tell the truth.*
> **(1 John 4:8)**

When Jim arrived at Phouc Vinh, he was greeted by a group of anxious soldiers. His arrival and that of the others in his cattle truck meant that others would be going home. For some unknown reason, one hardened combat veteran by the name of Lervaag, waiting to ship out, singled out Jim. Jim was his S-3 replacement. The S-3 was an alphanumeric designation that identified the task assigned, not by rank but by the job performed. Jim's S-3 meant he was in special operations. "You're gonna die within a week. You ain't got what it takes to survive here," Lervaag shouted in Jim's face. "You're an absolute wimp and a waste of space."

A heated exchange continued, and Jim had his first battle in Vietnam. It wasn't with the enemy but with this loud-mouthed soldier. Fists flew, punches were exchanged in a skirmish that lasted only a few minutes. To the cheers of the onlookers, in good old Iowa farm boy fashion, Jim cleaned Lervaag's plow. Apparently the guy had a reputation as a real bonehead, and many were pleased that Jim put him in his place, facedown on the ground. Those first short moments at Phouc Vinh set the tone for Jim's tour of duty in Vietnam.

In the comfort of our table at Smokey Row, Jim looked up at me and took a sip his coffee which, by now, was cold. "You know," he said, "My guys either loved me or hated me." When I asked how he managed that balancing act with his fellow soldiers, he replied, "Simple, I just never let them see me cry."

During his year at Phouc Vinh, Jim went on thirty-four major combat operations, some of which lasted as long as two weeks at a time in the field before returning to base camp. "I saw too many killed and wounded on both sides to even begin talking about." To survive and succeed, Jim commented, "You had to be pencil-sharp, know what you're doing and what resources were available." He often went attached to other units, assigned as a special operations detail. On one particular operation his, team wiped out an entire battalion of two hundred North Vietnamese regulars (NVR). For his actions in that battle, Jim received the US Army Commendations Medal for heroism.

One duty assigned to Jim, no doubt because he had completed a couple years of college before the army, was that of writing sitreps (situation reports). At the end of each day, he would compile information to be forwarded to headquarters, oftentimes from the field. That information included the number of wounded, fatalities, enemy kills, and location of the engagement. Too often, names appeared in the report of men he knew who walked beside him earlier in the day. It was hard enough to think about it, but now he had to write about it. It became a struggle to separate himself from the craziness of combat.

One incident that impacted Jim more than anything else was the day he worked as radioman and forwarded the grid coordinates called in to the artillery gunners. It had been a long day with dozens and dozens of rounds fired off that thwarted the advancement of the VC. The platoon sergeant came to Jim and told him that his evening replacement was sick as a dog. He asked Jim if he could pull double duty and work through the night. Jim quickly offered to fill in. The sergeant informed Jim that guy had yet to get settled in and hadn't the opportunity to find a tent in which to bunk down. Again Jim stepped up. "Tell him to take my tent and he can use my sleeping bag till the morning."

That night, multiple mortars rounds hit the encampment. When the smoke cleared the next morning, Jim was dumbfounded to find his tent took a direct hit. The soldier who slept in Jim's tent had been severely wounded and later died from the injuries. The guy was within a couple of weeks of ending his one-year tour of duty in Vietnam. Thoughts raced through Jim's mind. Why? What was the probability that this soldier would get sick that particular day? What were the chances he was asked to fill in for him? What were the odds that he wasn't in the tent? What were the percentages that the tent took a direct hit? Why was he spared and the other guy not? Divine intervention, perhaps? It became a memory of Vietnam that will never escape Jim's mind.

Jim's platoon was a tight-knit group. They knew one another well and totally relied on each individual to pull their own weight. The company commander, Lieutenant Colonel Charles Rogers (later awarded the Medal of Honor for his heroic actions on November 1, 1968), was on a first-name basis and always asked for Spence when headed out on a mission.

Jim's tour of duty in Vietnam ended exactly one year to the day of his arrival. He commented, "I wasn't sure if I was fit to go home or even if I deserved go home. I always viewed myself as a pretty tough guy but realized I wasn't tough at all. I had merely survived not by any physical strength within me or any acquired superior skill set, I was just lucky. Others were not. I felt an obligation to stay and help my buddies who struggled daily just to survive the day."

Jim headed back to the States in February 1967 and returned to Fort Riley, Kansas. With five months before his discharge, the army put Jim to work as an instructor for others soon headed for Vietnam. Uncle Sam even changed his MOS from weapons specialist, 1120B, to clerk typist, a 71B20. Jim chuckled and gave the reason for the change. "I was in the orderly room at Fort Riley and saw the clerk typist pecking away with two fingers as he attempted to type out a report. I offered to help him out." Little did the NCOIC of the orderly room know that Jim not only was pretty adept as a weapons specialist, he could also type seventy words per minute. The transition from a foxhole to an office desk became a no-brainer. The transition from Vietnam back to life in the States, however, would not be as easy.

Within days of his arrival at Fort Riley, Jim got word that his good friend Sidney Williams, from Crescent, Iowa, had been killed in a car accident the day he returned from Vietnam. Sidney and Jim went through basic training together, served in Vietnam together, and endured many a harrowing days in the war. He thought to himself, *How can something like this happen, to survive the war and make it home only to be killed in his small Iowa hometown with a meager population similar to that of Milo, about five hundred residents? It just doesn't make sense.*

A lot of things didn't make sense. As the young blond waitress at Smokey Row coffee shop came to our table and offered a coffee refill, Jim continued, "You know, I had people throw paper bags of human feces at me when I returned. They spit at me and spewed forth a litany of vulgarity directed at me and the uniform I wore. It was all I could do to walk away."

The last several months at Fort Riley, Jim traveled for several days at a time to nearby army facilities and shared his experiences and expertise about his time in Vietnam for those soon destined to follow his path. He remembered his encounter with Sergeant Lervaag when he first arrived at Phouc Vinh and used that experience as a tool of what not to do when he indoctrinated the new soldiers. The best lessons learned were the ones hardest taught. Jim had a briefcase full of hard-taught lessons he shared and a memory bank filled with names and faces of those he served with in Vietnam.

One particular character Jim recalled was a friend and fire team member by the name of Paul Gipson. Paul discharged in 1967, about the same time as Jim, and enrolled at the University of Kansas. There he played football, not as a young eighteen-year-old fresh out of high school but just a few years older with some serious life experiences tucked in his back pocket. Paul was drafted into the NFL in 1969 as the twenty-ninth overall pick by the Atlanta Falcons. He played a total of four years as a professional football player, two with the Atlanta Falcons, one with the Detroit Lions, and his final season with the New England Patriots. Jim went on to say, "Paul was a pretty good guy, a good soldier, a good athlete, and a good friend. It was fun following him and his statistics when he played on Sundays, wearing a different uniform but with the same determination as I witnessed when we served together in Vietnam."

At last, Jim returned to civilian life on September 12, 1967, with his discharge from active duty. He would soon head back to Milo and life as he knew it just two short years before. As a going-away celebration, he and a handful of soldier buddies headed to a bar in Kansas City to party and have a few beers. They were having a great time, throwing down a couple of suds and playing pool. Suddenly this guy comes into the bar and grabs a pool cue. Jim and his army buddies had their quarters lined up on the corner of the table to play the winner of the next game. The guy brazenly walked to the table, pushed the quarters on the floor, and announced that he had the next game. Jack Bretchsneider, Jim's good GI buddy from Racine, Wisconsin, quickly intervened. He told the guy to take a hike and wait his turn. Someone from the other side of the bar shouted, "Don't mess with these guys, they're just back from Vietnam."

A scuffle ensued and Bretchsneider punched the guy in the face. The dude left the bar, and the pool game continued. About fifteen minutes later, the guy returned. He busted through the door with a pistol in his hand and fired a shot into the ceiling. Jim dove under the pool table as the others sought cover elsewhere behind overturned tables. The gun-toting tough guy was looking for Jack. He saw Jim on his stomach under the pool table and pointed the gun right at him. He said, "Crawl out of there on your knees, you yellow belly."

Jim did as ordered. He convinced him to point the gun in a different direction and, with some nonverbal signs, indicated he and the others wanted no trouble. Again the gun-toting dude barked out, "Unless some of you are ready to die, I suggest you all leave now." Jim and his group quickly exited the bar and hightailed it down the street. How could it be that Jim survived all the thousands of shots fired at him in Vietnam yet nearly met his maker at some hole-in-the-wall bar in Kansas City. Jim never returned to that bar again and would never forget crawling out from under the pool table on his hands and knees with that pistol pointed at him. Welcome home from the war!

Today Jim is a retired school teacher with thirty-six years in the classroom. One of the proudest accomplishments during those years were the two state championship teams he coached in girls' cross-country track at Colfax High School. He was twice voted as state track coach of the year. He now lives in rural Jasper County, Iowa, and maintains an active lifestyle. He breeds, raises, and trains championship American leopard coonhounds and frequently travels the Midwest for coon hunting competition with his dogs. Always ready for the next challenge, Jim stays in shape by jogging three miles each day, lifting weights, and doing four hundred sit-ups. However, he remains old school to the core. He proudly states "I don't have a computer or cell phone. No satellite television either, just the three network channels from antenna reception. I do most of the cooking on the stove and don't own a microwave."

JAMES FRANKLIN GALBERT JR., SERGEANT, E-4

United States Air Force
July 20, 1965–January 6, 1969

F rank Galbert was the older brother of John Galbert. When I knew Frank, he lived on Main Street in the upstairs level above the restaurant his parents owned, adjacent to the Milo Locker. Frank was a different kind of guy. I didn't know him that well. He kept to himself to the point I would call him a loner. I didn't want to make that accusation without input from others to confirm my impression, but yes, others that knew him agreed. Frank had an unusual perspective on many things, clearly in another dimension, and as a result, he kept to himself or others steered clear.

Perhaps my most vivid memory of Frank occurred during a snowball fight outside the Milo Catholic Church when we were in our preteens. His brother John, Dan Reeves, Ben Hamilton, and I— all Milo boys included later in this book—were engaged in a serious snowball fight. Frank seemed to have the weakest arm of the group and, as a result, became the main target of everyone. He got pelted from every direction. He ran and took shelter in the open door that led to the basement of the church. All the kids followed him down the stairs with two or three snowballs balanced in our hands and continued to pelt him inside the church basement. When all our tightly packed white grenades were expended, we regrouped outside and resupplied ourselves with more. Again we entered the basement ready to toss the snowballs. This time, however, Frank weaponized himself with whatever he found. He grabbed a handful of butter knives from behind the kitchen counter and frantically threw them at his four attackers.

We retreated and planned another assault. Frank had since closed the basement door and waited for our return. We decided that John would quickly open the door and then step aside and the rest of us would rush in with another round of ammunition. I took the lead position with a snowball in each hand. John opened the door, and I jumped with my arm cocked ready to hurl the best fastball I could muster. *Wham*, Frank frantically screamed and then threw a butter knife. It caught me in the upper lip as if thrown by a crazed Comanche warrior. It pierced my lip and firmly stuck in my gum-line above my front teeth, like a Bowie knife thrown by Jim Bowie himself in his last-ditch effort as he defended the Alamo. I fell to me knees, and the blood gushed out. I reached for the butter knife with both hands and pulled it out. Nobody said a word.

I lived just one block away and ran home with my hands cupped in front of my mouth. When I came through the back porch door of my house, my mom freaked out. My cupped hands overflowed with blood. It was only a small wound, but I bled like a stuck pig. Off to the local doctor I went. Two stitches later and all seemed well. Word quickly spread amongst the kids our age that Frank knifed me. That wasn't exactly the truth, but I didn't bother to correct others when quizzed about it. Today I carry the scar on my upper lip that Frank Galbert gave me half a century earlier. That was my last true encounter with Frank.

Frank attended the Rosemount parochial Catholic school located just a few miles southeast of Milo in his elementary years. He bragged upon his arrival to the public school, "I'm the only kid to ever get kicked out of school at Rosemount." Perhaps the sisters who tutored Frank realized, too, that he was quite the character.

Right out of high school, Frank joined the air force. He enlisted on July 20, 1965, and headed to basic training in Texas. His advanced training in a technical school gave him the AFSC (air force specialty code) of 64730, a material facilities specialist. In layman's terms, Frank was a stock clerk.

His first duty assignment sent him to France in late 1965. Unfortunately, I was unable to determine the exact location where he was stationed in France, but most likely, Evreux-Fauville Air Base which was the front line base for USAFE (United States Air Force in Europe). His older sister, Georgia, simply confirmed he went somewhere in France.

The United States and France were at odds over the former's leadership role in NATO (North Atlantic Treaty Organization), particularly its increased involvement in Vietnam, a former French colony. Frank became a very, very minute pawn in the scheme of things. French President De Gaulle informed the United States government in April 1966, that all foreign troops must leave his country. De Gaulle then removed all French armed forces from NATO and stated he would remain an ally but only send French troops if Germany was invaded during the Cold War. He hoped to negotiate a separate treaty with the Warsaw Pact countries. At the same time, France had conflicts with insurgents in Algeria and wanted to keep ties with NATO so that it might bolster his position with the insurgents. But in no uncertain terms, he told America to get its troops out of his country. Thus Frank and seventy thousand Americans (which included dependents) left France in April of 1966 under Operation FRELOC (fast relocation from France).

After he left France, Frank landed in—of all places—Guantanamo Bay, Cuba. Again I found no documentation on his assignment there but got that information from his brother, John. Guantanamo Bay (known as Gitmo) is the oldest overseas US Naval facility in US history, a forty-five-square mile patch of real estate and waters located on the southeastern corner of the island. The United States signed a lease agreement with Cuba in 1903 and has maintained its presence there since, despite the communist takeover of Fidel Castro in 1959.

Frank was honorably discharged from active duty at Seymour Johnson AFB, North Carolina, on January 6, 1969. He served just three years, five months, and eleven days of his initial four-year obligation. Of that time served, two years, two months, and nine days were served overseas. Frank died on December 23, 1990, at the age of forty-four.

RICHARD A. MANLEY, SPECIALIST FOURTH CLASS, E-4

United States Army
December 6, 1965–December 5, 1967

Richard was the second oldest of four children. He live four miles east of Milo on a farm where the pavement ended. I best remember him by the car he drove, a black 1957 Chevy, one of the cars that has attained classic status in today's market. With an original purchase price slightly over two thousand dollars, the car now garners somewhere in the fifty-thousand-dollar range if in good condition. It was a sleek-looking car, and Richard fit the bill as its operator. He was a sleek-looking guy as most of the Milo girls in the mid 1960s would attest.

I remember an occasion when I, John Galbert, Terry Town, and Dan Reeves walked a couple of miles west of Milo and were rabbit hunting on property owned by Kent Wilbur. I was the youngest of the group as an eighth grader, the other three were freshman in high school. We came upon Richard, and his car parked on a dead-end dirt road. I chuckle now at the incident as once he realized he was spotted by our inquiring eyes, he and his unnamed girlfriend made a hasty retreat back to civilization. Oh, the joys of those teenage years and the not-so-innocent events of our youth.

Richard graduated from high school in 1964 and just over a year later was drafted into the Army on December 6, 1965. His trip to Fort Hood, Texas, for basic training was an eventful one. On the departure flight from Des Moines, one of the exit doors unexpectedly became ajar. The aircraft made an emergency landing in Kansas City. There the airline placed him in a hotel for an overnight stay. The following morning, he took a bus, 214 miles to Fort Leonard Wood, Missouri. Once checked in there, he again boarded another bus with other recruits for the 662-mile ride to Fort Hood, Texas. It was a lengthy but smooth trip on paved highways rather than a narrow, tree-lined, dead-end dirt road outside of Milo. This ride, however, lasted nearly twelve hours, and he did not spend the entire trip reclined in the back seat.

Once Richard completed the eight-week boot camp, his next stop with the Army took him back to Fort Leonard Wood for advanced training as a combat engineer where he earned the MOS of 12B20.

His first permanent duty assignment sent him to Fort Belvior, Virginia, located just twenty miles outside of Washington, DC, where he was assigned to Platoon B of the Ninety-First Engineering Battalion. Just thirty days into his assignment, new marching orders came forth. A large contingent of his battalion would be headed to Vietnam. As he stood in formation with others, the announcement came from the commander. Platoon A would go to Vietnam. Platoon B would remain at Fort Belvior. Richard was in Platoon B.

In 1967, the *Rowan & Martin's Laugh-In* comedy show debuted on television. It skyrocketed to the number one watched show in America with Goldie Hawn, Ruth Buzzi, Gary Owen, and the two characters, Dan Rowan and Dick Martin. During the show, Dan and Dick presented the "*Fickled Finger of Fate*" award to deserving people or organizations for their bonehead decisions or just pure bad luck. In Richard's situation, Platoon A was a prime candidate for the *Fickled Finger of Fate* award. It would be bad karma for Platoon A.

Richard's good friend from Mason City, Iowa, was in Platoon A. He would be killed in Vietnam.

The year 1967 saw the rise of racial riots in several cities across the country that included the Hough riots in Cleveland, Ohio, the Compton Cafeteria riots in San Francisco, California, the Marquette riots in Chicago, and political and anti-war protests coupled with racial riots in Washington, DC. Richard and hundreds of other soldiers from Fort Belvior were sent to nearby Washington, DC, in fall of 1967 and patrolled the streets armed with live ammunition and tear gas. As stated by Richard, "I never fired my weapon but dispensed several canisters of tear gas in an attempt to control rioters. Over 650 rioters were arrested during the looting and burning of vehicles and buildings in Washington, DC. It was a scary time, not just for me and those at the US Capital complex but for all of America." Richard went on to comment while in Washington, DC, during the riots, "I slept on a leather couch in the office of the Secretary of Defense, Robert McNamara, after my street duty ended each day."

Later that year, Richard received new orders and reported to the US Army's West Point Academy, where he trained about 130 cadets in combat tactical engineering, specifically explosive demolition. Recruits trained with light tactical rafts (LTRs) and the use of C-4 explosives used to blow up bridges. "I showed them how and where to strategically place the explosives then floated down the Hudson River with them and watched as they blew things up. It was fun duty."

After the short stint at West Point, Richard returned to Fort Belvoir, where he received an honorable discharge on December 5, 1967. He returned to his civilian job as a postal worker that began directly out of high school that was interrupted by his two years of active duty in the Army. He retired from the US postal service after thirty years and currently lives in Altoona, Iowa.

JERRY RAY FERGUSON, SERGEANT, E-4

United States Air Force
January 28, 1966–May 22, 1969

J erry grew up on a farm less than one mile north of Milo. Their family lived in a dove-gray Lustron house, a prefabricated metal home of about one thousand square feet that became the answer to the American housing boom of post WWII in the United States. It was the only such Lustron home in Milo. There he and his older brother, Denny, helped their father, Gerald Ferguson, with the dairy cattle farming operation. Denny joined the US Navy in 1958. That left Jerry with the bulk of farm chores before and after school from the time he was in his early teens until he graduated from high school in 1964. It was there that he learned the work ethic that served him well later in life. Nothing builds character with any greater meaning than rising at 5:00 a.m. each morning, seven days per week, knowing that livestock are dependent on a farmer's presence. That character building doubled down again at 5:00 p.m. with the repeated milking of the Guernsey cows.

In 1964, milk sold for 93¢ per gallon at the grocery store. The farmer's profit margin was razor-thin. Their operation had no automated manure removal system. A pitchfork or shovel, coupled with brute strength, served as the only means of cleaning the dairy barn. Jerry did his fair share of shoveling cow manure, a task that gave him an enhanced perspective about life in general. *When it gets too deep, it's time to clean house or move on.*

Jerry found time and participated in the upstart high school wrestling team at Southeast Warren as well as the school band. Jerry certainly was a likeable fella, well mannered, and a low-key type of guy. My recollection of him reminded me of Rick Nelson from the television show *Ozzie and Harriet*. He didn't sing but played a mean saxophone. What he didn't know in 1964 was the fact that he would soon be a "Travelin' Man" leaving the tranquil Milo community on a journey to points unknown. "At every stop, he owned the heart, of at least one lovely girl."

Right out of high school, Jerry enrolled at AIB (American Institute of Business) college in Des Moines. Upon completion of his education there, he obtained a job at Cars Incorporated, a Volkswagen dealership located at Fifteenth and Locust in Des Moines. There he worked in the office and managed the paperwork for the sale of vehicles.

In November of 1965, he received notification from the draft board that he would soon be up for induction into the US Army. Jerry wasn't too surprised at the notice. Between 1964 and 1973, 27 million men became eligible for the United States draft. Over 15 million were given deferments for education, family hardships, or some type of physical or mental condition. Government records revealed another 209,517 actively evaded reporting and gained the moniker "draft dodgers." About 30,000 actually left the United States and headed to Canada to avoid induction. Jerry dutifully checked in with the draft board and awaited the phone call to report. The draft board told him that within the next thirty to sixty days Uncle Sam would call. Not all that enthusiastic about joining the army, Jerry checked with the air force recruiters. There he was told the waiting list to wear the air force blue was quite lengthy. It would be six to eight months before they anticipated an opening. Jerry checked with the national guard units in hopes of joining but again was told, "Sorry, we're full at 100 percent manning." Resigned to the fact the US Army would be his destination, he continued to work at the car dealership and awaited the dreaded phone call.

On Monday, January 24, 1966, Jerry received a call. To his surprise, it was not the US Army that called but instead the US Air

Force. The recruiter informed him that someone had dropped from their enlistment commitment due to a family hardship. The question then arose—"Do you want the available slot with the air force?"

Jerry thought about it for a mere ten seconds. "Sure, I'll take it," he told the recruiter over the phone. Then he asked, "When do I need to report?"

The recruiter responded back, "You need to report next Friday, four days from now." With a simple yes answer, Jerry snuffed out the fuse that had been lit as a draftee with the US Army and a very strong likelihood that Vietnam would be his ultimate destination.

Jerry's enlistment in the USAF began on Jan 28, 1966. Like many other Milo boys, he took his first airplane ride en route to basic training, headed to Lackland AFB, Texas.

Boot camp with the air force gained the reputation as notably "easier" than other branches of the military. For one, it was only six weeks in duration. Some sarcastically referred to the organization as the "air farce." Jerry's basic training experience was most unusual. Just two weeks into training, a meningitis outbreak occurred. Four recruits were diagnosed with the bacterial strain of meningitis, and a fifth recruit died. Jerry's barracks was just across the street from the recruit who died. Subsequently the entire basic training base was put on lockdown, and the recruits were confined to quarters with limited mobility or interaction with others outside their barracks. At four weeks into the basic training, the USAF sent Jerry, via bus, to Amarillo AFB, Texas, where he finished the final two weeks of his basic training. Additionally Amarillo became his next duty assignment for technical training. Upon completion of advanced training, Jerry emerged with an AFSC (air force specialty code) of 64550, an inventory management specialist.

His first permanent set of orders sent Jerry to Williams AFB, Arizona, located near Chandler. There he was assigned to the 3525th Supply Squadron, Air Training Command. In Jerry's own words, "It was the most boring job in the USAF. I sat at a desk and shuffled documents for inventory control with an occasional trip to the flight line to verify receipt of an items." It was a far stretch from his experience on the dairy farm back in Milo. The chow hall offered buffet meals much like those of top-notch restaurants. Jerry continued by saying, "When we finished eating, we didn't even have to put our trays away, civilian contractors cleared the tables. I never had KP (kitchen duty) or guard duty after basic training."

Within a short time at Williams AFB, Jerry moved into an apartment off base and commuted to work. He said, "It was like a regular job as a civilian. I worked from 8:00 a.m. to 5:00 p.m. Monday through Friday. On weekends, a few buddies and I went on short trips and visited places like Disneyland, the Grand Canyon, or Las Vegas. It was pretty easy duty but absolutely the most mundane job I've ever had."

In the early days of May 1969, the air force presented Jerry with an interesting offer. They wanted to open their ranks for more enlistments. As a result, he was given the choice to re-enlist or be discharged. As quickly and unexpectedly as he joined the USAF, he was given two weeks to either sign up for another hitch or get out. Jerry opted for the latter. He discharged from active duty on May 22, 1969, after completing just three years, three months, and twenty-five days of his initial four-year commitment.

Jerry tried to poo-hoo his time in the military when reflecting on his USAF experience. "I didn't do anything special," he told me. "In fact, I had it pretty darn easy compared to what others went through." My response to him came from the lines of a John Milton poem "When I Consider How My Light Is Spent."

> *God doth not need either man's work or his own gifts; who bears his mild yoke, they serve him best. His state is Kingly. Thousands at his bidding speed and post o'er land and ocean without rest. They also serve who only stand and wait.*

> *All the inhabitants of the earth are accounted for as nothing, and he does according to his will among the host of heaven and among the inhabitants of earth; and none can stay his hand or say unto him "What have you done?"*
> —**Daniel 4:35**

RICHARD "DICK" COFFMAN, SPECIALIST FIFTH CLASS, E-5

United States Army
April 5, 1966–April 11, 1969

D ick was a tall lanky kid, three years older than me, who graduated from high school in 1964. He was a senior and I a lowly freshman during our school years together. I don't recall too much interaction with Dick during that time, but I did know he was well liked and respected by everyone. Dick almost seemed too mature to be a kid. He was responsible and never on the wrong end of any shenanigans. He was very reserved and overly polite, or so it seemed. He lived in a modest home, just a stone's throw from my grandparents' house, one block east of the Milo school and another block south. Dick didn't play any sports in school, but I do remember him active in band, particularly the marching band where he played the drums.

The US Army drafted Dick into the military on April 5, 1966. Like many others from Milo, he went to Fort Leonard Wood, Missouri, for basic training. He heard the same song and dance once in the grasp of the army that perked the ears of virtually every recruit. "If you sign up with a longer hitch with Uncle Sam, your chances of Stateside duty are greatly enhanced, and your chances of walking patrol in Vietnam with a carbine in your arms will be greatly reduced." Dick drank the Kool-Aid and signed up for an additional year of duty.

Without counsel, plans fail, but with many advisors, they succeed. ***(Proverbs 15:22)***

Dick's only counsel that day was his drill instructor (DI). In retrospect, he admitted his decision was flawed. No doubt, the DI smiled with his fingers conveniently crossed, tucked out of sight behind his back, when he made that statement and hoped it might offset any fib he told. Mark Twain satirically presented a few words of wisdom years earlier on such matters. He stated, "Figures don't lie, and liars don't figure." If Dick would have taken a moment to crunch some numbers in his mind, he would have quickly realized the truth. Draft inductions by the military in 1966 approached 35,000 per month. For the year 1966, 382,010 were drafted into service. That huge number did not reflect volunteer enlistments. At the end of December 1966, US forces in Vietnam totaled 389,000. Unbeknownst to Dick, his ticket to Southeast Asia had already been punched.

Dick endured boot camp. The daily routine of early morning calisthenics followed by long marches that heeled to the cadence of a raspy-throated DI became a routine for the next eight weeks. Dick was perplexed and not accustomed to the periodic smoke breaks afforded the recruits. He didn't smoke or drink when he entered the military. Oftentimes the smoke breaks paralleled the degree of nicotine addiction of the DI. In order for him to smoke, he let the recruits smoke. When the opportunity arose and the order "Light 'em if you got 'em" came down, cigarettes magically appeared. Dick watched in amazement as others puffed away with sighs of enjoyment as clouds of smoke filled the air, as if a mini fireworks display occurred. Some even smoked two cigarettes at once in double-time fashion. Finally Dick gave in and decided to try one. If the cigarettes gave the true enjoyment he observed on others, he certainly deserved the same. That wasn't the case, however. He didn't enjoy cigarettes. Peer pressure overwhelmed him, and he continued to smoke with the other troops. There was a significant difference, however. Dick did not inhale, a practice later used by a guy named Bill Clinton. He puffed away and exhaled all the smoke, but none entered his lungs. Because of his technique, his boot camp buddies soon nicknamed him Smokey.

After basic training, Dick's orders sent him to Fort Gordon, Georgia, on the outskirts of Augusta, where he received advanced training as a communications specialist with a MOS of 72B20. There he learned about the operation of teletype communications and cryptography. That duty required a secret security clearance and an extensive background investigation. In a letter received from his family, Dick was asked if he was in trouble because the neighbors approached his dad, Bill, and told him someone from the military was in town, asking questions about Dick. Dick's background checked out squeaky-clean, and before he left Fort Gordon, he was awarded the secret clearance.

Once the advance training wrapped up, Dick received orders to Fort Carson, Colorado. Upon his arrival, he discovered not a single teletype machine existed on the installation. With nothing to do that matched his MOS and his superiors not sure what to do with him, they assigned him to the motor pool. Dick said, "I spent a lot of time laying on a creeper underneath a vehicle, hiding and snoozing. I did very little." It didn't take long before senior leadership realized a mistake had been made, and it boiled down to round pegs being forced into square holes. Within a week, they again reassigned Dick for duty in the aviation department where he categorized aircraft parts. This time around, it amounted to square pegs being forced into round holes. Just a few days passed, and it became apparent that this didn't work well either. Dick knew absolutely nothing about aircraft or aircraft parts. Finally...finally, Dick was transferred to the orderly room as a company clerk. After nine months at Fort Carson, Dick again received marching orders. His destination became Vietnam.

Dick took a one-month leave and headed back to Milo before his departure. He gave much thought about his relationship with a girl named June, from Lynnville, Iowa, whom he met a few years earlier. It might not have been the wisest decision he made, to get married right before shipping out to a war zone; but at the time, he thought it was the best decision. Dick and June tied the knot on March 11, 1967, in a whirlwind wedding. A few days later, he left Milo for a quick six-week refresher course on the teletype communications equipment at Davis Station, California, located near Sacramento, before he headed for Vietnam.

In May of 1967, Dick arrived at Cam Ranh Bay, Vietnam. It was hot—stifling hot—and Dick experienced trouble as he adjusted to the heat. His legs and ankles swelled tight. He became uncertain if he could endure the climate for a full year. As fortune prevailed, within a day or two, he was sent north to Qui Nhon and, after a very brief stop there, on to An Khe in the upper highlands where the weather was less oppressive and noticeably cooler, particularly at night.

Upon arrival at An Khe, Dick checked in with the orderly room's first sergeant for assignment. When the first shirt asked Dick what he did at Fort Carson before his arrival in Vietnam, Dick responded quickly, "I worked in the orderly room."

"Well, that's what you're gonna do here, soldier, I need someone in the orderly room now," he rattled on as if giving dictation. "We'll get you settled in with a room today and report for duty first thing in the morning."

At An Khe, Dick was assigned to the 586th Road Runner Signal Company and performed communications duties at the base camp for the 1st Cavalry Division. The 1st Calvary Division continued in and out of An Khe on assorted missions and used the base to recoup, relax, and repair before the next mission. Before Dick's arrival in May of 1967, the 1st Calvary had their metal tested during the infamous battle at Xa Drang Valley in November 1965. They were a hardened group of soldiers. During Dick's 1967 tour of duty in Vietnam, the 1st Calvary Division, based out of An Khe, engaged in eighteen major battles with the enemy and numerous minor skirmishes. All the while, Dick remained on base and never once fired a weapon at the enemy or was himself fired upon. Thus was the duty of an orderly room clerk, and Dick was so grateful for it.

An Khe seemed secure to Dick. The base perimeter was lined with rows and rows of concertina wire as a protective barrier. There were assaults on An Khe from time to time. Dick noted that the locals grazed their cattle near the perimeter fence during the day. It was then that they nonchalantly cut the perimeter wire so that during the night, intruders could easily slip in. Numerous times, groups of two to three Vietcong infiltrated the base and attempted to blow up facilities. Every time they were stopped, dead in their tracks, no pun intended.

Well into the backside of his tour, Dick and his orderly room coworker, Randy Kelley from Florida, decided to take R & R (rest and relaxation) for a week and go to Australia. They made their way to Pleiku and caught a military flight to Cam Ranh Bay. From there, they intended to catch a military hop to Australia. It was at Cam Rahn Bay that Dick bumped into Larry Kubli of Milo who was at the terminal en route to Qui Nhon. They greeted each other in surprise and cherished their few moments together before Larry's flight departed. Dick's airlift to Australia remained uncertain. He got bumped from the flight by a higher ranking soldier who also wanted an R & R in Australia. Dick and buddy Randy Kelley hung out at the terminal at Cam Ranh Bay for two days, hoping to catch a ride but had no luck. They decided to head back to An Khe after three days of travel and still in Vietnam. Before Dick departed the terminal, he experienced yet another chance encounter. Ken Keeney, a US Marine who Dick knew, from nearby Indianola, Iowa, shouted out to him as he passed through the terminal. Yet again another ten-minute reunion halfway around the world. After his military service, Ken Keeney became a Warren County police officer and now is retired living in Milo. As the Disney song reminded Dick, "it's a small world after all."

Virtually everyone at An Khe performed, at one time or another, overnight guard duty at one of the many tall reconnaissance towers located around the base. The armed guards kept vigilance and a watchful eye as they looked for intruders with orders to fire if needed.

Dick and his orderly room buddy Randy were about their business one day when the first sergeant boldly announced to them that today was their day. He instructed them to requisition weapons and be prepared to stand guard. As they waited outside for more detailed instructions as to where to report, the captain came by and saw them with M16 rifles, helmet, flak jackets, and a bandolier of ammo that hung off their shoulder. The captain barked to his clerks. "So where do you two think you're going?"

Dick answered, "We've been assigned guard duty for the night."

"You're not going anywhere, get back inside, I'll take care of this." He barked at them. "Who came up with this cockamamie idea anyway? I can't get a thing done if I lose you two. Get back inside, pronto."

In unison, Dick and Randy answered, "Yes, sir!" Dick commented years later that was the closest he ever came to seeing combat during his tour in Vietnam.

Dick noted that his time at An Khe was not all work and no play. The Bong Son River flowed through the base, and on Sundays after church services, with an ever watchful eye, he and several others made their way down to the water's edge where they grilled steaks, swam, and drank a few beers. On a funnier note, the orderly room captain kept a huge python snake, caged in his office, as his pet. A few of the guys often ventured downtown and bought live chickens and fed them to the snake. It was cheap but gory entertainment. The first shirt was unaware of the situation and inadvertently strolled in during a feeding session and freaked out. He nearly tore the hinges off the door as he made his exit. Laughter echoed through the building at his departure.

Exactly 365 days after he arrived in Vietnam, Dick saw his tour of duty there come to an end. During his stay at An Khe, Dick recalled, "The only time I left the base was for a haircut." The local Vietnamese barber used a razor to cut hair, so the standing joke became, it would either be a high-and-tight haircut or a slit throat. "I never asked him for a shave."

Dick still had time to serve after he left Vietnam. His next set of orders took him to Fort Dix, New Jersey. He arrived there in May

1968 and worked as a clerk in the overseas processing station where orders were issued for European OCONUS (outside the continental United States) duty. He discharged on April 11, 1969.

As he returned to Milo, Dick literally clicked his heels as he skipped down the sidewalk, so thankful to be home with his wife and family and friends. It became time to get back to a normal lifestyle. He and June had difficulty finding a place to live in Milo. The small town afforded few vacant homes, either for rent or sale; but alas, an acquaintance, Johnny Baughman, had a small house on the east end of town that fit their needs. Thoughts of the 1939 musical *The Wizard of Oz* buzzed through Dick's head. "There is no place like home, there is no place like home."

Some time passed, and all seemed well. Dick's father asked him to go on a short fishing trip to nearby Lake Red Haw, a state park on the outskirts of Chariton, Iowa. Dick knew that fishing was a passion of his father. It wasn't the top item on Dick's things to do, but he thought, what the heck, it would be a good opportunity to re-connect with his dad. As they sat by the water's edge, and the sun began to set, an uneasy feeling overcame Dick. Dick blurted out, "We gotta go, it's getting dark."

"Not yet, let's wait a while longer. The fish are just starting to bite. Maybe we should stay all night," his dad, Bill, replied.

Again Dick blurted out, "But, but we don't have any guns."

His dad said, "What? No guns, we're fishing, son, not hunting."

Dick became even more tense. "The tree line is too close, somebody might be over there watching us. We gotta go, let's go now." Bill noticed the change in his son's demeanor and agreed to end the fishing trip. Bill made light of Dick's concerns that evening and poo-hoohed the entire event as a weakness in his son's manhood, or so it seemed to Dick.

Even though Dick never saw combat in Vietnam, never once fired a shot at the enemy, the strangle grip of PTSD (post-traumatic stress disorder) put a choke hold on him that night. He was, however, front and center and witnessed the madness of war while at An Khe. Out of nowhere, the tension, the uneasiness, the fear that burrowed itself deep into his mind boiled out that evening at Lake Red Haw.

Dick came home from the war, but the war also came home with him. What he thought would be a bonding experience between him and his father proved otherwise. Their father-son relationship withered away. They spoke very little for the next nine years until his father's death. War wounds run deep, and oftentimes no scars are visible. The healing process for Dick continues fifty years later.

As I sat with Dick in his man cave attached to his garage and took notes as we talked about his military experience, I felt a sense of complete reverence for him. Here was a man who perhaps felt he didn't do enough while in Vietnam yet gave so much. A tear streamed down his cheek as he told me, "I wish I knew what was wrong with me, but when visiting the Grand Ole Opry in Nashville, Tennessee, last month during a Memorial Day dedication for those who served in the military, they asked all who served to please stand. I did. Then they played the national anthem as Old Glory unfurled. I just couldn't help myself, I cried like a baby."

My comment then to Dick was, "God bless you and those like you that served." Dick Coffman, once a young Milo boy, was now a seventy-one-year-old man. Smokey represented all the goodness of Milo, all the pride of that community packaged into a compassionate and caring person. He was proud to be an American, proud to have served his country, and proud to be a Milo-ite. I was proud and thankful to know him and for the opportunity to tell his story. Dick retired from the US Postal Service after thirty-eight years carrying mail. He still resides in Milo today.

ALBERT J. WADLE, PRIVATE FIRST CLASS, E-3

United States Army
May 16, 1966–May 16, 1969

Albert, one of six siblings, lived a few miles east of Milo, just where the pavement ended and became a bumpy gravel road filled with potholes. I'd describe him as a rough-and-tumble guy who refused to back down to anyone. I best knew Albert when we both played on the high school football team. He wasn't the biggest guy, he wasn't the fastest guy, but he was one of the most dependable guys on the team coached by Bill Luse, particularly when the going got tough. During his senior year, the team went undefeated, a first for the school. Albert also wrestled for the green-and-white Warhawks and won the conference championship for the 133-pound weight class his senior year.

Albert's high school class had sixty students comprised of twenty-eight boys and thirty-two girls. One of those boys was a foreign exchange student from South Korea, Doo Hoon Hyun. Fifteen of the boys lived in Milo, and ten of the fifteen would eventually serve in the military, an amazing two-thirds of the Milo boys graduating class of 1965.

Exactly one year after graduation, Uncle Sam called. Albert knew the writing was already on the wall when he received his draft notice. He didn't want to join the military, and he didn't want to go to Vietnam. To avoid the latter, the recruiter told him if he would voluntarily enlist for three years instead of the minimum two years as a draftee, his chances of avoiding Vietnam would be greatly enhanced. Albert bought in to the sales pitch and signed up for a three-year hitch.

On May 16, 1966, he headed for basic training at Fort Riley, Kansas. Upon completion of basic training, he remained at Fort Riley for advanced training with a MOS of 64A10, light vehicle operator. A few weeks into training, he became gravely ill. He reported to his instructor his sickness but was told to "gut it out, you'll be fine." The end results of that illness proved to be a ruptured appendix. The army transported him to the base hospital for emergency surgery. When he recovered from the operation, he found himself back in the advanced training school but several weeks behind his initial group of trainees.

Alas, his training at Fort Riley came to a close. To his surprise, the next duty assignment kept him at Fort Riley where he worked for headquarters as a vehicle operator at the motor pool. For the next six months, Albert put in his time chauffeuring officers to various events in the area. One eventful morning, as the entire motor pool stood in ranks inspection, Albert received some fateful news. There were two lines standing at attention when the commanding officer announced, "Everyone in the second row will be deployed to Vietnam shortly." Certainly the luck of the draw for Albert—he was in the second row. He could just as easily have been in the front row, but today he just happened to be in the second row.

He recalled the words of the army recruiter, *If you sign up for an additional year, chances are you can avoid going to Vietnam*." Fellow high school classmate Terry Tigner, who joined the army the same time as Albert, didn't swallow the malarkey of the recruiter. Terry opted to take a chance as a draftee and only took the two-year obligation. Both didn't serve together at Fort Riley, but each quickly shared with each other their new destinations. Terry would be headed to Germany while Albert would be headed to Vietnam.

Albert reported to Oakland Army Base, California, in early December 1966, for his trip to Vietnam. The US Army transported him and about two thousand others via merchant marine vessel. There were three ships total that made the transpacific voyage. It took about thirty days to make the journey to Vietnam. In Albert's words, "It was a terrible trip. The food was lousy, and many got sick and puked their guts out, hanging over the deck railing. Maybe it could have been seasickness, but the grub they served tasted like crap."

One incident remained transfixed in his mind during the voyage. One soldier, who suffered the same ills as he from eating the bad food, broke into the ship's galley in search of something more appealing to his stomach. He got caught and was being taken to the brig. As Albert watched, the young soldier became very vocal, and a scuffle ensued. The soldier didn't like the food, he didn't like the US Army, he didn't like being onboard the ship, and certainly didn't like being sent to Vietnam. He broke free and jumped overboard into the South Pacific Ocean. Crew members immediately threw him a life ring and alerted the command bridge of "man overboard." As others gazed portside, the soldier pushed the white donut-shaped life ring away and swam in the opposite direction of the ship. Albert absorbed what he just witnessed in amazement. *The guy just committed suicide!* he thought to himself. By protocol during such overboard incidents, the ship remained in the area for twenty-four hours searching for the soldier. He was never found. Albert wondered how that soldier's death would be reported to his family, suicide, non-combat fatality, accidental drowning, or lost at sea?

A few days later, the convoy of ships arrived at Subic Bay Naval station in the Philippines. Albert and the others destined for Vietnam were given shore leave while the ship resupplied with food and fuel for the final leg of the trip. Olongapo City, just outside the gates of Subic Bay, had a reputation of a no-holds-barred and anything-goes environment for visiting troops. Of course before going ashore, the troops were give the standard speech of don't go to this particular bar, travel in pairs, don't drink the water, watch out for thieves and pickpockets, hookers are on every corner with God only knows what disease they carry, drug dealers are rampant, and con artists will trick you out of your last dime. Beware!

As if on a shopping trip with a checklist, the majority of troops rushed ashore and tried their best to experience the wonders of Olongapo City. Most returned back aboard ship flat broke, either stumbled down drunk or high on something, and within the next day or two, many needed a shot of penicillin for the conjugal visit. *Mabuhay*, Subic Bay.

Albert's next stop would be Cam Ranh Bay, Vietnam. He arrived there on January 3, 1967. Ironically that same day, Carl Wilson, founder of the iconic Southern California rock and roll band The Beach Boys, was indicted after being drafted and claimed conscientious objector status. Wilson's punishment before the courts was simply to perform free of charge at prisons and hospitals. Quite a different gig than the one in which Albert was about to engage. Upon arrival, Al was assigned to the 9th Division, 4th Battalion, 47th Infantry Division, Headquarters Company.

For the first two weeks in Vietnam, Al offloaded equipment from the three ships as a truck driver. His unit carved out of the jungle a new post named Camp Bear Cat, located near Biên Hòa, about twenty-two miles northeast of Saigon. Al worked out of Camp Bear Cat for about three months before a relocation to My Tho, sixty-five miles southwest of Saigon. At My Tho, Al worked out of headquarters company and drove a variety of vehicles doing somewhat mundane transportation duties.

On one particular morning, Al's task became a trip to the dump as he hauled trash for disposal in a deuce and a half truck. It would turn into an unforgettable day during his tour of duty in Vietnam. Al had made the trip before and knew the route. He also knew local villagers lived at the dump and sorted through the trash, looking for anything salvageable the GIs discarded. He also knew that as he approached, the local villagers literally rushed his truck and climbed aboard before he stopped, hoping to be the first to get a prized piece of his trash. That again was the case that morning. About six to eight kids scampered to the running boards on both sides of the truck as he backed up to dump his load. They quickly climbed into the bed of the truck and began their search. As they pushed and shoved one another, unbeknownst to Al, a young girl fell to the ground. He heard a loud scream and looked into his side mirror. He saw the kids pointing to the ground. Al stopped his truck, got out to see that he had just ran over a young girl—maybe eight to ten years old—and crushed her. She died right there, beneath his tires, in a pile of trash.

Al later revealed when I interviewed him for this book that of all the things he witnessed in Vietnam, all the shots fired, all the wounded and killed comrades, that moment when he ran over the little girl still haunts him today. There was no incident report filed with his superiors. There was no IG (inspector general) investigation performed, no insurance claim filed, or attorney seeking damages involved. It was as if a raccoon had been hit by a vehicle while driving a lonely back road in Iowa. The carcass left lifeless by the roadside, and the driver proceeded on. So it was that day in Vietnam. Another innocent casualty of war, and things just—*proceeded on.*

Things plowed on at My Tho, and frankly Al became disenchanted with the routine. Hauling supplies, garbage trips to the dump, and driving troops from point A to point B was easy enough, but just didn't give him the job satisfaction he wanted. He had conversed with others in the 47th Infantry Division and heard their stories of what transpired while in the jungle on patrol. Al had an epiphany moment and decided he wanted to see for himself what this Vietnam War was really like. On his own accord, without approval from his superior, he sneaked off on patrol with a group of his buddies. That very first night on patrol, the lieutenant, platoon sergeant, and RTO (radio, telephone operator) were gathered together discussing tactical movements that evening, when one of them tripped a bobby trap. The explosion severely injured all three and took them out of the war. Subsequently Al was assigned duty as the RTO for the remainder of the patrol. The three injured troops received immediate medevac extraction. That first night was a real eye-opener, and Al thought to himself, *What the heck did I get myself into?*

As they hunkered down for the evening, Al noticed that all the others in his platoon brought along a hammock on which to sleep, stretched between two trees. Al carried an air mattress. A rookie mistake for certain. Camped along the Mekong Delta, Al blew up his mattress and settled in as best he could with the bugs, the heat, and threat of enemy encounters. He awoke floating on water on his mattress. The tide came in during the night and caused the river to rise. Not quite like peeing in bed but almost as alarming. After several days, his group returned to the camp at My Tho, and Al checked in with his assigned unit at Headquarters Company.

His commanding officer at headquarters greeted him with less-than-warm handshakes and hugs. "Where in the devil have you been, Wadle?" he asked. Al told him of his adventure the last few days and his decision to see for himself what he had heard from others. His officer shouted to him, "If you like that so much, you're fired from Headquarters Company. Go ahead and join your buddies on patrol. You're transferred."

It was simple as that, a very matter-of-fact decision. Al went from riding around in a jeep and sleeping on a cot to wading through rice paddies and crawling through the jungles of South Vietnam. Yes, indeed, Al got a firsthand look at what the Vietnam War was really like, and it sucked big-time!

Soldiers always complain, just like Al and his buddies complained of the food aboard ship during the trip to Vietnam. Al's biggest complaint when in the jungles of Vietnam was the constant battle with jungle rot. Days on end with monsoon weather or wading in water through rice paddies brought forth a constant battle with one's own health. The GI boots had "weep holes" that allowed water to drain, but often those holes were plugged and were less than adequate to keep a soldier's feet dry. Open sores quickly developed and led to potential infections that took many infantrymen out of combat. Dry socks were just a faint memory for Al, but luckily he stayed one step ahead of the cellulitis that afflicted so many.

During the next six months, Al encountered only one significant battle with the Vietcong. His unit became engaged with the VC across the river and exchanged extensive gunfire in a firefight. The lieutenant called in air support to hit the other side of the river and put some serious hurt on Charlie. As happened more frequently than reported, the ordnance came down on Al and his unit. Fortunately Al was not injured by the friendly fire, but several within his group were killed and many others injured. A bonehead move, either by the lieutenant for calling in the wrong coordinates or the pilots who dropped their ordnance at the wrong spot cost some American soldiers their lives.

Most of Al's patrols, however, consisted of avoiding booby traps and half-heartedly seeking out the VC. On occasion, sporadic sniper fire gave them pause. It became a battle for each one in the patrol, a battle to just make it till the next day. Don't do anything stupid, don't be a hero, don't take unnecessary chances. Dummies and fools quickly die in the jungle.

On one of his breaks between patrols back at My Tho, Al took the time to relax and have a few beers. Well, perhaps more than a few beers, maybe several beers, as he recalled. He decided he had walked enough the previous week and needed a ride. He commandeered a jeep he found left unattended and hopped in and took a joyride to the Enlisted Club. When there, by chance he happened to encounter Cotton Beeler, a friend from nearby Indianola, Iowa. What were the chances of them meeting, he thought. "Let's have another beer."

When the two exited the Enlisted Club, an MP (military patrol) greeted them. Apparently Al didn't notice the markings on the front of the jeep. He didn't take just any jeep—he stole the colonel's jeep. Al and Cotton were taken into custody and placed in confinement at the My Tho jail. To his surprise, within hours, they both were released. The only punishment was to get a haircut. His hangover from the drinking served as a greater punishment, but that only lasted a short while. *That was too easy*, he thought. *Next time I'll take it downtown and see what I can get for a jeep on the black market.* He knew of others who had done it.

Exactly one year to the day, Al left Vietnam on January 3, 1968. To him the whole year 1967 had been a total waste. He left the country just in time. The Tet Offensive by the NVA began just a couple of weeks later, and the war ratcheted up yet again. Since he signed on for a three-year enlistment, Al still had some time left to serve. His next assignment took him to Fort Benning, Georgia.

Al made no bones about his feelings with the war and with the US Army. He hated the army, he hated Vietnam, and he hated the people of Vietnam. The entire Vietnam experience seemed like a bad dream. When he arrived at Fort Benning, he soon realized he was in like company. Nearly all the soldiers were leftovers from the war. They had the same attitude and really didn't give a hoot if anyone knew their feelings. They just wanted to get out and get back home. Al drove a truck at Fort Benning and made runs to and from the mess hall. He served his time with the army and discharged on March 21, 1969.

During Al's time in the military, he earned the Vietnam Service Medal, the Vietnam Campaign Medal with Device, and the Bronze Star.

CHARLES L. PUTZ, PRIVATE SECOND CLASS, E-2

United States Army
June 23, 1966–June 5, 1968

Charley Putz grew up on a farm north of Milo and was the oldest of seven kids. He was a tall slender fella and, for the most part, kept to himself. I knew his sister Shirley better than him since she and I graduated together from high school in 1967. Charley was two years older.

Charley received his draft notice in the spring of 1966, less than a year after he left school. On June 23, 1966, he raised his right hand and took the oath of induction into the US Army. "I do solemnly swear that I will support and defend the Constitution of the United States against all enemies, foreign and domestic; that I will bear true faith and allegiance to the same; and that I will obey the orders of the President of the United States and the orders of the officers appointed."

He departed Milo and headed to Fort Leonard Wood, Missouri, for basic training. Upon completion of boot camp, he remained at

Fort Leonard Wood for advanced infantry training and additional schooling with a MOS of 12C20, a bridge specialist.

His first duty assignment in January 1967, sent him to Furth, Germany, home of the 24th Engineering Battalion, 4th Armored Division, located near Nuremberg. He arrived after a fourteen-hour flight aboard a twin-engine turbo-prop aircraft that departed McGuire AFB, New Jersey, located adjacent to Fort Dix. Once at Furth, he quickly settled in at Johnson Barracks. As a member of the engineering battalion, he operated equipment designed for amphibious river crossings (ARC). Charley commented, "During my one year, four months tour of duty in Germany, my outfit performed only one ARC as part of a training exercise. Most of the time, I had guard duty or KP" (kitchen patrol).

Charley went on to say that his whole military experience was almost like a vacation. Prior to his enlistment in the army, he never strayed too far from Iowa, let alone a trip to Europe. The duty was real easy, unlike doing chores on the farm before and after school. In the army, he worked just forty hours per week and rarely any weekends. "My two-year hitch with Uncle Sam was a walk in the park." When quizzed about his memories of Germany, his quick response was, "The twelve-percent beer!" He went on to say, "Heck, when I got back home, I'd have to down a whole case of beer to get the same buzz as a few Bitburgers."

Private Putz returned to Fort Dix where he discharged from the Army on June 5, 1968.

LARRY KUBLI, SPECIALIST 5

United States Army
August 8, 1966–July 13, 1968

L arry graduated from high school in the spring of 1965. He grew up on a farm a few miles east of Milo. I remember Larry as a fast runner. He played running back on the football team and outfield on the baseball team, but his best sport, as recognized by many, was track. Larry was a quarter-miler and a hard guy to run down. As part of the mile relay team, he, along with Bob Ford, Larry Lancaster, and Dick Klein, won many races for the green and white of Southeast Warren High School. Their school record time for the mile relay in 1965 remained intact for thirty-four years until finally broken in 1999 with a time of 3:28.9.

Just one year after graduation, Larry received his draft notice. He left Des Moines, headed to Fort Leonard Wood, Missouri, for basic training in August 1966. Earlier in April 1966, the US Army announced that due to the growing man power needs of the Vietnam War, and to accommodate the thirty thousand to forty thousand inductees per month into the army, it would be expanding the basic training centers to include Fort Lewis, Washington. All recruits that initially headed to Fort Leonard Wood with Larry were sent elsewhere. All the other recruits were immediately shipped out to other locations except Larry. He sat alone in the barracks in Missouri for two days before getting new orders that sent him West. He was the only recruit sent to Fort Lewis from the hundreds of others that reported at Fort Leonard Wood the same time as he. He later found out that he would be part of the first basic training group from Fort Lewis since World War II.

Upon completion of basic training, Larry received orders to Fort Sill, Oklahoma, for a quick two-week course in advanced infantry training (AIT), followed by an eight-week course for advanced training as a light vehicle mechanic, a MOS (means of support) of 63030. With that behind him, and lucky as he could ever imagine, in September 1966, he remained at Fort Sill as a light vehicle mechanic for the headquarters group. He remained there until his next assignment directed him to Vietnam.

On July 21, 1967, Larry arrived at Cam Ranh Bay, Vietnam. There he was assigned to headquarters of the 35th Engineer Group. Larry stated the first thirty days of duty consisted of driving high-ranking military officers around the base, a somewhat mundane and downright boring assignment. Larry noted that the commanding officer of the 35th Engineer group quickly noticed his unenthusiastic demeanor as the military version of a chauffer. Without hesitation, Larry agreed with the commander's assessment. Within a few days, he was reassigned duty within the 35th Engineer Group and worked in the motor pool where he was in charge of inventory for repair parts of vehicles and stock shipment orders. Larry commented, "It was pretty easy duty, I was never once shot at or felt I was in harm's way. It seemed almost like Stateside duty."

Despite being in a war zone, even the headquarters group had inspector general (IG) inspections during Larry's time in the motor pool at Cam Ranh Bay. Every GI that has endured such an IG inspection can attest that there is a military way to conduct business, coupled with the inspector general's concept of doing business. Somewhere in the middle, a reasonable conformity to practice and policy met. That usually happened a day or two after the IG team inspectors left the area. In Larry's case, he recalled taking a full truckload of inventory parts for a day trip to the beach before the arrival of the inspection team. "Out of sight, out of mind, and out of the inspectors' view" became a policy not just of the motor pool at Cam Ranh Bay but multiple organizations throughout the military, regardless of which branch of service. For some strange reason, things just seemed to work smoother without prying eyes that peered over your shoulder questioning every single accountable item or action performed. The day after the inspection, Larry sent a crew to the beach to bring back the ratholed items, and business continued as usual.

One item that didn't escape the probing inspector's eye was Larry's personal locker at the motor pool. He was at the barracks when he received a notice to report to his duty section immediately. Larry was miffed at why he was called but soon found out. The inspectors opened Larry's personal locker and discovered his dog tags hanging on a hook inside the locker. That was a write up as relayed to Larry. He was to wear his dog tags at all times, not leave them in his locker. Larry commented, "I guess they just wanted to nit-pick the place and could find nothing better to correct than my lousy dog tags not being around my neck." For the next two weeks, the ranking NCO checked Larry to confirm the fact that he wore his dog tags. War is hell, or so they say.

Larry took on a new responsibility in the motor pool shortly after the IG inspection. He became the guy that qualified troops to drive specific vehicles and issued military drivers' licenses. Army regulation 600-55, the Army Driver and Operator Standardization Program for selection, training, testing, and licensing became his new mantra. Surprisingly many who arrived in country did not have a valid military driver's license. Not only did they not have a military license, a great number did not have a valid Stateside license. Larry recalled one particular soldier from New York City who had never driven a car. Larry grew up on a farm and had been behind the wheel of tractors, pickups, combines, and even motorcycles since age thirteen. He couldn't fathom anyone who had never driven a car. "So how did you get around back home?" Larry asked the young soldier.

The New Yorker answered back. "Oh, I'd take a taxi or ride the bus, sometimes the subway."

"Well, you got one on me," Larry told him, "I never rode in a taxi, bus, or subway train back in my hometown." Larry took the guy from the Big Apple out on the taxiway at Cam Ranh Bay when no aircraft were around and turned him loose. "This is the clutch, that's the brake, there is the shifting column, have at it. I'll watch from a distance." Luckily both survived the experience. Larry thought to himself, *And Uncle Sam is going to turn this guy loose with a gun.*

On March 4, 1968, Cam Ranh Bay took some mortar rounds from the Vietcong. Fuel bladders along the flight line were ignited. The air force fire department extinguished the extensive fire, but the base received only minor damage. Larry remembered the incident as the only time during his Vietnam tour that he felt any duress. During that incident, he was issued an M16 and remained near his duty station at the motor pool in a readiness posture. Yes, indeed he had his dog tags around his neck.

In April of 1968, a portion of the 35th Engineers Group relocated to Qui Nhon and established a base of operations there. Qui Nhon was a coastal city located in the Binh Dinh Province on the South China Sea, about 170 miles north of Cam Ranh Bay on Highway 1. A few days before the move, Larry flew to Qui Nhon on a C-121 Constellation (Connie) to facilitate the transition. When he went to the air terminal at Cam Ranh Bay to catch his plane, to his amazement, he saw another Milo boy also waiting for a flight. What a chance meeting when he greeted Dick Coffman. Dick was a 1965 graduate of Southeast Warren High school. After some hearty backslapping and handshakes, they went on their way, not to see each other again until back in Iowa.

Larry remained at Qui Nhon for only a few more months until his enlistment ended in July 1968. With great anticipation, he headed home. Larry compared his time in Vietnam as if it were a trip to the dentist office for a bad toothache. He knew he needed to go, he didn't want to go, he didn't enjoy the visit, and he was glad to leave. He winced a few times, clutched his fists in anticipation of pain, but everything turned out pretty good. He acknowledged that yes, God watched over him during that year. Many things could have easily gone sour, but by God's grace, Larry was headed home unscathed.

Larry's return to the United States was not without frustration. The aircraft scheduled to depart from Cam Ranh Bay with returning soldiers experienced mechanical problems. The army procured a second aircraft after a twelve-hour delay. Larry and the other returning troops, who were elated over the completion of the Vietnam tour of duty and finally headed home, had to temper their joy a while longer before liftoff. When finally airborne, the first leg of the return journey to the States took them through the USAF base in Yakota, Japan. Once there, another problem arose. There was no flight crew available due to the initial cancellation for the disabled aircraft from Cam Ranh Bay. Another five-hour delay surfaced while base operations at Yakota searched for a fresh aircrew to fly the thirteen-hour final leg to McChord AFB, Washington, adjacent to Fort Lewis. Finally Larry arrived at Fort Lewis in the early morning hours of Saturday, July 13, 1968. Yet again, another obstacle popped its ugly head. The army had no one available to out process Larry and the rest of the returning GIs at 2:00 a.m. The personnel office rousted some clerical administrators out of bed and got the out-processing task completed. The military lingo for such a chain of events is often referred to as a snafu (something normal all fouled up). As the sun rose on Saturday morning, July 13, 1968, Larry became a civilian once again. Hallelujah!

The number 1 hit on the Billboards top 10 that week was "This Guy's in Love with You," which was written by Burt Bacharach and recorded by Herb Albert. For certain, Larry wasn't in love with just any girl, he was in love with the good old USA. But even more than that, he was in love with Milo, the small community he called home. Larry managed to climb out of the dentist's chair after one year, eleven months, and six days. He returned home with all his teeth and a Pepsodent smile that even Shirley Temple and Clark Gable envied.

By midweek, Larry was back at the farm helping his father, Wayne, bale the second cutting of alfalfa hay. Oh, the sweet smell of freshly mown hay! Oh, the sweet smell of freedom!

RONALD E. CLARK, PFC

United States Army
November 21, 1967–May 14, 1968

I remember Ron Clark as a soft-spoken unassuming kid. He was of slight build and unusually polite to almost everyone, an uncommon trait for young teenagers in the early 1960s. He was another Milo boy that championed all that was good about the small community. Ron was two years ahead of me in school. I knew his younger brother, Dennis, much better since we both played on the junior high football team. Prior to his junior year in high school, Ron and his family moved to Indianola, the county seat, just twelve miles north of Milo. I didn't see him much after the move from Milo, unless we passed each other as we scooped the loop around the Indianola town square on a Saturday night.

I was a sophomore in college when I got word that he had been killed in Vietnam. Quite frankly, I had lost all track of him after graduating from high school and didn't even know he joined the army.

As often said, a lot of water has passed under the bridge since then. How could I find out what happened to Ron? Who had the answers to my questions about him? I turned to another old friend of mine, Jon Fehrer. Jon and I have been good buddies for over sixty years. Jon married Ron's widow, Debbie, and became the step-father for Ron's young son, Ronald Clark. Jon pointed me in the right direction with contact information about Ron Junior. I vaguely knew Ron. We had met off and on over the years during some social events with Jon's family. He knew who I was, but our relationship was merely acquaintances only. I had his phone number and called him and related the fact that I would like to hear what information he knew about his dad's time in the military. My query was well received. Ron told me, "I've got exactly what you need."

As coincidence played out, I arranged to meet Ron at his house in nearby Lacona, the hometown of my wife, to hear what information he might have about his dad, Ron. On that same day, I also scheduled a visit with a first cousin of mine, Bill Warbington, from Portland, Oregon. He just happened to be in the area, driving up to Lacona from Kansas City, Missouri, for a short hello with relatives. He was in Kansas City for the weekend as part of a Vietnam War reunion of his unit where he served as a helicopter pilot. The war was long over, but the memories for all who served remained vivid some fifty years later. Sharing those stories was caring for those who lived them.

As I walked onto the front porch of Ron's home, I tried to remember what he looked like, a skinny kid with blond hair and an unforgettable grin. Much like I remembered his dad, Ron. Before I could knock on the door, it swung open. There stood a middle-aged man, forty-nine years old with gray whiskers, still in his camouflaged shirt and pants from his wild turkey hunt earlier in the morning. "Come on in, Mike, I've been waiting for you," he said as he grabbed my hand with a vice-grip handshake.

I stepped into the house, and the first thing that caught my eye were the multitude of wild animals mounted on the walls, sitting atop the dining room table and the floor. A wild turkey peered at me, mounted on a perch near the ceiling. Two huge busts of antlered deer stared at me across the room. A small set of moose antlers occupied the dining room table. I quickly figured out, Ron was a taxidermist. He brought back to life various animals that seemed so lifelike I kept waiting for them to move.

As I continued to survey the room, I noticed in the far corner, a triangular-shaped wooden display case with a crisp folded American flag that neatly rested behind a glass window. Below I saw rows of military ribbons, and then the small snapshot of his dad in uniform. With that military display, Ron brought to life his dad's legacy, much like the wild animals that surrounded me, which were brought back to life through his taxidermy skills. The father he never knew was present, front and center. I felt as if I should stand at attention and salute. Ron gently took the display case and placed it on the table in front of me. The yellow Vietnam campaign ribbon with red and green stripes virtually jumped through its glass protective covering, as if shouting, "I was there!" Ron got a screwdriver and carefully took the only photo he had of his father out of the frame and handed it to me. "Here, you can make a copy if you want," he said. I bit my lip at that moment and reeled in my emotions.

"So what do you want to know about my dad?" he asked.

I told him I had a small amount of information that I retrieved from the Vietnam veteran's website, but it was very generic. "What can you tell me about your dad?" I asked him.

Ron went on to explain that he was born on August 5, 1968, about three months after his father was killed in action on May 14, 1968. All he knew about his dad was information he received from others and the generic information already posted on the Internet's virtual wall website. That information consisted of the following: "Ronald Emery Clark, age 22, PFC, US Army, A Troop, 1st Squadron, 11th Armored Cavalry, killed in action on May 14, 1968, Binh Duong, South Vietnam, hostile ground fire." Ron went on to say that he attended the twenty-ninth reunion of the 11th Armored Cavalry, Veterans of Vietnam, held in Las Vegas in September of 2014. There he met two soldiers who served with his father, Ed Brown from San Antonio, Texas, and Gerry Costa from Corning, New York. As Paul Harvey would say during his radio broadcasts, "And now, the rest of the story."

I called Ed Brown with the phone number given to me by Ron. After I explained to him who I was, how I knew Ron Clark, and my efforts at telling his story, Ed spoke with me on the phone for over half an hour.

"Yes, I remember Ron Clark. I was Ron's platoon sergeant." He went on to tell me their platoon engaged the enemy near Xuan Loc, not far from Cu Chi. A heavy firefight with the VC began on the afternoon of May 13, 1968, and continued through the next day. Artillery fire directed on the village all but flattened it. Then the USAF hit it again with multiple bombing runs. Their M113 armored personnel carrier (APC), affectionately called "green dragons," came under fire as well, but the rockets fell well short of their position. Ron's company amounted to eight APCs, with about thirty to forty troops, and accompanied by four tanks. Each APC was armed with a .50-caliber machine gun and carried up to a dozen soldiers. Most of the time, however, only four or five troops occupied the APC since it also served to carry ammunition, food, water, and other supplies for the soldiers while in the field.

There came a lengthy lull in the action, and Sergeant Brown received orders to proceed into the village. He thought it would be just a quick in and out, not much more than a body count of the VC since they clobbered them pretty hard the last two days. He told Ron to get in the APC on the right, he took the left side position, along with one other, and the driver. Within a few seconds, out of nowhere, a rocket-propelled grenade (RPG) slammed directly into the right side of the APC and exploded. Ron took a direct hit. The explosion threw his body to the left side of the APC and against Sergeant Brown. Ron died instantly. Ed Brown received multiple injuries, and the concussion from the explosion temporarily deafened him. Ed went on to say he spent nearly three years in and out of the Veterans Administration (VA) hospital for treatment of his injuries that fateful day. He has only partial hearing even today as a result of the blast.

Ed relayed to me what haunted him most. "The mystery and madness of that day, May 14, 1968, lives with me. I could have told him to get in the APC on the left and me on the right. It was a toss of the coin that cost Ron his life and saved mine. I can never forget that."

Ron Clark was posthumously awarded the Bronze Star and Purple Heart.

Ron became the first Milo boy to die during the Vietnam conflict. Unfortunately he would not be the last.

*The lot is cast into the lap, but its every decision is from the L*ORD*.*
—Proverbs 16:33

STEVE HINDMAN, SPECIALIST FOURTH CLASS, E-4

United States Army
January 2, 1968–October 18, 1969

S teve lived on a farm a few miles west of Milo. The homestead was directly across the dusty gravel road from the Dale Fridley farm. Steve was two years older than me. I got to know him best as a teenager when I worked for his dad, Ray Hindman, when I helped the family bale hay in the summer. It was hard work, I'll attest, but the joy I took in the labors outweighed all the sore muscles and sweat I endured. The fact that Ray had enough confidence in my ability and allowed me to drive their blue-and-gray 1965 Ford 5000 tractor from the field to the barn gave me such elation. Steve drove the tractor that pulled the hay baler, so we rendezvoused every hour or so in the field and switched my empty hay wagon for a full one that I pulled back to the barn and unloaded.

Ray and his wife, Roberta, were the nicest people. I first met them at the Milo United Methodist Church years earlier when I attended Sunday school as a preteen. Both taught Sunday school classes at the church for years. Steve's younger sister, Patty, was a year behind me in school.

When gathering information from Steve about his military experience, he commented, "We all have crossroads in our lives, and the paths we take often lead us in unknown directions." Steve's crossroad in life began with a high school typing class taught by Mrs. Mabel Maulik. His mother insisted that he learn how to type. Steve's reply was typical. "Why do I need to know how to type, I'm going to be a farmer?" His mother's perseverance prevailed, and Steve took the typing class. Little did he know how that decision would impact his future.

Upon completion of high school in the spring of 1965, Steve enrolled in an automotive school located in Omaha, Nebraska. Already adept at fixing cars and machinery around the farm, this schooling, he thought, would be an added touch for his future profession as a farmer.

In late 1967, the Warren County draft board notified Steve they needed his presence at their office. Steve was drafted into the US Army on January 2, 1968, and reported to Fort Bliss, Texas, for basic training. Upon completion of basic training, Steve entered advanced schooling as an auto mechanic with a MOS of 63D20.

His first assignment sent him to Fort Belvior, Virginia, with the 81st Engineering Company. Within days of his arrival, the senior enlisted officer asked the question to his company, "Does anyone know how to type?"

Steve immediately raised his hand. "I do, sir!" Thus Steve packed up his tools and headed to the parts department of the motor pool. "On my best day, I could type thirty-five words per minute," Steve confessed. "I never again touched a wrench while at Fort Belvior." He typed purchase orders and requisition requests for automotive parts.

On April 4, 1968, things changed not only for Steve but for America. On that day, Martin Luther King Jr. was assassinated as he stood on the balcony of the Lorraine Hotel in Memphis, Tennessee. Chaos reigned in the black communities across America. On April 5, Steve, along with 13,600 other federal troops, were sent armed to walk patrol in the black communities of Washington DC, and maintain the peace and assist the overwhelmed law enforcement. "It was a scary time," Steve recalled. "We climbed into the back of a truck, then drove through the city. One soldier at a time jumped out and took up a position at each intersection. We were issued an M14 rifle and three rounds of ammunition. I'm not joking, just three rounds of ammunition!" He continued, "At night, we slept in the back of convoy trucks with nothing more than a canvas cover for protection from the elements. Later we moved into a school gymnasium." Marines with machine guns were at the steps of the US capital and the Third Infantry guarded the White House. On April 5, 1968, rioters came within two city blocks of the White House before they retreated. That incident marked the first such occupation of any US city since the Civil War.

Eighty percent of the Washington DC police department in 1968 were comprised of white officers. The population of Washington DC, at the time was 67 percent black. Black unemployment hovered at 30 percent. The riots continued for six days. The King assassination was not the sole reason for such violent riots. A buildup of tension within the Washington DC black community had festered for some time around issues of housing segregation, unemployment, and strong-arm police tactics within the black community.

On April 11, President Lyndon Johnson signed the Civil Rights Act of 1968 (Fair Housing Act) which prohibited discrimination concerning the sale, rental, or financing of housing based on race or religion. He also declared the next Sunday as Martin Luther King Jr. Day, a day for all Americans to mourn, and ordered all flags across the nation to be lowered to half-mast. That action became the precursor of the MLK holiday recognized today but not officially enacted for another fifteen years in 1983 under the Reagan administration.

For Steve, that week in April was an eye-opener. He never once had any contact with black people back in Milo. There were none. The over-the-top hatred against the established government witnessed by Steve from the Washington DC population became a memory etched in his mind he will not forget.

About four months into his assignment at Fort Belvior, Steve received orders for Vietnam. He wasn't the least bit surprised. He became hesitant, however, to tell his parents about his new destination but knew he had to. He was surprised at their response. He certainly didn't want to go. His mother told him, "If it's God's will that you go. Do not fear, as He will always be with you."

> *Do not be conformed to this world, but be transformed by the renewal of your mind, that by testing, you may discern what is the will of God, what is good and acceptable and perfect.* (**Romans 12:2**)

Steve arrived in Vietnam on October 15, 1968, and found himself at Dĩ An, a town in the Bình Dương Province located about twelve miles north of Saigon. There he was assigned to the 3rd Squadron, 17th Air Calvary, 816 Signal Detachment. Upon his arrival, one of the very first questions asked of him was, "Can you type?"

"Well, of course," he told the sergeant. And so it was. God continued to watch over Steve, and the typing class in high school again paid huge dividends. It was a crossroads moment for Steve. He became the dispatcher for the vehicle maintenance shop and pecked away on his typewriter for this entire tour of duty.

Steve told me, "I never fired a shot the whole time I was in Vietnam. I never drank a beer, never took a shot of whiskey, or smoked cigarettes or marijuana, and never once gambled playing cards. Well, let me refine that," he continued. "I did gamble but not playing cards. I played lots and lots of ping-pong at the recreation center. One day, a guy came in and challenged me to a game. I told him sure."

Before he even picked up his paddle, the challenger asked, "What do you want to play for? How about $5 per game?"

Steve told him, "No, let's just play for the fun of it." The guy insisted that the fun of the game was playing for money. Steve gave in and agreed to play for $5. Steve won the first game.

Immediately his opponent demanded, "Double or nothing on the next game." And so it went, on and on and on. Each game became a double up. Steve could tell the guy was getting real ticked off that he was losing, so he offered to stop playing. His opponent could lick his wounds and quit anytime. Finally Steve made an offer, feeling sorry for the rookie ping-pong player. "I'll play till we're even on money or you're broke." The amateur took the challenge. Sometime later the soldier tossed his paddle on the table, opened his wallet, and tossed out $1,600 cash. The loser walked out of the room and grumbled under his breath. Steve had no intentions to hustle the guy. He just would not let him win. The cash amounted to nearly six months' pay. Steve took the money and went to the dispatch office and locked it in the safe.

It didn't take long for word to spread that Steve was top dog at the game of ping-pong. A good buddy of his, Ray Skipper from Texas, teamed up with Steve, and the pair became unbeatable. These events were years ahead of the movie *Forrest Gump,* released in 1994. However, the character of Forrest Gump mimicked Steve's prowess at the game of ping-pong.

Steve's tour of duty in Vietnam ended on October 16, 1969. He returned to the States and was given an early out on his enlistment. He was astonished as he walked through the passenger terminal in California while in uniform. People made snide remarks at him, vulgar hand gestures, and a few even spit in his direction. He felt proud that he answered his country's call to duty but confused about his reception in America. Who were these weird people?

Years later, when attending a Fourth of July parade in St. Louis, Missouri, Steve heard cheers from the crowd as soldiers who had just returned from the Iraq War marched in formation. He stood and cheered too. He told me, "And then the cheers became really loud. A group of Vietnam veterans marched together at the end of the parade. They wore blue jeans, had long hair, and old fatigue uniforms that didn't button up. A chill ran up my back, and I got goose bumps up my arms. And yes, I teared up. I was proud once again. Proud to be an American, proud to be a soldier, and proud to be from Milo."

God's will prevailed, just as his mother, Roberta, told him. As our discussion came to an end, Steve relayed to me a story about his great-grandfather. "You know, he fought in the Civil War and came home without a scratch."

"That had to be something," I told him. "Especially with the high casualty rate back then. Of the 1,264,000 soldiers killed in all of our nation's wars, 626,000 were killed in the Civil War. Another 475,883 were injured."

Steve went on, "Amazing how things work out. My great-grand-father was killed after the war when a horse kicked him in the head as he mowed hay." My thoughts flashed back fifty years earlier to the days that Steve and I worked in the hayfields on his father's farm. Yes, for both of us, life had been like a box of chocolates. We never knew what we were going to get.

LOREN EDWARDS, SPECIALIST FIFTH CLASS, E-5

United States Army
April 8, 1968–April 7, 1970

L oren was a late comer to the Milo community. He moved there from Des Moines at the beginning of his junior year in high school. He fit right in with all the crazy youngsters that roamed the streets, seeking out mischief. Loren graduated from high school in 1966. His family lived at the west end of Main Street, just north of Buck Bales' garage, in a very modest house. Loren wrestled on the high school wrestling team. He was just one of the guys that blended in among so many others.

Loren was just a little squirt of a guy, and his passion rested in cars. In the fall of 1967, he bought a brand-new 1966 black Dodge Coronet. It had a 383 cubic-inch engine with a four-speed manual transmission and white leather interior. He became the envy of every guy in town who ever dreamed of such a street rod. The price of the new car then was about $2,500. A large sum at the time.

With the fast and fancy car came fast and crazy times. Loren admitted he wasn't the best behaved kid in town and had his share of regretful moments. As he later said, "You don't think ahead about troubles, with all the shenanigans I pulled. Instead I gave more thought to how to get myself out of a jam." That ideology held true for most of the Milo boys who screeched their chrome-rim wheels at every stop sign in town. For the younger kids, Milo was a playground, a parklike setting. For the older guys with cars, it was a drag strip. With no police patrols in the town of five hundred residents, it became open season for just about anything mischievous that could be conjured up. It was easier to ask for forgiveness later rather than permission at the moment.

Loren got married on August 7, 1967. There was no exotic honeymoon for him and his wife, Pam. The very next day, he reported to the Warren County draft board with the thought that his goose was cooked. To his surprise, he wasn't inducted into the military. At least not for the moment. Just seven months elapsed before his draft notice found its way to his mailbox. On April 8, 1968, Loren was drafted into the US Army.

When he in-processed at Fort Des Moines, he recognized one of the soldiers that conducted the enlistments. Finally he approached the fella and asked him who he was. "You sure look familiar." Loren quizzed him. "What's your name?" The soldier recognized Loren, but he too could not put a name with the face. After some back-and-forth questions, Loren discovered the guy was a classmate of his, way back in elementary school in Des Moines. His first lucky break, so to speak.

"Do you want to be a marine?" asked his former classmate.

"No, emphatically no!" Loren responded.

"Well, get back in line, and when you do, count so that you are standing in an even-numbered position." Loren jumped back into line, counted down, and squeezed in at number 16.

Just as his classmate warned, every third inductee became a marine. At number 16, Loren became a member of the US Army. That same day, he boarded a plane and headed to El Paso, Texas, home to Fort Bliss and his new residence for the next eight weeks of boot camp.

An incredible event happened once at Fort Bliss. When he began his boot camp and assigned a platoon, defying even the best of Las Vegas odd makers, he encountered Larry Johnson and Fred Fridley. Both were Milo boys, both had graduated with him in high school, and both were in the same platoon. All three bunked together in the cubical room of the concrete barracks. Added to the astronomical odds of the three Milo boys being together, another anomaly occurred. A few weeks into their boot camp, they discovered yet another Milo boy was bunked just a few doors away. Dan Reeves of Milo, also a 1966 graduate, had just arrived before for the long Memorial Day weekend as a new recruit. They paid him a surprise visit and dog-piled him as he napped in his bunk. Of the nine Milo boys who graduated together in 1966, four found themselves together at Fort Bliss in the spring of 1968. After half an hour of handshakes, backslaps, and shared memories, they departed. The foursome never met again until after the war.

Loren completed basic training in early June of 1968. His next stop took him to Fort Huachucka, Arizona, for a two-month long school as a supply technician. His MOS was 76J40.

Finished with the supply school, Loren's next set of orders took him to Okinawa in the Ryukya Island chain of the South China Sea in October 1968. The Ryukya Island chain, also known as Nansei Islands, was part of the sixty-four island Kyushu chain that stretched to within one hundred miles of Taiwan. There Loren was assigned to the 2nd Logistical Command Headquarters, 70th Medical Depot, part of the US Army Hospital. His responsibility was enormous. Loren supplied all of South East Asia (SEA) with needed emergency medical supplies. That encompassed everything within the US military's medical inventory that ranged from eye glasses to bandages and morphine. Loren manned a desk equipped with a hotline, answered twenty-four hours per day, seven days per week, that had the capability to receive calls from field hospitals in Vietnam. When a life-or-death situation arose and specific medical needs were requested, Loren dispatched the required items immediately. A F-104 Starfighter out of Naha Air Force Base, Okinawa, flew the priority items within hours of the request. It proved to be a very satisfying job for Loren, knowing that his actions saved lives of American soldiers.

From fiscal year 1967 through fiscal year 1969, the total volume of medical supplies that passed through the medical depot on Okinawa jumped from $28.5 million yearly to $71.5 million. In that same period, shipments received jumped from 482 short tons per month to 932 short tons per month. Loren was front and center on the tail end of that time frame and had his finger on the huge, huge deliverance of medical supplies to soldiers in need that served in SEA.

Loren's wife, Pam, joined him in Okinawa in late October of 1968, even though Loren's military assignment was classified as an isolated tour. That simply meant that since he was not a career soldier, the US government would not pay for her travel expenses to Okinawa, nor would they recognize her presence and make available government on-base housing. Loren and Pam were not concerned with career military status, they just wanted to be together. She was pregnant, and it was important for them to be together for the birth of their first child. Pam sold the 1966 Dodge Coronet and obtained the money for an airline ticket. They rented an apartment off base and were as happy as two ticks in a bear rug. Their son, Grayson, was born March 2, 1969.

Okinawa, also called The Rock, was an island just sixty-five miles long and thirteen miles wide. It had been occupied since the end of WWII by the United States and strategically located in the South China Sea. The USAF flew B-52 bomber missions from Naha AFB over Vietnam. Loren received verbal orders to report to work extra early on one particular day. He was also told to wear his battle dress uniform (BDU) instead of the normal khaki office attire. He arrived before dawn and waited in his car just inside the main gate near the supply warehouse. He noticed a crowd gathered outside the gate as the sun came up. About two hundred local nationals came to the base and protested the US presence on the island. Most were college kids from the university, and the political tension in Okinawa between the local nationals and the United States boiled over. Communist political activists infiltrated the group and promoted the anti-American agenda.

As the base commander approached the installation in his staff car, the protesters rushed the vehicle and pounded it with wooden clubs. They broke several windows and dented nearly every corner of the staff car before it reached the safety inside the main gate. Loren watched from his parked car and pondered why he had been instructed to wear the BDUs to work that day. The general calmly got out of his vehicle once inside the gate and did a quick walk around and examined the damage. He got back inside the vehicle and drove off.

Within twenty minutes, the general returned. When he got out of the car, an M16 rifle hung over his shoulder. Behind him followed a cadre of US Marines who were also armed. They marched through the main gate in bulldozer fashion and pushed the protesters to the side of the road and into the ditch. It was a serious moment for the protesters involved, and it was a very serious moment for US relations with the local nationals. Finally things calmed down, the entrance road to the base remained clear, and the protesters dissipated. Loren jumped out of his vehicle and headed to his office.

One particular duty day, Loren received a call from the first sergeant. The first shirt told him to go requisition a sidearm and check out a jeep from the motor pool. He was tasked to escort a prisoner from the brig to the hospital for a psychiatric evaluation. Loren asked, "So who is this guy I am to get?"

"His name is Matthews. He was arrested at the airport, attempting to leave the island and has been absent without leave (AWOL) for several weeks after he collected his variable re-enlistment bonus (VRB). He was wearing a red zoot suit when picked up. I understand he has been a fixture in the Naha City red-light district."

Loren dutifully headed to the brig with a military-issued .45 caliber pistol, a Colt Commander, strapped to his side. There he found his prisoner for the escort to the hospital. Matthews walked out handcuffed, and to Loren's surprise, he knew the guy. He couldn't remember his first name, but Matthews and Loren went through basic training together back in 1968 at Fort Bliss, Texas, in the very same platoon. Matthews was a tall black dude, about 6'4", and walked with a swagger like that of a drum major from some college marching band. Once he spotted Loren, he too recognized him as the little chalk-white squirt from basic. "Hey, my main man Ed, what's up?" He spoke as if they were long-lost friends.

"What in the world is going on, Matthews?" Loren asked him.

"Oh, just a little mix up, Ed. I'm fixin' to get it straightened out soon. You with me, bro?"

On the ride to the hospital, Matthews came on hard to Loren. "If you just stop and let me get out, man, nobody will know nothin'. We be friends from boot camp, right? Don't ya'll remember me?"

"I do," answered Loren, "I do. I also remember my wife and son. If you escape while in my custody, I'd find myself behind bars, just like you. If you even so much as attempt to run, I'll shoot you in a heartbeat."

Loren made it to the hospital with his prisoner without further conversation. He waited a couple of hours while the medical staff completed their evaluation of Matthews. On the return trip to the brig, not a word was spoken. Loren never saw him again.

After nineteen months of duty in Okinawa, Loren headed back to Oakland, California, where he discharged from the army on April 7, 1970. From there he made a beeline back to Iowa and set up his residence in Des Moines.

It was good to be back to the heartland of America. The cost of a gallon of gas hovered around 36¢ per gallon. The average price of a new home pegged at $23,450. Postage stamps cost just 6¢. The Dow Jones Industrial Average reached 838 points, and the average income in America stretched just above $9,000 per year.

Prior to Uncle Sam's call for him to serve his country back in 1968, Loren worked in the auto parts business. He returned to his love for cars and car parts as a civilian in Des Moines where he managed The Auto Parts Warehouse for two years, then the Rissman Auto Warehouse. An opportunity arose for a manufacturer's representative in the auto parts business, and Loren jumped at the chance. He and his family relocated to Mulvane, Kansas, in December 1979, and life seemed good. The new job required extensive travel, and Loren found himself on the road frequently. He often wined and dined clients and viewed that as a requirement of the job. He also found himself alone many times at far-flung hotel rooms that stretched as far west as the Colorado border. Loren filled his empty time with alcohol. He justified it as part of his job to entertain customers. It soon became a problem, not for just himself, but his wife, Pam, also drank when he was out of town. When home, they went out together and celebrated. Of course that included more alcohol consumption. "It got bad," Loren said. "We argued often when together, all focused on alcohol. The arguments encouraged me to be away from home even more, and the cycle of drinking continued." In January of 1980, while on a drinking binge, Pam attempted suicide. Something, they thought, had to be done, something.

Pam knew the bus driver who picked the kids up on Sunday morning and transported them to Sunday school at the church in Mulvane. What she didn't know was that he pulled double duty. In addition to driving the Sunday school bus, he was also the pastor of the Nazarene Church. She reached out to him and confessed both her and Loren's problems. On March 2, 1980, both Loren and Pam found themselves on their knees at the altar of the Mulvane Church of the Nazarene. Loren mentioned that never before had he been to the altar of any church, let alone kneeling and weeping. He was a broken man and needed divine assistance. That evening, both Loren and Pam gave their lives to the Lord Jesus Christ. They lived a sinful life for years. Now they asked for a new beginning.

> *Do not be deceived: God is not mocked, for whatever one sows, that will he also reap. For the one who sows to his flesh, will from the flesh reap corruption, but the one who sows to the Spirit will from the Spirit reap eternal life. And let us not grow weary of doing good, for in due season we will reap, if we do not give up.* (**Galatians 6:7–9**)

As if someone had flipped a light switch, their lives began an upward climb rather than a downward spiral. Loren's story, however, did not end there. The lyrics from the song "Amazing Grace" reverberated in his ear, "I once was blind, but now I see."

In 1982, Loren quit his job as a manufacturer's representative for automotive parts. He had a new calling. He would no longer fix broken cars with new parts. He wanted to repair the hearts and souls of broken individuals, like himself—*thee* Loren Edwards, one of the Milo boys. He entered the Nazarene Bible College in Colorado Springs, Colorado. For the next twenty-seven years, he pastored churches in Upstate New York, Maryland, Iowa, Kansas, and Missouri.

Today Loren and his wife live in Casa Grande, Arizona, where he retired from the ministry. He continues to work a part-time job. He's a bus driver. Of all things, a bus driver.

THEODORE DANIEL REEVES, SPECIALIST 5

United States Army
May 28, 1968–May 28, 1971

There is a time for everything, and a season for every
activity under heaven. A time to love and a time to
hate, a time for war and a time for peace.

—Ecclesiastes 3:8

There was a kid from Milo who lived about two city blocks directly west from me. I knew him well, oh so very well. As preteens, we both were members of our local Boy Scout Troop 136. He delivered the daily newspaper to the north side of Milo while I handled the south side paper route. In high school, he was the wingback on the football team while I played the halfback position. We ran together on the school track team as the opening and final leg of the mile relay. We went hunting and fishing together as youngsters, rolled corn silk cigarettes and then smoked them in the secrecy of his garage, got into fistfights, and then afterward would stay overnight at either his house or mine. For sure, we were pretty tight. More than just real good friends, Dan was my mom's brother. Yep. Dan was my uncle and just four days shy of being a full year older than me. I stood up with him as a groomsman on his first marriage. He was my first choice as best man for my wedding in August 1969, but Dan was in Vietnam at the time.

After graduating from high school in 1966, Dan completed an automotive technical school in Kansas City, Missouri, in July 1967, and shortly thereafter began his first job at Crescent Chevrolet in Des Moines. He was there less than a year when he received his draft notice and entered the US Army on May 28, 1968.

He attended basic training at Fort Bliss, Texas, and arrived on Memorial Day weekend, a holiday. Normally drill instructors (DI) were right on top of the new troops, but the confusion of the holiday gave Dan a little reprieve from the in-your-face tactics of the instructors. A small moment of quiet time was a big deal, and Dan took advantage of it. He dozed off on his bunk in the barracks just a day or two into his enlistment, contemplating his future in the US Army.

Out of nowhere, in the middle of the day, two guys crept into the dorm and dog piled Dan as he slept. They jumped on top of him and began pummeling him with slaps to the head and mild punches to the gut. What a wake-up call! Dan wasn't sure if this was some kind of initiation into the US Army or the instructor's idea of a lousy joke. He got his hands up, rolled out of the bunk, and took a defensive stance, ready to lay a couple of fist punches on his attackers. Then the two attackers began to laugh. Dan blinked and couldn't believe his eyes. Holy smokes, it was Fred Fridley and Loren Edwards of Milo. Two former high school classmates. What a reunion! They, too, were at Fort Bliss doing basic training, and they, too, had a reprieve from the DI for the holiday, so they took advantage of the free time. "How in the world did you know I was here?" Dan asked. "How in the world did you find me?"

Fred piped in, "By chance, we saw a listing of the new recruits posted on the bulletin board of the orderly room as we passed through. We took a chance that you were the same Theodore Daniel Reeves we knew. What are the odds of that? It was you."

They jabbered on for about an hour about the good times in high school, old girl friends, and cars, then hurried back to their unit before chow call. "We'll catch up with you later," Loren said as they split ways. Unrealized at the moment, they would never again cross paths until their military service was over. Fred spent a tour of duty in Vietnam and was in country the same time as Dan but never saw each other again in uniform. After his time in the service, Loren never returned to the Milo area. Dan learned later that Loren went into the ministry somewhere out east. He never saw Loren again.

About a week into basic training, the light came on for Dan. It became apparent that ground pounders (infantry) were in high demand, and if he preferred not to carry a rifle and wade the rice paddies of Vietnam, he needed do something and do it fast. Based on his extremely high mechanical aptitude test scores, the US Army offered Dan an advanced school as an aircraft armament repairman, the MOS (means of support) of a 45J20. What came out of that was a quick discharge from the US Army and subsequent and immediate re-enlistment. That translated into a three-year hitch with Uncle Sam instead of only two. Out of boot camp, Dan headed to the Aberdeen Proving Grounds, Maryland. There he began advanced training. In very simple words, he fixed the guns on rotary aircraft.

Hello, Vietnam! Dan arrived in country on a Monday, April 7, 1969. The day was hotter than a firecracker on the Fourth of July, and the heaviness of the humid air made a sweltering August day riding a hay wagon back in Iowa seem like a walk in the park. He became just one of the already 543,000 US troops there. The month of April 1969, saw the total number of US soldiers killed in Vietnam exceed the 33,629 previously killed during the Korean War.

Just the week before, on March 28, 1969, President Eisenhower died after he suffered his seventh heart attack, the first of which was in 1955. Gone was the man who first opened the door for the United States regarding Vietnam's political struggles. Now Dan was there, and hoped to pull that door tightly shut, not with diplomacy and handshakes but with bullets.

Within a few days, he found himself at Camp Coryell near the village of Bam Me Thout, located in the Central Highlands, just south of Plieku. As he stepped into the company's orderly room so that his presence there could be documented, he heard two Huey helicopters lift off. It was a common event repeated dozens of times per day. As the orderly room sergeant introduced himself and began to process Dan into Camp Coryell, a huge explosion interrupted their conversation. The orderly sergeant looked outside and saw that one of the choppers went down immediately after liftoff. "Come on, Reeves, time to get your feet wet," he shouted to Dan.

Both ran outside and jumped into a jeep. As they raced toward the downed Huey, they saw that it had just cleared the base perimeter fence and crashed into—of all places—a church. They heard no gunfire, and the sergeant spoke out loud as he talked to himself, "Either he went down due to pilot error, or the thin mountain air didn't give him enough lift or maybe both."

When they pulled up near the church, Dan saw the door gunner and crew chief as they limped away from the Huey. They hadn't been airborne long enough to even snap on their safety harness and jumped out immediately upon impact. The jeep came to a stop about twenty yards in front of the church. A Vietnamese man hurriedly ran past them from the crash site with the door gunner's M60 machine gun balanced over his shoulder. He stumbled several times as he kept the twenty-three-pound weapon in a tight grip by the barrel as he headed for the nearby village. The sergeant again spoke out as if in a conversation with himself, "That no good son of a gun is stealing our weapons. Stop, stop, I said stop," he shouted. He then pulled his .45 caliber handgun from his waist and fired four shots at the fleeing man. He turned to Dan and said, "Go get that M60. He won't be doing that anymore."

Dan was still seated in the passenger side of the jeep, glassy eyed at what he had just witnessed. Dan stuttered slightly then asked, "Holy crap, man, why did you…"

And before he could even finish the sentence, the sergeant piped in, "Welcome to Nam, Reeves, it's just another day in the armpit of this hellhole country."

Once settled in at his duty station, Dan became the "gun guy" for the 155th Assault Helicopter Company, Falcon Gun Platoon.

There were about 250–300 troops assigned to Camp Coryell which was a small air base that supported a few air force Cessna 172s (T-41 Mescalaro) as observation aircraft and about forty UH-1H Huey helicopters. A good portion of those choppers were armed gunships that flew patrol every day. Others were called slicks and ferried troops in and out of combat zones or served as medevac extraction helicopters.

It didn't take Dan long to see there was a problem with the 7.62 caliber miniguns mounted on the Hueys. There had been an ongoing problem with gun jams that greatly reduced the capability of the miniguns and the aircraft's ability to fight while in flight. The 7.62 round fired so hot and so fast through the revolving barrels that any burst of ammo longer than three seconds tended to warp the barrels. That caused misfires and misdirection of the rounds that did make it into the firing chamber.

When back at the technical school in Maryland, Dan finished second in his class as overall top graduate. He told me, "The only reason I was second was because the top guy was a college graduate and was better at taking written tests than me. When it came to hands-on stuff, diagnosing and repairing the equipment, I was the best time and time again."

Soon word spread that Reeves was the gun guru for the miniguns. Now that things were up and running as designed, pilots readjusted their gunsights and with a grease marker put crosshairs on the front of their Plexiglas windshield. That practice became the precursor of the modern heads-up display (HUD) used on today's aircraft.

The Vietcong assaulted Camp Coryell on a regular basis with mortar rounds. Several days per week during the early morning hours, the base would get hit. The incoming rounds alternated between the flight line, hoping to hit an aircraft, and the other side of the base that contained support equipment and troop quarters. Bunkers were positioned throughout so when that familiar *thud* sound was heard, soldiers would grab their carbines and helmet and head to the nearest bunker before the mortars hit the encampment. "For almost a year, I slept with one eye open and never once got a full night's rest," Dan told me. It didn't take a medical degree in psychotherapy for me to understand why Dan slept with a loaded pistol in his bed for years after the war ended. It freaked his wife out, but for years after, like many Vietnam veterans, Dan fought the war over and over again.

Two months passed and a familiar face showed up at Camp Coryell. A guy by the name of Rigoberto Rodriguez who went to gun school with Dan in Maryland greeted him. He was in the same aircraft armament repair course but two phases behind Dan. He followed the same path and ended up at Bam Me Thout. They were buddies back in the States, went to class together, socialized after class, and had a few beers and pizza on occasion. Dan's wife, Carolyn, and Rodriguez's wife, Tina, even hung out together when the guys were in class.

Rigoberto—Dan called him Rigo—was a soldier of slight build, maybe 150 pounds. That didn't concern Dan. What did bother him was how naive he seemed in the midst of so much peril. Like a big brother, Dan took him under his wing and gave him instruction, not about gun repair but common sense survival tactics. He continually harped and harped, "When on guard duty, never turn your back on the perimeter wire. Never ever fall asleep when on watch. Always have your weapon within reach as well as your helmet. Always be cognizant of the closet bunker. Always keep your eyes open and think. Think about what if this, what if that, how am I going to react, and where am I going to go if things go south quickly. Situational awareness is key to survival here."

Two days later, Camp Coryell received a mortar attack. Dan scrambled to the bunker with explosions on both sides of the compound. It was no relay race on the high school track team—it was a run for his life. He dove into the bunker and cowered down as the mortars continued. Suddenly Rigo shows up—last man in. "What took you so long to get here," Dan screamed at him. "You're a dead man if you pussy foot your way here, remember that."

Rodriguez answered him, "I got caught up in my sleeping bag."

Dan replied, "What? Your stupid sleeping bag held you up?"

Rigo answered, "Man, I had it zipped up to my neck, and the zipper got stuck, and I couldn't get out of it." The conversation continued when the mortar attack stopped.

Dan lectured him again, "For god's sake man, unzip the damn sleeping bag and toss it over you like a blanket. When those mortars come, you've got just seconds to make it to the bunker. You have no time to waste screwing with a stupid sleeping bag zipper."

Humbly, Rigo mumbled, "Okay, okay."

Three days passed, and at about 2:00 a.m., the familiar thud noise filled the air and then another and another. Someone in the barracks shouted, "Mortars, mortars!"

Within seconds, the camp siren sounded the warning reminiscent of a whining tornado siren back in Iowa. *Boom, boom, boom,* the explosions pounded the camp. Dan began a sprint from his hooch to the nearest bunker. He wore only a pair of white government-issued (GI) boxer shorts and his boots. Dan grabbed his helmet, his M14 rifle, a bandolier of ammo and made a frantic dash to the bunker some forty to fifty yards from his hooch. As he ran, he saw his buddy Rodriguez already near the bunker. Rodriguez had been assigned his first guard duty that very night, stationed outside the bunker. As Dan approached, he saw him on a cot, outside the bunker, struggling to get out of his fully zipped-up sleeping bag. He had been asleep again! Finally after what seemed an eternity, he kicked free and dove headfirst into the sandbagged entryway of the bunker, just as a mortar exploded some ten yards away. Rigo flopped forward like someone had kicked him in the buttocks. But no, it wasn't a boot. The concussion shock from the mortar shell and shrapnel pushed him forward. Only his upper torso safely made it to the entryway. From the waist down, his lower body took the fragments of the nearby explosion. Dan had yet to reach the safety of the bunker but far enough away that the mortar fragments missed him. He was at Rigo's side within seconds. Blood was everywhere. Rodriguez was hit and hit bad. Someone shouted, "Get the medics here, call them on the radio, hurry."

Two guys showed up with a stretcher. As Dan related, "I picked him up to put him on the stretcher, I got one arm under his shoulders, my other arm reached below his hips. I couldn't pick him up. His hips and legs were like a jackrabbit that had been shot a close range with a shotgun, just mangled and mashed something terrible.

Somebody help me, somebody help me, get him on the stretcher!" Two other guys held his hips and legs as best they could and eased them onto the stretcher. Rigo had been in Vietnam just seven days, and things were headed south for him real fast.

The mortars stopped, and Dan stood outside the bunker in disbelief and shock at what just transpired. Luckily Rigo was the only one hurt. Thoughts raced through Dan's mind. He thought of his buddy's wife, Tina, back in Maryland, and then he remembered an envelope that Rigo gave him the first day they met at Camp Coryell. He told Dan, "If anything happens to me, send this letter to my wife." *My god*, Dan thought, *Rigo had only been here just seven stinking days! He can't be dead, he can't be dead!*

Dan quickly jogged to the flight line just as the medevac helicopter lifted off with Rodriguez onboard, heading to the Cam Rahn Bay hospital. The medics were still there. "Is he going to make it?" he asked.

The senior medic shook his head and said, "He was alive when they took off. If they can get him to a field hospital quickly, he has a chance. He has lost a lot of blood."

The other medic looked at Dan and said, "You're hit too, get over to the camp dispensary." His adrenalin still pumping, Dan reached to his side and felt for any wounds. "I don't think I'm hit," he said.

"You're soaked in blood, soldier. It's dripping off your shorts," the medic fired back. "Let me walk you over for a checkup."

Once at the dispensary, Dan still insisted he wasn't hit, but the medic had him strip down to look for anything obvious. He still only wore just his skivvies and boots. Sure enough, no injuries, but his GI-issued boxer shorts were totally saturated, dripping with the blood of his buddy Rodriguez.

Months later, while still in Vietnam, Dan received a letter from Rigo's wife. He was in a wheelchair as a result of his injuries and unable to walk. He would be that way for the rest of his life. Dan responded with a letter and gave her his account of that eventful early morning attack on Camp Coryell. Dan told me, "I don't know how many times a flashback of that night awoke me from my sleep over the past forty years. I thought maybe there was something else I could have done to change the outcome. It haunts me. It's a reality I can't escape that's burned into my brain, which no twenty-year-old kid should ever carry."

He kept in touch with Rigo after the war. About ten years later, Rodriguez's wife contacted Dan and informed him that he had died from complications of his injuries.

"As sad as it seemed, the routine of war, the mortar attacks, the dead bodies, and my wounded buddies became way too easy to accept as normal business as usual." Dan pondered. "It became so easy to simply shrug my shoulders and say…just another day in Vietnam."

Daily the choppers returned from missions for a quick turn-around, taking on more ammo and fuel before immediately heading back out. Dan checked the miniguns for any maintenance problems and reloaded both ammo bins with two thousand rounds of the 7.62 cartridges, as well as another two thousand rounds for M60 machine guns used by the door gunners. The M60, hung by a bungee cord, connected to the top of the side door and pumped out 550 rounds per minute. The turn time was relatively short, and there was a constant hurriedness on the ground. The choppers served as the lifeline to the troops in the field, and any time not in the air was wasted time.

It was just another ordinary day of war in Vietnam, or one could say. Huey's constantly in and out of Camp Coryell, landing on the AM-2 matting (aluminum matting). The AM-2 matting provided some sense of a runway or parking ramp for aircraft in remote regions of engagement. Its use dated as far back as WWII. The matting consisted of nothing more than six-foot or twelve-foot sections of one-by-two-inch steel rectangles that snapped together and then anchored to the ground by cruciform stakes. The sections could be as long or as wide as the base commander envisioned.

As Dan approached one particular inbound gunship, he noticed the door gunner slumped forward. As he got closer, it became obvious that he was injured. As it touched down, a medical crew rushed in and helped the door gunner out of the chopper. He had been shot in the elbow, hit by ground fire, and was in no condition to go airborne any time soon. Dan refilled the ammo boxes and checked the guns. Everything was thumbs-up. The petroleum oils and lubricants (POL) crew quickly fueled the chopper, and it was ready for liftoff again. The pilot turned to Dan and yelled, "Hey, Reeves, get in, I need a door gunner. I was told by the command post on company radio frequency that none are available. You're the only guy available who knows how to operate the M60. Hurry, there are guys in trouble, we need to get airborne immediately."

Without so much as giving it a second thought, Dan jumped aboard. Once airborne, however, he began to think to himself, *Nobody knows I'm onboard as a door gunner other than the pilot, I'm not qualified for flight duty, what the hell am I doing?*

The pilot barked at him on the radio headset and informed him that they were headed to a fire base that was under attack by North Vietnamese regulars. The flight time was about twenty minutes. Located atop a mountain somewhere in the jungle, US forces had positioned howitzer artillery cannons to strike enemy forces along the Ho Chi Minh trail when grid coordinates were called in for a particular location. The M102 howitzer fired a thirty-three-pound shell with a range of seven miles. As they approached the mountain, Dan noticed that Agent Orange had been used to clear the forest canopy and ground foliage some one hundred yards in all directions around the fire base. As he looked to the right, Dan observed another three Huey gunships and two more on his left trailing some fifty yards behind.

The pilot of Dan's UH-1H dipped forward and banked hard to the left as he approached the mountain. Dan lunged forward and slammed between the seats of the pilot and copilot. "Holy crap, Reeves, get your damn monkey harness on, or you'll be out the door on the next pass," the pilot shouted. It never dawned on Dan that it might be a good idea if he was tethered in. He didn't have any flight training. This mission was on the job (OJT) at its best.

As they made their initial approach, Dan's eyes widened. It looked as though tiny black ants were running up the mountain right into the open field. He leaned out the door, pointed the M60 machine gun downward, and began firing while the pilot triggered his guns and popped off three-second bursts from the miniguns. His chopper broke away, and the next Huey made a pass repeating the maneuver and then the next in similar fashion, and so it went for nearly thirty minutes. On the backside, Dan peered down and could not believe his eyes. There were more Vietcong (VC) coming from the timberline rushing up the mountain. But to his disbelief, the VC stopped for a second, then picked up the weapon from a dead VC who had been killed. These gooks were going into battle and not everyone was armed. They waited for a comrade to get killed, then advanced and retrieved a weapon to fight on. Holy crap, Batman!

As his Huey made a final pass, Dan saw, out the corner of his eye, a group of about four or five Vietcong soldiers that ran into a small thicket of bamboo trees that still offered some cover. He radioed to the trailing gunship about their location. They were right there and fired off a pair of 2.75 rockets. Two rockets fired simultaneously from each side of the Huey so as not to throw the gunship off balance. No doubt one rocket would have been enough, but either way, the entire thicket was obliterated.

When they landed back at Camp Coryell, the first duty at hand was to service the guns. Dan's muscles were taut, and his heart pumped as if he just finished another quarter-mile run on the first leg of the mile relay team back in high school. The pilot, a warrant officer who himself looked as though he, too, was right out of high school yet to get his first shave, walked past Dan and said, "Hell of a nice job, Reeves. Glad to have you onboard."

A few days passed, thoughts flashed through Dan's mind. What happened earlier in the week was dangerous. That wasn't what he signed up for, but admittedly, it provided a tremendous rush. He knew that flight pay was an extra $50 per month, and that stacked up huge against his $254 per month base pay as an E-5. Dan was in country for less than six months and decided to volunteer for flight duty as a shotgun rider, which provided some much needed relief for the other "men at the door." Not every day, however, part-time would be a better fit. Just being in harm's way two to three days per week would be good enough.

As the saying went, the life span of a door gunner in Vietnam was about five minutes.

It was a Friday, September 5, 1969. Dan received a message from the Red Cross. His wife, Carolyn, had given birth that day to their first child, his namesake, a son named Theodore Daniel Reeves. They called him Ted. Dan bought a box of cigars from the small post exchange (PX) at Camp Coryell and cheerfully handed them to all his GI buddies. What else could he do, he thought to himself. *I should be there, but I'm not. I'm halfway around the world in this outhouse of a country.* He was just five months into his tour of duty, and it would be another five or six months before he could hold his son. Unfortunately monumental events such as this, when fathers were at war in Vietnam, were a common thing for many, many soldiers.

That same day, September 5, 1969, the US Army formally filed murder charges against Army Lt. William Calley for his role in the death of 109 innocent Vietnamese civilians in what was termed the My Lai Massacre, which occurred on March 16, 1968. Fourteen soldiers in 1st Battalion, 20th Infantry, 11th Brigade of the 23rd Division were all charged. Only Lieutenant Calley was sentenced to life in prison. Charges against all others were dropped. The Court of Military Appeals later reduced the sentencing to twenty years, then the secretary of the army again reduced the sentence to ten years. In 1974, after serving less than a third of his sentence, President Richard Nixon paroled Lieutenant William Calley. Most of America viewed Calley as a plain-and-simple scapegoat for the atrocities of war brought forth by the United States.

After six months in the country, GIs were given a two-week R & R (rest and relaxation) at a location of their choice. Many would catch a military hop to Hawaii or the Philippines and rendezvous with their spouse and try to regain some sense of normalcy outside the war zone. However, when Dan's rotation approached, his commanding officer denied his two-week reprieve from the war zone. "Why?" Dan asked.

"Because you are just too damn valuable to let go that long," his commander answered him back. Apparently, Dan had gained the reputation as the go-to guy when the gunships had trouble with their armament. In fact, Dan became the regional expert and would oftentimes be ferried by helicopter from one base to another to ferret out mechanical issues with the guns. Most of the time, it would be an all-day trip, but the actual time examining and fixing the guns amounted to an hour or less. Dan was a sharp cookie, no doubt about it.

On just about every sortie, Dan's helicopter flew very near the MARS (military affiliated radio station) not too far from Pleiku. Each morning, his alarm clock awakened him to the familiar call at 6:00 a.m., "Good morning, Vietnam." The MARS station brought a little taste of America to the troops in Vietnam with top hits like "Sugar, Sugar" by the Archies and "Proud Mary" by Creedence Clearwater Revival or songs by Sly and the Family Stone, "Hot Fun in the Summertime" and "Everyday People." The music group Animals released one of the all-time favorite tunes of the troops in 1965, "We Gotta Get Out of This Place."

Years later in 1987, after the war, comedian actor Robin Williams starred in a Vietnam-era movie entitled *Good Morning, Vietnam*, which portrayed a rebel disc jockey, Adrian Cronauer, who served as the DJ on the MARS station from 1965 to 1966. He was adored by the troops but loathed by his military superiors for his irreverent tendencies. When Cronauer left, a guy by the name of Pat Sajak stepped into the radio booth at the MARS facility in 1969 and belted out the familiar words to the troops, "Good morning, Vietnam." Private Sajak bungled the 1969 Christmas message by President Nixon to the troops in Vietnam when he cut off the live broadcast prematurely. Little did Dan know, or anyone else as a matter of fact, that Pat Sajak would become a television celebrity across America as the game show host of *Wheel of Fortune*.

The days became a jumble of mixed-up meaning. Tuesday or Sunday, Wednesday or Saturday, they all seemed the same. There were no weekends off and precious little time to relax. The Camp Coryell soldiers were involved in one thing or another nonstop, day after day. A sixty-hour workweek became common. But what the heck, in a war zone, you're on duty 24-7. Gee whiz, what else could one do, anyway? It was get ready for battle, go into battle, recoup from battle, fix up, clean up, and suck it up. Dan put a pencil to the numbers. Based on his E-5 pay status, in 1969, plus the extra $50 per month for flight pay and with the assumption he only worked forty hours per week (which he didn't), he made something in the range of $1.25 per hour. Of course, since he was married, his wife, Carolyn, received a $110 per month housing allowance. Uncle Sam was getting a real bargain with those kind of wages.

It was the early months of 1970. Dan awoke at 6:00 a.m. sharp from a night that was free of mortar attacks. He reached up and cranked the volume knob on his single speaker Sony radio that hung by a bungee cord suspended against the plywood wall near his cot. The bungee cord had seen better days when it held a twenty-three-pound M60 machine gun at the door of a Huey but still enough strength left to suspend the little Sony. "Good morning, Vietnam," it shouted to him. Yes, he preferred that wake-up call to the traditional reveille, common at Stateside military installations. And no, he didn't jump out of his cot and stand at attention while the bugler played "I can't get 'em up, I can't get 'em, I can't get 'em up in the morning." But he did have a bad case of nocturnal penile tumescence (morning wood) that stood at attention and needed immediate relief as the first priority of the day. He rubbed his eyes and made sure he was 100 percent awake and then scurried to the latrine. Others filtered out of their barracks and fell in line as if in a cadence march, not on the parade ground, however, but stepping in beat to the forty paces to the biffy. Apparently, the chow hall was low on saltpeter that month, but who cared?

As he stood at the urinal and bled off his bladder, he did a quick finger count and realized that hey, it was his day to be door gunner. As he headed back to the tent to get his fatigue pants, he heard another nearby radio tuned in to the MARS station. The disc jockey said, "Hey, all you soldiers out there, I've got a new record release for you today. Would you believe the name of the song is 'War'? Let's give it up for Edwin Star."

There was a little scratchy noise in the background for a second or two, and then the lyrics began, "War, huh, yeah, what is it good for, absolutely nothing. Oh war, I despise, 'cause it means the destruction of innocent lives, war means tears to thousands of mother's eyes, when their sons go off to fight and lose their lives. I'll say it again…

War, huh, yeah, what is it good for, absolutely nothing." Within seconds after the first few lines were aired, every grunt, swabbie, jarhead, flyboy, and ground pounder within earshot at Camp Coryell stopped dead in their tracks and just—listened. Somebody mumbled, "My god, finally the knuckleheads back home got it right."

Dan headed to the small mess hall located about seventy-five yards from his hooch. It was a concrete building constructed years before in the 1950s by the Dutch and French during their brief involvement with Vietnam. There he grabbed a quick cup of coffee, loaded it up with sugar, then piled some powdered eggs on a slice of toast, and topped it off with ketchup and a dash or two of hot sauce. He ate while he walked to the gunships parked on the AM-2 matting on the airfield. What he didn't know then was that today would be no ordinary day, indeed it would not.

He performed the preflight check of the miniguns and the M60 machine gun at the door. The pilot made a final walk-around on the chopper, and they pulled pitch within a few minutes. And yes, Dan strapped on the monkey harness. On the headset, the pilot told the crew they were headed for coordinates about thirty klicks to the south where some ground troops needed air cover before crossing a river to an area where some VC had been reported by a T-41 Mescalaro the day before. They flew unaccompanied, and if all went as planned, the grunts would successfully cross the river, and the chopper would be back at Camp Coryell in slightly more than an hour. Dan belched and almost lost the powdered eggs he gobbled down earlier for breakfast. *Oops, too much hot sauce*, he thought. Well, at least it wasn't the combat-rations the troops on the ground dined on.

About ten minutes into the flight and before the altitude safety threshold of three thousand feet, trouble began. *Zip, zip, zip, zip.* Four rounds of small arms ground fire hit the gunship. The crew chief shouted over the headset, "Anyone see where that came from?"

In unison, both rotor heads screamed, "I think it came from our two or three-o'clock position. You see anything now?"

Dan yelled, "I see smoke, we're hit. I think they got the transmission."

"Ah, crap," the pilot blurted out as his sphincter tightened, and his voice raised three octaves higher. "I'm starting to lose it. We're going down, hang on."

The gunship filled with black smoke as the transmission fluid sprayed against the hot engine and burned the throats of the entire crew. Dan stuck his head out the door. His lungs struggled to find oxygen, then finally he sucked in some good air. He looked down and saw nothing but trees, nowhere—but nowhere—a spot for a hard landing. If they fell into the treetops, the helo would flip and most likely explode. His heart pounded as if it were about to jump out of his chest. "I see a spot, a small clearing below," the copilot shouted. "Over there, over there!"

"For god's sake, man, it's no bigger than a picnic table. Can you make it? Can you make it?" screamed the crew chief.

"It's all we got, it's all we got. Dear Jesus, help me get this bird down," begged the pilot. He glanced at his gauges. The rate of descent was slightly over seven hundred feet per minute and increasing. "Hold on, hold on, baby," he talked to the Huey. "Brace, brace!"

The tail of the gunship clipped a branch of a Hopea tree about forty feet in the air and tipped sharply forward. The helicopter, in auto rotation with just a smidgen of effective transitional lift (ELT), struggled to flare, but the Huey dropped straight down and hit the ground with a huge thud. Jesus put them on the picnic table.

Moans and groans filled the flight deck. Dan unfastened his monkey harness. He was bruised but uninjured. "Hey, hey, let's get the hell out of here." He jumped out the side door and looked back for the three others to follow. Nobody moved.

"I'm hurt, man, give me a hand," came a voice from inside. Dan peered in and could see all three other crewmembers had various injuries. The pilot appeared to have a broken back, and he couldn't move; the copilot had a broken leg, and the crew chief suffered a broken arm and some rib injuries. Lucky, in fact, that everyone was alive, but even luckier that he himself escaped serious injury.

Dan did a quick triage assessment. He first helped the crew chief with the broken arm and ribs out of the Huey and told him to make his way into the jungle. He went to the rotor head and tried to grab the pilot and pull him out, but he screamed out in agony. "I can't move, I can't move at all."

He went to the other side and asked the copilot if he could walk. "I don't think so, my leg is broken pretty bad."

Dan eased him out, threw the copilots left arm over his shoulder, and together they limped into the jungle where the crew chief had stopped some twenty yards into a thick wooded area. Dan spoke out loud. "How am I going to get the pilot? I can't even touch him and he shouts out in pain."

"Leave him in the seat, take the whole seat out of the chopper," the crew chief told him. "There is a release pin underneath the seat that lets the whole thing come out. Pull that pin and carry him, seat and all if you can." Dan went back to the downed chopper, smoke still pouring from the transmission fluid spilled against the engine. He knew the VC would soon be there with so much smoke rising, it would surely mark their position.

Just as the crew chief stated, Dan easily found the release pin for the pilot seat. He made the disconnect on the pin and tugged on the seat. The pilot cried out in pain again. "Damn it, you're going to have to suck it up 'cause if I leave you here, you're either going to burn to death if this thing catches on fire, or the gooks will find you and shoot you." With one steady lift, Dan raised the seat with the pilot still harnessed in and carried him to where the other two crewmembers awaited.

Dan's mind raced at a thousand miles per hour. "Our goose is cooked, we're in deep doo-doo. I've got three guys who need medical help, the radio is out, nobody knows we are here, and I expect the VC will be paying us a visit soon."

The copilot chimed in, "I let command post know on the radio we were going down before we crashed. They know we are out here somewhere."

Dan said, "Let's pray they find us soon."

A few minutes passed, and it dawned on them that nobody had a weapon. Dan went back to the Huey and found the standard issue .45 caliber handgun kept onboard. He grabbed a phosphorus grenade and wedged it behind the copilot's seat, then took a roll of wire from the emergency repair kit. Carefully he pulled the pin on the grenade and gave it a hair trigger release and then tied the thin wire to the pin and strung the wire far enough out that it almost reached their position in the jungle. If the gooks showed up, he had a booby trap surprise in store.

Hours went by, and nothing but dead silence other than the moans of the pilot from his broken back. Night set in. No rescue helicopter, nothing. Dan could hear his heart beating in his chest. He sat next to the pilot with the .45 handgun cocked and ready to fire. His hands shook like that of an old man. *Scared* was not the right word to describe the emotions that night. There were no words, no words to even remotely express the fear generated with each heartbeat. "My eyes were as wide open as a dinner plate when hiding in that jungle. I don't even think I blinked once. I just stared off into the jungle looking for any sort of movement or sign that the VC were coming."

Was today the day he and the other three would meet their Maker? Hopefully not! Jesus found them a landing spot and got them on the ground alive. They all quietly prayed, *Dear God, please send help!*

Several more hours passed, and it was total darkness. The pilot's injuries seemed to worsen. His moaning increased and became louder and more frequent. Dan put his hand over the pilot's mouth to keep him quiet, knowing the noise would give away their position. "I damn near suffocated the guy that night," Dan later told me. "He moaned with almost every breath, and I had to shut him up. Then the crew chief mentioned, 'There should be some morphine in the medical kit that's still on the Huey. If he had some of that it might keep him more comfortable.'"

Dan thought about it for a few minutes. Was it worth the trip back to the Huey, and would his movement give away their position? If things kept on as it had been, the pilot's moaning would do that, anyway. Like a snake slithering toward it unsuspecting prey, Dan quietly crawled by the light of the moon and made his way to the downed Huey. He grabbed the medical kit and again made the crawl back to their hiding place. He popped the cover on the small canvas bag. What the heck! Nothing but bandages, rotten, stinking, no-good bandages. The drug users at Camp Coryell had ransacked the medical kit on the helicopter and stole the morphine for their drug habit! So they waited for daylight. Fingers crossed, hammer cocked, eyes wide open, and the pilot continued to moan in pain. "Oh, Lord, hear our prayers."

As the early light of dawn creeped in, a heavy fog surrounded them. It provided a nice cool reprieve from the heat of the jungle that had all of them soaked in sweat and drained what little energy each of them had left. Dan's mouth was cotton-dry. They all needed a drink of water.

Suddenly Dan whispered, "Did you hear that, did you hear that? There's something out there." Everyone's sense of sight and sound peaked instantly.

"Yep, I heard it, over there." The crew chief pointed his good arm in the direction of the helicopter. "Here they come." Dan began to crawl toward the line attached to the grenade in the Huey with the .45 handgun in his right hand, cocked, and his finger on the trigger. The line was just fifteen feet shy of their position.

"Wait till there are more than one of them near the helicopter before you pull the wire." One of them whispered.

Dan reached the wire. He held it tightly in his left hand, ready to give it a hard jerk and blow the hell out of the gooks sneaking up on them. Waiting, waiting to see some movement. Suddenly he saw something just beyond the Huey in the tree line, still too far away to detonate the grenade. "Come on, you lousy bums. I've got a surprise for you," he quietly whispered to himself.

Dan squinted to see through the morning fog. There at the edge of the tree line behind the Huey, one of them stood up. "Come on, come on, just a little closer." All of a sudden, Dan's heart jumped in his throat. The guy pulled out an orange placard—yes, an orange placard—for sure it was an orange placard! Dan jumped up and yelled, "Hey, hey, we're over here, we're over here." He turned to the helicopter crew behind him and shouted, "They're our guys, they're here for us."

The orange placard was a color code used for identification exactly in instances such as this. The colors rotated from day to day, and Dan knew that today was *orange*! His new favorite color, bright *orange*!

The GI walked toward Dan. When he got closer, Dan saw he was a Green Beret and looked as big as a linebacker on a professional football team. He had to be six feet and five inches tall and weighed about 230 pounds. His biceps stretched the sleeves of his rolled-up fatigue shirt. For certain, a very welcome sight.

"Everybody okay?" he asked.

"No," Dan told him. "There are three back in the jungle who need medical assistance. One is pretty bad with a broken back."

"We'll get you guys out of here in no time," the green beret told him. "We were all around you most of the night but waited till daylight to signal our position. There are six of us here, and the other five are still in the jungle, giving us cover just in case any unwanted visitors show up. We have a couple of choppers en route to lift you guys out of here."

"I'm okay, I don't need a medevac, just some clean underwear. Last night was kind of iffy," Dan told him. "I'm used to sleeping in a cot, walking on cement, and taking a crap in a porcelain toilet. This jungle business ain't my cup of tea. Thanks, man, thanks a lot. God bless the Green Berets. Oh, and another thing I forgot to mention," Dan inserted at the last minute. "The Huey is booby-trapped. I put a phosphorus grenade behind the copilot's seat with the pin partially pulled out and connected to a wire."

"Thanks for that heads-up, Reeves. I'll take care of it in a minute."

By then. the familiar *whoof, whoof, whoof* noise emitted by the rotor blades of an approaching helicopter could be heard in the distance. The Green Beret walked over to the downed Huey, reached in and grabbed the grenade, pushed the pin back in tightly, and then clipped it on his shirt for later use. Dan thought to himself, *This guy is good. He's done this before. Sure as hell glad he's on my team.*

The approaching Huey medevac hovered above the crash site and lowered a basket down and hoisted up the two badly injured pilots. Dan and the crew chief, despite his broken arm, opted to walk out with the green berets to a landing zone a klick or two away. Before they left, a second chopper flew in, dropped a cable down to the wreckage of Dan's crippled Huey. One of the Green Berets connected the cable to the "Jesus nut" on the rotor, and away the two choppers went, one in tow. Dan thought to himself, *Jesus got this gunship down safely with us on board, and now He is lifting it out.*

As they walked out of the crash area and toward the landing zone, the big strapping green beret turned to Dan and said, "It would be all right now if you uncocked your .45 and put it back in the holster."

For a second or two, Dan forgot he even had the gun but then raised his right arm, looked at the gun still cocked, his finger still on the trigger, and then complied with the request. After a huge sigh, he said, "Oh, I've been a little on edge the past twenty-four hours, you might say."

Dan had been at Camp Coryell long enough that the shine on his boots was long gone. Things at the gun shop were running as well as possible under the conditions of war. He noticed, however, several unopened wooden crates stored in the munitions warehouse. They had been there since his arrival, and he had never investigated their contents. On a curious note, he took a pry bar to see what they might contain. Some had mortar shells which were delivered to the wrong unit. To his surprise, about three or four other crates contained the screw-on barrels of the M240 coaxial machine guns, the same as used on the M60 machine guns. *Who in the heck ordered these?* he thought to himself. *Perhaps another bungled shipment of government equipment?*

It wasn't too many days afterward when he heard the roar of twelve M60 Patton tanks chugging into Coryell. They all lined up and parked on the AM-2 matting near the helicopters with cannon muzzles pointed away from the camp. Dan had no idea why they were there, other than perhaps a day or two of rest and some needed maintenance. "Aha," he whispered to himself. "I've got something they might be interested in." He went to the warehouse and grabbed three gun barrels and tossed them over his shoulder and headed to the flight line. About halfway there, the crew chief of one of the M60 tanks saw him and virtually ran to him with open arms.

"And what do you have here, my good man?" queried the salty Big Boy. He knew damn well what Dan carried on his shoulders and was anxious to relieve him of the heavy load.

As if in a high etiquette conversation with a foreign dignitary, Dan retorted in his best rendition of an English accent, "Well, kind sir, I have what I believe to be brand-new barrels for your wee pea shooters which are in overabundance for me. Dare I ask, are you interested in procuring them?"

The tank crew chief immediately dropped the baloney and the silly foreign accent, then quickly responded, "Damn straight I am." By then, several other tank drivers saw the two together at the edge of the ramp and gathered around Dan. "We've fired so many rounds through our tank-mounted M60 machine guns that the rifling is totally gone. It's like we are throwing out knuckleballs when firing on a target. How many barrels have you got?" they all asked in unison.

"Enough, enough for each of your tanks," Dan responded. "But the question is, what's it worth to you?"

"So what do you want, cowboy?" one asked in his best John Wayne impersonation. "We have a collection of Vietcong (VC) flags to offer, or how about a ring of ears?" A ring of ears was a perverted way some soldiers kept track of VC body counts by cutting off the left ear of dead gooks and clipped them on a looped wire. The foul odor was beyond description. This wasn't a new practice by any means. In fact, the American Indians did something akin to this macabre practice over 250 years prior when they collected scalps from their dead enemies after battle.

"Not interested," Dan countered. "What else you got? Any booze?"

"Yep, we sure do," Big Boy answered. "If you have enough replacement barrels for all our tanks, I've got a deal you can't resist." Dan shook hands, and they consummated the deal. He received two cases of Old Grand-Dad Kentucky bourbon, a case of Cutty Sark blended Scottish whiskey, plus an additional four cases of Falstaff beer. Big Boy nodded to his crew, snapped his fingers, and pointed toward the tanks. Like pack rats going to their nest, the tank crews went into their iron holes and within minutes had the goods stacked in front of Dan.

"Follow me," Dan ordered. Just like the pied piper, the tank crew fell in line and followed Dan to his stash of gun barrels and made good his end of the bargain. Two days later, the tanks departed, all with newly installed M60 machine gun barrels and ready again for action with the six thousand rounds of the 7.62 mm ammo each tank carried.

Word filtered down to command from the intel unit that Camp Coryell could possibly be the target of attack by the NVR (North Vietnamese regulars). As a result, the base was put on high alert. That in itself was a misnomer. To those in a war zone, every day was high alert. As a result of the alert, extra guards were posted. Dan got the call that put him on one of the guard towers for an overnight watch. The towers were nothing more than elevated shelters, lined with sandbags atop four-by-four-inch beams about thirty feet in the air.

Dan and two other soldiers occupied the eight-by-eight-foot confines of the guard tower for the late night shift till dawn. Staying focused and scanning the horizon for unusual movement was difficult. *Boring* might be a better word, with hours and hours of nothing. But in the words of a battle-seasoned veteran, nothing was a good thing. Suddenly, Dan caught some movement running toward the building that housed the base generator. Yes, three figures raced closer and closer. Dan released the safety on his M14, drew his weapon down, and fired off three quick rounds. He dropped one NVR just yards from the generator building. The other two ran inside the building. Within seconds, the base alarm sounded. Then the mortars began to fall. The third mortar exploded right at the base of the tower and splintered one leg of the guard tower. Gradually under the weight of the sandbags, the tower began to tip and, in slow motion, fell downward. Dan jumped as it fell, and when he hit the ground, rolled like a paratrooper on a bad jump. As he looked up, he saw the canine handlers turn their dogs loose and sent them into the generator building. They weren't German shepherds but some other strange-looking breed. They didn't bark, they didn't growl. Within a minute, the two dogs exited the building and ran to their handlers. Blood dripped from their mouths. Dan got up and asked, "Did they get 'em?"

"You betcha they did," fired back one of the handlers. "They ripped out their throats before they knew what happened. Good boy, Bruno, good boy."

All this happened within five minutes. Three dead gooks, three shots from his M14, and three mortar rounds that hit the base. As if an afterthought, Dan remembered the two other GIs that were in the guard tower with him when it fell. He hadn't seen or heard from them since that last mortar hit. He limped over to the downed tower and shouted out. It became painfully apparent that he badly sprained his ankle from the jump. Damn! There was no answer. Maybe they took cover somewhere else, he thought, as the guard tower was smashed upon impact. A few other soldiers gathered, and Dan asked if they had seen his two buddies when the tower fell. "Holy cow, man," one buck private said, "You're the only one we saw jump."

They began to further examine what was left of the guard tower. Sure enough, two bodies were buried in the busted boards and sandbags. The sandbags had turned to hardened cement from months and months of exposure to the elements. They crushed the two who failed to jump upon impact on the thirty-foot fall to the ground. "Yep," the buck private said. "They're DRT."

"What did you say?" Dan asked.

"I said they are DRT, dead right there."

Several days passed since the base had been attacked by the three NVRs. Dan's mind raced as he thought of what would be next. Was the previous attack just a means of testing the preparedness of Camp Coryell? Would they be back and in greater force? There wasn't a whole lot of regular infantry assigned to Camp Coryell to provide a fighting force. Most of the few hundred guys were pilots, mechanics, armament repairmen, cooks, fabrication, and an assortment of support personnel. However, when the alarm sounded, all grabbed their small arms weapons and did what soldiers do in times of war—improvised.

Dan jawed with the sergeant from the fabrication shop located adjacent to his gun shop. "We need more firepower if they hit us again, don't you think?" Dan asked him. "Our M14s and M16s are okay, but there are limits to what the carbines can do. I've got an idea, but I'll need your help."

The next few days, Dan spent on a scavenger hunt as he lined up various items needed for his special project. He ventured down to the flight line and tossed his idea out to the guys who worked on and flew the T-41 Mescalaro. Sure enough, they were onboard with his brainstorm and made available what items he needed. Then back to the fabrication shop with a rough sketch drawn on paper of what he needed welded together. Parts here, parts there, and in a short time, his idea became a reality.

The final product was a spare minigun from one of the Huey gunships which mounted on a swivel and placed atop a tripod, about four feet high. It took five guys to put this new high-powered jerry-rigged weapon into place. Two guys carried the minigun, one guy carried the batteries that electrically fired the rounds, one guy carried the 7.62 ammunition, and the fifth guy carried the tripod. Dan knew the gun worked just fine but wasn't certain how it would perform mounted on his homemade tripod and swivel. The minigun fired two thousand rounds per minute and had some serious kick. Would the tripod withstand the fierce punishment from the gun's recoil was a yet-to-be-answered question. He set it aside in his gun shop in hopes of test-firing his contraption in the not-too-distant future.

A couple of weeks had passed, and Dan almost forgot about his tripod-mounted minigun. It had yet to be baptized by fire and remained inside the gun shop. While at the chow hall keeping his intake of saltpeter at acceptable levels, one of the guys from the fabrication shop quizzed him, "Have you got your new gun ready to go?"

Dan replied, "I think so but haven't had it in the field as yet."

"Well, the latest briefing from the commander said we might be in line for another assault on Coryell, did you hear that?" the fab guy retorted.

"No, I hadn't. Let's set it up the day after tomorrow and see how it goes," Dan answered as he gulped down the last of his glass of powdered milk.

"Sounds good. Get in touch with me, and I'll give you a hand," the fab shop sergeant replied.

> *But in the cities of these peoples that the LORD your God is giving you for an inheritance, you shall save alive nothing that breathes, but you shall devote them to complete destruction.* (**Deuteronomy 20:16–17**)

That very night, chaos broke loose at Camp Coryell. The alert siren sounded in the early morning hours as small arms fire could be heard in the distance. Then a couple of mortars hit. Dan jumped out of his bunk and ran for the gun shop. He yelled to his five helpers to follow him and get the minigun. He didn't even bother to grab his M14 carbine, but instead his entire focus became the minigun. Within five minutes, the crew had the gun in place beside one of the bunkers. The fab guy used a screwdriver and stabbed it into the linkage of the 7.62 ammo and loaded it into the chamber. All five of Dan's crew worked in sync readying the gun. "Batteries are connected, ready to go."

Two flares fired off in the distance and lit up the sky. Dan got his first clear view of what was coming. Dozens and dozens of NVR troops raced toward Coryell, approaching the concertina wire that surrounded the camp. Dan knelt frozen behind the tripod, in disbelief of the sight. The fab sergeant firmly rapped him on the helmet with the screw driver and shouted, "Kill 'em, Reeves, kill 'em now!" Dan fought for words to come out of his mouth, but his first attempt was nothing more than a whisper.

It was a sphincter-pucker moment. He took a deep breath and, with a guttural shout, yelled, "Everyone, down, everyone, down now!"

Dan made one pass from right to left across the field of fire with the minigun. That recognizable sound filled the air in three second bursts. *Vvvvvvvvvpppppppp. Vvvvvvvvvpppppppp. Vvvvvvvvvpppppppp.* Another pass from left to right followed. His ammo guy again stabbed the screwdriver into the 7.62 linkage and reloaded another two thousand rounds. Again a series of three-second bursts from right to left. *Vvvvvvvvvpppppppp. Vvvvvvvvvpppppppp. Vvvvvvvvvpppppppp.* Then back again to the right. *Vvvvvvvvvpppppppp. Vvvvvvvvvpppppppp. Vvvvvvvvvpppppppp.* Four thousand rounds fired in little more than two minutes. And then—all was quiet. Not a sound anywhere. Reflecting back on the moment, Dan commented, "It was so quiet, you could have heard a mouse fart."

The fab sergeant thought to himself, *Oh well, so much for the field testing of the tripod-mounted minigun. I guess it worked to perfection.*

Within a couple of hours, the sun slowly creeped into the sky, giving a first glimpse of the field of fire. Still there remained dead silence. Everyone squinted, peering out of their bunkers to the perimeter wire. Was anyone or anything still out there, or had it become a full-scale retreat by the NVR?

After it became evident that the immediate threat of a second assault by the NVR wasn't happening, a contingent of South Vietnamese Army regulars (SVA) ventured out toward the perimeter of Camp Coryell and checked the status from events of the previous night. Dan stood up and slowly walked toward the concertina wire, still with a dry cottonmouth from his actions hours earlier, he couldn't even muster up a spit. Oh my god! There were bodies everywhere, stretched for about one hundred yards clear back to the grove of the rubber trees. The SVA dragged bodies off the wire and into a pile for removal. Dan stopped counting bodies at seventy. As they worked their way further out into the rubber trees, the muffled sound of a .45 caliber pistol popped. Then another. A few minutes later yet another. There were wounded NVR regulars who had taken refuge among the rubber trees. The SVA took no prisoners. There was no mercy.

About an hour later, in the early morning before the heat became too stifling, three, deuce and a half trucks arrived, and the SVA began loading corpses for disposal. Yes, three trucks full of bodies.

Before the last truck pulled away, the base commander came down to the area just outside the bunkers. "What the blankety blank," he barked. "Who is responsible for this?" Nobody said a word, but instead, all eyes turned toward Dan. "I want to see you, Reeves, in my office in one hour. Got it?"

"Yes, sir," Dan answered.

Not quite sure what was in store for him with the commander, Dan headed toward the command post as ordered. Years later, when reflecting on the incident, Dan said, "I don't remember the major's name, but he was a black guy. I do remember he was from Iowa because when I walked into his office, an Iowa flag hung on the wall. I commented on that, and he told me he graduated from the University of Iowa. Once I told him that I was from Iowa, too, the tension level dropped."

"Did you rig that gun on the tripod?" he asked.

"Yep, I sure did," Dan answered.

"Don't you know that such actions are against military regulations?" the major continued.

"What actions?" responded Dan.

"You are not authorized to alter military equipment and use it for anything other than its intended purpose," the major said, spitting that sentence out, as though reading it directly from a manual.

"Well, well, I thought we needed more, more firepower," Dan stammered as he prepared for a butt-chewing from the commander.

"Well, you know what I think we need?" the major replied in an elevated voice. "I think I need you to show me how that damn gun works. Genius, soldier, absolutely genius! Meet me at the bunker—if the gun is still there—in thirty minutes. I want to see with my own eyes what that damn gun can do."

As stated, the major and an entourage of lesser-ranking officers rendezvoused at the bunker. Dan gave a two-minute briefing on how it operated, and the major eagerly fired off a few bursts. "Great balls of fire. This thing is wicked! It shakes your eyeballs right out of their sockets and knocks any fillings out of your teeth." A second lieutenant took a turn and simply walked away after another few bursts, shaking his head in amazement. He might have been afraid of it.

The major asked Dan, "So how long did it take you to put this thing together?"

"Oh, about three or four days," Day replied.

"No, no, I don't mean how long it took to make it. I want to know how long it took to get this gun in position ready to fire?" the major asked.

"I'm guessing five minutes, maybe ten on the high side. It took five guys to get it in position," Dan answered.

"Here is what I want you to do, Reeves," ordered the major. "I want you to fabricate another minigun just like this one, except mount it in the back of a jeep. That way five troops won't be needed to get it underway, and the response time can be greatly reduced. Hell bells, we will be able to take this to any location on camp at a moment's notice, even out of camp if necessary."

So it was ordered, and so it was done.

That day at Camp Coryell was no ordinary day. Dan stepped up and pretty much singlehandedly thwarted a full-scale assault against the three hundred men fighting the war at Bam Me Thout. There was no official ceremony with military awards pinned on Dan's chest that recognized his heroic feats, there were no marching bands that celebrated the achievements of the day, only the gratitude and ultimate respect by his fellow soldiers. That was something earned, which could not be bought. Thus was the camaraderie of the United States soldiers. Events such as this happened daily somewhere in Vietnam.

There were a few occasions when daily operations at Camp Coryell veered to the left of normal. Dan recounted some strange hunting expeditions he became involved in as a door gunner. Fresh meat was a scarce commodity in Vietnam. To remedy that situation, aircrews often would go deer or wild boar hunting. Unlike hunting back in Iowa, when groups of hunters would tromp through the woods and push the deer out where other hunters waited to get a clear shot, the soldiers improvised. Two helicopters worked in tandem with a marksman at the door. One chopper flew low and slow and pushed the wild game into a clearing. The second helicopter flew a little higher and in front with sharpshooters at the ready. As the wild game ran from the chasing helicopter, they became easy targets for the gunship. Dan had a scope-mounted rifle that bagged many deer as he sat perched in the doorway of an Iroquois chopper. "I even bagged a wild boar once," he recounted. "Man, was that good eatin'!" He continued, "Once we had a kill, we'd land and throw them in a cargo net suspended below the helicopter and fly back to base. The maintenance sergeant was a butcher in civilian life before the army grabbed him, and he waited with knife in hand. He lifted the deer by their hind legs on his engine hoist, and in no time at all, we had steaks ready for the grill."

Their airborne hunting expeditions were no secret to anyone. One day, a group of green berets approached Dan with an interesting request. The green berets worked closely with the Montagnards in their battles with the VC. The Montagnards were a group of indigenous Vietnamese who lived a nomadic life in the mountains and became fierce fighters alongside US Special Forces. During the French's occupation of Vietnam in the 1950s, they also encountered this ethnically distinct group of villagers that lived in the upper highlands. The French called them Montagnards, which meant "mountaineers." American GIs abbreviated the name and used the slang word *Yards* to identify them. Their unusual request was straightforward. A tiger prowled the village of the Yards and had attacked and eaten several children. The four-hundred-pound tiger (*Panthera tigris corbetti)* had an appetite for human flesh, and the green berets wanted him dead. The Yards even told them that the tiger usually could be found on a sandbar in the afternoon, sunning himself, but was too elusive to sneak up to on foot. Could the deer hunters keep an eye out for the tiger?

On the second hunting trip after he received notification of the probable location of the tiger, Dan's gunship saw him as they hovered five hundred feet above. Sure enough, he lay on a sandbar in the river. Dan dialed his scope onto the tiger and popped off three quick rounds. The tiger never had a chance. The chopper landed on the sandbar and put the tiger in the cargo net, lifted off, and headed back to Camp Coryell. They notified no one of their bounty, but as they approached the airfield, a crowd began to gather. Within moments of touchdown, two yards in the company of three green berets pulled at the netting even before the rotor blades stopped turning. They quickly pulled the dead tiger free and began gutting him with their knives. Dan watched, mesmerized at what unfolded before him. The older Yard pulled at the entrails of the carnivore, then stabbed his knife into its stomach. He reached in and pulled something out. It was the tattered remains of child's clothing. He screamed out something in his native dialect that Dan couldn't understand. No translation was necessary. The Montagnards completely skinned the tiger, took its pelt, and walked away with the carcass still on the tarmac.

A few weeks later, they returned and paid a visit to the base commander. The yards presented him with the tiger's pelt. It was cured and tightly stretched between a bamboo frame. It was their way to say thank you for ridding their village of the child killer. Dan never saw the pelt again. In today's overseas market for fur traders, a tiger's pelt in good condition garners a price tag somewhere between $35,000 and $45,000.

Dan served his tour of duty in Vietnam, to be exact, eleven months and twenty-two days. He anxiously twiddled his thumbs at Bien Hoa airbase for five days awaiting the ride home. Finally, on March 30, 1970, a charter aircraft flown by Flying Tiger Airlines arrived. About two hundred GIs boarded and loudly cheered as the stretch DC-8 lifted off. Once airborne, a stewardess dressed in a candy-striped uniform walked the aisle with a can of aerosol deodorant in each hand and vigorously sprayed it above the heads of the soldiers. None had showered, shaved, or brushed their teeth for nearly a week. In no uncertain terms, she told them, "You guys stink!" They could have cared less. A full-bird colonel sat next to Dan on the flight back to the States, and they struck up a conversation. The DC-8 first stopped in Japan for a refuel, then headed east to Seattle. As Dan walked through the terminal at SEA-TAC airport searching for the connecting flight to Kansas City, a young blond girl spit on him as she walked by. He instantly turned in rage and aggressively approached her with clenched fist, ready again to fight the enemy. The colonel grabbed him by the shirt and pulled him back. "Easy, Reeves, easy. Pay her no mind." Dan obeyed the order from his superior. Coincidentally, both Dan and the colonel were heading to Kansas City.

Upon landing in Kansas City, Dan was just a hop, skip, and jump from Milo. To his dismay, the flight to Des Moines was delayed and would not leave for nearly eight hours. He just couldn't wait another eight hours to see his son for the very first time, his wife, and parents. Kansas City was only a short three-hour drive to Milo, so he headed to the rental car agency. Dan was tuckered out to say the least. He had been traveling for nearly twenty hours, still in his jungle fatigues, long overdue for a shower, and his patience was paper-thin. The ticket agent at the rental car agency told him he could not rent a car because he was not an NCO. Their policy restricted rentals to the lower-ranking soldiers. Dan showed the agent the rank on his sleeves. "I'm a specialist 5, that's an NCO," he shouted. "Are you stupid? What's going on here?" The discussion continued and seemed to be going nowhere fast.

Suddenly as if sent from heaven, Dan's travel buddy, the colonel, appeared. He pointed to the eagles on his shoulder. "You see these, son?" he barked out. "If I told you he was an NCO, would that be good enough to get him a car?"

The young rental car agent simply answered, "Yes, sir! He can have any car he wants."

Dan selected a brand-new 1970 red Ford Mustang. He virtually ran to the lot and jumped in and then pointed it north on Interstate 35 and hit the accelerator. It had been a year since Dan had driven a car, and he had not forgotten how to drive. His anxiety and excitement to be on the final leg of his journey home became overwhelming. He looked at the speedometer, and it registered one hundred miles per hour.

Needless to say, the trip to Milo did not take three hours. His return to Milo for some much deserved rest and relaxation (R & R) was long overdue. He longed to see his wife, Carolyn, and his son, Ted. He hoped to clear his mind of what he had witnessed, of what he had done in Vietnam, but discovered that would be a daunting task. The effects of his fighting in the war haunted him for years. The daily struggle in Vietnam—the death, the destruction, and personal survival—left a scar deep within him that popped its ugly head on a regular basis. Post-traumatic stress syndrome (PTSD) became a reality and haunted him nearly fifty years after the war.

Dan still had about a year left on his enlistment. He spent that time at Fort Rucker, Alabama, located eighty miles south of Montgomery. There he provided range support for the Huey helicopters and its weapons system. The job was identical to his task in Vietnam without the frequent mortar rounds or door gunner duties.

Dan arrived at Fort Rucker on May 4, 1970. It was another typical Monday in May, or so it seemed. Two days earlier, Dust Commander won the ninety-sixth running of the Kentucky Derby at 15–1 odds. On May 4, the New York Knicks beat the Los Angeles Lakers in game 5 of the NBA playoffs, 107–100, and eventually went on to win their first NBA title with Willis Reed named as the most valuable player (MVP), alongside teammates Walt Frazier, Cazzie Russel, and Bill Bradley. The Los Angeles Lakers, led by Wilt Chamberlain, Elgin Baylor, and Jerry West, pushed the series to a full seven games before losing four games to three.

Those events mentioned were insignificant and paled in comparison to actions taken by the Ohio National Guard on May 4, 1970, when they responded to student protests at Kent State University. That day, US military personnel fired upon unarmed US citizens at a peaceful college campus demonstration of the Vietnam War. Four students were killed, nine others wounded. That single event triggered a nationwide political and social revolt that divided America more than any gruesome evening news report broadcast live from the jungles of Vietnam. It marked the beginning of the end for the Nixon administration and a turning point in the resolve of Americans for the war and its soldiers.

Dan put his time in at Fort Rucker and finished out his enlistment. He saw many familiar faces on the flight line he recognized from Camp Coryell that cycled back to the States, both pilots and ground crew. The names all became a blur, but the memories of his days at Bam Me Thout remained as vivid as they were in 1969. Specialist 5 Dan Reeves discharged from active duty on May 28, 1971.

Well done, good and faithful servant! You have been faithful with a few things; I will put you in charge of many things. Come and share your master's happiness! **(Matthew 25:21)**

Dan retired as a printing press operator and lived in Hartford, Iowa. He was a member of Milo American Legion Post 263. He would often call me when stressed about one thing or another. In his words, "Do you want to go to the rifle range and decompress?" Guns had been part of his life for well over fifty years from the time we were old enough to go rabbit hunting alone and tromp the brush and scare up a few cottontails. Guns became a fixation for him, bolstered by his expertise in repairing them and his time in the military. He had a stockpile of guns that ranged from pistols, rifles, and shotguns. We often joked about our supply of ammunition that envied that of a small-town hardware store. We'd regularly hop in his car and head to Banner Pits rifle range and fire off a few hundred rounds, despite our failing eyesight, and still joked with each other who had the better aim. I had talked with him multiple times during our short rides together about what was on our minds. I knew that Dan had been receiving PTSD counseling for some time from the veterans hospital and medication as well to keep him on an even keel. However, as well as I knew Dapper Dan, I never dreamed in a million years how the stress gnawed away at him over the years. Dan left Vietnam in 1970, but like so many of the young men who served there, Vietnam never left him. Nearly fifty years after he left Bam Me Thout, the war finally ended for him on June 22, 2019, when he took his own life with a handgun. I don't think of Dan as just another statistic of the Vietnam War, yet he was.

In Shakespeare's play *Julius Caesar*, Marc Anthony speaks of the death of Caesar. "The evil that men do lives after them, but the good is oft interred with their bones." Thus, the evil of war that Dan experienced is easily remembered, but let us not forget the good he brought forth.

* ⭐ *

LARRY W. JOHNSON, SERGEANT E-5

United States Army
April 8, 1968–April 17, 1970

L arry Johnson was a scoundrel when I knew him in high school. His orneriness and sometimes hot temper found him in the principal's office on a weekly basis, or so it seemed, for she-nanigans in the hallways or boys' restroom. Larry struggled academ-ically and, as a result, ended up graduating with me in 1967 rather than in 1966. He attended most of the athletic events during his high school years but never participated in any of the organized sports or extracurricular activities. The reason for his faithful attendance at ball games, no doubt, was attributed to the soft spot in his heart for one of the cheerleaders, Linda Ballue. They would later marry.

He was a fella who charted his own course and followed his inner compass regardless of what others thought. The toughness he exhibited in his early teenage years served him well in the following years. Larry couldn't be characterized strictly as a loner, but he wasn't afraid to take a stance on any issue even if others veered in a different direction. He would stand alone if necessary.

I lost track of Larry after those high school years and had no idea where he went or what he did. I knew he served in the US Army but had little information beyond that. I asked questions to those in the community I knew who might steer me in the right direction. Through the magic of social media (Facebook), I received a response. Bruce Edgington, who graduated in 1968, had married Betty Ballue,

174

Linda's sister. Bruce lived in Minnesota. He told me Larry had died of a heart attack in 2011. Bruce gave me the contact information for Larry's son, Larry Johnson Jr., who lived in Lamoni, Iowa. I made the phone call and exchanged several text messages with Larry's son. I initially thought Larry's military story would be lost, like so many others, because I didn't see much useful information forthcoming. About the third contact, I asked Larry Jr if he had any documents that could give a picture of his dad's time in the military. Suddenly a treasure trove of material sprang forth. He told me, "Oh yes, I've got a copy of his Bronze Star award as well as his Purple Heart award. I also have a six-page letter he wrote to the Veterans Administration when he applied for benefits that related to PTSD issues he was experiencing." Herein lies, pretty much in his own words, Larry's military story.

The US Army drafted Larry on April 6, 1968, and two days later, he was aboard Trans-Texas Airlines headed to Fort Bliss, Texas. He noted that the flight encountered a severe storm while en route, and one of the aircraft's engines failed. The aircraft limped onward to Fort Bliss, where it made an emergency landing. Basic military training began immediately upon touchdown.

Larry finished boot camp in July of 1968, then proceeded as ordered to Fort Ord, California, for advanced infantry training (AIT) where he earned the MOS of 11B40, light weapons infantryman. In his transcript, he referred to the comments frequently made by the instructors, "If you don't pay attention here, you're gonna die in Vietnam!"

In October 1968, Larry completed his AIT. His next stop took him to Fort Benning, Georgia, at the Non-Commissioned Officer Academy. He graduated there as an E-5 after just three months of schooling in leadership skills and a mere total of eight months in uniform. In 1967, the army implemented the NCO Academy as a means to bolster its enlisted leadership due to the number of casualties of career NCOs from hostile action caused by the Vietnam War. At the time, it was a revolutionary and controversial idea. The young newly enlisted soldiers were called shake and bakes, or instant NCOs, or whip 'n' chills. It took a while for older NCOs to accept these new E-5s since they themselves had served years to attain the same rank. The challenges of the Vietnam War called for a new course of action for the troops in the field. Vietnam was a junior leaders war that encompassed small areas of combat rather than large-scale operations. The bulk of the fighting fell on the shoulders of junior officer and NCOs. Larry became one of many new NCOs soon headed to Vietnam. Records revealed that of the 546 graduates of the NCO school at Fort Benning, Georgia, that Larry attended in January 1969, 28 would die in Vietnam.

In late January 1969, Larry boarded a chartered commercial aircraft filled with young soldiers like himself and departed Oakland, California, with Vietnam as his final destination. The flight took over sixteen hours with stops in Hawaii and Guam. Bien Hoa Air Base became visible out the window as they approached the airfield, but rather than make an immediate descent, the aircraft circled the field for over half an hour. The pilot informed the soldiers that the base was under attack and hoped that things calmed down before landing. Larry stated, "The stewardess were frantic and crying as they walked down the aisle upon our descent. They told us to get off the aircraft as quickly as we could. We landed, and as our plane taxied to the parking ramp, I could hear gunfire."

As Larry rushed off the aircraft and sought shelter, the repugnant aroma of Vietnam immediately caught his attention. It was a strange funky smell, unlike any other he knew. It wasn't like the stench of an Iowa hog lot on a hot dry day, but a god-awful stench comprised of open latrines, rotten fish, burning JP-4 fuel, jet engine exhaust, and what he termed *the smell of death*.

Larry soon processed through the orderly room and documented his presence in Vietnam. As an NCO, he was given an additional three-day orientation of the dangers in Vietnam. He wondered what in the hell they could tell him that he hadn't already thought of a hundred times over. This stint would not be a picnic in the park.

The next day, Larry headed to Duc Pho, located along Highway 1, halfway between Da Nang and Qui Nhon. Upon arrival at the Duc Pho orderly room, he glanced at the list of arrivals and departures from the unit roster. Also on that list were the names of those killed in action (KIA) for the 4ᵗʰ Battalion. There were about twenty names listed as KIA. Larry asked the sergeant where he wanted him to go. The reply was a sobering, "Charlie Company, 4ᵗʰ Battalion, 21ˢᵗ Infantry Regiment," known as Americal. Larry would be headed into the teeth of the tiger. He was issued a weapon and, that very night, sent out on perimeter patrol where he encountered his first firefight.

"That first night on perimeter is one I'll never forget," Larry commented. "A trip flare went off, and I opened fire immediately in the direction of the flare. Four .50 caliber machine guns sprayed the area with lead, and then we called in artillery. At daylight, helicopter gunships flew above us and relentlessly riddled the area with lead. We had a full response against the intruders."

As that first day drew to a close, Larry and several others were taken to a helipad and boarded a helicopter, along with multiple boxes of supplies and ammunition, then ferried off to join his assigned unit. Upon arrival at a tree-covered hilltop, given a numerical identification, they touched down and quickly unloaded the supplies. There were several dead VC bodies stacked like cordwood near the tree line. Larry watched as they were loaded onto the chopper, then hastily lifted off. Larry remained transfixed on the Huey as it became smaller and smaller in the sky. To his amazement, it hovered at about one thousand feet, probably a mile away, and tossed the dead enemy soldiers out the side door.

Larry checked in with the company commander, Captain Hopkins, and was assigned as squad leader of the second squad of the second platoon. He then met others in his squad. The point man had a ponytail tied around the barrel of his shotgun taken in combat as a scalp from a dead VC soldier. The medic had a string of gold teeth tied around his helmet. Both war trophies represented a macabre way that demonstrated their hatred for the enemy and their power and dominance over them. The act of collecting body parts during the Vietnam War was not that uncommon a practice. In addition to scalps and teeth, other body parts included ears, fingers, and the prized trophy—a severed penis.

Larry continued to make the rounds and greeted each member of his platoon. Each platoon in Vietnam usually consisted of three squads comprised of eight soldiers in each squad. Larry remained on that hill for two days until the platoon had been replenished to full strength. Those first few days became the first time Larry regularly dined on C rations and SPs (sundries packets).

C rations consisted of small cans marked "M" (meat), "B" (bread, normally crackers), "D" (dessert), and an accessory pack (salt, pepper, sugar, instant coffee, a four-pack of cigarettes, and a couple squares of toilet paper). Each ration contained 1,200 calories. One pack out of every twelve contained a can opener, referred to by the troops as a "John Wayne."

Those first few days in the field, Larry slept on an air mattress and covered himself with a poncho. In his words, "The poncho was just thick enough to keep the mosquitoes from sucking your blood, and by morning, the air mattress leaked the air until it was flat. At daylight, a quick body check for leeches became the routine, and I often needed a lit cigarette to burn them off my skin." Larry continued in his narrative, "If the VC didn't get you, the elements would."

A few days later, his platoon set out on his first mission. They walked for two days and found themselves in a rice-covered valley. Shots quickly rang out but not directed to his unit but instead the first platoon. Larry's squad took cover on the dike of a rice paddy.

That night, Larry and his squad settled in and smoked and joked until just after dark. Larry decided to move his men to a new position, about two hundred yards away, in the cover of darkness. Later that night, that decision proved to be genius. Their previous position was hit by mortar fire in the early morning hours and likely would have devastated Larry and his entire squad.

At daylight, the platoon moved forward and approached the nearby village where the VC mortar fire came from the night before. Larry called in support with artillery fire as a precaution while his guys were about two hundred yards out. When the barrage stopped, Larry and his platoon rushed the village with weapons firing. At the edge of the village, his troops ceased fire as people virtually sprang from beneath the ground. Most were women, children, and a few old men. Then something happened—he wasn't sure what set it off but the guys in his squad opened fire and killed two women directly in front of him. Larry was ticked off about the unnecessary kills and approached those who fired with the intent of taking some type of discipline against them. As he approached, those involved began laughing. They had been in the field much longer than Larry—heck, he was just a week into his tour. Maybe they knew something he didn't. Larry decided to just let it go, checked his emotions, and restrained any thoughts of discipline against his troops.

The next order came from platoon sergeant Gant. Larry's squad was to sweep along the river by the village and check for any VC. When he presented this order to his squad, they all hesitated and wanted to sweep right through the middle of the village. Larry gave the order some thought, then asked another squad if they would trade assignments. Sergeant Gant approved the switch. He told Larry, "Your guys are older and meaner." Larry thought to himself, *Older? I'm just twenty-one? Meaner?* He wasn't sure but he knew his squad had already tasted blood and were anxious to finish the sweep.

The village was about a mile long, so another round of artillery was called in to hit the farthest end. His men proceeded on, right through the middle of the village. When finished, several VC had been wounded and apprehended by the squad on their flank as they tried to outrun Larry's squad. A handful of VC were killed. Larry had been in Vietnam less than two weeks and already had witnessed the worst of the worst.

Larry lost track of how many missions he went on. Only a few stuck in his mind. It was March 1969, and his squad flew to yet another rice paddy. As they touched down, they received ground fire but was unaware they were targeted as the chopper noise drowned out the *pop, pop* of incoming rounds. When the choppers lifted off, it became obvious that all kinds of VC were after them. Larry returned fire and killed several VC. A helicopter gunship circled above them and peppered the surrounding perimeter with minigun fire as well as smoke to provide cover for other squads arriving. It was a hellish day, but the next morning brought forth a more fierce battle. Larry's platoon was ordered to take the hill beyond the rice paddies. As the lead group began its ascent up the hill, they encountered a machine-gun bunker manned by the VC. Several of his guys were hit. The heavy gunfire had them pinned down, and they couldn't return fire for fear of hitting their own wounded near the bunker. Larry gritted his teeth as he could hear his own soldiers cry out for help. They could do nothing to help them. Those cries for help haunted Larry. "Why me, God, why me?" he heard again and again, shouted from the distance.

Finally a plan was put together to assault the hill and, hopefully, rescue the wounded. A helicopter gunship was called in to take out the bunker before further casualties arose. The choppers used rockets and their miniguns and poured what they had on the bunker. When the gunships departed, Larry's squad charged the hill. The air assault did the trick and completely obliterated the machine gun bunker. However, all the wounded GIs who cried for help the previous hour were also killed by the friendly fire. The ranking lieutenant entered the bunker and opened fire on the already dead VC. In anger, he wanted to make certain all were dead. When his carbine was empty, he placed it on the ground and grabbed his knife. With a guttural scream, he cut off the penis of one of the VC. A few dozen yards outside the bunker, they found the bodies that fell victim to the VC machine gunner and friendly fire. As Larry walked toward the bunker, he saw a black US soldier, dead and burning from the phosphorus rocket attack. In his written narrative, Larry commented that it was an image so profound, he could never forget it.

Whoever strikes a man so that he shall die, will be put to death. (Exodus 21:12)

It was June 12, 1969. Larry's unit was called into action again. An entire company of US troops had been shot up pretty bad and were in the middle of a battle. Larry's platoon jumped aboard a transport helicopter and rushed to the battle. His group was the first in, but only half his platoon was on the ground. A perimeter was quickly set up so that the rest of the company could join them. Air force jets hit the area hard with munitions as well as US Army gunships. Larry commented in his transcript, "It was quite an air show."

As other members of his unit were airlifted in, the VC fired mortar rounds at their position. Two in Larry's company were killed and several wounded. During the battle, Larry was hit in the back with shrapnel. The battle continued, and despite his superficial wound, Larry crawled out of his foxhole toward those more severely wounded to check on their injuries. The machine gunners ran low on ammunition, so Larry called for a helicopter drop for more ammo. He crawled to the dropped ammo, grabbed what he could, then crawled to each machine gunner, and tossed them the precious bullets. The guns were so hot that a crew around each machine gun dumped oil on the barrels to keep them from overheating and warping the barrels.

Sergeant Gant, the platoon leader, had worked his way a distance from Larry during the fight. There came a break in the battle, and the troops huddled up to tend to the dead and wounded. Sergeant Gant, a black guy, had been wounded. He had taken shrapnel to the neck. As he boarded the medevac helicopter for evacuation, he looked at Larry and said, "The platoon is yours now."

Larry responded to him, "Shut up, your talking will just worsen the wound." They squeezed hands, looked each other in the eye, and nodded. Larry told Gant, "You'll be all right." He lifted him by stretcher into the helicopter, and Sergeant Gant flew off with several other wounded. They would never see each other again.

Within minutes, the company commander, Captain Hopkins, came to their position. He asked who was the ranking man. All the soldiers standing there pointed to Larry. Larry stood up and shook the hand of the captain. In a very matter-of-fact voice, Hopkins said, "You're the new platoon leader, Johnson." Then he casually walked away.

A second medical evacuation (medi-vac) helicopter arrived to pick up more injured. There were dead US troops as well that needed removed. Sergeant Kaye came up to Larry and said, "Help me get these bodies out of here." Larry asked if it would be okay if he carried the end with the boots. It was his way, even if in the slightest manner, to distance himself from the death and destruction. By then, the bodies were stiff. Larry grabbed the boot end of a soldier and lifted him onto the chopper.

When all the dead and wounded had been evacuated, Captain Hopkins called all platoon leaders together. His order was this, "We're going back down the hill and clear the area."

Larry gulped, then thought to himself, *What a time to be a platoon leader.* When the order was passed down to the men, everyone thought they had breathed their last breath. When the trek down the mountain began and they encountered no resistance, Larry murmured, "Thank God the VC had left their positions. Enough fighting for this day."

It was October 25, 1969. Larry had been in Vietnam seven months. The US Red Cross contacted his commanding officer. Larry's older brother, Gary, had been killed while riding as a passenger in a single car accident on Vandalia Road in Des Moines, Iowa. Larry was granted immediate bereavement leave and left Vietnam, headed back to Iowa for his brother's funeral.

After a thirty-day bereavement leave in Milo, Larry had just a couple of months left before his twelve-month tour of duty in Vietnam ended. The US Army elected to send him to Fort Riley, Kansas, to finish out his enlistment there where he trained soldiers destined for Vietnam and honed their survival skills in the jungle.

It was there at Fort Riley that Larry again met up with high school classmate John Galbert who was also a member of the 4th Battalion, 21st Infantry Regiment in Vietnam. The very same outfit as Larry and served at the very same time but never went on patrol together. John was wounded on January 10, 1970, and was getting treatment at the Irwin Hospital at Fort Riley.

Larry discharged from the US Army on April 17, 1970. He spent seven months and one day in the jungles of Vietnam. He received the Vietnam Service Medal, the Combat Infantry Badge, a Purple Heart, and Bronze Star. In civilian life after the military, Larry was an over-the-road truck driver. He died of a heart attack in 2011.

ROBERT C. GILLESPIE, CORPORAL, E-4

United States Marine Corp
August 26, 1968–May 18, 1971

B ob and I graduated together from high school in 1967. We knew each other for years, growing up as little tykes in Milo. One of my fondest memories of Bob takes me back to the early 1960s when he lived on the far south side of Milo. Bob lived at the bottom of Drake's hill. Streets in Milo at the time had no names, but two other kids our age lived across the street from Bob. They were John and Becky Drake. That's how, as youngsters, we pinpointed locations in Milo—by who lived on the street. In the wintertime, the block-long downhill stretch of the road that ran past John and Becky's house, and finished at the bottom of the hill at Bob's residence, became the hot spot in town during the winter when snow-packed roads became the playground for toboggans and sleds. We rode our sleds down that hill time and time again and then slid halfway up the next hill until darkness forced us to head home. A dozen or so kids made Drake's hill their Olympic tryout camp for days at a time. Of course, numerous snowball fights ensued as those trudging back up the hill could not resist the temptation of throwing a tightly squeezed snowball and peppered those sliding down at breakneck speed. Kids freely shared sleds with one another, sometimes riding in tandem, either sitting upright or lying on top of one another while they attempted to force others into the ditch or crash before reaching the bottom. Everyone had a blast.

183

I've passed through Milo many, many times in the past fifty years during the winter months and don't ever recall seeing kids sliding down Drake's hill like our crowd of hooligans from years past. It must have been, no doubt, a special moment, a special time, and a special place reserved only for the boys of Milo.

Bob joined the United States Marine Corps one month shy of his twentieth birthday and headed to Camp Pendleton, California, for basic training. Only a handful of Milo Boys from the Vietnam era became marines. The USMC motto, "A few good men," certainly described Bob.

As I gathered information about Bob's military service, it became difficult. Bob died of pancreatic cancer in January 2005. He kept his military past buried from those close to him. His older brother, Jerry, who joined the US Army Reserves in 1963, knew very little other than Bob served as a mechanic in the USMC and went to Vietnam. His wife and only son were unable to share any information other than some photos. Like so many Vietnam veterans, Bob's thoughts about his role in the military—what he did, what he saw, and his opinions about the war—died with him. However, through military records, public after-action reports from the USMC, and conversations with other Milo boys who knew him and served with him, Bob's story unfolded as if I had rubbed a magic lamp and a genie appeared.

Bob joined the US Marines on August 26, 1968. He spent thirteen weeks at basic training located at Camp Pendleton. Upon completion of basic training, the USMC sent Bob to auto mechanic school, an eight-week course, also located at Camp Pendleton, where he completed his advanced training as a MOS 3516.

In the spring of 1969, Bob headed home to Milo for leave after his advanced schooling. While there, a unique set of circumstance befell Bob. While riding his motorcycle on a gravel road east of Milo, he became involved in an accident when he popped a wheelie coming out of a ditch. He didn't see the car coming, and it hit Bob and tossed him into the air. As a witness to the accident stated, "He was tossed as high in the air as the telephone poles alongside the road." Bob suffered internal injuries and a broken leg and was taken to the veterans hospital in Des Moines. As a result of his injuries, Bob stayed home in Milo for nearly two months on convalescent leave while his motorcycle wounds mended.

In July of 1969, Bob left Iowa and headed back to Camp Pendleton. While on the aircraft en route to California, Bob became ill with a bad case of the flu. When he arrived at Lindbergh Field in San Diego, he was so incapacitated he could hardly walk across the terminal to the baggage claim area. He missed the bus that carried troops to Camp Pendleton. He called the base and told them of his poor condition, but their cold response was simple, "You missed the bus, soldier, take a taxi."

Bob didn't have enough money for a cab and, not knowing what to do next, made a collect call home and told his parents of his dilemma. As his story unfolded, his older sister, Shirley, had a sister-in-law (sister of her husband) who lived near San Diego. Bob's sister, Shirley, contacted her and asked if she could pick her brother up at the airport. Bob had never met the sister-in-law, but she found him slumped on a chair at the passenger terminal. She took him to her home and, for the next few days, nursed him back to health. Bob knew he needed to get to Camp Pendleton and pronto, so as soon as he felt up to par, his sister's sister-in-law took him to the marine base.

The USMC greeted Bob with open arms the minute he checked in at Camp Pendleton. The familiar phrase "suck it up, buttercup" resonated with him as they placed him in the brig for being AWOL (absent without leave). Despite an attempt to justify his absence due to sickness and missing the commuter bus to the base, the USMC offered no sympathy. Bob spent three days in the military jail. Between his initial military leave, coupled with two months of convalescent leave at home and over a week traveling to California, Bob approached almost three months of freedom from the corps. It wasn't much longer before he received new marching orders with a destination he knew was inevitable. He would be headed to Vietnam.

Bob arrived at Da Nang, Vietnam, in May of 1970, and assigned to the 3rd Marine Division. There he worked not as an auto mechanic but in the vehicle maintenance parts supply facility. Da Nang was one of the largest US military installations in Vietnam and served as an air operations center for the USMC, the USAF, and the Vietnamese Air Force. The base was well secured but not entirely free from hostile attacks. During Bob's time at Da Nang from May 1970 to December 1970, the base was hit eighteen times by rocket and mortar attacks, most frequently in the early morning hours. Fortunately personal injury from those attacks were at a minimum, but significant damage to structures and some aircraft were incurred.

There was an occasion one day where Bob ventured to the other side of the base and checked out the USAF chow hall. The USMC grub was okay, but he just wanted a change of diet and scenery. As he made his way through the food line, loading his plate with air force chicken (mostly wings and landing gear), some instant potatoes, and canned gravy, he then spied an empty table across the room. He sat down to enjoy the meal, then nonchalantly glanced up at the adjacent table. "Holy cow," he muttered to himself. "It can't be!" But yes, indeed, it was! There at the next table sat Roger Hasting. Bob jumped up and nearly knocked his drink from the table as he lunged over to greet him. Roger and Bob graduated together from Southeast Warren High School just a few years earlier. Roger lived in nearby Liberty Center and joined the USAF about the time Bob signed on with the USMC. What a reunion it was! Handshakes, backslaps, and hugs were abundant as if long-lost brothers had reunited. "This is unbelievable," Bob said, "just unbelievable. What are the odds that we meet like this, halfway around the world?"

Roger was just as surprised at the chance meeting and agreed, "Pretty crazy, man, pretty crazy."

They both caught up on news they shared from back home. Bob asked Roger, "So what do you do over here in this hellhole of a country?"

"Ah, I work in supply in the top secret compound. Nothing too exciting," Roger replied. "How about you?"

Bob grinned and came back at him with what Roger said was his standard answer, "I've got the best job ever. *I guard the beer in the rear.*"

As slight as that statement seemed, behind it stood a significant meaning. Beer was a most important commodity in Vietnam. For soldiers, alcohol and combat went hand in hand. After returning from a combat mission, a ritual of knocking down a cold brew became commonplace. Its consumption brought a taste of home to the troops and, with enough gulps, blocked out the misery of war. An official report estimated that total beer sales through the various PXs (post exchange) throughout Vietnam amounted to a staggering $4 million per month. With the consideration that the price of beer was a meager 15¢ per can, the five hundred thousand troops in Vietnam in 1969 guzzled about 32 million cans a beer per month. When the logistics of American beer fell short, the troops drank the local beer called *Ba Muoi Ba*, or 33 as the GIs called it. The fact that 33 contained formaldehyde as a preservative did little to slow down consumption. Patrons of the brew discovered the aftereffects as they stood in front of the urinal, screaming as they emptied their bladders. Until their digestive system became accustomed to the formaldehyde, a horrible burning sensation occurred during discharge as the lining of the urinary tract became irritated from the preservative.

As a firsthand testament to the alcohol consumption, I deferred to the recollections of my first cousin, Bill Warbington, who piloted Hueys in Vietnam with the 192nd Assault Helicopter Group out of Phan Thiet. On one particular mission, his helicopter took on heavy ground fire. He coaxed it back to base with thirty-nine bullet holes and the front Plexiglas window shot out as he did a controlled crash-landing on the tarmac. Somewhat shaken by the event, he and his copilot made their way directly to the officers' club for a few shots of whiskey to settle their nerves and check the content of their underwear. Within an hour, a member of the maintenance team came to them and reported, if they could fly it to Cam Rahn Bay, the depot there would requisition a brand-new Huey. The repairs to damaged hydraulic and fuel lines had been quickly cobbled together. Not 100 percent sure if it was airworthy, the few shots of whiskey at the club bolstered their confidence. They climbed aboard and headed out. They flew out over the ocean to guarantee no ground fire and made their destination. Once on the ground, the process seemed like that of picking out a new car and trading in an old worn-out clunker. What a bargain, he thought to himself, a twenty-two-year-old signing for a $1 million piece of equipment. Bill took care of the paperwork at the operations center while his copilot headed off.

Ready to head back, his copilot was nowhere to be found. Bill did the preflight walk-around, checked all the fluid levels. He even cranked it up and hover-taxied for ten minutes to make sure everything was in perfect order. Finally his copilot ran onto the tarmac waving his arms. Bill set the Iroquois down, and the copilot climbed aboard. They were airborne. Bill watched as his partner reached into his flight bag and pulled out a full bottle of Old Grandad bourbon whiskey. He twisted the cap off and tossed it out the window. "We won't need this anymore."

The flight back to their base lasted ninety minutes. When they landed Bill commented, "I couldn't find my nose with both hands, don't know how I found the runway?" Ah, if the general public only knew the secret stories of the war.

At Da Nang, Bob and Roger kept in touch almost on a daily basis after duty hours. With Bob as the beer guard, every meeting was well supplied and fell within the realm of the auto mechanic training he received as a MOS 3516. To say they stayed "well oiled" should suffice.

Roger's DEROS (date expected to return from overseas) of July 8, 1970, quickly approached and he was "short." His office held a going-home party for him on China Beach on July 4. Roger invited Bob to attend.

The atmosphere seemed unreal to Bob. All kinds of mixed-rank soldiers whooping it up and having a great time. Guys bobbed in the surf as waves jostled them, steaks cooked on the grill, beer chilled in tubs of ice buried in the sand, loud music played over a speaker wired to a smaller Sony radio, and even a few American gals attended and wore cut-off fatigue pants and tightly fitted T-shirts. Roger motioned to Bob, "Hey, come with me, I want to introduce to somebody."

With that they walked to the tub of ice buried in the sandy beach and grabbed a couple of cold beers. Standing there was a full-bird colonel. Roger called him by first name, then said, "Hey, Jim, I'd like to introduce my high school classmate from Iowa. This is Bob Gillespie, he's in the marines on the other side of the base." Roger turned to Bob and said, "Jim is my squadron commander, hell of a good egg."

Jim reached out for a handshake with Bob. "Good to meet you, Bob. Did you say you went to high school together?" Bob nodded his head. "How amazing is that?"

Bob thought a moment about a proper response. "Kind of crazy, isn't it?"

Jim released his grip on Bob's hand and said, "This whole lousy war is crazy. Let's hope we all get out of here together."

Bob didn't say much for the next few minutes, but when he walked away with Roger, he asked, "How could you go up to a colonel and call him by his first name, let alone call him a 'good egg?' There is no way in God's green earth I could greet a marine colonel like that. They don't put up with that kind of disrespect."

Roger's response was simple, "Marines versus air force."

Bob pondered that meeting with the USAF colonel that day and later told Roger, "You know, I see all these USAF airplanes fly in and out of Da Nang. They're all flown by officers. It takes a whole bunch of enlisted guys to get that one pilot into the air. No doubt they trusted the guy who packed their parachute or the guy who loaded the ammo and bombs or the guy who fueled the jets or the avionics guys that calibrated their onboard instruments. On the other hand, the jarhead USMC officers commanded hundreds of enlisted troops, then sent them out to fight in the jungle while they remained in the rear. Now it all made sense. Or maybe not?"

The MACV (Marine Assistance Command in Vietnam) implemented Operation Keystone Eagle in July 1969, which involved the gradual removal of the Third Marine Division from Vietnam. That meant good news for Bob. He arrived at Da Nang in the middle of the transition and knew his time there would be short. The removal of the Third Marine Division took place in three increments. The First ARNV (Army of the Republic of Vietnam) gradually replaced the USMC as the US government encouraged them to take a bigger role in the protection of their country.

Bob left Vietnam in the final phase of Operation Keystone Bluejay, a few months after Roger Hasting's departure in July 1970. Bob had been in Vietnam slightly over six months. From Vietnam, Bob headed to MCAS (marine corps air station) Iwakuni, Japan, and was immediately assigned to Marine Support Squadron 17 that provided logistical ground support to the air station. Iwakuni's military population approached five thousand troops. There his assigned duty became that of a MP (military policeman) in lieu of his normal MOS as an auto mechanic. Due in part to the short time before his own DEROS.

There was a handwritten poem inscribed on the back of a photo taken of Roger and Bob on July 4, 1970, while together in Da Nang. I quizzed Roger about its author, and he didn't know. Bob's wife also didn't know its origin. Perhaps Bob wrote this himself, but regardless of the poet, it's worth sharing.

For us, it was the six o'clock news
For them it was reality
We called for pizza
They called for medics
We watched children play.
They watched children die.
We learned of life.
They learned of death.
We served dinner.
They served their country.
Our passion was success.
Theirs was survival
We forgot.
They never will

A man of many companions may come to ruin, but there is a friend who sticks closer than a brother. **(*Proverbs 18:24*)**

Bob's enlistment ended on May 18, 1971, when he discharged from active duty in San Diego, California. In total, he served eleven months and twenty-seven days overseas with equal time spent between Vietnam and Japan. Bob received the Vietnam Service Medal for his wartime service.

Bob died of cancer on January 4, 2005.

ALAN TED GODLOVE, SERGEANT, E-5

United States Marine Corps
August 26, 1968–November 10, 1970

Ted Godlove grew up in Milo along with his older brother, Edsel, and younger brother, Lee. His family lived at the far west end of Main Street. In all the years I knew Ted, I never once heard anyone call him by his given first name, Alan. Ted was a member of the Milo Boys Scouts troop 136 as a young kid. I later knew him as a member of the high school football team. He was a year behind me in school. Ted wasn't a big guy, but the coach played him in the line anyway, no doubt due to his tough and scrappy nature. Ted only participated in football his freshman year. In his words, "A skinny 135-pound kid had no business going up against other players fifty to sixty pounds heavier and not expect to get the snot knocked out of them time and time again." He gave up sports after one year, but his competitive nature never left him. A distinctive characteristic of Ted, as I vividly remember, was his jet-black hair. He reminded me a little of Elvis Presley with his slouched stature, olive skin, greased-back black hair, and a very easygoing personality.

Ted became known among those who followed the Milo boys' story as a member of the gang of five. On August 26, 1968, just a few short months after he graduated from high school, five rough and ready guys from the area volunteered for induction into the USMC, all on the same day. Ted, along with Bob Gillespie, fellow high school classmates Bradley Graham of Milo, Larry Flynn of nearby Lacona, and friend Dick Collins of Indianola raised their right hand and officially became jarheads.

All departed the tranquil surroundings of small-town Iowa and embarked on a journey that took them first to Camp Pendleton, California, for basic training. Once there, they separated only to see one another occasionally as they their platoons passed one another like two ships in the darkness of night during the eight weeks of training.

With basic training completed, additional orders followed and directed them to their next assignment. All, that is, except Ted. He was the only one in his platoon that did not receive orders for his next assignment. The USMC sent Bob to automotive school, a MOS of 3516. Brad received orders to become a MOS 3421, paymaster. Larry Flynn went to artillery with a MOS of 0811, and Dick Collins became a machine gunner, MOS 0331. As for Ted, his next duty would be a shot in the dark, no pun intended. His gunnery sergeant quickly realized the snafu (something normal all *fouled* up) and made an on-the-spot decision. Sarcastically he spouted, "For the love of God, Godlove, you're going to recon, HUA!" (heard, understand, acknowledge).

Within a few days, Ted found himself in reconnaissance advanced training, still at Camp Pendleton. After several weeks, Ted had multiple MOS ratings as a 0331, machine gunner, and 8651, 8541, scout/sniper as well as an MOS 8662, parachute qualified. Members of recon units were comprised of the corps' elite soldiers, called upon to accomplish missions that ranged from point reconnaissance to direct action. To complicate matters, emphasis on special operations added a new dimension to recon's personality, one that seemed to confirm—yes, indeed—Ted certainly was a marine's marine.

Next stop for Ted became Vietnam. On April 3, 1969, he arrived at Da Nang, Vietnam, and assigned to the First Marine Division, Alpha Company, First Recon Battalion. What caught his attention when he first stepped foot in Vietnam was the oppressive heat and unbearable stench of open air sewers and latrines. Reflecting back on that moment, he commented, "That perhaps was the easiest thing to endure during my nineteen months and ten days in Vietnam, the horrific odor." But like a terrible stink, the lousy smell of war stuck with Ted after his departure and lingered with him some forty-plus years into his future.

As a recon soldier, Ted became part of an eight-man team that was regularly airlifted by helicopter from the reasonably safe base of operations at Da Nang Air Base and inserted into the jungles for a week to ten days at a time. Their mission was not to search out and attack the Vietcong but rather to hide and observe the enemy's movements, troop strength, base camp locations, and type of equipment used. During the first year in Vietnam, Ted became involved in thirty-four such long-range missions. To say that the multiple encounters with the VC were simply "watching" their movements would be incorrect. His team participated in too many firefights to remember. Oftentimes, as stated by Ted, "the quickest on the trigger survived." Ted quickly rose through the ranks from an E-1 private to E-5 sergeant. That rapid progression was amazingly quick, but in Ted's own words, "I got promoted by default because many within our group were badly injured or killed. I was simply next in line, and the line moved quickly." In that first year of combat, Ted was the only remaining original member of his platoon. All the others were either injured and sent home or killed in action.

As a patrol leader, Ted employed a tactic of having his guys crawl on their stomach to advance through the jungle about fifty feet to one hundred feet off a trail. "It wasn't like John Wayne hacking his way through the brush with a machete," he said. "The undergrowth had about an eighteen-inch clearance close to the ground that made movement easier than tromping through the tangled mess of vines. It also gave us a better line of sight, as low as it was, than peeking around the taller foliage looking for movement. By avoiding trails, we also avoided the high probability of booby traps set by the VC."

In addition to his M16 carbine, Ted carried a Remington 700 bolt-action sniper rifle in a sling over his shoulder. From his experience, he noted, when VC soldiers walked down trails in the jungle, for the most part, they carried their AK-47 rifles slung over their shoulders. They were so close he could hear their voices in casual conversation as if they were on a walk through a park. He could detect women's voices among them as well. Ted insisted that his guys carry their weapons in hand, ready to fire at a moment's notice with their thumb on the safety. The motto to his patrol, "When encountered, first to fire is first to survive." The AK-47 required the removal of the dust cover before firing. The few seconds to unsling the weapon and remove the cover became the edge that Ted's men relied on.

Not every encounter resulted in the exchange of small-arms gunfire. Ted himself called in grid coordinates for artillery rounds to be fired upon enemy encampments which his patrol located. He went on to say, "On one occasion, I called in the coordinates and the battleship USS *New Jersey* fired rounds from offshore. It was more impressive than a B-52 bombing. I initially asked for a spotter round."

They replied, "We don't do spotter rounds." Then all hell broke loose.

During the Vietnam War, the USS *New Jersey* expended 12 million pounds of ordnance, only 1,500 pounds shy of the battleship's total ordnance expended during all of WWII. Ted commented, "I guess you could say I accounted for a few thousand pounds of metal fired on the VC."

On one of his missions, early on during his time in Vietnam, Ted lay in the underbrush of the jungle with several others on his patrol, waiting and watching VC movements. Suddenly they heard voices, and a group of twenty VC appeared, perhaps fifty feet away, on the trail. Ted and his team remained motionless and let the VC pass and made note of the type of small arms they carried. Just a few minutes later, more voices follow. Again the marines remained quiet and held their breaths without the slightest of movements. This time, sixty North Vietnamese Regular Army troops in uniform paraded past them. They stopped and chattered among themselves. Ted not only heard their voices but was close enough to smell the odor of marijuana they smoked. Another noise ahead of them in the bushes aroused the marines' senses. Ted pushed the selector switch on his M16 with his right thumb, from safety to full automatic, ready for an assault. A squeal came from the bushes. A wild boar suddenly ran across the trail in front of the NVR, and they fired their AK-47s at the pig. The boar raced into the jungle—directly toward Ted's patrol. They held their fire knowing they were vastly outnumbered. The pig raced past Ted, only ten feet away, then abruptly swerved to his right. The NVR, in hot pursuit, fired away at the boar. They wanted fresh pork for dinner that evening. More shots were fired by the NVA, then shouts of joy as they downed the wild boar. Ted quietly breathed a sigh of relief, pushed the selector switch back to the safety position. The NVA feasted that night on fresh pork. Ted and his patrol survived that potentially disastrous situation. They slowly crawled further away from the trail, grateful that they were not discovered by the pig hunters.

On September 19, 1969, Ted and seven others were inserted by helicopter into the jungle near Quang Nam on yet another recon mission. That afternoon, his buddy Frank Montez from Salinas, California, heard noises on the knoll ahead of them and smelled food cooking. Frank and Private Head moved closer to investigate. A lone VC spotted them and opened fire. Frank returned fire and killed the gook. Two more VC appeared and retrieved the body, and the fight was on. The eight marines soon were surrounded by superior numbers. A firefight ensued and continued from late afternoon, about four thirty, into the early morning hours of the next day, September 20. Ted called in air support to beat back the VC. Bullets flew everywhere. Gunships fired from the sky, the marines fired from the ground, and the VC fired at both.

At 0400, a helicopter was able to get in and attempted the extrication of the recon team. PFC Head had been shot in the foot. Of the eight-man team, Ted and Frank were the only two not hit by enemy fire. In the darkness of night, Ted turned on his flashlight and guided in the Huey. His light drew immediate fire. Frank held PFC Head's arm, draped around his own neck, as he, Ted, and Head scrambled to the landing zone. For support, Frank interlaced his other arm onto the harness of Ted's tactical vest. *Zap!* A single round hit Frank Montez, and all three tumbled to the ground. Ted shouted out, "Lord Jesus, don't let me die!"

Ted recalled a calm that overcame him. He later reflected on the moment. "I don't know if it was ten seconds or ten minutes. It was as if no time constraints existed. I was somewhere in a segment of time previously unknown to me. It seemed as though there was some kind of electrical field around me. A zapping noise pierced the air. Light flashing sensations surrounded me, and I remember free falling through a golden tunnel. It sounds crazy, but my life passed before me like a fast-forward slideshow. Then I saw a figure in the distance. I couldn't see the face, but He spoke to me. '*You have to go back.*'" *My god, was that Jesus?* he thought to himself. *Am I dead?*

Flat on his back, Ted blinked his eyes as he looked up. He heard the heavy *whop, whop, whop* noise caused from the chopper blades that pushed against the night air. He turned his head to the right and saw his buddy Frank Montez. Frank had taken a hit to the head and was killed instantly. Half of his face was gone. Ted grimly recalled Frank's hanging cheek tissue that flapped freely in the wind from the rotor wash of the chopper as it settled in. He jumped to his feet and grabbed Frank and threw him on the floor of the Huey, then went back and lifted PFC Head into the chopper. The five other wounded grunts from his patrol hobbled to the LZ, and Ted helped them onboard as the Huey pulled pitch and *di di maud* from the hellhole. As the Huey reached altitude, Ted glanced down at the area they just left. It was lit up like a Christmas tree on Times Square. The air force pounded the area with napalm once they got word that the extraction had been completed. *Kill 'em,* he thought to himself, *kill every one of the bastards!*

Five days later, PFC Goldmeyer, part of the recon team died from his wounds. Frank Montez also died in the early morning darkness. Of the eight-man team, two were killed and another five wounded. Ted exited the ordeal as the only person unscathed. The

USMC later posthumously awarded Frank Montez the Silver Star for his heroic actions on September 20, 1969. Ted knew the true story but never contested the corps' honor to his friend Montez for the award. He knew who guided the Huey in and who carried the wounded onboard.

> *And I was with you in weakness and in fear and much trembling, and my speech and my message were not in plausible words of wisdom, but in demonstration of the Spirit and of power, so that your faith might not rest in the wisdom of men but in the power of God.* **(1 Corinthians 2:3–5)**

After that mission to Quang Nam, Ted felt a sense of ease come over him. Gone was the battlefield fear, the constant reminder that death walked beside him each moment in the jungle. That release of fear would serve him well into the future. He continued to have close calls and simply shrugged his shoulders. Twice he thought he had been hit by rifle fire, only to find that his canteen attached on his web belt took the round. He felt the impact, he felt warm fluid running down his leg, but it wasn't his blood. *How lucky can a guy be?* he thought to himself. On yet another occasion, while in a skirmish with the VC, the stock of his M16 stopped a bullet destined for his chest. His weapon shattered in his hands, but he never received so much as a scratch. What else would one expect from a marine who had met Jesus and was told, "You must go back."

In the fall of 1969, Ted was between missions and had a few days to recoup from the rigors of the jungle and the unknown danger that lurked behind every tree. He took the time to relax and had a few beers at the Da Nang recreation compound. While engaged in a game of billiards, he looked up, and lo and behold, in walked Larry Flynn, his high school classmate and comrade in arms who enlisted in the USMC with Ted. Larry just happened to be passing through Da Nang and knew Ted's unit, so he took a chance he might find him. What a joyful rendezvous it proved to be. They played a few games of pool and reminisced of their innocent days back in Milo and Lacona. Despite the fact that they were hardened combat veterans, back home in Iowa, they were not old enough to legally consume alcohol. Larry spoke out with a phrase taken from the movie *The Wizard of Oz*. "Well, Toto, I don't think we are in Kansas anymore—*I mean Iowa*. Here's to us."

Ted chimed in. "That's for sure, Toto, damn straight. We aren't in Iowa anymore. Here's to mud in your eye." They tipped their warm cans of Schlitz beer and guzzled it down. They looked at each other with empty beer can in hand, laughed out loud, and together sang the familiar jingle, "*Yep, when you're out of Schlitz…you're out of beer.*"

Little did they realize the significant meaning of their toast, "Here's mud in your eye." The origin behind that toast for good health can be traced to biblical times as noted in John 9:15. There Jesus healed a blind man when He rubbed mud in his eyes. "I once was blind, but now I see." With that toast and God's blessing, Ted and Larry were in good hands. They both would eventually return home from battle unscathed.

On April 18, 1970, I was home on leave back in Milo, fresh out of boot camp with the USAF. That same day, halfway around the world, Ted was twelve days shy of his twentieth birthday and conducted duties as a patrol leader of a six-person long-range reconnaissance team in the Thuong Duc area of Quang Nam Province of Vietnam. While on patrol, his team encountered a numerically superior enemy force that approached his guys. He told his troops to hightail it to a suitable landing zone, while he remained behind alone and delayed the advancement of the VC. As the enemy approached, Ted detonated four antipersonnel mines that killed four VC soldiers. He engaged the others with small-arms fire, then directed air strikes on the enemy positions and aborted the attack. As a result of his actions that day, the USMC awarded Ted the Bronze Star with a combat distinguishing device.

Over 2.7 million US soldiers served in Vietnam during the war. Of those 115,000 were Iowans, and just a handful were from Milo. Hundreds upon hundreds of crazy stories were told by those who returned to the disbelief of those back home. A story surfaced that involved weird encounters with a creature that inhabited the thick undergrowth of the Vietnamese jungles. The locals called it *batutut*. The GIs who saw the bipedal hairy creatures called them rock apes. Ted witnessed, multiple times, the rock apes that roamed the jungles, oftentimes in groups of a dozen or more. They were bigger than a chimpanzee but smaller than a gorilla. They barked like a dog. Some stood as tall as six feet and were covered with hair that ranged from brown to black. The documented rock apes were akin to the Bigfoot creature often spotted in the Pacific Northwest of America. Ted told the story of hearing something coming through the jungle. Not sure if it was the enemy, Ted quietly held his position. Worried that the commotion created by the rock apes would give his position away if any VC were in the area, Ted found a rock and threw it at them to scare the primates away. To his surprise, the apes picked the rock up and threw it back. Others recounted the same story. Thus the rock apes turned from a myth to a reality for some of troops that frequented the choking jungles of Vietnam, and so the name stuck.

On another occasion, when based at a LZ, one of the marines in Ted's outfit went to answer the call of nature in the early morning hours. A makeshift latrine had been constructed with a fifty-five-gallon drum cut in half to collect the human waste. The marine stepped inside the latrine and began his business on the two-holed facility. Only the light of the moon guided him, and once inside, it was pitch-dark. The marine sat down and lit a cigarette. The glow of the match revealed someone sitting next to him on the second hole. To his disbelief, there sat a rock ape. Before the match hit the floor, the marine bolted from the latrine as if shot from a cannon with his fatigue pants at his ankles. He told others of his encounter with a rock ape, and they went to investigate, armed with their M16 rifles. By the time they arrived, apparently the intruder had finished his business too as nothing was found.

During yet another insertion into the jungle, Ted's recon team encountered heavy enemy forces and needed an immediate extraction. He radioed for a helicopter to pull his six-man team out of harm's way. Within a short time, a chopper arrived, but with no clear LZ nearby, his team was extricated through the jungle forest with a STABO harness (stabilized body). The STABO device was a highly effective means of extracting or inserting soldiers when ground landings were impossible and allowed them hands-free capability to use their weapons while hanging in the air. Ted and his team snapped their carabiners onto the line and began liftoff. They came under immediate fire as the UH-1H Iroquois pulled away. The rescue helicopter was hit by ground fire and began to lose altitude with Ted and his crew dangling beneath. It became evident the chopper was going down.

The pilot fought to keep the battle-damaged Huey under control during the rapid descent. He guided it toward a nearby river knowing that if it hit the trees, those hanging freely would be seriously injured, if not killed. Ted hit the water and found himself and the others being dragged down the river. Thoughts of drowning in Vietnam never entered Ted's mind until now, but it became an instant reality. Ted tried to disconnect his tethered line, but his own weight and the force of the Huey was too much to overcome. Suddenly the rescue chopper hit the water and flipped onto its side. Ted popped to the surface. It was a hard landing and could have been much worse. Ted disconnected his carabiner and made his way to the shoreline. Others followed. The helicopter crew bailed out and also made their way near the marines. All, including the aircrew, escaped without any major injuries. Within minutes, a second Huey hovered above them that observed all the events prior to the crash. *Hooray for the backup team*, Ted thought to himself. Nobody said a word. They didn't need to. All rushed to the airworthy chopper, hopped aboard, and ascended upward into the heavens, destined for friendlier territory. As the Huey reached altitude, Ted shook his head and tried to put the day in perspective. He couldn't.

On November 10, 1970, Ted Godlove discharged from the USMC back where it all began, Camp Pendleton, California. To say he served his country honorably and with distinction would be a gross understatement. During his two years, two months, and fifteen days of active duty with the USMC, of which one year, seven months, and ten days were in Vietnam, Ted received the National Defense Service Medal, the Vietnam Service Medal with two devices, the US Navy Commendation Medal with valor, the Vietnam Campaign Medal with device, the Republic of Vietnam Cross of Gallantry with palm and frame, the Bronze Star Medal with valor, and the Combat Action Ribbon.

Shortly after discharge, the remnants of Vietnam still lingered with him back home in Iowa. He went to his family doctor, Dr. Adeline McCormick, an icon in the Milo area for years, with a leg ailment. Upon examination, she found a festered wound in his left leg. Ted could have gone to the veteran's hospital but thought it was no big deal. What Dr. McCormick found shocked her. A fragmented piece of shrapnel had worked its way to the surface of his left leg. Ted recalled the incident in Vietnam but thought it was just a scrape, a superficial wound, nothing to worry about. "I wish I had kept that small piece of metal as a souvenir of my time in Nam," he told me. Instead, he tossed it away. Ted never reported that injury while in Vietnam. "I didn't want a Purple Heart," he insisted. "Never bothered with the paperwork." That's just the kind of guy Ted was. The commonly used phrase "been there, done that" fits Ted perfectly. He added, "I've got the T-shirt too."

BRADLEY A. GRAHAM, MASTER SERGEANT, E-8, RETIRED

United States Marine Corps
August 26, 1968–September 30, 1989

I knew Brad since the days we played Little League baseball for the Milo Mustangs. He lived just a block south of the gazebo on Main Street in the heart of town. Our mutual enjoyment of sports continued as we grew older, and eventually we found ourselves as teammates on the high school athletic teams. Brad was quite the rascal that seemed to be in such a hurry headed somewhere but not sure of his destination. He wanted to do everything and try everything as if he had a limited time to find his niche in life. The guys that hung out with Brad had a nickname for him. We called him Trax. The story behind that nickname came from his penchant to smoke cigarettes at a very young age. By young, I mean about twelve or thirteen years old. He smoked nonfiltered Camel cigarettes stolen from his dad's supply. As his nicotine habit increased in his young teen years, sneaking just one or two of his dad's smokes just didn't meet his needs. He bragged to those who knew him that he *bought* his cigarettes at a small gas station located across the street from the Honnegers grain elevator in Indianola, adjacent to the railroad tracks on Highway 65. The name of that small gas station was Trax Gas.

At the tender age of eighteen, just a few short months out of high school, Brad joined the Marine Corps on August 26, 1968. He would soon find his niche in life, if not as a grunt, perhaps a POG (person other than a grunt). I quickly discovered that Brad's military experience with the USMC was far from the open book I anticipated. Unfortunately Brad died in 2011 of chronic oppressive pulmonary disease (COPD) at age sixty-one. Much of his twenty-one-year military story disappeared with his death. I attended his funeral in Milo as did a number of other boys of Milo.

As I attempted to piece together Brad's story with the USMC, I continued to run into dead end after dead end. The more I encountered those dead ends, the more determined I became to bring to light his story. I spoke to his mother, Betty, who was in her nineties, and she offered little information other than a small box of his military documents. I spoke to his two younger sisters, Sandy and Teri. They were just little girls when he enlisted in the marines and had little memory of when he joined. I spoke to his children scattered across the country from Virginia to Arizona to California. In a phone conversation with his adult daughter, Heather, she began to cry when I told her I knew her dad and was seeking information about him. She told me she never really had a father-daughter relationship with her dad. He divorced her mother when she was just an infant and didn't see him again until years later when he suffered from COPD. She told me he had multiple marriages and children from each of those marriages. Determined to find more about Brad, I pressed on.

I reached out to one of his high school classmates, Larry Flinn, who lived in Albuquerque, New Mexico, and who joined the USMC with Brad under the buddy enlistment program. Larry turned out to be a gold mine of information. They stayed in touch off and on over subsequent years. Much of Brad's story is credited to Larry.

Brad performed his USMC basic training at Camp Pendleton, California. After a stint there, the corps sent him to advanced training where he earned the MOS of 0151, administrative clerk. Larry joked with him and called him the "Remington raider," the moniker given to those adept at pecking away on a manual Remington typewriter. That was in sharp contrast to Larry's MOS of 0811, artillery and mortars. Larry continued on, "Brad was what the Marine Corps called a *house mouse*. He just shuffled papers and quietly sat at a desk most of the day and hoped nobody noticed his presence."

Brad received military orders to Vietnam in the spring of 1969. He arrived at Da Nang Air Base about April 1, 1969, and assigned to headquarters, 1st Marine Aircraft Wing. In a letter written to his friend Larry, dated May 20, 1969, he said, "I've only got 306 more days left." Brad spoke of his activity beyond the mundane house mouse duties in the office. "We've been getting hit the last three or four nights. I've been doing guard duty on the perimeter fence next to the rice fields out on the dark corners. On the six-hour shift, I walk perimeter. I like the four-hour shift better just sitting on outpost where I can watch for them coming. I'm getting used to it. I witnessed 'Puff' (a C-47 gunship known as Puff the Magic Dragon) as it blew the hell out of somebody on the other side of Freedom Hill last night and watched those tracer rounds coming down."

Brad never once spoke of any skirmishes during his time at Da Nang. However, he referred to the boring and mundane duties of working in an office atmosphere during the day and guard duty at night. He did comment, "I was drunk a lot, almost every day."

On June 26, 1969, Brad received word through the Red Cross that his father, Bill, had died from a heart attack at age forty-four. Just three months into his tour of duty in Vietnam, Brad headed home to Milo on bereavement leave and attended his father's funeral. He returned to Vietnam in early August and served another eight months at Da Nang. He quickly fell back into the routine of drinking. Brad's moral compass pointed him in the wrong direction as several references in his letters to Larry mentioned drunkenness and encounters with bar girls. Larry provided me with copies of those letters. They were very graphic and filled with obscenities and activities that would cause a drunken sailor to blush, certainly not the kind of letter that would be sent home to a mother.

Like many young soldiers, Brad became consumed with the underbelly life that existed during the off-duty hours in Vietnam. There were no rules that could not be broken or moral standards that could not be ignored. He came home not with a Purple Heart but scars on his soul that remained with him years and years after. At the young innocent age of twenty, he met the devil in Vietnam, face-to-face, and shook his hand, not understanding the consequences.

What comes out of a person is what defiles him. For from within, out of the heart of man, come evil thoughts, sexual immorality, wickedness, deceit, and foolishness. All these evil things come from within and defile a person. (**Mark 7:20–23**)

After his tour of duty in Vietnam and a short trip home on leave, Brad's next set of orders sent him to Camp H. M. Smith, Hawaii, about October of 1970. Camp H. M. Smith was located on the island of Oahu, near Pearl Harbor. There he continued his duties with the USMC as one of Remington's raiders. While at Camp H. M. Smith, Brad met his former drill instructor (DI) from basic training. Drill instructors, particularly USMC drill instructors, carried the reputation of being real tough on their recruits. Brad remembered just how far off the charts his DI treated him and others. Brad now felt he had the upper hand. With unrestricted access to the pay records at headquarters, Pacific Command, in what could be called a payment in kind, Brad intentionally altered his former DI's pay records and created financial havoc for the DI as repayment for the hard times he bestowed on Brad. Touché, drill sergeant, touché.

His next duty assignment sent him to Okinawa. For a while, he simply fell off the radar screen for the next several years. I found no documents as to his exact location or his duration at any specific USMC bases, other than recollections from his younger sisters. As told by them, Brad went from Hawaii to Okinawa for a couple of years. His training records indicate that in 1980, he became a COBOL (common business-oriented language) programmer. In 1982, he returned to the United States and found himself stationed at Bethesda, Maryland. There he continued with the USMC's newly implemented computer system for duties as an automatic data process equipment operator for the Fleet Marine Forces (ADPE-FMF). In 1985, a new set of orders sent him to Arizona, to Marine Corp Air Station Yuma, Arizona. His last set of orders, dated in 1988, sent him to Kansas City, Missouri. There he worked in the Marine Corps Central Design Program Activities (MCCDPA). The MCCDPA responsibilities included issuance of all orders for IRR (individual ready reserves) and MTU (Marine Training Units) personnel and maintenance of financial records for RPMC (Reserve Personnel, Marine Corps) and O and MCRA (operation and maintenance of continued resolution agreements) appropriation funds. Alas, after twenty-one years in the Marine Corps, Brad transitioned well beyond the title of a Remington raider. No doubt he became a full-fledged computer geek.

Brad honorably discharged from the USMC on September 30, 1989, after twenty-one years of active duty service where he attained the second-highest rank of E-8 for enlisted personnel. During that time, he received the Vietnam Service Medal with two devices, the Vietnam Campaign Medal with device, the Vietnam Meritorious Service Commendation Medal Civil Action with palm and frame, the Vietnam Meritorious Unit Commendation Medal with Cross of Gallantry with palm and frame, the Navy Achievement Medal, Sea Service Deployment ribbon, the National Defense Service Medal, the Good Conduct Medal, and the Rifle Expert Badge.

EDWIN LAWRENCE ALLEN, FIRST LIEUTENANT

United States Army, Special Forces Green Beret
March 18, 1967–September 18, 1970

No one I ever knew used the name Edwin or Lawrence when referring to this newcomer to the Milo community. In school, everyone called him Larry. Larry moved to Milo the summer of 1964, before his senior year in high school, and quickly assimilated with the Milo teenage crowd. Not long after his arrival, he earned the nickname "Tidball." I often wondered how he acquired such an odd nickname. In fact, most of the guys I knew called him Tidball instead of Larry. An interesting story behind his newfound moniker surfaced within months upon his arrival to the streets of Milo.

Larry was always up for a good time despite any potential dangers that lurked behind teenage shenanigans. He, and two other Milo boys, Bob Gillespie and Ben Hamilton, decided, as a Halloween prank, to tip over outhouses that lined many of the alleys in town. There were a number of folks in Milo in the early 1960s who still did not have indoor plumbing. Larry, Bob, and Ben took it upon themselves to tip toilets one evening. It just wasn't one outhouse but several that ended up on their side adjacent to a large stinking hole in the ground. What they did not know at the time was someone observed their mischievous prank and called the authorities. Apparently a county sheriff was in the area, and his quick response caught them red-handed in their dastardly deed.

They didn't go to jail for their pranks, but they did have to return to the scene of their crime and upright all the privies they had previously toppled. Then the law enforcement officer gave them a true tongue-lashing about their wrongdoings. He referenced a similar incident back in the 1930s when a Milo resident shot some pranksters as they tipped over his outhouse. His shotgun put lead pellets into the backside of some ornery youngsters. The last name of the guy who took the worst of the buckshot was Tidball. Once word spread among Larry's peers in school about the incident, as the ringleader of the outhouse-tipping team, by default, Larry garnered the nickname Tidball by all who knew him. Jerry Ferguson confirmed the Tidball story. Tidball was the maiden name of his grandmother. The person shot was Charles Tidball, the brother of his grandmother.

Larry and his siblings lived west of Milo, on an acreage near the Fridley family. He played defensive back on the high school football team his senior year. That year, the Warhawk football team went undefeated, a first ever occurrence in the history of the small school, a record that still stands today. Of course, that was before the high school playoffs became a reality for the state of Iowa or the class division among schools. However, anyone back then would tell you the team would have advanced far into the playoff if one had existed. The team was pretty good. A bunch of hard-nosed young men that never knew the meaning of *quit*. That toughness served well for many on the team in the years to come, particularly Larry.

Two years out of high school, Uncle Sam knocked on Larry's door and requested his services in the military. On March 19, 1967, Larry was drafted into the US Army and headed to Fort Benning, Georgia, for basic training. After a very, very short time, he elected to volunteer and extended his enlistment after being selected for officer school. Once basic training wrapped up, Larry headed to Fort Bragg, North Carolina, for the twenty-week officer training school (OTS). Upon completion of OTS, he was commissioned as second lieutenant, as an infantry officer, on October 18, 1967. Further training sent him to the grueling special operations warfare school which included psychological operations, special forces, and airborne jump school. The 1966 Barry Sadler song "Ballad of the Green Berets" pretty much identified the tough rigors of special forces. As the tune stated, "One hundred men will test today, but only three win the green beret." Special forces demanded the best of the best, and that didn't mean just muscle strength but intellectual excellence and an unstoppable mindset. Larry completed the training and became an officer in the Green Berets, Special Operations, Airborne on September 27, 1968. The motto of the special operations soldier, *De Oppresso Liber*," which is Latin for "to free the oppressed."

The next stop on Larry's military journey sent him to Vietnam. In October 1968, he arrived at Song Be, located about two kilometers from Phước Bình in Southern Vietnam where he was assigned to 5th Special Forces, Detachment B-34 as a young lieutenant. No specific details of his personal activities in Vietnam are known. Larry died in 2014 of cancer. Like many other Vietnam veterans, he spoke very little to others of his personal war experiences, including his wife of thirty-five years, Cheryl. Her only recollection of his Vietnam story he shared with her involved his survival skills. He and his fellow troops were in a very remote location and low on supplies. Larry told her they shot a monkey and ate it, cooked over an open fire. What can be determined, however, based on his MOS, coupled with his location at Song Be, Vietnam, and declassified secret after-action-reports from the 5th Special Forces at Song Be, things in the area were helter-skelter.

As a psychological warfare officer, Larry would have engaged the local population in an attempt to win the hearts and minds of the Vietnamese civilians. Techniques involved medical aid to civilians injured by the war and dissemination of literature to the general populous about the evils of the communist political agenda and the ideological objectives of the United States. All was not smiles and handshakes by the farthest stretch of the imagination. Additionally special forces trained and led unconventional forces against the enemy in direct action. The special forces detachment identified sympathizers to the Vietcong (National Liberation Front) NLF and carried out assassinations of prominent opposition leaders through Operation Phoenix. The Vietnamese called it *Phụng Hoàng*, named after a mythical bird that appeared as a sign of prosperity and luck. Operation Phoenix began in 1965, before Larry's arrival in 1968, and carried on until 1972. As a special ops officer, Lieutenant Allen would have been heavily involved in the program during his time in Vietnam. For the duration of Operation Phoenix, military after-action-reports from the 5th Special Forces revealed as many as 81,740 sympathizers were "neutralized" and another 41,000 NLF operatives and VC informants killed. As a psychological warfare officer, Larry too would have been involved as an observer in the interrogation of captured VC. However, techniques used to obtain information as identified by eyewitness authors of other books chronicled gruesome torture conducted by South Vietnamese soldiers.

In June 1969, the death of a suspected double agent by the name of Thai Khac Chuyen, and subsequent cover up, led to the arrest in July of seven officers and one noncommissioned officer of the 5th Special Forces Group (Airborne) B-57. That elimination became known as the Green Beret Affair. Chuyen worked with the 5th on Project GAMMA when the Green Berets learned he might be a bad egg. Several of their own special forces people were unexpectedly killed. He underwent ten days of rigorous interrogation before he was shot and dumped into the sea. The American press picked up the story which only fueled the antiwar sentiment back in the United States. Finally, in September 1969, the secretary of the army announced that all charges would be dropped since the CIA, which likely had some involvement, refused to make its personnel available as witnesses. Even though Larry was not involved in that particular incident, he was adjacent to it as a member of 5th Special Forces Group (Airborne) B-34, and this event served as a glimpse into the craziness of special forces activities.

The 5th Special Forces Group served in Vietnam from 1965–1971 and was one of the smaller military groups in Vietnam. Despite their size, they were *the* most decorated unit and involved in fourteen campaigns. During that time frame, eighteen Medals of Honor were awarded to members of the 5th Special Forces, nine given posthumously. As for 1st Lt. Larry Allen, he received the Vietnam Service Medal, the Vietnam Campaign Medal, and the Bronze Star Medal with palm.

What Larry witnessed and participated in during his twelve months in Vietnam, from October 1968 to October 1969, made it glaringly clear why he never spoke of his time there. Most people today who have never served in the military and, more specifically, never fought in a war have little—if any—comprehension to the horrors of war as witnessed by Larry. It was a long journey for Tidball, one that took him from tipping outhouses in Milo to tipping the scales on the battlefields of Vietnam. In both cases, memories were vivid. One he could laugh out loud about. The other, he refused talk about.

*I am the man who has seen affliction under the rod of his wrath; he
has driven and brought me into darkness without any light; surely
against me he turns his hand again and again the whole day long. He
has made my flesh and my skin waste away; he has broken my bones;
he has besieged and enveloped me with bitterness and tribulation;
he has made me dwell in darkness like the dead of long ago.*
—Lamentations 3:1–6

JAMES R. HELLER, CAPTAIN, 0-3

United States Air Force
January 2, 1969–November 10, 1973

Jim grew up on a farm about three miles east of Milo. He was the third oldest of his seven siblings. To say that he was a tall drink of water would be an understatement. Jim stood six feet and four inches and was one of the tallest kids in high school. I best knew Jim when we both played on the high school basketball team. Jim was a towering senior who dominated the game beneath the basket. I rode the pines in a support role as a lowly freshman. Dick Cory, our high school coach, remembered Jim's performance on the hardwood. "He wasn't a prolific scorer. Larry Niles, the other big man held that title, but Jim's rebounding and defensive skills were the backbone behind the team's success. Most importantly, his leadership and demeanor was a tremendous asset, perhaps the best I've witnessed in over thirty years of coaching." During Jim's senior year, 1964, the team recorded a 15–3 season and eventually lost to our archrival, the Corydon Falcons, in the sectional tournament. It wasn't until 1967 that the Iowa High School Athletic Union divided the high schools into class divisions based on their enrollment. The Southeast Warren Warhawks competed valiantly despite a very low student body that hovered around two hundred students when compared to the big city schools with enrollment in the thousands.

After graduation from high school, in the spring of 1964, Jim went to college at the University of Northern Iowa, located in Cedar Falls. After he received his bachelor's degree, he applied to the University of Iowa's law school, located in Iowa City, and was accepted. Things appeared to be on a fast track for success, until late fall of 1968. It was then Jim received his draft notice from the US Army. It became decision time. It only took a few minutes to weigh the differences between the US Army and the other military options. Jim chose the United States Air Force and made a beeline to the recruiter's office. In the blink of an eye, Jim became a flyboy and headed to Lackland AFB, Texas, where he bypassed basic training requirements and went directly to officer candidate school (OCS). There were many in the military who used the phrase "ninety-day wonder" in reference to those who were allowed to skip basic training and go directly to OCS without the rigors of the traditional basic training indoctrination. Jim was indeed a ninety-day wonder.

Jim earned his "butter bar" commission in March of 1969 at Lackland AFB. I was there exactly one year later from February through April 1970. Perhaps the only experience we shared while in San Antonio was our trip to see the Alamo, a must-see visit for USAF trainees as they squeezed a few moments of free time for a quick history lesson. Just as the Texans shouted, "Remember the Alamo," back in 1836, when Mexican president General Antonio López de Santa Anna reclaimed the Alamo Mission near San Antonio and killed all those who defended it, Jim and I remember the Alamo for a different reason.

Jim's first assignment sent him to flight school at Reese AFB, located in Lubbock, Texas. Yes indeed, Lieutenant Heller would be a flyboy. The USAF had height restrictions for its pilots. Jim measured in at seventy-six inches, just below the maximum height threshold before disqualification for flight status. The USAF flight school consisted of a forty-day ground program followed by twenty-five flight hours as a screening course before the next step of specialized flight training. Jim's first training flight was in a glider and eventually on to a T-41, the military version of a Cessna 172. A memorable event that Jim vividly remembered and chuckled about was his recollection of the school's mandatory parachute jump. "I did two of those," he told me. "Two was plenty for me."

Jim's fight training continued, and he spent time in the cockpit of the T-37 Tweety Bird, a twin engine two-seater (side by side) jet with a speed capability of 425 mph and range of 930 miles. The T-37 became the transition aircraft for pilots in training, progressing from the piston poppers to the jet engine. It was a forgiving aircraft with wide track landing gear, and most pilots were able to solo in the jet after as little as six hours of instructor in-flight training. Because of the high-pitch scream of its twin engine, those who flew it referred to the Tweet as a six-thousand-pound dog whistle. It's relatively low ground clearance made entry into the cockpit as simple as swinging a leg over the lip of the waist-high cockpit.

Nearly six months into flight training, an unforeseen medical issue arose, and Jim required throat surgery. The air force sent him to Valley Forge Army Hospital located in Phoenixville, Pennsylvania. The Valley Forge Army Hospital was the only hospital in the army named for a location rather than a person. The hospital first began serving the military in 1943 and continued through 1974.

Jim was devastated about his need for the surgery and its unfortunate outcome. The USAF's medical eligibility requirements for pilots brought Jim's flying career to a screeching halt. He reflected on his short time at the hospital as he lamented his circumstances. Jim commented, "As I was being wheeled down the corridor of the hospital on a gurney headed to the operating room, I saw a soldier in the hallway. The young man had no legs and no arms. I thought to myself, how shameful of me to be discouraged by the misfortune of throat surgery. I was given a private room during my recovery period. The soldier with no arms or legs was kept in a ward with multiple beds, I couldn't understand the disparity of the treatment he received when compared to what I experienced. It just didn't seem right." That epiphany moment would serve Jim well for years to come when he would later not only serve but also render judgement on others.

Once fully recovered, Jim was reassigned to Benton Air Station, located in Sullivan County, Pennsylvania, about 120 miles northwest of Philadelphia. Sullivan County was the least populated county in all of Pennsylvania. There he was assigned to the 648th Aircraft Control and Warning Systems Squadron (ACWS). Benton Air Station was a very small radar site. Jim was one of only five commissioned officer on the entire base. As a result, he held many responsibilities. His primary duty included the tracking, monitoring, and identification of all aircraft in US airspace and guided interceptor aircraft to vectored locations to confront any enemy aircraft that approached US airspace. Additional duties included officer in charge (OIC) of the motor pool as well as the small base exchange (BX).

Perhaps the worst duty during his entire military career occurred while at Benton Air Station. He became part of the team who notified the next of kin of the death of their family member. Military protocol required that notification be done in person within eight hours of the death of a soldier. The team was comprised of one uniformed officer, a chaplain, one medical representative, and one public affairs officer for high-profile deaths. The duty was horrible as described by Jim who was the notification officer. "It was just a tremendously sobering experience to deliver the tragic news on the doorstep of the family of the deceased soldier." Such a task was a sacred duty of the military and needed the utmost professionalism offered by the military. Notification officers were to be extremely courteous, passionate, and respectful with excellent communications skills at all times when with the deceased soldier's family. Jim fit the requirements perfectly despite his reluctance and disdain for the job.

While stationed at Benton Air Station, Jim was selected to appear in the 1970 edition of the *Outstanding Young Men of America* in recognition of his outstanding ability, accomplishments, and service to his community, country, and profession. That award was based on a new program he implemented that lightened the workload and created a substantial financial savings.

After two years at Benton Air Station, Jim received new orders to McChord AFB, Washington. There he was a member of the 25th Air Division, Air Defense Command (ADC). The unit flew the

THE BOYS OF MILO

F-106 Delta Dart and provided the air defense posture of the north-western section of the United States. Jim was a member of the battle staff command, and in his words, "I did a lot of computer stuff."

While at McChord AFB, Jim enrolled in night classes at the University of Puget Sound and continued to pursue his law degree. Jim discharged with the rank of captain from the USAF in November 1973, but not before setting a record at the Madigan Army Hospital, located at adjoining Fort Lewis. Jim's wife gave birth to twin sons, Brian and Brent, in 1973. Never before had the hospital delivered such huge twins whose delivery weight measured in at eight pounds for one child and eight pounds and two ounces for the other. Jim was a big guy, and he passed his genetics on to his twin sons.

After his honorable discharge, Jim continued his pursuit of his law degree under the GI Bill. In 1975, he earned his jurisprudence degree from the University of Puget Sound and worked in private practice until 1985. It was then that he was elected to the bench as a judge for the Pierce County District Court. Jim served thirty-two years in that capacity before his retirement. Jim currently lives in Gig Harbor, Washington.

HENRY LONG, SPECIALIST FOURTH CLASS, E-4

United States Army
April 24, 1969–April 15, 1971

enry lived in town, about a block south of the grain elevator located on the far east end of Main Street. He and I graduated from high school together. A couple of years later, we encountered each another at the Guy Hornaday Buick dealership in Indianola. He worked as a full-time mechanic, and I was a car jockey that worked part-time while going to college.

The army drafted Henry into service on April 24, 1969. He completed basic training at Fort Polk, Louisiana, then another short stint there for advanced infantry training (AIT). His MOS was 11B20, light weapons infantry.

His first assignment in July 1969, sent him to Aschaffenburg, Germany, as part of the 3rd Infantry Division. Aschaffenburg was a small US Army installation located on the Main River, about thirty kilometers south of Frankfurt. Henry and a buddy from St. Marys, Iowa, Gary Shultz, reported to the orderly room upon arrival.

Upheaval reigned down that day. The company clerk found himself in a jam with his superiors and was on the verge of a court martial. He had issued fraudulent leave requests for the soldiers stationed there. Henry said, "The guy cooked the books and issued phony leave requests in return for a substantial fee from the troops. I don't know how much he made on the scheme, but an E-3 earned about $150 per month, and he was driving a Jaguar."

The company first sergeant asked Henry, "Do you know how to type?"

Not knowing what other options might be available, Henry responded, "Yes, sir, I do." Mable Maulik, the typing teacher from our high school days, would have been proud. Henry and his Iowa buddy, Gary Schultz, became the new staff within the orderly room. They pecked away on their manual typewriters and became astute with the use of and the Venus circular eraser and the messy onion-skinned carbon paper. The clerk typist duty worked well for Henry for the next year.

In July 1970, the easy duty at Aschaffenburg came to a screeching halt. Henry received orders for Vietnam. After a thirty-day leave back in Milo, Henry headed to Vietnam as an infantry soldier. He arrived there in August and reported to the 1st Battalion, 6th Infantry Division, 198th Infantry Brigade.

His assigned platoon, comprised of about twelve men at landing zone (LZ) Dottie, located about fifteen miles from Chu Lai, was out on a mission when Henry arrived. He would wait a few days before he joined them. In the meantime, his first work assignment at base camp in Vietnam became a "crappy" one. He burned human waste. Outdoor latrines used fifty-five gallon barrels to collect the human excrement. Henry's duty entailed the gathering then disposal of the waste. Certainly a *crappy* job to say the least. The disposal method involved fifty-five gallon barrels which were cut in half, then a few gallons diesel fuel poured into the barrels and saturated the feces. A smaller amount of more volatile gasoline was added to the mixture for easy ignition, then set ablaze. Like a witch's brew stirred with a stick, Henry and others on this detail toiled away for as many as four hours to dispose of the waste. Huge plumes of black smoke filled the air, and the aroma of diesel fuel and human excrement would be forever etched in each soldiers mind.

A couple of days later, Henry headed out on his first mission with the platoon. Each mission lasted about two weeks, tromping through the jungle, then back at base camp for two days. The missions were dangerous, and the goals were very straightforward: find and destroy enemy forces in the area of responsibility (TAOR), to include interdiction of enemy forces and supplies.

Operation Nantucket Beach began in May 1970, and ended on March 1, 1971. Henry's platoon, along with others in the 6th Infantry Division, engaged the VC numerous times with heavy firefights during that time frame. Military records obtained from the 6th Infantry's after-action reports confirmed twenty-six engagements during Henry's time at Camp Dottie. In total, the 6th Infantry destroyed 78 bunkers, 1,430 tunnels, and 40 mines and booby traps. US forces killed during Operation Nantucket Beach amounted to 254, a huge number compared to the 6th Infantry Division's strength of about 450 men. A total of 817 US soldiers were wounded in the year-long Operation Nantucket Beach operation. There were 481 confirmed enemy combat deaths and 32 VC captured. Henry was in the midst of it all and defied the odds of death or injury.

Henry left Milo in 1969 as an impressionable young twenty-year-old. He returned as a seasoned combat veteran with unquestionable resolve and courage. He spent nine months in Vietnam, searching the jungles near Chu Lai for the enemy. One of his greatest challenges among the bamboo and banana trees was the constant unrelenting battle with insects. Mosquitoes, chiggers, fleas, biting flies, and ticks overwhelmed those in the field. They carried diseases such as malaria, scrub typhus, Lyme disease, dengue fever, and sandfly fever. In particular, the never-ending buzzing of mosquitoes was the worst. Any veteran who spent time in the jungles of Vietnam will acknowledge the millions upon millions of mosquitoes that served as a pesky opponent. During the Vietnam War, over forty thousand cases of malaria were reported as a result of the Anopheles mosquito bite.

The US Army issued bug spray in the form of the chemical N, N-Diethyl-m-toluamide, or better known as DEET. The two-ounce bottle of bug juice, oftentimes seen in photographs of GIs while in the jungle, were strapped to the side of their helmets. For the most part, soldiers rejected bug juice as ineffective. Post-war surveys revealed that only 11 percent of soldiers used the repellent regularly while 45 percent never used it. Some insisted that the odor emitted when applied gave off a smell strong enough for the enemy to detect when in close proximity. Some referred to it as mosquito food. Soldiers, however, found an ingenious way to use the 25 percent alcohol mixture. They mixed the repellent with peanut butter, then lit the concoction like a Sterno heater to warm rations. Post-war evaluations of the bug juice also revealed that it actually enhanced the absorption into the skin of the Agent Orange defoliant.

Henry was on the tail end of his tour in Vietnam. He had just a week or so before his discharge from the US Army, which would punch his ticket back to Milo. However, the mosquitoes and malaria grabbed ahold of him. Henry self-diagnosed the disease. He had the fever, the sweats, the nausea, the headaches associated with malaria. He scratched at the mosquito bites on his arms to the point they became open wounds. Soldiers in the field affectionately called them "gook sores." He also knew if he reported his illness, he likely would be sent to a field hospital and then on to a medical facility at Da Nang or Cam Ranh Bay for several weeks. He wanted out of Vietnam and was determined not to stay a day longer than necessary.

> *But a certain man drew his bow at random and struck the king of Israel between the scale armor and the breastplate. Therefore he said to the driver of his chariot, "Turn around and carry me out of the battle, for I am wounded."* (**2 Chronicles 18:33**)

Henry left Vietnam and was discharged from the US Army at Fort Lewis, Washington, on April 15, 1971. He caught the first flight out of SEA-TAC airport to Des Moines. The very next day, he checked in at the veterans administration hospital in Des Moines.

Yes, he had malaria. He stayed confined in the hospital for thirty days. The irony of this entire ordeal became the fact that the quinine drug treatment for malaria was *not* available in the USA. On his own accord, Henry wrote to his buddies back in Vietnam and asked them to send the needed drug that was readily available there.

The Chinese documented the disease of malaria as early as 2700 BC based on ancient Chinese records. Treatment for disease with quinine has been used for over four hundred years when discovered by Jesuit missionaries in South America in 1630. It's derived from the bark of the chinchona tree. As legend has it, a Native Indian who suffered from malaria staggered through the jungles of South America. His thirst overcame him, and he drank from a pool of stagnant water. The water was saturated with the bark of the chinchona tree. To his surprise, he recovered. Thus the discovery of a medicine recognized by the World Health Organization as one of the most vital in the world.

Henry was lucky in many ways. He avoided combat injuries and death in the midst of war's madness. He skirted the serious malaria sickness that infects—even today—over two million per year and kills nearly 450,000 from third world countries.

Rarely does he speak of his time in Vietnam, other than acknowledgment that he was there. Tucked away are his combat infantry badge, his Vietnam Campaign Medal, and his Bronze Star. Tucked away are the memories of evil times. Not tucked away, however, is the reverence for those who know Henry and their appreciation of his service to his country during difficult times.

Henry retired as an iron worker and, today, lives in Pleasant Hill, Iowa, with his wife, Wanda.

JOHN ALLEN GALBERT, SPECIALIST FOURTH CLASS, E-4, MEDICALLY RETIRED

United States Army
January 30, 1969–November 9, 1972

John was the youngest son of Frank Galbert Sr. and Adeline Galbert. His family owned and operated a small restaurant (Adeline's Restaurant) located on the south side of Main Street, adjacent to the Milo Locker. The family lived on the second floor above the restaurant. There was no connection between Adeline's Restaurant in Milo and the 1967 Arlo Guthrie song "Alice's Restaurant," but yes, "You could get anything thing you want, at Adeline's Restaurant." It was even located just about half a mile from the railroad tracks where the Chicago, Burlington and Quincy (CBQ) ran daily routes that traversed the track from Chariton through Lacona, then Milo, and ended in Indianola.

As a youngster, I spent many hours with John and his older brother, Frank, along with many other young Milo teenage boys, honing my skills in the back room of the restaurant where we played penny poker and another card game called 2 or 22. With just a few dollar bills and a handful of change, we entertained ourselves endlessly. Our only vice as youngers was gambling. Well, almost the only vice. Occasionally I stole a smoke or two from my mom's pack of Salem cigarettes and brought it with me to the card game.

While in high school, John and I, along with Dan Reeves and Terry Town, hunted together almost every fall and winter weekend. John and Dan dated sisters Carolyn and Pat Veasman from Indianola, whose family owned some prime hunting ground. They later married those girls, their high school sweethearts, if for anything, to lock in hunting rights.

On January 30, 1969, the US Army drafted John into their service at the tender age of twenty. He headed for basic training at Fort Benning, Georgia. Upon completion of boot camp, John went directly to Fort Polk, Louisiana, where he began his advanced infantry training and emerged with a MOS of 11B20, light weapons infantryman.

After a short twenty-one-day visit back home in Iowa, John's next set of orders took him to Vietnam. He arrived there on May 20, 1969, and assigned to Company D, 4th Battalion, 21st Infantry, 11th Brigade, Americal Division, located near Chu Lai. John found himself at Fire Base Debbie, smack-dab in the middle of a war.

As an infantryman, John went on patrol with about twenty to twenty-five troops and offensively sought out enemy forces. He often carried the M60 machine gun, a 23-pound weapon that tasked even the fittest soldier after several hours of trudging through the mud and unbearable heat of the jungles. His fight wasn't solely with the VC but the ever-present swarms of bugs and pesky mosquitoes. John weighed perhaps 150 pounds.

As crazy as the war seemed, even a crazier coincident arose. To John's disbelief, he encountered fellow Milo boy and high school classmate Larry Johnson, assigned to the same company at Fire Base Debbie. They spoke frequently and wondered aloud, "How in the world did we end up here together?" Both became hardened combat veterans as the months progressed. To keep the bizarre perspective of war in check that played heavy on his mind, John often used humor to deflect any chance of fear that would unexpectedly jump up and grab him. As he watched Larry leave one morning on a patrol, John spoke to him in his best Elmer Fudd cartoon voice, "Lawwy, be vewy, vewy quiet, you're not out hunting dem scwewy wascal wabbits."

John completed eleven combat assault mission in the first seven months during his tour of duty in Vietnam. Those missions lasted from seven to ten days each and usually involved multiple engagements with the VC. Many shots were fired, many fellow soldiers wounded or killed in action. John had been lucky. During the Vietnam era, 9,087,000 Americans served in the military (1965–1975). From that number, 2,709,918 served in Vietnam. From that number, over 303,704 received combat injuries, and 58,148 were killed in action. The odds of being a combat casualty and injured were about 10–1. The odds of being killed in action were 185–1 or .5 percent. John's days of playing penny poker as a teenager back in Milo were pretty productive. He often beat the odds and left the table with a pocket full of loose change. The stakes, however, had changed in Vietnam. John was all in with the US Army in Vietnam as a combat infantryman and only hoped he could beat the odds and eventually walk away. He played the cards that were dealt, and he knew there would be no bluffing this time.

January 10, 1970, marked a momentous occasion for those back in the USA. Disney World in Orlando, Florida, opened its doors to the general public for its Preview Center which treated guests with a glimpse of what they could anticipate in the very near future for phase 1 of the $3-million vacation magic kingdom. In a few short months, over eight hundred thousand people toured the facility for a peek of what was to come, even before the gates to Disney World opened. Advance tickets to the amusement park sold for $3.50.

January 10, 1970, also marked a momentous day in the life of John Galbert. Again that day, he and several others went out on his twelfth patrol. On this trip, John carried an M16 rifle. The platoon sergeant asked John to keep an eye on a new troop who just joined the outfit. This would be his first mission. John gave him the short skinny of what to watch out for before they headed out. He was a black dude and seemed to have some degree of situational awareness. Blacks comprised 11.6 percent of combat soldiers in Vietnam. To John, skin color had no bearing on the task at hand. Whether the newbie could be relied upon and able to carry his own weight became the question. The newbie took up position number 2 behind the point man. John fell in right behind him in the third positon as they headed out on patrol. They cautiously made their way down a trail and scanned the jungle for any signs of Charlie. They creeped along for about twenty to thirty minutes when instantly, *kaboom*! The newbie stepped on a trip wire and an antipersonnel booby trap exploded. The shrapnel hit the black soldier in the back and knocked him down. John took the impact head-on. It threw him backward to the ground, stunned and dazed. He got up and ran back down the trail before he succumbed to his injuries and fell to the ground again. John took a direct hit with multiple wounds to his head, chest, and abdomen. He yelled for help, but no words came forth. The gaping chest wound let his air escape through his chest. John immediately stuck his finger into the hole in his chest and tried again to inhale. It worked that time, and he again yelled for help. "I'm hit, I'm hit," he shouted. Both John and the newbie were taken by a medi-vac helicopter to a rear field medical facility. After stabilized, they immediately flew him offshore to the USS *Repose*, a medical ship with more advanced facilities than the field medical tent. The medical staff aboard the USS *Repose* performed two life-saving operations on John. The shrapnel took John's right eye, penetrated his lung, and punctured his stomach. John eventually lost his right eye.

After two days in recovery aboard the USS *Repose*, the military again flew John via medical transport to Japan. He remained in Japan at a US military hospital for two months. When recovered well enough for a more lengthy trip back to the United States, the army sent him to another medical facility, Irwin Army Hospital, located at Fort Riley, Kansas. There he had three more surgeries. His stay there lasted a full year as he recuperated and performed rehabilitation from his wounds.

To his surprise, friend, fellow classmate, and company comrade, Larry Johnson of Milo visited John at Fort Riley. Larry too had been hit with shrapnel from a booby trap but only received superficial wounds. Not severe enough to earn a ticket home from the war but enough, however, to earn him a Purple Heart. Larry's older brother, Gary, had been killed in a car accident back in Iowa. Larry returned to Milo on a thirty-day bereavement leave from the army and attended the funeral. He had just a few short months before his tour of duty in Vietnam ended, so rather than redeploy him back into the war, the army sent him to Fort Riley to train troops with his firsthand knowledge of combat operations for soldiers bound for the jungles of Vietnam. It was a good reunion.

In late October 1970, once again, the US Army transported John to Fitzsimmons Army Medical Center located in Aurora, Colorado, for further evaluation. John remained there a mere two weeks. Because of the extent of his wounds, he would not see further active duty, and the army deemed that no further medical procedures would improve his condition. He received a 100 percent medical retirement from the US Army on November 9, 1972. Today John still carries in his chest shrapnel from that eventful day of January 10, 1970.

John served one year, ten months, and fourteen days on active duty with the US Army. Seven months and one day were in Vietnam. John earned the Purple Heart, the Vietnam Campaign Medal with devices, the Vietnam Service Medal with devices, and the Combat Infantry Badge.

John's story does not end there, however. In 2007, he received a phone call from a young man from California seeking his Boy Scout Eagle Badge. John himself was once a scout with Milo Boy Scout Troop 136. The scout's father also served in Vietnam and returned to the country long after he served to put to rest all the emotions he carried as a result of being there during the war. In his journey through Vietnam, he came upon an old man selling dog tags of US soldiers. The old man had a whole fistful of American dog tags. The veteran bought every single one of them and brought them back to the USA. As his son grew and progressed through the ranks of scouting, he needed a special project to earn the rank of Eagle Scout. Without so much of a second thought, the father handed his son the dog tags he brought home. "Find these men and return their dog tags to them," he told his son. The young teenager somehow tracked down John, who lived in Georgia, and returned to him the very dog tag that had been blown away from his neck and chest when he was hit with the explosion from the antipersonnel mine thirty-seven years earlier. John was speechless and grateful. The dog tag, along with John's military awards, were placed in a display case which is now in the safekeeping of his adult son, John Junior. The journey for John came full circle.

John died on February 24, 2019, a short time after he underwent heart surgery.

dented dog tag of John Galbert blown from around his neck, returned by Boy Scout

He heals the brokenhearted and binds up their wounds.
—Psalm 147: 3

THE GARDEN STATE

I n April 1970, on my ten-day leave between basic training and my first duty assignment, my wife, Judi, and I packed our car to the gills with what little belongings we owned. Judi and I left Iowa, headed for New Jersey. A weird memory burned into my brain on that trip was the ironing board that had been given to us a short nine months earlier as a wedding gift. It stretched between the bucket seats on my 1968 Opal Kadet and reached far into the back seat. A soldier needed a freshly starched and ironed uniform. I suppose that stupid ironing board represented some kind of confidence builder that things would be just fine.

This trip just wasn't a deployment to a new part of the country that neither of us ever before witnessed. We viewed it as a long-overdue honeymoon and soaked every minute of the wonderment as we cruised down the toll roads headed to New Jersey, the Garden State.

Within two days of our arrival at McGuire AFB, we procured off-base housing in an old rundown three-story rental property located on Garden Street, in Mt. Holly, New Jersey. What a deal for us! It was cheap, it was fully furnished, it was close to the base, but it was a dump. We did receive $110 per month in housing allowance from the military, and that all but covered the monthly rent. I distinctly remembered my military take-home pay amounted to $60 every two weeks. That was less than I made pumping gas back in Iowa during my college days. I thought, *What in God's name have we gotten ourselves into?*

AIRMAN WILLIAMS REPORTING FOR DUTY, SIR!

A t last, the day arrived. My first duty day at the fire station became unforgettable. Believe it or not, I liked it. No, I loved it. I was as green as they came, regarding the knowledge required for firefighters, but I eagerly accepted any and all guidance. Technical Sergeant Roger Miller became my training supervisor. Our paths crossed again nearly thirty years later at the National Fire Chief's conference in Dallas, Texas. After his retirement from the USAF, he accepted a Department of Defense (DOD) position as the fire chief at Quantico Marine Base, Virginia. I had climbed the ladder in the civilian sector as well and served as the assistant fire chief at the Des Moines International Airport under the guidance of the Iowa Air National Guard. Small world, I thought. To my surprise, he remembered me when we met by chance at the chief's conference.

There were about eight of us newbies who arrived DDA at McGuire. We hit the books hard and soaked in as much knowledge as possible in the classroom setting at the fire station. Back then, no professional certifications existed as they now do. The firefighter 1, firefighter 2, airport firefighter as well as many other higher educational certifications simply did not exist. My air force specialty code (AFSC) was a 571X0, better known as a fire protection specialist.

We spent the afternoons on the floor working with other troops and a contingent of civilian firefighters employed at McGuire. Vehicle familiarization, equipment checks, radio procedures, driving classes, hose lays, communications procedures, airfield familiarization, aircraft identification, and physical fitness training dominated the remainder of the day. Quite frankly, much of the practical knowledge received during that initial training came from the civilian firefighters who mentored us green-horned troops like young pups that needed some serious potty training.

My gratitude went out to those individuals, some now gone. Mr. Ed Sary, Mr. Frank Kranz, Mr. Archie Taylor, Mr. Kenny Fort, Mr. Joe Tomasella, Mr. Ben Flannigan, Mr. Olie Johnson, Mr. Frank Burk, Mr. George Rogers, Mr. Dickie Emmons, Mr. George Kirk, and the list could continue on. I learned so much from them, not just about firefighting but about life in general and becoming a good man.

I reached the point in my early career when I thought maybe, just maybe, I might know a thing or two. I had perhaps six months on the job under my belt. I received my second set of stripes and moved up in rank from airman to airman first class. Knowledge and rank can be a dangerous thing for some, and I was no exception. A little bit of knowledge can be even more dangerous, and the power of authority through rank became a volatile mix for others. That became a tremendous lesson for me thirty years later in my professional firefighting career. I previously worked for a whole bunch of knuckleheads, rumdums, and boozers in my younger days who perfectly defined the Peter Principle that constantly put people one rung higher up than their competency level warranted. They thought they walked on water, and everyone should bow in their presence in awe of their status. Someone once asked me years later what I thought to be the single most significant factor to become a solid leader in the fire service. My answer led me to the words spoken by Jesus in Mark 10:45, *"I did not come to be served, but to serve, and give my life for many."*

A buddy of mine from basic training, Gary Pickel, showed up one day at the fire station. Of course, I gave him the very important person (VIP) tour of the fire station and attempted to display my depth of knowledge. I guess he swallowed all my malarkey as he just kept shaking his head and saying, "Neat stuff." He just received his first PCS assignment to McGuire from his advance technical school.

We were good amigos during basic training and solidified our friendship at McGuire. Gary, or "Dill Pickle," as everyone called him, worked with radio and telephones and eventually retired from the USAF on the presidential communications staff in Washington DC. I certainly never received or was never offered a VIP tour from Pickle for his duty section. "Top secret," he always told me.

I told him, baloney, he didn't do a thing except answer the stinking telephone. Gary was from nearby, Reading, Pennsylvania. Within a short year at McGuire, he married his hometown sweetheart, Janice. I was honored to be a groomsman in their wedding. We are still in touch with each other through the magic of Facebook.

THE GRIM REAPER
PAYS A CALL

Who said death is dead? He's fully alive, traveling around the world, throwing shadows, and soaking in the sun. Visiting the young and old; placing bets and dicing regrets, for the worse or a better off place. When the Grim Reaper comes to call, words fail, they're just too small.

Mid-September came upon McGuire AFB in 1970. Things moved quickly for Judi and I. Technical Sergeant (TSgt) Ron Risk, one of the senior firefighters at the station, hooked me up with a job on my days off from the fire station where I worked at the Airman's Club. The extra money earned matched my military wage. I told him I had never worked in a restaurant or bar before. His words were, "Don't worry, Willie, it's a piece of cake."

I immediately thought of my buddy Ed back in Iowa, lugging sides of beef, driving around in his Corvette, making three dollars per hour and sitting on draft selection number 363. In the back of my mind, I heard him whisper, "Hey, Willie, how you doing?"

"So just what will I be doing at the Airman's Club?" I asked TSgt Risk.

"We need a dishwasher. That's it, just a dishwasher. Can you handle that?"

My slow response was a long drawn out, "I guess so. How much does it pay?"

In the long run, that opportunity worked out well. With good connections through the Airman's Club, I parlayed a strong work ethic scrubbing dishes, then put a bug in the ear of the manager of the Non-Commissioned Officer's (NCO) Club. They needed a hostess to seat dinner guests in the late afternoon till closing. Judi needed a job, we needed the money, and luck was with us. She became a hostess, I became a dishwasher. We were loaded with money, or so we thought. I took a moment to do a quick calculation of my military pay. My monthly base pay was $138 as an airman first class. I worked fifty-six hours each week at the fire department. That math revealed a whopping $.62 per hour in wages. Of course I got $110 per month in housing allowance. Certainly the dishwasher's job made a big difference in our income. I was paid $1.65 per hour. We made do and survived.

One early afternoon, my buddy Pickle arrived at the club with some coworkers from his telephone-answering service. I had just bussed some tables and made room for more customers. My white kitchen apron was messy with spaghetti sauce spattered all up the front. I had a damp rag in my right hand I used to wipe clean the tabletops and a rubber tray full of dirty dishes in my left hand, balanced on my hip. I tried to avoid him, but he came right up to me and introduced his telephone friends to me. "Hey, guys, this is my good friend Willie from Iowa, we went to basic training together."

He peered down at my apron and then said, "You look good, Mike, you look real good." My face turned as red as the spaghetti sauce. Again humiliated by a friend. This time, I wasn't hugging a gas pump, I was the lowly kitchen help from the back room. I bit my lip to control my frustration with the situation.

> *It shall not be so among you. But whoever would be great among you must be your servant, and whoever would be first among you must be your slave.* (**Matthew 20:26–27**)

I called the Dill Pickle later that week and asked if he and his wife, Janice, would like to go out for a pizza and a few beers that Saturday evening, hoping to regain his confidence in me as a stand-up guy who didn't take offense with his rude comments earlier. He responded, "No, we can't go, I'm broke till payday." With that, I smirked. Spaghetti sauce splattered on one's self isn't such a bad thing after all. Enough said on that subject.

We lived in Mt. Holly, about ten miles west of the base. To stay abreast of events back home, I subscribed to the local county newspaper from Indianola, the *Record Herald and Tribune*, just to keep tabs on events back in Iowa. Judi and I didn't have a phone in our apartment, so the only correspondence available came though letters or a short walk to the phone booth on the corner near our apartment. The *Record Herald and Tribune* was a small-town newspaper that inherently plugged its pages with advertisement from local merchants, area high school sports scores, as well as Simpson College sporting events. Other than that, no meaty stories surfaced. I often joked about the articles written on the front page that depicted crazy ridiculous stories. One particular story went into detail how lightning struck a small maple tree in town, and over one hundred sparrows were found dead on the ground. That wasn't exactly the stuff that garnered a Pulitzer Prize for news reports. However, it kept us in touch with things back home to some degree.

We both arrived home after our stint working at the NCO and Airman's Club. It was late, after 10:00 p.m. I checked our mailbox as I entered the entryway to our apartment. "Oh, look, the newspaper arrived today," I said in jest. Eager to see what non-news made the front page, I immediately began to read. Within thirty seconds of reading the newspaper, my hands began to shake. "Judi, Judi, oh my god. Art Wright is dead!" Yes, the *Record Herald and Tribune* brought us tragic news that day.

We last saw Art in February of 1970, at the Pizza Hut. That was just seven months ago. I continued to read. There wasn't a whole lot of information to obtain a true grasp of what happened to Art, other than the fact that he had been killed in Vietnam.

The next morning, when I arrived for work at the fire station, I rushed into the chief's office and used the Automatic Voice Network (AUTOVON) phone system, common in the military, and made a free phone call back to Iowa. The call confirmed what we already knew. Art died on September 5, 1970, as a result of enemy action; he had stepped on a land mine. Art was just twenty-one years old. His wife, Carol, was eight months pregnant with their first child due at any time. Military records revealed that Art was assigned to A Company, 4th Battalion, 503rd Infantry, 173rd Airborne Brigade. He died as the result of an explosive device, in the Binh Dinh Province of South Vietnam, most likely the same type of booby trap that nearly killed Mike Crabb three years earlier. We were sick to our stomachs. Such a terrible, terrible tragedy.

The war in Vietnam came front and center each night on the evening news. America viewed it, up close and personal, with all the cruelty and gore choreographed to entertain or scare the bejesus out of worried parents, sisters, wives, brothers, and children. The intent of the reporting by those from the major networks, CBS, NBC, and ABC, and the intense presentation of the war on live battlefields of Vietnam, by the likes of Chet Huntley and David Brinkley, along with Eric Sevareid, undoubtedly changed the perspective of war through the eyes of television.

One of the best recognized statement from the news media came from the "most trusted man in America," Walter Cronkite. In a CBS special broadcast a few years earlier, February 27, 1968, Cronkite concluded, "To say that we are closer to victory today is to believe, in the face of the evidence, the optimists who have been wrong in the past, to say that we are mired in a bloody stalemate seems the only realistic, yet unsatisfactory conclusion."

We stopped watching the evening news segments on our four-teen-inch black-and-white Emerson television. It made us cringe. We mourned the loss of our high school classmate and friend Art Wright. We prayed for his family. Then the realization, as put forth by a mid-sixteenth-century statesman, John Bradford, "There but by the grace of God, go I."

RUDY WADLE, SPECIALIST FOURTH CLASS, E-4

United States Army
November 28, 1967–November 27, 1969

Rudy lived in the country a few miles east of Milo, just beyond where Highway G-58 pavement ended. Six months after graduating from high school, Rudy received his draft notice in the mail. Certainly not much time to enjoy the pleasures of his youth. Rudy reported to basic training at Fort Bliss, Texas, on November 28, 1967, for eight weeks of intense training. He was just eighteen years old. Upon completion of basic training, the US Army sent him to Fort Huachuca, Arizona, for advanced training as a truck driver as well as an infantryman.

April 2, 1968, marked Rudy's arrival at Lai Khe, Vietnam. Lai Khe was located on Highway 13, northwest of Saigon. It was a garrison town for the South Vietnamese Army and coinhabited by the US Army's 1st Infantry Division, and a busy hub of activity and the home base of the US Army's 227th Assault Helicopter Battalion (AHB). Rudy commented that Lai Khe received harassment mortar and rocket fire every single day he was there. He later found out that the NVA used the Lai Khe base as a target for training its artillery crews.

It was there on the "Thunder Road," Highway 13, where Rudy drove about every imaginable military vehicle, ranging from jeeps, to deuce and a half trucks, to tankers, and even a bulldozer. He transported troops, hauled ammunition and explosives, fuel, water, post exchange (PX) items, and his favorite cargo—beer. There were no city or county police officers monitoring Highway 13, looking for speeders and possible drunk drivers. Rudy knew that, so he made certain when his favorite cargo was his shipment, he never went thirsty on the trip. Thunder Road was a two-hundred-mile stretch of road that ran north from Saigon to Quan Loi. Thunder Road got its name from the radio call sign of the unit located in Quan Loi, which was Thunder, thus the road trip garnered the nickname Thunder Road. As Rudy stated, "I was just a peon and was given about every job imaginable." The truth is, he did a heck of a lot more than herd trucks up and down the graveled Highway 13.

On one particular road trip, Rudy received orders for an emergency shipment of ammunition destined for a camp nearly a three-hour drive north. They needed the ammo, and they needed it now. There was no helicopter available to airlift the amount of ammo requested. Time was of the essence. Rudy jumped into his truck, put it in gear, and double-clutched his way several miles down the road when he was forced to stop by some military police (MPs) who had used two jeeps to block the road.

"Get out of the way, you guys, I'm in a hurry." Rudy barked at them.

"Ah, whatta you got in the back," one of them asked. Rudy figured out real quick what was up. They were wanting to intercept what they thought was a PX delivery with maybe some nice goodies aboard, and hopefully some beer.

Rudy shouted again, "I'm in a real hurry, guys, get out of my way." Both of the MPs walked to the rear of Rudy's truck for an inspection. Rudy put his truck in low gear and pulled forward, pushing both jeeps into the ditch. He was bound and determined to get the ammo to the guys in the field, just as ordered. He looked in his rearview mirror as he pulled away and saw the two MPs standing in disbelief. That particular moment was perhaps a precursor for a future 1979 television series, *The Dukes of Hazzard*, as Bo and Luke Duke again foiled the plans of Boss Hog. No, Rudy wasn't running moonshine, not that time anyway. He was bringing one the most important items to the battlefield—ammunition.

Most of his convoys were comprised of three to four vehicles that made mad dashes up and down Thunder Road, usually lasting two to three hours. On just about every road trip, his convoy received sniper fire and periodic mortar fire from the NVA hoping to get in a lucky shot. On one memorable trip, two mortar shells exploded behind his truck and directly in front of the vehicle following him as he floorboarded his deuce and a half down the rough and bumpy gravel road. Rudy got on the radio and shouted in the hand mic, "You better speed up. They are zooming in on you!"

To which the driver of the other truck responded, "It's you they are aiming for, not me. They're lousy shots." Both drivers pressed on with their cargo, giving only an instant thought to the true danger that surrounded them.

Once at his destination, Rudy offloaded the cargo to resupply US camps located up and down the highway between Saigon and Quan Loi. At that point, Rudy boarded a helicopter and accompanied the supplies that were parceled out, and then airlifted to fire bases in the jungle where ground troops eagerly awaited his arrival. Once in the field, Rudy provided fire cover and usually stayed at the firebase for several days before making a return trip to Lai Khe, then would repeat the cycle again. "I spent a whole lot more time in the air delivering supplies than I did driving them down the road," Rudy said. "And the ride was much smoother."

Rudy wasn't one to miss the opportunity for a good time. It was the Fourth of July 1969. Not much to celebrate in Lai Khe other than the fact he wasn't on Thunder Road as a moving target or flying supplies to remote firebases. He recalled the July 4 celebrations held back in Milo. It was a big deal for the town. A huge parade stretched down Main Street and through town led by the Milo American Legion Post 263, followed by Milo's fire trucks with siren screeching, antique cars and old tractors, horseback riders, and various community groups like Boy Scout Troop 136 and the high school marching band. Kids games in the city park, pony rides, Little League ball games, water fights by fire departments from neighboring communities, bingo games, a dunk tank, foot races, and even some boxing matches were the events of the day. Homemade pies from the community churches along with hamburgers on the grill were sold at the concession stand in the city park. In the backyards of homes throughout the town were ice chests filled with watermelon and cold beer where friends and neighbors freely shared whatever their guests might enjoy most.

That evening, at ten o'clock, thousands of people gathered near the Milo baseball field at the school to watch the fireworks. It was a tradition, not just for Milo residents but everyone throughout the entire county. Grandparents took their grandkids to watch, teenagers walked with their girlfriend or boyfriend hand in hand and made goo-goo eyes at one another as they strolled the few blocks from the park to the ball field. Young parents brought their toddlers and helped them light sparklers and enjoy the excitement. Such activities helped everyone understand just why we celebrate the Fourth of July in America. It was good times for all.

With the thoughts of the July 4 celebration back in Milo running through Rudy's mind, it was just too much to discard. "We need to shoot off some fireworks," he told some of his GI buddies. As if an order had been given by a ranking officer, several soldiers grabbed their M16 and began popping off magazine after magazine, shooting into the air. The star-shaped flash of light from the muzzle of their carbines, coupled with the loud pops of the expended cartridges, actually seemed like a mini version of the Milo fireworks display.

After just a few minutes of celebration, everyone suddenly stopped. No further away than one hundred yards, the recognizable sound of multiple AK-47 Kalashnikov rifles answered back. As if a dozen woodpeckers were hammering away on an old hollow cottonwood tree back in Iowa, the *ratta tap, tap, ratta tap, tap* continued. "My god, they're shooting back at us," someone shouted.

Rudy piped in, "They're not celebrating the Fourth of July, that is for sure." That armed response confirmed what everyone already assumed. The village of Lai Khe had its share of NVA sympathizers, and they were mixed among the villagers, just a stone's throw away.

The ranking sergeant chimed in, "Let's call that good enough, boys. We might need our ammo later on."

Rudy's closest call to death while in Vietnam came not as a result of enemy action but instead from a near accidental poisoning. Of the 58,200 deaths of American soldiers in Vietnam, 9,107 were accidental and another 938 were due to illness. Rudy's encounter with a bad decision might have placed him in one of those groups.

He and several GI buddies were drinking beer one day and feeling pretty good. At some point, early in the evening, their entire supply of alcohol had been consumed. Still thinking they needed a buzz, they decided to go on a search-and-destroy mission in the village of Lai Khe. Actually it was just a plain and simple beer run. They searched for anything with alcohol that they could drink that would keep the party going. Rudy, along with several other soldiers, went armed from hooch to hooch in the village, rousting out the local Vietnamese families from their homes and scouring for alcohol to satisfy their thirst. Already three sheets to the wind, Rudy saw a wine bottle on the shelf and grabbed it. The frail wrinkled old man of the Vietnamese family shouted out, "Number 10, number 10."

Rudy pulled off the cork and took a swig and then swallowed a mouthful of something from the wine bottle. "What the heck is this?" he demanded.

He handed the bottle to one of the other GIs for further examination. One whiff was all it took to figure out the contents. Rudy swallowed kerosene! Within seconds, his throat began to burn, and he became lightheaded. Already pretty intoxicated, the introduction of kerosene into his system became an even greater toxic mixture. He began to wobble, then fainted and fell to the ground. His soldier buddies carried an unconscious Rudy back to the base. They didn't bother to take him to the medical tent but instead lifted him over the perimeter fence and dropped him in the grass to sleep it off. Little did anyone realize the seriousness of the situation. As little as twelve ounces of consumed fuel can be fatal to an adult. Consumption of a petroleum product like kerosene can cause blindness and long-term respiratory damage.

The next morning came, and Rudy awoke, lying just inside the perimeter fence where he had been tossed the night before. He felt as though he had been run over by a truck. He had puked on himself during the night and was very weak. His guts hurt, and his head throbbed with the worst headache ever. Thank the Lord, however, he was alive. To say he had dodged a bullet that night might have been an understatement. War is hell, but so is stupidity. Oftentimes the two walk hand in hand, unaware of the dangers that lurk.

*O simple ones, learn prudence, O fools learn sense. (**Proverbs 8:5**)*

During the monsoon season, the road trips up and down Highway 13 challenged every type of vehicle and even the best of drivers to reach their destination. It was plain and simple, the roads were a lousy muddy mess. Floodwaters ran knee-deep to waist-deep over the roadway in some places. For a young kid like Rudy, who liked to go four-wheeling in the mud, this job was the cat's meow. Except for the fact that some gook likely would be shooting at you and ruin your day.

The year 1968 marked the bloodiest year of the Vietnam War. Estimates from the US Military Assistance Command revealed 181,150 North Vietnamese were killed while US forces lost 14,584 soldiers, a 57 percent increase from 1967. Those huge numbers were attributed to the Tet Offensive launched by the Vietcong in January 1968, and the US response to those attacks. The year 1968 saw US troops in Vietnam jump to record high of 536,100.

Rudy and many other boys of Milo were a part of those statistics and were center court for much of the action. That year marked the beginning of the end for any hope of a victory for the US. Peace protests and antiwar movements became commonplace back in the States. On March 31, 1968, President Lyndon Johnson announced, "I will not seek, nor will I accept the nomination for another term as your President."

In late September 1969, Rudy's tour of duty in Vietnam ended. His next set of orders sent him to Fort Belvoir, Virginia, where in his words, "I goofed off for eight weeks before finally being discharged from the Army on November 27, 1969.

Rudy witnessed more than his fair share of death and destruction that reigned down in Vietnam during his tour of duty. It became impossible to avoid it. He brought home memories, some good and some bad, but he also brought home a treasure trove of artifacts as a reminder that yes, he served and served honorably. I was humbled to see his collection of photographs, pay stubs, Vietnamese currency, maps, and a painted image of himself on a circular velvet cloth that he sent home to his parents. What caught my attention, however, was a war souvenir taken from the body of a dead North Vietnamese soldier. It was a simple homemade spoon, held by a string around

the neck of the soldier. It had been carefully shaped, hammered and fabricated from a flat piece of aluminum, most likely from the skin of a US aircraft, with the initials of its owner scratched along the handle. One would not think such an item would be a reminder of war or death but instead a reminder of life.

Many, many years after the war, the metaphor of Rudy's souvenir spoon came boldly forth. Rudy opened a successful restaurant in the nearby town of Lacona called Rudy's Rendezvous. There he served up delicious meals and poured his exuberant personality into the community. One could easily say Rudy's spoon fed those from miles around back to life, not to dwell on the evils he endured but to trumpet the goodness of all men. Job well done, Private Wadle.

And I commend joy, for man has nothing better under the sun but to eat and drink and be joyful, for this will go with him in his toil through the days of his life that God has given him under the sun.
—Ecclesiastes 8:15

JOHN F. SARGENT, SPECIALIST FOURTH CLASS, E-4

United States Army
November 28, 1967–November 18, 1969

John was the third oldest of seven children, six boys and one girl, who lived about five miles south of Milo in a small yellow house on the gravel road near the Rosemount church turnoff. Of his five brothers, John was the only one who served in the military. John and I were classmates in school and graduated together in the spring of 1967. He was a soft-spoken fella that interacted well with everyone and never on the wrong end of any typical teenage pranks or shenanigans. John was a member of the high school track team in 1967 which broke five previous school records on various events.

Just six months out of high school, John received his draft notice and joined the US Army on November 28, 1967. That same exact day marked the enlistment of Rudy Wadle, another classmate of John and I. Both John and Rudy reported to basic training at Fort Bliss, Texas, and endured the rigors of boot camp together.

John completed his initial basic training and headed home for a short visit during Christmas and the New Year holiday. Rudy headed elsewhere. After a brief stop in Milo for John, his next journey for Uncle Sam sent him to Fort Knox, Kentucky, for advanced training with an MOS of 11E20, an armored tank crewman. That eight-week course proved an eye-opener for John as to the magnitude and military might brought forth by armored tanks and the dangers associated with those who operated the iron behemoths. During a training session at the range, twelve tanks lined up and fired upon old cars from a distance. The tank adjacent to John's had a misfired round. Protocol required that the chamber not be opened immediately upon a misfire. The trainee did not follow protocol. The chamber was opened and an explosion occurred that killed one crew member and seriously injured the other three. Training for the remainder of the day was canceled. The very next morning, however, as John related his story, "we were back at the range firing more rounds but adhered very emphatically to protocol." Military records revealed that between 1967 and 1969, sixteen such misfired tank artillery rounds occurred and caused death or injury to tank crewmen.

On April 4, 1968, Martin Luther King was assassinated at the Lorraine Motel in Memphis, Tennessee. Things at Fort Knox took a dramatic turn for John while stationed there. Tank training stopped. Fort Knox was located a short 39 miles south of Louisville. He and 150 other soldiers from Fort Knox were sent to Louisville, Kentucky, home of the Kentucky Derby as well as boxing champion Muhammad Ali, along with another 250 from other military installations to patrol and curb any civil unrest within the city limits. The relative small contingent of police in Louisville were woefully unprepared for such violent disturbances. As stated by John, "A total of 400 of us soldiers were issued M-16 rifles and several rounds of rubber bullets and positioned throughout the city. Groups of us rotated throughout the day and night. We stayed in tents erected on a local high school football field. It was an uncertain time and not sure what would be in store for those of us deployed there." Riots, looting, overturned cars, and fires were set by the mobs. Military patrols continued until June 4. Two teenagers were killed by police with 472 arrests made before things became somewhat normal.

After his short eight-week stint at Fort Knox, John received new orders to Fort Richardson, Alaska, located five miles north of Anchorage. Alaska, by military definition, is considered outside the continental United States (OCONUS) and thus, John's military records reflects overseas duty for the one year, six months, and twenty-five days assigned there with Troop F, 10th Calvary, 172nd Infantry Brigade.

John distinctly remembered a miserable bivouac at Fort Richardson that placed him and others into the harsh elements of Alaska. For three weeks his group camped in tents when outdoor temperatures plummeted to minus eighty degrees. He went on to say, "We had to leave our tanks running nonstop twenty-four hours a day or the fuel would jell." John continued about the cold, cold weather, "There was a rope stretched between our tent and the chow tent. We grabbed that rope to guide us through the snow, high winds, darkness, and cold temperatures so we would not become disoriented and later found dead, frozen in the tundra." He recalled one particular incident where he made the frigid, icy trek for a breakfast of biscuits and gravy. He opted to carry his food back to his own tent where it seemed somewhat warmer than the chow tent. By the time he returned, following the rope line, his food tray was frozen solid. He placed the grub atop the small, portable Yukon heater in his tent to warm his food. That, in a nutshell, was the epitome of a rough bivouac, colder than a Minnesota's well diggers gizzard.

When at Fort Richardson, in late 1968, John's entire unit received orders to Vietnam. It would offer a stark change in climate for him. However, just one week before the unit's scheduled departure, the Army rescinded the orders and changed the destination to Korea. Then before John could pack his duffel bag, the orders to Korea were canceled. That suited him just fine.

John wasn't much of a party animal. When others in his unit had some free time, they made a beeline to several off-base destinations that offered booze, women, and loud music. John refused to go along with the crowd and often stayed on base. He told me he sent out over eighty Christmas cards one particular year to people he knew back in Milo. That became his source of dealing with the faraway places and loneliness in such a remote location. He reflected on the good memories of growing up in Milo. He missed the Fourth of July celebrations in the city park. He missed the Santa Clause visits to main street when the white-bearded man in the red suit handed bags of candy to the kids who crowded around not a sleigh, but the city fire truck. He missed the quaint eatery, The Farmerette Café, where he drank coffee and socialized with friends as well as Joe and Virginia Biddle who owned and operated the establishment. Memories such as those don't fade over time but become even more vivid with each passing year. The Farmerette Café, once a mainstay of the Milo community, no longer exists. Joe and Virginia, close friends of John, are also gone. Gone, too, are the nickel scoops of ice cream, penny candy, and the peppermint-flavored candy cigarettes.

John honorably discharged from the Army at Fort Lewis, Washington, on November 18, 1969, after serving one year, eleven months, and twenty-one days. John retired after thirty-nine years as a contract mail carrier for the United States Postal Service and currently lives in Ankeny, Iowa.

LESLIE TOWN, SPECIALIST FIFTH CLASS, E-5

United States Army
September 25, 1968–January 11, 1972
Air National Guard, Master Sergeant, E-7, Retired
August 10, 1986–December 10, 2004

L es lived in town, no pun intended, about one block south of Main Street. His grandfather O'Fair Town and later, his father, by the same name, Fair Town, operated the only barbershop in Milo for years and years. And so it went, he always had a nice clean haircut. The long-hair hippy look that became prevalent in the 1960s evaded Les. He didn't play any school sports, but I remember that he played the trumpet in the school band and, along with me, sang in the high school chorus. I knew on my best day, I couldn't carry a note, not even in a paper bag, and only participated in chorus because my girlfriend was a good singer and a good-looker. It served as another opportunity to make goo-goo eyes at my future wife, Judi Bishop. Les and I never spoke to each other about our musical talents, but I think he would agree. He too carried a paper bag.

Les graduated from high school in May 1967, and slightly more than a year later was drafted into the US Army on September 28, 1968. That same day, the Beatles song "Hey Jude" hit the Billboard's spot as the number 1 song in America and held it for nine weeks. As Les left the easygoing lifestyle in Milo and headed off to basic training at Fort Polk, Louisiana, he only wished he "could *take a sad song and make it better.*"

Upon completion of basic training and AIT (advanced infantry training), Les acquired the MOS of 11B10, light weapons infantryman. The writing was already on the wall, and Les knew it. His first set of orders sent him to Southeast Asia. On March 3, 1969, he arrived at Dĩ An, Vietnam, located about twenty miles north of Saigon, and assigned to the 1st Infantry Division, Company A, 1st Battalion.

As an infantry soldier in Vietnam, Les found himself out in the jungle, where he hunkered down at various LPs (listening posts) with his platoon. As odd as it seemed, orders were not to engage the enemy unless first fired upon. Many tense days were spent in the sweltering heat and insect-infested plush greenery of South Vietnam. Firefights ensued with VC forces despite efforts to remain hidden in the undergrowth. Les soon realized what a miserable situation surrounded him. After several days in the field on LPs, his team returned to nearby firebases, only to trek out again after a day or two of rest. Two locations etched into his memory were Firebase Red and Firebase Fort Apache. The refuge of the firebases offered minimal security for Les.

He recalled sleeping in a bunker located beneath the barrel of a 105 howitzer. It offered little as a sanctuary from battle and even less as a place of quiet rest. All night long, the artillery shells fired off just a few yards above Les's bunker. The decibel range for the 105s measure 190. The generally accepted standard range for noise exposure during an eight-hour period was 85 decibels. Les seemed grateful that, at the moment anyway, he personally was not under fire. However, without any type of hearing protection, his eardrums were continuously exposed to double the acceptable norm. If you spoke to Les today, and his first response is, "Huh? What did you say?" You'd understand why. During the short moments of sleep, rats awakened him as they crawled across his chest. Les commented, "Oh, I wasn't afraid of them, they just startled me, and I'd brush them off and tried to get some much needed shut-eye."

From Dĩ An, helicopters ferried Les on more than twenty-five assault missions in just three short months. Each mission proved to be akin to a game of Russian roulette. One never knew when a chambered round had their name on it. It was a game he wasn't anxious to play. He pondered a plan to get away from the daily madness of an infantry soldier and made a decision in June 1969, just ninety days after his arrival in Vietnam.

Les extended his enlistment in the US Army to three years in exchange for reassignment to a different MOS. Luckily for Les, he left the battlefield and became a truck driver. Les shuttled thousands of tons of cargo that included ammunition, fuel, and food rations along Highway 1 in support of US forces in need, often times in long convoys with other supply trucks. He double-clutched his rig, all the while dodging occasional enemy small-arms fire until his tour of duty in Vietnam came to an end on May 3, 1970. When he left, he was awarded the Vietnam Campaign Medal, the Combat Infantry Badge, the Vietnam Service Medal, and the US Army Air medal for his twenty-five-plus assault missions on the helicopter.

On his return to the US, he made a quick visit with family and friends in Milo. His military orders directed him to his next duty station, Kelly Barracks, located in Stuttgart, Germany, home of the 7th Corps, headquarters for US Army's African Command. He arrived there in late May 1970. It didn't take long for Les to realize he didn't like the assignment. There were more officers at the installation than enlisted, and his duty assignment became that of a chauffeur who drove high-ranking officials to command staff meetings, luncheon engagements, and various errands beneath the dignity of his superiors. Again just as he did as an infantryman in the jungles of Vietnam, Les made another situation assessment. He didn't care for all the pomp and circumstance, the crisp crease of heavily starched uniforms, the shiny Corfam shoes, the opening of doors for four-star generals, as if he were a concierge at New York's Waldorf Astoria, or the dozens of hand salutes required in the course of the day's work.

Les had enough and wanted change. This was not what he envisioned. Within three months upon his arrival in Germany, Les did the unthinkable and volunteered to go back to Vietnam. The US Army gladly honored his wish and issued orders back to the chaos he left just four months earlier.

Les flew back from Europe to McGuire AFB, New Jersey, adjacent to Fort Dix, via a military aircraft. There the army's transportation office gave him cash to purchase commercial airfare to Fort Lewis, Washington, where his departure back to Vietnam would originate. Of course, Milo would be a definite layover while en route. However, with the several hundred dollars cash in hand for the plane ticket, Les had other desires. He went through the money like a knife through hot butter and had a good time on Uncle Sam's dime. Out of money, he hitchhiked from New Jersey back to Iowa.

Milo had changed little in the two years since he left. Some of the old crowd of friends he used to carouse with still could be found on a barstool at the South Side Tavern located on Main Street. Some had yet to turn twenty-one, not old enough to buy a cold beer, but they patronized the bar anyway as the lone source of social entertainment in the community. Farmers popped in for a quick cold beer between loads of grain they had just unloaded at the Cooperative Elevator located just a block away. Corn market prices were at a low of $1.44 per bushel, and farmers held on to the previous crops in anticipation of a market increase. With the upcoming fall harvest just weeks away, local farmers were forced to empty their grain bins in preparation for the fall harvest. Otherwise, their 1970 fall crop would have to be stored outside.

As much as Les wanted things to be the same as it was before he left, they just weren't. The faces were the same. Shorty Baumgarten, the five-foot-five farmer from south of town, still told the same jokes; Orville Kennedy, a WWII Purple Heart veteran, could be found hovering over the huge slate pool table that consumed the south end of the bar; and Bob Rodgers sat in the corner, involved in a heated pitch game. It wasn't the fact that Milo that changed, he thought to himself, maybe, just maybe he had changed.

As Les looked up, through the front door of the tavern, in walked Rudy Wadle, a good friend and high school classmate. Rudy's parents, Leonard and Irene Wadle, owned and operated the South Side Tavern. The old friends greeted each other with handshakes and smiles. Rudy had just returned from Vietnam the previous year. "Are you through with the army yet?" he asked Les.

Almost embarrassed to answer, Les replied, "No, I extended my enlistment. I'm home on leave now and headed back to Nam for a second go around."

Rudy was dumbfounded. "You gotta be kidding me? You're headed back…when?"

"I leave Fort Lewis in about a week," Les answered.

"Oh no, that's just not right," Rudy chided. "Did you hear about Art Wright?"

Les shook his head and said, "No. He's in Vietnam the I last heard."

"Not anymore, he was killed on September 5 when in Nam, his funeral is next Monday, the twenty-first. Are you still going to be here then?"

Les intended to hitchhike to Fort Lewis and had to be there soon. He thought to himself, if he stayed in Milo another three days, he would report late for his return trip back to Vietnam. His decision was a no-brainer. He stayed for Art's funeral and only allowed four days to make his way to Fort Lewis.

Bad luck befell Les. Local police in Yakima, Washington, picked him up for violation of the state's hitchhiking laws, a mere 168 miles from his destination. As Les relayed his story, "I couldn't believe it. It was okay to hitchhike in Iowa. I rode around in a paddy wagon for most of the day as the local cops picked up other hitchhikers on I-82. Apparently there were a significant number of people avoiding the draft and making their way to Canada on foot. Les spent three days in the Yakima jail. Once he had an opportunity to tell his story to the judge, that he was in the military and only trying to get to Fort Lewis because he had orders for Vietnam, the judge let him off the hook and released him from jail with no penalties. When Les arrived at Fort Lewis, he knew he was in trouble. He missed his scheduled flight to Vietnam. Military authorities were not happy. They issued an Article 15 against him, a nonjudicial punishment that carried an array of circumstances that ranged from reduction in rank, forfeiture of pay, and time in a military jail. Les received a fine of $500 to be systematically withheld from his pay and additionally required to purchase his own airline ticket to Vietnam at a cost of $256. Les never felt so glad as when he climbed aboard the chartered aircraft to Vietnam to simply get out of dodge.

Les arrived at Biên Hoa Air Base, Vietnam, on October 10, 1970, for his second tour of duty. Biên Hoa was located about sixteen miles from Saigon. He reported to the 1st Logistics Division, 446th Transportation Company where he once again resumed his duties as a truck driver. There he drove a Kenworth truck and shuttled supplies from docks on the Saigon River to depots at Long Biên and Cam Rhan Bay. He later drove a daily route from Tan Son Nhut to Long Biên that carried mail. Les was never one to let grass grow under his feet. There was always a nervousness about him that kept him at near-full throttle most of the time. That included not just his personal demeanor but the manner in which he drove his trucks. His theory became, "The faster I drive, the less chance I become a sitting target for ground fire."

And yes, indeed, ground fire was a common occurrence. He carried a shotgun in his truck along with a cache of grenades and C-4 explosives, just in case things went south and got out of control. On one particular trip, as Les barreled down the road with the accelerator buried in the floorboard, MP checkpoints on the narrow winding road blipped past him like fence post on a rural Iowa highway back home. Les commented, "I was doing almost 75 mph, and the MPs were attempting to flag me down for going so fast. Finally I stopped, and beyond all reason and logic, I was issued a speeding ticket. Imagine that," he said, "a friggin' speeding ticket in a war zone!"

As a result, Les temporarily lost his military driver's license. He became relegated to the motor pool and began changing tires on the rigs he previously drove. Removing a flat tire from an eighteen-wheeler and breaking it down by hand with a hammer and pry bar was no easy task. Les hated the job and wondered how long this duty would last. A few short weeks later, he once again climbed into the cab and hit the roads. In his own words, "There were a lot of young guys fresh to Vietnam, still wet behind the ears, who weren't experienced drivers, and they wrecked several of our vehicles." I assumed that at the tender age of twenty-one, Les considered himself a tenured veteran of the road and master behind the wheel of the big rigs.

In addition to dodging tracer rounds from the VC as he herded his truck down the road, other obstacles often arose. Two wheeled wagons pulled by caribou or small motorcycles with sidecars driven by locals crowded the roadways. Traffic jams were a common sight and caused not by a logjam of huge trucks like his own but under-powered puddle jumpers and even people on foot with carry-poles across their shoulders, loaded down with huge bundles that hung on each side in a careful balancing act. The whole scenario brought forth such frustration for Les toward those who blocked his path. On one occasion, as he approached a checkpoint, a bottleneck of traffic brought movement to a slow crawl. The MPs at the checkpoint were doing their best to hurry things along, but his patience wore thin. Les repeatedly blew the air horn on his Kenworth to no avail. An MP approached and looked up. Again Les laid on the horn with some accompanying arm and hand gestures. The MP flipped his rifle off safety and quickly fired a few rounds into the front tire of his vehicle. The slow crawl of traffic instantly came to a dead stop. It became a moment in which Les later realized he should have reeled it back a notch or two. He settled back in his seat and turned up the volume on the radio in his rig and clasped his hands behind his neck and took a deep breath. As if on cue, the AFN blared out the 1965 Roger Miller hit "King of the Road." As the lyrics were belted out loud and clear, Les chuckled to himself and sang along, "I'm a man of means by no means, king of the road. Whoop-poop-poopie-do."

According to comments made by Les when he reflected on his military experience, especially while in Vietnam, "Time there wasn't all dodging bullets or breathing diesel exhaust fumes. There was plenty of downtime with not much to do, downright boredom, in fact." Les was forthright and freely admitted that he smoked quite a bit of marijuana that reduced the tension he felt during his time in country. Government statistics reinforced that statement when reports released after the war revealed marijuana usage peaked at 34 percent among US soldiers. The weed grew wild in the jungle and was easily obtained without too much ingenuity. Marijuana was readily available on the streets from local vendors, already prerolled and packaged. The GIs called the package of smokes "park lane" or genuine "craven A." The military knew about this, but for the most part looked the other way. The extreme violence of combat traumatized many GIs, and as a result, 31 percent suffered from PTSD. The cannabis use, in the minds of some, provided a means of psychological decompression and allowed, in some small way, an avenue to cope with the sheer horror and craziness of the war as it unfolded before them.

Despite all the bumps in the road, blown-out tires, traffic citations, an Article 15, and admitted marijuana use, Les was promoted to specialist 5. He completed his second tour of duty in Vietnam and headed back to CONUS (Continental United States) on October 10, 1971. His next set of orders sent him to Fort Riley, Kansas, home of the First Infantry Division and the Big Red One. Once checked in and ready for duty, after just three short months, he received a pleasant surprise. The army offered him an early out. Les jumped at the offer and discharged from active duty on January 11, 1972.

After fourteen years away from the military, Les felt the itch again. At the urging of his brother-in-law, he joined the Iowa Air National Guard in Des Moines, as a member of the 132 Fighter Wing on December 10, 1986. He was a little surprised at their eager acceptance of him back into the military, especially with his past marijuana usage documented in his medical records and his not-so-young age of thirty-seven. There he became a fuels journeyman, AFSC (air force specialty code) 2FOXX, and drove POL fuel tankers from the storage facility to the flight line and serviced the A-7 Corsair and later the F-16 Falcon aircraft assigned to the unit. Les served a total of eighteen years with the air national guard, the last two in Arkansas when he transferred to the 189th Airlift Wing, located at Little Rock AFB.

He retired on December 10, 2004, as an E-7 master sergeant. When I last saw Les at our high school's fiftieth class reunion in 2017, we talked briefly about our time in the military. I too spent twenty-two years with the 132 Fighter Wing, Iowa Air National Guard, and our paths frequently crossed. He told me, "The last eighteen years was a walk in the park, a piece of cake. Not once did I get a speeding ticket by the sky cops, not once did I take on enemy fire, and not once did my own guys intentionally shoot out my tires."

And I answered back, "And not once did you run into any potholes on the tarmac or potheads smoking a doobie."

GARY CHUMBLEY, BOATSWAIN'S MATE THIRD CLASS, E-3

United States Navy
January 1969–September 1971

Gary grew up on a farm a few miles west of Milo. We knew each other even before our school days in kindergarten began. My mother operated a beauty salon in our home, and Gary's mother, Betty, was a frequent customer. When she came to town for a haircut, she brought along Gary, and we played together outside while our moms did the snip-and-clip things that women do when making themselves beautiful. That seemed a strange thing for us, making such a fuss over their hair since our own hairstyles were nothing more than a quick buzz cut. That seemed okay with us at the time.

Within a year out of high school, Gary stepped forward and took the pledge to defend and protect our country when he enlisted in the US Navy in January of 1969. He completed his basic training in San Diego, California. Regardless of which branch of service any of the Milo boys joined, the indoctrination employed by the drill instructors mirrored one other. It was no different for Gary. It was a strange psychological tactic familiar to all who served. A constant barrage of insulting remarks shouted at point-blank range into Gary's face regarding his intelligence, his appearance, his self-esteem, and even his family members and girlfriend back home. Vulgar references to each recruit's manhood were abundant, and profane language filled every single sentence directed their way. Of course, the required response was nothing but "Sir, yes, sir." *Maggots, dummies, scumbags,* and *pukes* were some of the milder terms applied to Gary and all the swabbies, grunts, jarheads, and flyboys that ever marched on the parade grounds to the cadence of an overbearing drill instructor.

In some perverted way, this manner of doing business with young recruits worked magic. The minute they stepped off the bus at the basic training station, their personal identity was temporarily kidnapped, symbolically taken away with a buzz haircut and their civilian clothes tossed aside. While standing naked in formation, a designated inspector walked in front of them checking each soldier's genitals for any obvious medical issues. Then the command came forth, "Bend over and spread your cheeks." A subsequent backdoor inspection took place. From that point forward, all the trainees became one. Gone was their modesty, and gone was their personal identity. Each had nothing, from that point forward, to hide from one another. As if under some magical spell, Gary and all the boys of Milo became transformed into government issue (GIs) soldiers.

With basic training completed, Gary began advanced training on the USS *Neversail*, a landlocked replica at one-third scale of a seaworthy vessel. Gary learned the skills of a boatswain's mate. His responsibilities entailed the care of the ship's hull and all its components, including its rigging, anchors, cables, sails, deck maintenance, and small boat operations

After completion of advanced training, his first duty assignment sent him to San Francisco, California, at Naval Station Treasure Island, a 568-acre manmade island in San Francisco Bay. It was there he was united with the USS *Rehoboth*, a 310-foot ship with a crew of 215 that performed oceanographic survey duties.

Gary's first trip out to sea was unforgettable. After a short operational run beyond Treasure Island, the captain of the ship, upon return, rammed the USS *Rehoboth* into the dock, damaging the ship and severely damaging the dock. Gary's thoughts were, *Whoa! What the heck, am in in McHale's navy with Earnest Borgnine at the helm?* As a result, the Treasure Island commander prohibited the captain of the bungled docking from ever steering into his port again. That duty fell upon a more skilled yet subordinate officer.

When the USS *Rehoboth* left port in the spring of 1969, it headed toward the South Pacific Ocean on a top secret mission. The crew performed an ocean floor survey for an under-ocean communication cable to connect Hawaii, Okinawa, the Philippines, Japan, and Taiwan. During the entire deployment, a Russian trawler shadowed the *Rehoboth*, attempting to determine the intent of its activities. As Gary recalled from memory, the ship zigzagged back and forth across the South Pacific Ocean with enough nautical miles to sail around the world two and one-half times.

With such tropical weather, Gary's uniform of the day simply became dungarees and a tan. As they approached Zamboanga, Peninsula of the Philippines, one of Gary's buddies called out to him from atop the crow's nest. "You gotta come up here and smell the fresh air of the Philippines. I can see the island. It's beautiful." Not to miss out on a wonderful event, Gary scurried up and took it all in. "Can you smell that?" his sailor buddy asked.

Gary took in a deep breath and then another. "Holy crap, man, that smells like fish guts!"

"Yep, that's kind of what I thought too." His buddy laughed.

When in port at Zamboanga, it marked the first time since the Korean War that a US military ship had visited the port. While at least a mile offshore, local Filipinos paddled their small banca boats out to sea alongside the USS *Rehoboth*. Gary thought to himself that these rickety poor excuse for seaworthy boats might be suitable in a small fishpond back in Iowa, but certainly had no business out in the deep ocean waters. What the young Filipinos were seeking was money—American money. The sailors aboard the *Rehoboth* would toss coins into the water, and like seagulls diving for food, the

Filipinos dove to catch them before sinking too deep. It was cheap entertainment for the sailors and a huge payday for the locals.

While in the South Pacific, the *Rehoboth* charted the waters of Challenger Deep, the deepest and most unexplored part of the ocean located in the Mariana Trench near Guam. The Mariana Trench is 15,580 miles long and 43 miles wide. It's depth is an amazing 35,462 feet deep. At that depth, the water pressure is an unbelievable 16,099 psi. Gary watched in awe as the ship's camera brought images to the surface. He commented, "I wish I could have had some pictures of that, but since it was a classified mission, that didn't happen. It's real hard to comprehend the magnificence brought forth by such a place on earth."

The *Rehoboth* docked at Pearl Harbor early in 1970 and was decommissioned on April 15, 1970. Gary was glad to get his feet back onto solid ground. With a relative short time before his enlistment expired, he was reassigned to the USS *Tawakoni*, a 205-foot vessel designed for salvage and towing of other ships. It carried a crew of seventy-six sailors but also performed surveillance of Soviet electronic trawlers in the Gulf of Tonkin.

Gary discharged from active duty with the US Navy at Pearl Harbor in September 1971.

And God said, "Let the waters under the heavens be gathered together into one place, and let the dry land appear." And it was so."
—Genesis 1:9–10

WILLIAM ZIMMERMAN, WARRANT OFFICER 2

United States Navy
May 19, 1969–April 3, 1972
United States Army, Medically Retired
July 23, 1974–August 17, 1984

Bill Zimmerman stayed with his grandparents for much of his formative years, growing up in Milo. His father, Ivan, was a career army man and relocated many times with changes in duty stations. Bill called Milo his home and considered it the place where his roots were planted. Bill lived just two houses north of me and was a few years younger. It wasn't me, but someone gave him the nickname Pinky. I often referred to him as Pinky Zimmerman, the neighbor kid. The nickname came from *Pinky Lee*, the children's television show that aired in 1954. During the thirty-minute episodes, Pinky Lee performed as a high-energy character with slapstick antics for easy laughs from his audience of young kids. Bill fit that character to a tee, as I remember him, and even looked like the Pinky on television. Thus the name stuck.

Bill turned eighteen in March of 1969 and registered for the draft. His lucky number became 29. He knew before long, Uncle

Sam would knock on his door. He asked the draft board for an early medical exam even before his number was called. When he reported to the Fort Des Moines Military Processing Center for his exam, it became an eye-opening moment. As he sat in the hallway, he noticed about twenty-five guys in their undershorts, sitting on chairs aligned against the far wall. A burly looking marine, who appeared to be nine feet tall with six-foot wide shoulders, busted through the double doors and loudly addressed the draftees. He barked out. "Stand up and shut up. When I point my finger at you, go through the double doors and report to the desk."

Then he started down the line. With every fifth man, he pointed and screamed, "Marine, marine, marine, marine, marine!" Bill took this all in. He knew right then and there, three things: Number 1, he would not be drafted. Number 2, he would not be a marine. Number 3, he would not go to Vietnam. The very next day, Bill hurried to the navy recruiter and signed up.

Bill left for naval boot camp in May 1969, headed to San Diego, California. Upon completion of basic training, Bill received orders in August 1969, for a six-week signalman school located at Pearl Harbor, Hawaii. There he also received training for inshore, undersea, warfare group (IUWG). The IUWG performed harbor patrol and swimmer interdiction on small patrol boats.

In October 1969, the USN sent him to Coronado, California, for survival, evasion, resistance, and escape training (SERE). That training lasted six weeks. Bill began to see the writing on the wall. Well, at least two of three of his wishes would come true. He was not drafted, and he wasn't a marine. Vietnam loomed on the horizon based on the type of training he already received.

In November 1969, Bill went to Camp Pendleton, California, for a short two-week course in weapons training. Immediately afterward, another two-week course at Long Beach, California, in small patrol boat indoctrination.

In December 1969, Bill arrived at Cam Ranh Bay, Vietnam. When the aircraft door opened, and he exited onto the tarmac, his first full breath of air smelled of jet fuel mixed with the stink of human waste. What a combination of aromas, he thought. Neither appealed to him. The extreme heat nearly overwhelmed him as he tugged on the strap of his blue navy seabag. No, this wasn't a hot summer day in Iowa adjacent to a hog lot, it would be his home for a full year.

He initially served in the IUWG-1 Unit 2, Harbor Entrance command post that monitored all vessels at the entry point of Cam Ranh Bay. In April 1970, he transferred to patrol boat duty as part of the IUEG-1 Unit 2. On patrol boat duty, Bill cruised the backwaters of the Mekong Delta in an olive drab eighteen-foot fiberglass Boston Whaler, propelled by an eighty-five-horsepower outboard Johnson engine. A crew of just two men manned the small boat as it navigated through the tributary waterways near Cam Ranh Bay. His mission was simple: keep the rivers clear of underwater mines so that the main shipping lanes were clear for larger vessels and engage any hostiles if the opportunity arose. The crew carried only their M16 rifles, shotguns, flares, and grenades. No protective armament existed, just a flak jacket and helmet. It was a risky venture by any standard. Overall statistics for patrol boat duty during the Vietnam War were not good. Thirty percent of those that served in that capacity were either killed or wounded.

On Bill's very first mission, he and his crewmate encountered three bodies that floated in the river. Uncertain whether they were VC or perhaps US troops, Bill was instructed to jump in and retrieve them. As the lowest-ranking sailor onboard, he did as ordered. He approached the first and reached out as he swam closer. The stench was beyond anything he ever imagined. He grabbed an arm and pulled. The skin on the dead man's arm peeled off in Bill's grip and exposed the decayed muscle beneath. Bill freaked out. He swam back to the boat as quick as his splashing legs and arm strokes would allow. Once onboard, he simply shook his head and thought to himself, my god! Bill stated it took several days for the stench to dissipate. All the soap and water he could muster wouldn't do the job. It was as if had been sprayed by a skunk on the country roads that surrounded Milo. The lingering odor served as a stark reminder of the morbid environment in which he patrolled. Many of Bill's patrol missions received periodic ground fire from the shoreline. With little firepower of their own, the crew marked the enemy location and powered away as fast as the boat could go. As tense as the moment seemed during the daylight, night missions often raised the hair on the back of each sailor's neck. In Bill's own words, "The patrol boat missions were filled with hours and hours of pure boredom, then suddenly punctuated by a few moments of sheer madness. Other than that, I killed a lot of fish with concussion grenades."

With just two weeks left on his Vietnam tour, Bill left patrol boat duty and was reassigned to the naval support command at Cam Ranh Bay. There he issued US equipment to the Vietnamese Navy. In a blink of an eye, his tour came to end. He defied the odds as a patrol boat operator, unscathed from injury. The Christmas gift to himself was his ticket back to the United States of America. He thumbed his nose as he departed Cam Ranh Bay with no battle wounds, or so he thought.

In January 1970, he reported to the USS *Richard L. Page*, DEG-5, a 414-foot guided missile frigate harbored at Newport, Rhode Island, that carried a crew of 228 sailors. The USS *Richard L. Page* conducted drug interdiction operations along the East Coast of the United States in 1971, then steamed to the Caribbean with a stop in Guantanamo Bay, Cuba (Gitmo). On the return trip to the shipyard in Boston, Massachusetts, the USS *Richard L. Page* encountered the second longest hurricane on record. Hurricane Ginger rated a category 1. The eye of Ginger measured 80 miles wide. Winds clocked at 110 mph pummeled the Caribbean and eastern coastline of the United States from September 6 through October 2. Bill rode out the storm aboard the USS *Richard L. Page*, hunkered down below deck. Bill was tickled pink to finally set foot on dry land at Boston.

In May 1972, Bill jumped ship, so to speak. He transferred to the USS *Paul*, DE-1080, a 438-foot Knox-class frigate with a crew of 234 sailors. It too was docked in Newport, Rhode Island. On his first voyage aboard the USS *Paul*, the captain set a familiar course. Bill headed back to Gitmo. Once there, a new set of orders directed the ship to the Western Pacific (WESTPAC), off the shore of Vietnam. That marked Bill's second tour of duty in Vietnam.

On January 27, 1973, representatives of the United States, North and South Vietnam signed the Paris Peace Treaty. That, in effect, ended all US military involvement in Vietnam. South Vietnam, however, continued to battle against the North Vietnamese due to their unwillingness to recognize the Vietcong's Provisional Revolutionary government. That treaty, in all reality, was a saving-face gesture by the US government. Early on the morning of March 29, 1973, two months after the cease-fire, Bill's ship, the USS *Paul*, received shore artillery fire while off the coast of Vietnam. The ship returned fire. In Bill's words, "Our ship fired some of the last naval rounds of the Vietnam War."

Bill separated from the US Navy in San Diego in April 1973 as an E-4, third class petty officer. During his three-year, eleven-month stint with the Navy, he saw two tours of duty in Vietnam. He received the Navy Combat Action Ribbon, the Navy Unit Commendation Ribbon, the Vietnam Service Medal, the Vietnam Gallantry Cross, the Vietnam Civil Actions Ribbon, the Republic of Vietnam Campaign Medal, and the Republic of Vietnam Naval Service Medal.

In summary of Bill's time with the US Navy, in his own words, he stated, "It's better that my children not know everything that happened in Vietnam. I went there as an impressionable eighteen-year-old kid from a small town in Iowa and looked death straight in the eye. It looked back at me with hollow sunken eyes. There were some good memories and many bad ones. As a veteran now, and reflecting back, all who served in Vietnam, to a large extent, let the bad memories rule our lives. It is not what we choose but has become a fact of life. The good memories are the vivid faces of fellow soldiers we served with, whose names we do not remember. They are faces that come in the night and whisper in our dreams. They constantly stand beside us in our long-lived wasteland called the passing of time."

Listen, I tell you a mystery: We will not all sleep, but we will all be changed. **(1 Corinthians 15:51)**

Bill enjoyed civilian life, but for him, civilian life proved to be a tough row to hoe. He worked for a while as a farmhand, then became a well-digger, and even raised turkeys for a short time. Nothing seemed to click. Just nine months out of the uniform, he rethought his decision about the military. In January 1974, Bill enlisted—of all places—in the US Army.

Of course, he skipped basic training, with his past naval service, and went directly to a thirteen-week-long school at Fort Sill, Oklahoma, as a ballistic meteorology repairman with a MOS of 35D. He followed that with another nine-week school at Fort Sill as a field meteorology crewman. The duties of a ballistic meteorology soldier involved the gathering of atmospheric conditions that enhanced the on-target precision of artillery fire based on varying weather conditions. Bill monitored, repaired, and coordinated equipment that measured atmospheric temperatures, wind direction, humidity, air density and matched that data with specific weaponry trajectories in conjunction with local maps and charts. Once his schooling was completed, he remained at Fort Sill as an assistant instructor.

In April 1976, Bill received orders to Camp Page, South Korea, and was assigned to the 1st Battalion, 42nd Field Artillery. Camp Page, also known as K-47 Air Base, was located near Chunchon, South Korea, about forty-eight miles north of Seoul. The battalion provided artillery support in protection of the demilitarized zone between North and South Korea. At any given time, Camp Page had about seven hundred US soldiers on station, supplemented by about the same number of civilian South Koreans employed by the department of the army.

After a one-year isolated tour at Camp Page, Bill once again received marching orders. This time, in April 1977, the army sent him to Fort Knox, Kentucky, where he was assigned to the 3rd Battalion, 3rd Field Artillery. Fort Knox is best known as the location for the United States gold depository, located thirty-five miles south of Louisville. Bill's tour of duty at Fort Knox was uneventful. Job well done, Pinky. No gold bullion came up missing. As of April 2016, the depository had on hand 4,582 tons of gold. That amounted to 147.3

million troy ounces. At a value of $1,226 per ounce, the total value exceeded $180 billion.

In June 1980, Bill relocated to the US Army Recruiting Command (USAREC), located in Alexandria, Virginia. There he became a touring exhibit specialist. His duties included the transport of a mobile movie theater that presented the US Army's recruiting message at schools and fairs in the local area. That duty captured the opposite end of the spectrum from his duty as a navy seaman aboard a Boston Whaler that cruised the waterways of the Mekong Delta in Vietnam eleven years earlier. He no longer sought out the bad guys that hid in the jungles along riverbanks but instead searched for good guys—eighteen-year-old kids, like he once was, with a desire to "be all you can be." He didn't carry an M16 but instead recruitment brochures. The only incoming rounds he received were rapid-fire questions from high school kids who wanted to know why they should become a soldier.

Bill's assignment was tough duty. There remained a bad taste in the mouth of America about the military for many years after the Vietnam War. However, recruiting numbers for the army showed an increase from 758,852 enlistments in 1979 to 781,419 enlistments in 1981. Traditionally enlistments increased in direct correlation with national unemployment rates. From 1979–1981, the unemployment rate in the United States hovered around 6 percent. With enticements offered by the military through the GI Bill for educational benefits and housing, Bill kept pace with the recruiting demands.

In October 1981, Bill received orders to Schofield Barracks, Hawaii, and was assigned to headquarters of the 25th Field Artillery where he served as section chief. It was there that he received a direct appointment to warrant officer-1 as a field artillery radar technician. That represented a huge increase in rank from an E-7, sergeant first class to warrant officer, W-1.

One year later, in October 1982, he headed to Fort Riley, Kansas, to headquarters, 1st Infantry Field Artillery. There Bill shouldered the responsibility for six field artillery radar sections with seventy-nine troops and $160 million in equipment. While at Fort Riley, Bill enrolled in the local college and took a few courses he hoped would enhance his military career. He eventually graduated from Middle State Tennessee University a few years later with a bachelor's degree. In one of those early classes, he encountered a nurse. She noticed some things about Bill that gave her some concern. She previously worked with GIs who experienced PTSD and saw those symptoms coming out in Bill. She confronted him and suggested he get a medical evaluation. Bill heeded her advice and, as a result, got the help he needed for PTSD. He medically retired on August 17, 1984, after fourteen years of combined military duty.

His military awards included: the Navy Combat Action Ribbon, the Navy Unit Commendation Medal, the Vietnam Gallantry Cross (unit), National Defense Service Medal, Vietnam Civil Action (unit), Republic of Vietnam Campaign Medal, Republic of Vietnam Naval Service Medal, the Army Meritorious Medal, Army Good Conduct Medal with two devices, the Army NCO Development Ribbon with three devices, the Army Overseas Service Ribbon with one device, Expert Rifle Badge, and Sharpshooter Pistol Badge.

Bill's story does not end there. In 1984, as he sat in a small dive bar in Tennessee and reflected on his past, a blond-haired lady sat down beside him and struck up a conversation. She even offered to buy him a drink. She asked Bill, "Do you know who I am?"

To which he replied, "No." That must have been the answer she was looking for. A relationship developed, and two months later, they were married. The blond-haired lady was none other than Roni Stoneman of the acclaimed Stoneman family band. The Stoneman band had their own weekly television show, and Roni made frequent appearances on the television show *Hee Haw* that first aired in June 1969, and continued in syndication for twenty-three years. Roni was best known on the show as the ironing board lady, Ida Lee Nagger, and recognized as the first lady of the banjo with her bluegrass style of pickin'. Their marriage only lasted two years, but during that time, Bill became her booking manager and hobnobbed in Nashville with the likes of Roy Clark, Buck Owens, String Bean, Grandpa Jones, Minnie Pearl, Jeannie C. Riley, and numerous other country music stars. Bill and Roni's common denominator upon their split in 1986 was the number 5. Both had been married five times.

Today Bill Zimmerman lives in Red Banks, Mississippi, and enjoys the retired life. When asked what he does in retirement, his quick response was, "Nothing, and I'm getting damn good at it."

RICHARD C. RODGERS, SPECIALIST FOURTH CLASS, E-4

United States Army
September 14, 1970–April 21, 1972

R ick lived on a farm northeast of Milo, the eldest son of Charles and Anita Rodgers. I first met Rick as a member of the Milo Boy Scouts. He was a year behind me in school. As twelve and thirteen-year-olds, we enjoyed many campouts together. His dad, Charley, was actively involved as a leader of the scouts. As we grew into our teen years, I often found myself at his farm where I worked for his dad. Rick drove the tractor, and I stacked bales of hay on the wagon. We also walked soybean fields beside each other as we pulled butter print weeds, sometimes called velvet leaf.

I remembered Rick as one of the nicest most polite kids in Milo. He never cussed, he never got mad about anything, he never teased others, and he certainly didn't smoke. As teenagers, many of the boys of Milo caroused around town late at night and found themselves involved in some crazy ridiculous pranks. Not Rick. He was a true gentleman even as a teenager. Reflecting back, Rick was perhaps the most spiritually grounded young per-

270

son I knew. Even more spiritually grounded than my good friend Bob Lord who was a PK (preacher's kid).

Out of high school, Rick enrolled at the community college in Des Moines, where he studied mechanical technology, the precursor for a degree in engineering. He graduated in May 1970, the same month that the Beatles movie *Let It Be* premiered. That same month, college kids protested the bombing in Cambodia on the campus of Kent State University in Ohio. Four students were shot, and the nation erupted in protest of the Vietnam War. The month before, the largest antiwar protest took place in Washington DC, when twenty thousand demonstrators took to the streets and demanded radical change in the American society.

Rick pondered his situation. As if scripted by the Charles Dickens novel, *A Tale of Two Cities*, "It was the best of times, it was the worst of times." Political and economic unrest enveloped America and reached the small town of Milo. It became a stressful time. He knew his inevitable fate after college. Uncle Sam would soon be knocking at his door. He had a low number in the draft lottery and figured the writing was already on the wall. He didn't want to get drafted into the military or volunteer for active duty. It became a time for deep thought and a whole lot spiritual self-reflection.

The Lord of hosts has sworn: As I have planned, so shall it be, and as I have purposed, so shall it stand. **(Isaiah 14:24)**

It became a fork in the road for Rick—what to do? He decided to take a chance and roll the dice. It didn't take long before snake eyes appeared. He received his draft notice in August, and on September 14, 1970, he found himself headed to Fort Leonard Wood, Missouri, for basic training.

Upon completion of boot camp, the army sent him to Fort Gordon, Georgia, for an MOS of 95B-10, military police. What caught Rick's attention from the time he left boot camp and well into his advanced schooling was the diversity of the troops that surrounded him. It wasn't so much the racial diversity, but his Midwestern roots and upbringing on the farm greatly contrasted with others. He recalled the time the instructor asked the question, "Who here does not have a driver's license?"

Several hands shot upward. Rick had trouble absorbing the fact that the big city guys didn't know how to drive but instead took the subway or bus for transportation. In fact, he soon discovered there were a lot the city guys that didn't know things he assumed were common knowledge. He immediately realized he had a leg up on the others, not only during basic training but the advanced schooling as well. He kept a photo his mother sent him in his locker. One of the soldiers from New York saw it and commented, "Is that a park near where you live?"

Rick chuckled and told him, "No, that's my home where I grew up. It's the backyard overlooking my mom's flower garden and an open field." That comment solidified the fact that Rick, as well as all the boys of Milo, truly grew up in a blessed community. *Utopia* is defined as a place free of conflict and full of happiness. Utopia is derived from the Greek word *eu-topos*, which means "a good place."

Rick took two trips back to Milo during his advanced schooling. One for a Christmas break for several days in December 1970, and another two weeks upon graduation from the military police school.

In February 1971, military orders sent Rick to Fischbach Army Depot, Germany, a classified facility located near Dahn, where he became part of the US Army Europe (USAREUR) Command, 100th Military Police Detachment. Fischback was a nuclear missile storage site used during the height of the Cold War not too far from the Black Forrest. Rick commented, "My job wasn't so much that of a policeman but more of a security guard for the numerous bunkers on base. I did go on several convoys and escorted the transfer of missiles from one location to the other. Never once did I see what was kept inside the bunkers."

In May 1971, Rick received a surprise visit from someone he knew from Milo. Ray and Thelma Pehrson, along with their daughter, Marieta, sought him out and an evening with him for dinner at a local German restaurant. Ray farmed west of Milo and knew the

Rodgers family. They accompanied their daughter to Germany to join her husband, Dave Grissom, who was also stationed in Germany with the US Army at Flak Kaserne in Augsburg, Germany.

Not wanting to miss out on the opportunity to sightsee in Europe, Rick and two of his GI buddies, Jerome Bumgartner and Joe Kennedy, took Jerome's 1961 Volkswagen Beetle on a three-week road trip. They toured Italy, France, Austria, and Switzerland.

When Rick summarized his time in the military, he thought it was pretty good duty. In fact, he suggested everyone could benefit from serving a stint in the military. The challenges of military basic training and meeting people from various backgrounds from across the country was a great education. Buried in the writings of ancient scholars are the thoughts, "The grasp of a man's knowledge is not measured by any book he has read or scholarly degree carried in a pocket, but more importantly by the number of miles he has walked with his fellow man." Rick was grateful for the opportunity to walk a few miles with the diverse group he met while in the military.

The army offered Rick an early discharge. He jumped at the opportunity. He flew from Germany to Philadelphia, Pennsylvania, then bussed to Fort Dix, New Jersey. He discharged there and became a civilian once again on April 21, 1972, after just seventeen months in uniform. Ironically at the time, I was stationed at McGuire AFB, adjacent to Fort Dix in April of 1972. When he arrived at Fort Dix, we were just a few miles apart. My duty station was next door at McGuire AFB. If either of us would have only known.

MY FIRST PLANE CRASH

I t seemed like just any other ordinary day at the crash/rescue fire station at McGuire AFB. It was Saturday, January 16, 1971. The weather that day was actually quite mild in New Jersey, unlike the cold bitter winters of Iowa in the early months of the year. It rained off and on most of the day, with some drizzle into the evening hours. The temperatures hovered in the forties. Certainly a good day to hunker down at the station and practice my card-playing skills with some of the guys and hoped the alarm bell would not ring that evening. For certain, we played for cash, despite not having too much to spare. I remember one crazy airman by the name of Charlie Potts. He lost his entire paycheck playing high card draw within hours of cashing the puny amount we received every two weeks. Yes, it was me. I took Charlie's money. My conscience got the best of me when I later saw him ask another troop for a quarter to buy himself a soda.

Proverbs 13:11 came to mind, *"Wealth gained hastily will dwindle, but whoever gathers little by little will increase it."*

I certainly needed the extra cash but decided not to be that kind of guy. I hollered at Pottsie and asked him to join me in the dayroom. "I'm going to give you back this $60 if you promise never to play cards for money at the fire station again," I scolded him.

He stammered, "What? What? You gonna give me the money back?"

"Yes, Pottsie, here's your money back. Don't be that stupid again, okay?"

Right after the evening meal of air force chicken and cold potatoes served by the cooks from the main chow hall, who transported our food in insulated field cans to the station for our consumption, I headed with most of the guys for the television room and tuned in to the *Dean Martin Show*. The *Galloping Gourmet*, Graham Kerr, would have done a backflip had he eaten with us that evening. However, I made a return trip to the kitchen and grabbed a few cookies to top off the meal.

I had just finished my second cookie, and the alarm claxon rang out. The claxon had three distinct tones. One tone stood for a structural fire, another tone was for an impending in-flight emergency for an aircraft on short final approach that had some kind of issues. The third tone was a  definite crash landing. When that tone sounded, everyone knew big trouble lay ahead. I had only previously heard that tone during the morning bell tests. This was no test. We had one down!

This was the stuff we trained for, this was the stuff we anticipated in our mind but hoped it never came to pass. I ran to my crash truck, an AS32P-2. The truck was the top-of-the-line crash vehicle that carried 2,300 gallons of water with a 200-gallon foam tank. It was a beast. We headed down the runway at full speed as the air traffic control tower (ATC) directed us to the scene. It was dark, and I could see a huge orange glow in the distance beyond the perimeter fence.

When my truck arrived on scene, we immediately began dispersing our agent of protein foam on the downed aircraft. *Unbelievable*, I thought to myself, *unbelievable*. The magnitude of the crash so overwhelmed me. The smoke, the smell, the mangled metal fuselage, the destruction in all directions of smashed trees and flattened fencing became almost too much to comprehend. It seemed as if one hundred cars crashed together in one spot. Not much of anything remained that closely resembled an airplane. I remember distinctly our truck dumped eight separate loads of water on the fire. Two other trucks did the same, and still it burned and smoldered. That amounted to nearly fifty thousand gallons of water.

Finally the adrenaline rush I felt subsided. We had been on scene for an hour. That was my first crash. I was no longer a rookie.

I was mesmerized that night by an entire series of events. There was no rescue of passengers. All perished immediately. The aircraft was a C-130 cargo plane under contract with Saturn Airlines. Things began to settle down, and the fire chief released some equipment from the scene when it became apparent there was nothing else we could do.

I walked up close to the flight deck and peered in at ground level. My god, the pilot was still strapped in his seat. His flight suit burned completely through and a huge chunk of his left forearm hung in open view, his face completely blackened, and all the hair on his head singed away. An image of the sides of beef hanging at the packing house blipped on the radar screen of my  mind. "Holy Jesus," I murmured. The stench of burned bodies is an odor I can never forget.

Daylight crept in before I headed back to the station. Several military firefighters were held over for duty that morning to aid in the recovery of the aircraft and fatalities. I volunteered to go back to the scene and provide fire watch as the grim task of body recovery began. I will never forget that day, January 16, 1971.

That day, I became baptized as a professional firefighter. A baptism of fire.

Death is naked before God: Destruction lies uncovered.
—Job 26: 6

WHEN IN ROME, DO AS THE ROMANS

In the year AD 390, a Roman by the name of St. Augustine wrote a letter to Januarius. In that short letter, written in Latin of course, he made suggestions for travelers to Rome. In the letter he said, *Cum Romanian venio, ieiuno sabbato; cum hic sum, non ieiuno: sic etiamtu, ad quam foste ecclesiam veneris, eius moem serua, sicuiquam non vis esse scandalum nec quemquam tibi.* Again in 1777, Pope Clement XIV referred to those same words that were first translated into English. That phraseology and advice has been handed down for centuries and still used today. Translated, it simply meant, "When in Rome, do as the Romans do." Never one to shun words of advice from my elders, I took to heart what I already figured out on my own.

Judi and I had a wonderful experience on the East Coast. There were so many things to see and do. We tried to absorb as much as possible, squeezed between our work schedules. Sightseeing was pretty inexpensive and a perfect avenue to spend a weekend seeing what we had only read about in our high school history classes. We ventured into Philadelphia and touched the Liberty Bell located in Independence Square. We went to New Hope, Pennsylvania, where Washington crossed the Delaware River on his famous attack against British troops in Trenton, New Jersey. We traveled to Valley Forge, Pennsylvania, and watched Revolutionary War battles reenacted with cannon and muskets shots directed toward the advancing Red Coats. We walked beside the small wooden cabins where Washington's troops endured the winter of 1777–1778.

I quickly figured out, after some keen advice from by buddy Dill Pickle, if I wore my uniform to a sporting event, someone usually gave us free tickets. Judi and I witnessed our first Major League baseball game courtesy of free bleacher seats at old Connie Mack Stadium. We watched the hapless Philadelphia Phillies struggle to win. We became instant Philly fans despite their losing record of 73–88, in 1970, a horrible fifteen games under five hundred. I became entranced as I watched the likes of Tim McCarver, Jim Bunning, Greg Luzinsk, Don Money, Larry Bowa, and a young twenty-year-old outfielder named Oscar Gamble run onto the field. I gritted my teeth and thought, *If only—yes, if only—Simpson baseball Coach Larry Johnson would have given me a chance, I knew, I just knew I could play with the likes of these Major Leaguers.* And so went the dreams of young kids and old men. My brother-in-law Bob Bishop once told me, "If ifs and buts were candy and nuts, we all would have a Merry Christmas." How prophetic those words resonated with me.

Connie Mack Stadium opened in 1909 and closed at the end of the 1970 season. The Phillies moved into new Memorial Stadium in 1971. Old Connie Mack Stadium, located at the intersection of Lehigh and 20th Street, suffered vandalism by fire in 1971. It remained vacant for another five years and eventually razed in 1976. Gone was the first Major League Baseball stadium I ever visited. Gone too was my childhood dream of playing professional baseball.

By the spring of 1971, I had washed enough dishes at the Airman's Club that gave me the idea that I could afford to buy a motorcycle. A good decision, I thought. I bought a new 1971 Suzuki 350 motorcycle for $600 and continued with my plan. When in Rome, do as the Romans. Judi and I buzzed up and down Route 38, on over to Spring Lake Heights, and even Atlantic City. We enjoyed every bit of New Jersey as possible, as well as the East Coast.

We took a weekend trip to Washington DC, not on the motorcycle, and saw all the famous monuments: the Smithsonian Institute, Ford Theater, the US Capitol, the Jefferson Memorial, the Washington Monument, and Arlington National Cemetery. We were still on our honeymoon, it seemed, doing so many things we only dreamed about as teenagers.

Again we expanded our travels and ventured into New York City. We visited all the customary sites: the Empire State Building, the Statue of Liberty, and Greenwich Village. What stuck out in my mind as a gee-whiz moment was the public transportation on the subway. Absolutely nothing remotely compared to that experience for this small-town Milo boy.

Another air force buddy from the fire station, Don Cornell, lived in Rochester, New York. He asked Judi and I to join him and his wife, Barb, when he went home for a long weekend to visit her parents. "Heck yes," was our reply. They lived just a hop, skip, and jump from Niagara Falls. I thought, *This is the destination where thousands of young married couples flock to for their honeymoon.* It was neat, really neat. The boat trip under the falls in the Maid of the Mist spooked Judi somewhat, but we got it all recorded on film. We never left any stone unturned or any opportunity pass us by. We had the world by the tail and was loving life to its fullest.

FREDERICK LEROY FRIDLEY, SPECIALIST FIRST CLASS, E-3

United States Army
April 8, 1968–Mar 23, 1970

I best knew Fred when we were teammates on the high school football team. He grew up on a farm a few miles west of Milo along with his younger brother, Ron. If there is such a thing, Fred was a typical farm kid. He was a stout young man, built as strong as an ox yet, for such a superior physique, a very soft-spoken individual. Fred was a lineman on the football team and easily knocked opponents on their keister as he punched holes in the defense for the ball carrier. I remember Coach Bill Luse switched Fred to fullback in short yardage situations when the team needed a first down or a score. He wasn't a fast runner, but he plowed through defenders like a tank and was tough to bring down. That ability would bode well for him in the not-too-distant future.

Just like fellow classmate Dan Reeves, Fred also worked at Crescent Chevrolet in Des Moines immediately after high school.

His tenure there lasted no longer than Dan's as he received his draft notice early in 1968. On April 8, 1968, Fred left Milo, headed to basic training at Fort Bliss, Texas. After eight weeks of boot camp, he received another eight weeks of advanced training as a mechanic for heavy equipment at Fort Hood, Texas. His means of support (MOS) was a 63c20, general vehicle repairman.

Home on leave before shipping overseas, Fred left Des Moines in late March 1969, just before farm-planting season kicked into action. His dad, Dale, and sixteen-year-old brother, Ron, would have to plant the seed that year without him. His destination would be a place with no row crops of corn and soybeans, or rolling hills of alfalfa hay, but instead rice paddies and banana trees. Gone for the time being was the image of their old orange Allis Chalmers tractor that pulled a six-row corn planter. His new view would be water buffalo that pulled a single-blade plow through the knee-deep waters of a rice paddy, while a dark-skinned farmer tirelessly walked behind, hoping to keep the plow upright.

Fred's trip to Vietnam mirrored many others before him. He left Fort Lewis, Washington (flew out of McChord AFB), aboard a Seaboard World Airlines DC-8 with stops in Hawaii and Guam before landing at Cam Rahn Bay, Vietnam, located about two hundred miles northeast of Saigon. The flight lasted twenty-one hours. With the crossing of the international date line, by the clock, he actually arrived before he left.

Fred arrived in Vietnam on April 4, 1969, and spent three days in Cam Rahn Bay. He was scheduled to depart for Pleiku within twenty-four hours. However, the aircraft providing transport, with a 2:00 a.m. departure for the 260-mile flight, experienced a hydraulic leak prior to takeoff and cancelled the sortie. The next day, Fred boarded another aircraft, but before takeoff, the aircraft cancelled the flight due to a flat tire. The crew told those aboard headed to Pleiku that there would be a two-to-three-hour delay and please return to the tarmac in a couple of hours. They would be notified over the public address (PA) system when to report back to the aircraft. After the twenty-one-hour flight to Vietnam and the 2:00 a.m. scheduled departure for the first flight, Fred was dog-tired. A good time for a smoke break and maybe an hour nap, he thought to himself. He went outside the air operations area on the flight line, smoked two quick cigarettes, and then lay back on a bench for a short hour nap. When he awoke, he looked at his watch and saw that three hours had elapsed. Right on schedule, or so it seemed. He walked to the tarmac, looked out onto the parking apron, and saw his aircraft was gone. Apparently he slept through the overhead PA announcement about its departure. Oh well, Fred reminded himself of Murphy's Law. "Anything that can go wrong, will go wrong." Finally on day 3, Fred caught a flight to Pleiku and hoped to catch up with his gear that departed a day ahead of him on the flight he missed.

Once at Pleiku, Fred was assigned to the 1st Battalion, 69th Armored Division. The primary mission of the Pleiku Air Base was forward air controller (FAC) missions coordinated with the South Vietnamese and also as a base for United States special operations forces (initially called air commando units) in the Central Highlands. It was a joint-service base, with units from the army, navy, and marines stationed there as well as the air force which operated and maintained the base. With its diverse units, a wide variety of propeller-driven aircraft operated from the base, along with a large number of helicopters.

The day Fred arrived in Pleiku, his first assignment involved digging ditches with a shovel. It certainly was not what he envisioned, but orders were orders. "To say it was hot would be an understatement," Fred mentioned in an audiotape sent back to his family in Iowa. "It was miserably hot, but at least we had plenty of water to drink." Day two began with indoctrination training for new arrivals. "There were about three hundred of us in a classroom, listening to some staff sergeant tell us all about the dangers of Vietnam, customs within the country, booby traps, and the like," Fred continued in the audiotape.

About fifteen minutes into the briefing, a rocket attack hit the base. Guys scrambled out of the classroom and headed for the nearest bunker and sought shelter from the incoming rockets. Fred ran to the first bunker he saw, only to find it already crammed full of GIs. He ran to a second bunker about twenty-five yards away. It too was completely full of GIs. No room for anybody else. Fred remembered the ditch he dug the day before and made a beeline there and dove in headfirst and buried his face into the dirt. "I laid there for an hour and a half before crawling out," he said. It was a poignant ending for the training class that informed him of the dangers in Vietnam.

Fred commented, "Pleiku was a dump. The village had a stinky distinctive odor that just wouldn't go away. The whole place was nothing but shacks and grass huts. We'd be driving up and down the dirt roads and these"—in Fred's own words—"'mountain yard kids' would come out of the tall grass and run toward us with their hands stretched out, wanting us to give them money or some C rations. Most were totally naked, but some wore just a T-shirt. A sad sight, indeed."

At Pleiku, Fred worked in the motor pool where he serviced and repaired every imaginable vehicle in the army's inventory. He often found himself on a M88 vehicle, tank retrieval (VTR), that would venture out into the field and recover broken-down or damaged vehicles from enemy fire. The VTR had a crew of four with one mounted .50 caliber machine gun and eighteen M-72s Light Anti-Armament Weapon System (LAWS). The M-72s were a one-shot 66 mm unguided weapon designed for use against tanks. As the name implied, the VTR's mission was to recover tanks and other heavy-tracked vehicles and tow them back to base for repairs.

The VTR, in essence, was a mobile repair shop that carried heavy equipment tools, a portable welder, and a hoist to lift tank engines or smaller vehicles such as jeeps. One such trip took him to Camp Smith, some fourteen miles from Pleiku. It was the journey there that Fred became acutely aware of the rough terrain of Vietnam's jungles and the damage it could quickly inflict without any enemy aggression. His M88 threw two tracks while traversing a creek embankment. It took nearly a full day to make the repairs on the spot. Fred said, "I took the blame for damage to the vehicle. It was my first time out in the field, I was the lowest-ranking guy, so we just chalked it up as a rookie mistake that sidelined us for a full day. Nobody got hurt, it was a good day from that perspective."

Fred had only been at Pleiku for slightly over a month when he was reassigned to the 173rd Airborne, Armor Unit at An Khe, a short drive east on Route 19. When he arrived at An Khe, Fred was pleased to discover he would be assigned to Headquarters Company. Normally headquarters meant sweet duty, and for the most part, it was a cushy job. However, when he reported to the senior noncommissioned officer (NCO), he discovered things weren't as nice as he initially envisioned. The sergeant showed him his living quarters. It was just an empty room. No furniture, no bunk, no desk, and no storage locker. Fred was told, "You're going to have to scrounge whatever you can for your accommodations. It's up to you to find what you need."

That night, Fred slept on the floor with his M16 rifle at his side and used his folded duffel bag as a pillow. The next day, he took a walking tour of the An Khe and began gathering up items to transform his new hooch into his new home for the next year. He found an old building partly destroyed from a mortar blast that had seen better days and salvaged some lumber. He located an empty hooch on the far end of the base and commandeered a bed with several broken springs, but it did have a useable mattress. From several empty ammo boxes stacked atop one another, he fabricated some shelving. With a little Iowa farmer's ingenuity and some nails, he built a table and a chair from the salvaged lumber. He found some copper electrical wires that had been tossed in a nearby dump pile that served him well once he stripped off the insulation. With a twist or two from a pair of pliers and the copper wire, the springs of his bunk were fixed. "Almost as good as baling wire, a farmer's best friend. It can fix about anything, good enough," he figured, "Good enough for now."

At An Khe, Fred worked at the motor pool. The daily routine there was a little more rigid than at Pleiku. He attributed that to his assignment at headquarters. He reported for work at 6:00 a.m., stood formation at 7:30 a.m., and then worked on equipment for most of the day until 5:00 p.m. The morning formations closely resembled boot camp back in the States, almost to the point of being a joke. Here he was in a war zone, mortar and rockets falling on a regular basis, guys getting shot, and he and the eleven other guys in the motor pool were getting gigged at morning inspections for hair-cut violations and unpolished boots. Added to that schedule were frequent kitchen patrol (KP) duties and overnight guard duty from tower checkpoints around the base. Fred didn't mind washing pots and pans every now and then. "It's no big deal," he hold the folks back home on the audiotapes he sent. "Everyone uses paper plates and plastic utensils, so the duty isn't that rough. It could be worse."

Three guys at a time from the motor pool would pull guard duty at night, each taking a three-hour watch while the other two slept. That too, as Fred reported, was a piece of cake, unless you pulled the middle shift. Fred was about as easygoing a guy as anyone could imagine. It seemed like nothing ever got under his skin. Until one day, late in the afternoon at the motor pool, a young wet-behind-the-ears second lieutenant showed up.

Fred just finished replacing a wheel bearing on a deuce and a half truck as his normal duty day wound down. Suddenly in strolled the lieutenant and inquired about *that* particular truck Fred had worked on. He wanted it ready to go early the next morning. Fred told him it would be good to go within the next thirty minutes. As the butter bar performed a cursory inspection of the truck, he noticed the bed had quite a bit of dirt and chunks of dried mud strewn from front to back. He also noticed the cab had dirt clods on the floorboards.

"I want this truck bed cleaned out, as well as the cab's interior when I pick it up in the morning," barked the lieutenant.

Fred acknowledged his request and politely answered back, "Sir, I am the mechanic. I fix the broken vehicles. It is the responsibility of the operator to clean it."

The butter bar took a deep breath and attempted to authoritatively lower his voice in response, "I want this vehicle cleaned up. That's an order, you understand, soldier?"

Fred had already put in ten hours that day making an assortment of repairs on vehicles that were damaged by idiotic operators, no doubt akin to this knucklehead lieutenant. He gritted his teeth and, without looking up, dutifully answered, "Yes, sir."

Early the next morning, about two o'clock, May 15, 1969, the Vietcong (VC) launched a mortar attack on An Khe and hit the petroleum, oil, and lubricants (POL) depot. A huge fireball arose in the sky, unlike anything Fred had witnessed before. The flames licked hundreds of feet into the night sky and lit the area up for all to see the magnitude of damage. The boiling black smoke could not blanket the horror before them. Fred and another guy from the motor pool were on the reactionary team. They grabbed their weapons and headed toward their defense positions in anticipation of the VC overrunning An Khe. His counterpart was hit by shrapnel from a secondary explosion at the POL depot as they ran. He immediately went down. Fred went to his aid and then called for a medic. He would be okay but suffered a serious wound to his upper left leg. With his buddy in the care of the medics, Fred ran on to his predetermined defensive position. The night was chaos at its finest.

Things were crazy the remainder of the night. It was daylight before firefighters brought the flames under control. Fred later heard that over 150 assaults were made that very night on various US military locations in Vietnam. Fred glanced at the Seiko watch he purchased from the PX back at Fort Hood. It read 5:45 a.m. He headed toward the motor pool and prepared for yet another day with little to no sleep. As he approached the entryway, he saw the knucklehead lieutenant driving the deuce and a half truck toward him. He mumbled to himself, gave a half-hearted salute, and wished the young butter bar a mud-free trip that day.

Growing up on a farm, Fred figured out how to fix problems with easy and efficient solutions. It just seemed a natural thing for him. That was the reason his peers at the motor pool held him in such high regard. One phrase often repeated for those in the military was, "Can do, will do." That was Fred. He became the go-to guy when troubles arose. He was a hands-on fella, not afraid to let a little dirt and grime stop him from tackling the most difficult repairs.

There were times, however, when nothing made sense to Fred. That became an issue for him the morning after the attack. At roll call that morning, the motor pool troops were subjected to an in-ranks inspection and checked for any violations of Army Regulation 670-1. Fred thought to himself, *Are you kidding me? Most of the guys have been up all night securing the base, my buddy seriously injured, and the nincompoop pencil pushers from headquarters wanted to check for haircuts and shined boots! This is just plain stupid!*

Everyone who served in the military has encountered such bizarre demands by one of their superiors. It's affectionately called the Peter Principle. The Peter Principle recognized a tendency in most organizational structures, particularly the military, that allowed every soldier to climb the hierarchal ladder through promotions until they reach a level of their own incompetence. Such demands reflected a power play by those in charge. Their thought process became, "We're doing this not because it makes no sense, not because it's needed, not because it is a learning moment. We're doing this because I say so, and I am in charge."

Fred realized then that he needed to get away from the desk jockeys and two-fingered typists who sat on swiveled chairs and called the shots, all the while locked away in their remote headquarters office space. They obviously were out of touch with reality. As it turned out, Fred wouldn't have to wait long.

> *We ask you, brothers, to respect those who labor among you and are over you in the Lord and admonish you, and to esteem them very highly in love because of their work. Be at peace among yourselves. And we urge you, brothers, admonish the idle, encourage the fainthearted, help the weak, be patient with them all. See that no one repays anyone evil for evil, but always seek to do good to one another and to everyone.* **(1 Thessalonians 5:12–15)**

August 28, 1969, marked a turning point for Fred during his Vietnam tour. That day, a crew member of a Patton M48 armored tank completed his tour of duty. Fred received an assignment to replace the crewmember headed back home. His duty was simple. He accompanied the tank as its personal mechanic. Wherever it went, he went. Gone were the morning formations and in-rank inspections at the motor pool. His daily encounters with the paper-shufflers and pencil pushers became a thing of the past. Fred would be out on patrol for days and often weeks at a time.

The fifty-four ton Patton tank, vintage 1952, was a behemoth beast. It carried a crew of four with a 105-millimeter main gun and three 7.62 caliber machine guns. The 810-horsepower twin-turbo engine pushed the mass of metal up to 30 mph at top speed.

One of Fred's first trips out of An Khe sent him and several other tanks to a place affectionately called Happy Valley. The Happy Valley area was a major stronghold of the Vietcong (VC). The military's phonetic alphabet for the letters VC were Victor Charlie. Fred and his crew found themselves in Charlie's backyard. Happy Valley served as a storage area for Charlie's supplies where they shuttled ammunition and provisions south on Route 614. Fred and his tank crew's mission was to interrupt those activities and support ground infantry as needed. The valley was the sight of many fierce engagements with the enemy. Fred arrived with his tank crew just a month after Operation Oklahoma Hills ended, a three-month long clear-and-search mission by the marines. During that time, 44 US Marines were killed and another 439 sustained injuries that required medical evacuation. Another 456 US noncombat injuries were incurred. A body count of 589 dead VC somehow didn't make up for the lost 44 Marines. Despite the majority of the heavy lifting completed in the few months prior, it still remained a very hostile area. Fred preferred to call it Unhappy Valley.

Happy Valley's terrain consisted of dense undergrowth and elephant grass that grew up to ten feet tall. Critics initially thought the M48 tank would be ill-suited for the jungles of Vietnam, but they were proven wrong. The shock and firepower brought by the likes of Fred and his crew provided invaluable support for ground troops engaged in battle and defense of firebases.

Fred's tank commander (TC) preferred to stay off the beaten path as much as possible. Rather than drive down an existing roadway, Fred followed orders and steered the tank through the underbrush and jungle and easily knocked down bamboo trees that stood in his way. The danger of land mines planted by the VC along established roadways made the route least traveled the safest. Bulldozing through the jungle became a wise command decision. On an audio-tape sent back home, Fred told the story of getting his helmet ripped from his head as he peered out the driver's portal of his tank. A bamboo tree fell on the tank, rapped him on the side of the head, and nearly knocked him unconscious. Oftentimes the top-mounted exterior machine gun got ripped from it mounts by falling tree limbs.

About every week to ten days, Fred's tank crew returned to An Khe to refresh themselves from the daily grind of plowing through the jungle. He kept an Iowa flag in his hooch that hung on the wall as a reminder of home. Alongside was a *Playboy* calendar he used that counted down his time left in Vietnam. He hadn't updated it since his return from the first mission to Happy Valley. He got out his ink pen and marked the days already served. He had 208 days left.

Virtually all the information of Fred's Vietnam experience and for his story in this book came from audiotapes sent home to family. His daughter, Jenny, graciously gave me the opportunity to listen to his audio diary that she had copied onto a digital disc. As she and I met in the parking lot of Walmart for the exchange of information, she said to me, "Here, my dad gave me these tapes before he died. Thank you for telling his story. I wish I knew more," she told me as a tear trickled down her cheek. She wanted to know more yet not certain she could bear it all. She was proud of her father and his service for his country. What greater legacy could a father leave a child?

Much of what happened to the boys of Milo who served in Vietnam will remain a mystery. Some stories go untold, not because they are forgotten but because of the horribly vivid memories within the inner fiber of each soldier. Like a festered wound, the stories stay locked within their lips and slowly poisoned their soul. Some, like Fred, remained trapped in a battle within their own mind. For too many, the war is still being fought nearly fifty years later. Almost to a person, each Milo boy interviewed who served in Vietnam is a documented post-traumatic stress disorder (PTSD) sufferer.

Fred's audiotapes sent back home to Iowa stopped in late August 1969. We can only surmise that his assignment to the tank crew, doing missions in the battle-plagued Happy Valley region of Vietnam, kept him way, way too busy for an idle moment to send them home. Or what he experienced his last several months in Vietnam was not what he wanted to tell his family. Most likely, it was both.

Fred spent eleven months and eighteen days in Vietnam. He was awarded the Vietnam Campaign Ribbon as well as the Republic of Vietnam Gallantry Cross, with palm leaf for feats of valor and heroism in combat with hostile forces, the Vietnam Service Medal, the Army Commendation Medal, and the two Overseas Service Bars for duty of six months in a combat zone. Fred discharged from active duty with the US Army on March 23, 1970, at Fort Lewis, Washington. Fred died at age sixty-three, on September 15, 2011.

GARY LOUIS WADLE, E-4

United States Army
August 18, 1970–March 20, 1972

G ary was a typical rural Iowa boy that grew up on a dairy farm a few miles south of Milo. He was one of six kids that helped with the milking operation. He had four older sisters, Nancy, Anita, Mary, Kathie, and a younger brother, Jim. He knew hard work and, at times, as a teenager, took full responsibility of the dairy cattle when his parents embarked on an occasional trip out of state. As Gary relayed his upbringing on the farm, he commented, "For some reason, I never got to go on those three to five day trips my parents took. My younger brother, Jim, always went, but for some reason, Kathie and I remained on the farm and took care of all the chores and milking. As a youngster, I only left the state of Iowa a few times, and that was a short drive to the Lineville, Missouri, to buy fireworks."

Gary's time on the farm was short-lived. Just fifteen months after graduating from high school in 1969, he was drafted into the army. His first trip with the military took him to a familiar place—Missouri. Not his usual firecracker run to Lineville but a little further south to Fort Leonard Wood, Missouri, just 345 miles from home.

After basic training, Gary went to Fort Ord, California, for AIT and graduated with a MOS of 11B20, an infantryman. Like so many of the ground pounders the army produced, he needed no Ouija board to predict his destination. But he did ask the question, "Will I go to Vietnam?" The Ouija board planchette floated across the board and rested upon the word *yes*! As he lifted his finger, as if by magic, it drifted over to "GOODBYE."

The presidential election held in November 1968, put Richard Nixon into the White House early in January of 1969, based in part on his campaign promise to end the war in Vietnam. It became a precarious time in America. By 1969, the American death toll in Vietnam exceeded fifty thousand. Antiwar rallies were rampant across the country as protesters burned their draft cards in defiance.

While on an Asian tour in Guam, on July 25, 1969, President Nixon introduced what became known as the Nixon Doctrine (also recognized as the Guam Doctrine). In that announcement, Nixon stated the United States would keep its treaty obligations with its Asian allies, but America would encourage and expect those Asian countries to be responsible for their own defense. This doctrine would later be known as the Vietnamization plan that allowed America to back out of the Vietnam War and find *peace with honor*. The South Vietnamese, in turn, needed to stand up for the defense their own country and limit their dependency on US forces.

On April 28, 1970, Nixon authorized the invasion of Cambodia by US forces to disrupt the supply line from North Vietnam. That decision became a controversial one. US Secretary of Defense Melvin Laird argued against the decision. Presidential Assistant Henry Kissinger's top three aides who were members of the National Security Council resigned in protest of the action. Was Nixon really wanting peace for America and removal of US troops from war-torn South East Asia with his Vietnamization plan or was he ratcheting up military efforts with the invasion of Cambodia?

Over 250 state department employees sent a letter to then Secretary of State William Rogers and criticized the decision. United States Senator John Cooper from Kentucky and Senator Frank Church from Idaho drafted legislative initiatives that limited the war-making powers of the president. The bill passed the US Senate but was defeated in the US House a Representatives. What emerged was a modified version of the bill that prohibited the introduction of US troops into Laos or Thailand. Confusion and indecision ruled the political arena which queued up the music to which the military danced.

Draft-age Americans became equally frustrated. Because of the Cambodian invasion, Kent State University organized an antiwar protest on May 4, 1970. During that protest, Ohio National Guard soldiers opened fire. Four college students were shot and killed. The antiwar movement in America became even more emboldened. Just ten days later, another college campus protest at Jackson State College in Mississippi resulted in the death of two students and twelve wounded when state police opened fire on a women's dormitory.

All these events played out during Gary Wadle's enlistment. He became an unwilling pawn to the craziness of the political decisions made on his behalf as an American soldier. He wondered, did anyone have a clue? Just as the Ouija predicted, Gary received orders for Vietnam. The chain of events that followed left no doubt in Gary's mind that, indeed, not everyone was on the same page of sheet music. While at Fort Ord, California, his orders sent him to Fort Dix, New Jersey, where he would embark on his trip to Vietnam. Crazy, he thought, simply crazy. New Jersey was 3,009 additional miles in the opposite direction from Vietnam.

Unknown to either him or myself, we both were in New Jersey in April 1971. Gary to Fort Dix and myself on duty at adjacent McGuire AFB. When he passed through the airport terminal headed for Vietnam, I was on duty with the USAF less than fifty yards away, located at the flight line crash rescue fire department. Like two ships that passed in the darkness of night, we never saw each other.

Gary arrived at Da Nang Air Base in Vietnam on April 8, 1971. He reported to the orderly room and awaited his duty assignment and location. To his surprise, the desk sergeant told him to "hang loose" for a day or two at the transient barracks and check back in.

In 1970, there were 334,600 US troops in Vietnam, down from the record number of 536,100 in 1968 at the height of the war. In 1971, that number dropped in half to 156,800, and down even lower to 24,200 in 1972. Gary arrived in Vietnam at a time when things began to ramp down in conjunction with Nixon's Vietnamization plan. Could the Ouija board have been wrong? Two days later, Gary checked back with the desk sergeant. The response he received left him dumbfounded. The sergeant told Gary his orders for Vietnam and been cancelled, and he would be reassigned. Gary stuttered and stammered as he tried to get words out of his mouth. "What? Why? When? And most importantly, where?"

With an envious reply, the desk sergeant told him, "You heard me right, you lucky dog. Why? Because the army says so. When? You ship out in three days. Where? You're going to Germany. Any other questions?"

Gary's two older sisters, Mary and Kathie, were cheerleaders for the high school sports teams back in the mid-1960s. They performed all kinds of acrobatic jumps, backflips, and cartwheels as they encouraged the student section of the crowd to jump and shout with joy with each touchdown and team victory. While in school, Gary couldn't do any of that stuff on his best day. But that day in Vietnam, he didn't need to because he walked on air as he headed back to the barracks and packed for his trip out of Vietnam. He was there for just one week, hardly time for a cup of coffee. His recollection of Vietnam were summed up in a few short words, "It was miserably hot, and a stinky odor filled the air."

> Then the king said to Ittai the Gittite, "Why do you also go with us? Go back and stay with the king, for you are a foreigner and also an exile from your home. You came only yesterday, and shall I today make you wander about with us, since I go, I know not where? Go back and take your brothers with you, and may the LORD show steadfast love and faithfulness to you." (*2 Samuel 15:19–21*)

Gary flew back from Vietnam through Fort Lewis, Washington. Then after a brief stop in Milo, he returned to Fort Dix, and then on to Germany. In his first twenty years growing up in Milo, he never strayed too far from the farm and, for the most part, never left Iowa. In a few short months, under the direction of Uncle Sam, he traveled coast to coast in the United States—twice—and made the 12,666-mile trip from Vietnam to Germany.

Gary arrived at Hohenfels, Germany, located just sixty miles from the Czech border near the small town of Parsberg. There he was assigned to Company B, 2-6 Infantry Brigade, USAREUR (United States Army, Europe), part of NATO's Central Army Group. While there, he performed joint military maneuvers with multinational forces. When quizzed further about exactly what he did during his time in Germany, Gary grinned and simply stated, "I drank lots of German beer and fraternized with the locals." At $.25 per beer, a single Deutsche Mark went a long way in 1971 with a conversion rate of $1.00–3.66 DM.

Gary discharged from active duty with the US Army on March 20, 1972, at Fort Dix, New Jersey. He served one year, seven months, and three days with the US Army, of which one year, one month, and twelve days were spent overseas. His military award included the German Occupational Medal, the longest active military award of the US Armed Forces.

DANNY LEE
DYKSTRA, E-4

United States Army
March 30, 1971–December 18, 1972

I first met Dan Dykstra in 1961, on the Little League ball field in Milo, when he was just ten years old. It was my last year on the team as one of the older boys, a 140-pound pitcher, just a few months shy of my thirteenth birthday. It was Dan's first year. Dan played a tough third base and had a very deliberate side-arm throw to first base that had so much zip and velocity, it always tailed away from the runner. Dan and his younger brother, Dwayne, grew up on a farm east of Milo. Both were involved in sports from those Little League days through high school. Even years later, Dan and I reconnected as young men who competed against each other on the local fast-pitch softball team. He still played a tough third base, and I still pitched. His throws still tailed away from the runner. My pitches went from overhand fastballs to underhanded, hard-breaking curveballs. Those were great years.

Dan graduated from high school in the spring of 1970 and enrolled at Iowa State University that fall. His advanced education became short-lived. He quit school that first year, and by the spring of 1971, Uncle Sam knocked on his door.

The draft number of 125 in 1971 became the pivotal number. Anyone's draft number above 125 became safe from conscription. Dan's draft number, based on his birthday of November 29, was drawn at number 99. Dan held a distinctive honor. He became the very last person during the Vietnam era to be drafted into the US Army from Warren County, Iowa. For the year 1971, the military drafted into service just 98,000 troops nationwide, down significantly from the 382,000 drafted in 1966. The war began to wind down but not before latching onto the third baseman from Milo. Dan left for basic training at Fort Leonard Wood, Missouri, on March 30, 1971.

Upon completion of boot camp, Dan's next stop sent him to Fort Polk, Louisiana, where he received AIT (advanced infantry training) and emerged with a MOS of 11B20R6, a light weapons infantryman. Dan developed some concern about his next destination in the army. The entire group of recruits that finished AIT at Fort Polk, just ahead of him, all were sent directly to Vietnam. Dan assumed the worst and hoped for the best.

> *But blessed is the one who trusts in the LORD, whose confidence is in him. They will be like a tree planted by the water that sends out its roots by the stream. It does not fear when heat comes; its leaves are always green. It has no worries in a year of drought and never fails to bear fruit. (**Jeremiah 17:7–8**)*

Once Dan completed AIT, he received good news. He would not go to Vietnam. He took a short leave and returned to Milo before his next assignment.

In July 1971, the US Army sent Dan to Fort Bliss, Texas, to the air defense training school where he was assigned to the US Army Air Defense Command. There he received instructions on visual aircraft identification, not just for US aircraft but aircraft worldwide. That became a tremendous undertaking. Of the thirty soldiers in the program, half washed out before completion due to the rigors of instruction. Worldwide, in 1970, there existed hundreds of various types of aircraft for identification. Those ranged from propeller-driven piston poppers to turbo props to jet engine, fighter aircraft, cargo carriers, assault aircraft, bombers, observation planes, electronic jammer aircraft, and passenger aircraft. Various configurations included above-wing fuselage, overwing fuselage, swept wing, and tail draggers. Engine configurations also identified the type of aircraft as well as landing gear types. Indeed, it became a daunting task to simply look into the sky with binoculars and identify the type of aircraft and which country flew the aircraft.

Once Dan finished the aircraft identification course, he continued training at Fort Bliss with a classified air defense program that focused on the FIM-43 Redeye missile. The Redeye was a man-portable shoulder-fired weapon that launched a surface-to-air missile with a conventional high explosive warhead that used an infrared-sensing device as a means to home in on low-flying aircraft. The FIM-43 Redeye became a gigantic leap forward for ground troops in lieu of the conventional .50 caliber antiaircraft machine gun. The Redeye weighed a mere eighteen pounds and had an effective firing range of 14,800 feet with a 2.35-pound explosive warhead. Its speed could reach Mach 1.7 to hunt down its target.

The FIM-43 Redeye had some operational shortcomings, the most significant being a head-on engagement. With the heat-seeking infrared homing devices, the missiles could only engage the aircraft once it had already left the area and most likely dropped its ordnance. The Redeye was, however, the direct predecessor to today's highly effective FIM-92 Stinger missile.

While at Fort Bliss, Dan became involved with the training of both Turkish and Israeli soldiers on the use and implementation of the FIM-43. Though he never fired the Redeyes at a live target in a war zone, he conducted multiple demonstrations of the weapon for the foreign trainees.

To his surprise, in September 1971, Dan received orders to Fort Carson, Colorado, and assigned to the 1-8th Infantry Battalion. Just like many Milo boys who were reassigned, the actual job performed at their new destination often failed to match up with their MOS. Dan was an infantryman with missile training. At Fort Carson, the army assigned him as a mechanic at the motor pool. His agricultural background and mechanical aptitude learned when he helped his dad, Bob, on the family farm east of Milo served him well. There he fixed broken machinery and performed periodic maintenance on trucks, tractors, combines, augers and a plethora of other farming equipment. A 1914 edition of the *Country Gentleman*, a publication from a Philadelphia agricultural journal, first said it best, "You can take the boy out of the country, but you can't take the country out of the boy." The US Army certainly got a bargain when Dan signed on and put on the uniform of a US soldier.

Dan discharged from active duty on December 18, 1972, at Fort Carson, Colorado. He served one year, eight months, and nineteen days.

ROBERT OHNEMUS, CHIEF PETTY OFFICER, E-7, RETIRED

United States Navy
July 26, 1971–December 31, 1991

B ob grew up on a small farm three miles east of Milo along with his younger brother, Bruce. He graduated from Southeast Warren High School in 1969. It was on the farm, during conversations with his father, Carl, that Bob determined he wanted no part of the US Army. His father served in the army during the Korean War and had nothing good to say about his military experience. On the other hand, his mother's three brothers all had previously served in the US Navy and had gleaming reports of time spent

sailing the seas. As it became apparent that Uncle Sam would soon be knocking on Bob's door, he elected to join the navy on July 26, 1971. On that same day, the *Apollo 15* spacecraft launched its fourth mission to the moon. Little did Bob know at the time, the role he would play in future Apollo missions.

Bob performed his basic training at the Great Lakes Naval Base in Chicago, and upon completion of his advanced schooling as an aviation supply technician, the USN assigned him to an Essex-class aircraft carrier, the USS *Ticonderoga* (CVS 14), out of San Diego. It carried a crew of 1,615 sailors and about eighty aircraft at any given time. It was aboard the *Ticonderoga*, on April 27, 1972, that his ship participated in the splashdown and recovery of the *Apollo 16* module as it returned from the moon mission with astronauts John Young and Charles Duke aboard. He watched from the flight deck as the module splashed into the Pacific Ocean, 216 miles southeast of Christmas Island.

Again on December 19, 1972, the USS *Ticonderoga* served as the recovery ship for the Apollo 17 mission, the last of the Apollo series, with astronauts Gene Cernan, Harrison Schmidt, and Ronald Evans aboard. It was also the sixth and last of the lunar module missions. The crew returned to Earth with a successful splashdown 350 nautical miles southeast of American Samoa and brought back to Earth 243 pounds of moon rocks for further examination by scientists. During the mission, the crew spent seventy-five hours on the surface of the moon and traversed 30.5 kilometers in the lunar rover vehicle. Bob was front and center, eyes wide open, as the Milo boy witnessed these historic events in the US space program firsthand.

In 1973, Bob received a new assignment aboard the aircraft carrier USS *Kitty Hawk*. The ship maintained a crew of 5,624 sailors (one hundred times the population of Milo) and about eighty-five aircraft. The *Kitty Hawk* sailed out of San Francisco en route to the South China Sea with a stop at Pearl Harbor. On December 11, 1973, somewhere west of Hawaii in the Pacific Ocean, during some routine maintenance performed on the ship's fuel oil systems, a gasket failed and sprayed atomized fuel into the number 1 engine room. A fire broke out which put the ship at general quarters for thirty-eight hours. Thick black smoke filled the bowels of the ship, and all personnel were ordered topside on the flight deck. Two of the ship's three engines were shut down during the fire. Subsequently the *Kitty Hawk* began to list at 7 degrees on the portside. As a result, many of the aircraft were shifted to the starboard side in an attempt to balance the ship until the fire could be contained and two of the propulsion systems restored. After three days, the *Kitty Hawk* gingerly slipped into Subic Bay, Philippines, for repairs. Six sailors died in the fire, another thirty-four were treated for smoke inhalation and minor injuries to include some broken bones. Bob made it through the disaster unscathed. Ironically I was just a few miles north on the McArthur Highway stationed at Clark Air Base during that time frame. Neither Bob nor I were aware of the each other's location. Bob's tour aboard the *Kitty Hawk* ended in January 1975.

Bob certainly earned his sea legs after four years aboard two carriers. By then, he made the commitment to make the USN a career. He enjoyed the military and the opportunity it provided him.

Samuel Johnson, an English writer who lived in the 1700s, might have had it right when he said, "No man will be a sailor who has contrivance enough to get himself into a jail; for being in a ship is being in a jail, with the chance of being drowned…a man in a jail has more room, better food, and commonly better company. Thus is the life of a sailor."

Well, that wasn't quite the way it was, according to Bob Ohnemus.

Shore duty took Bob to Pensacola, Florida, from 1975–1978. While there, he had a chance encounter with two other Milo boys, Steve Canter and Dick Van Syoc. Both of them career navy men as well. Bob recalled drinking a few beers at Richie's lounge located just outside the main gate at the naval station on West Navy Boulevard when in walked two swabbies he knew. Who could have imagined that? The lounge still exists at the same location today, some forty years later.

Yet another shore duty for Bob came forth after his Pensacola assignment. In 1978, Naval Air Station Cubi Point became his next stop. Cubi Point was located adjacent to Subic Bay, Philippines. Cubi Point served as the primary maintenance repair and supply center for over four hundred carrier-based aircraft of the US Navy's Seventh Fleet in the Pacific. As an aviation supply technician, Bob kept busy ordering parts and facilitating repairs for the multitude of aircraft in and out of Cubi Point.

It wasn't a situation of all work and no play, however. Any GI who passed through Subic Bay or Cubi Point invariably had a story to tell about their adventures in Olongapo City, the bar-laden, massage parlor community nestled just outside the gates of the naval base and the San Miguel beer consumed. The average age of a sailor at either Cubi Point or Subic Bay was about twenty-two. Stepping foot into a bar on shore leave after several months at sea, full of testosterone and a pocket full of money, left many a drunken sailors wondering, "What happened?" With little fiscal or moral restraint, many a sailor fell prey to the ill vices that lingered at every corner. Many of the bar girls wore numbers on their dresses instead of their name. It was just easier to remember. "I'll have a number 6, and can you supersize it?" The Irish Rovers, a musical group capitalized on the long known shanty song first heard in 1839, "What Shall We Do with a Drunken Sailor?" The lyrics are known by every swabbie that sailed the seas.

> Hey, hey, up she rises, hey, hey up she rises
> What shall we do with a drunken sailor
> Shave his belly with a rusty razor
> Put him in a long boat till he's sober
> Early in the morning.

Bob left the Philippines in 1981 and headed back to the United States. His destination became the naval training center at Meridian, Mississippi. There he became an instructor for new recruits learning the trade as an aviation supply technician. He served as an instructor for four years. In June of 1981, he received a promotion to chief petty officer. The rank held a dual role, that of a technical expert and as a leader but with greater emphasis in a leadership capacity. Advancement to chief petty officer was recognized as the most significant promotion in US Naval enlisted rankings.

In November 1985, Bob again received orders for a new assignment to NAS Keflavick (NASKEF), Iceland. It was located on the Reykjanes Peninsula in the southwestern portion of Iceland. NASKEF provided all support facilities, including aviation operations, particularly the P-3 Orion aircraft as well as support for twenty-five different commands to include the USAF, USMC, US Army, US Coast Guard, as well as components from Canada, Demark, Netherlands, and Norway.

While Bob was assigned at NASKEF, he again was present at a historic location. It was at NASKEF, on October 11, 1986, that President Ronald Reagan and Soviet leader Mikhail Gorbachev met and discussed the multibillion-dollar American Strategic Defense Initiative (SDI), better known as the Star Wars Initiative, where space technology incorporated a protective shield as a defense against a nuclear attack. Reagan refused to budge on the program and accused Gorbachev of attending in bad faith. The meeting ended the next day and, as history proved, marked a turning point in the Cold War between the two countries.

Not to stay in one place too long, Chief Petty Officer Ohnemus left KASKEF in November 1988, and headed back to NAS Meridian, Mississippi, where he again assumed the role as an instructor.

His final assignment placed him aboard the USS *Nassua* (LAH-4) from December 1990 through April 1991. The USS *Nassua* was a Tarawa class amphibious assault ship that carried a crew of 964 sailors and was part of the Command Amphibious Group 2 with admiral staff that sailed the Persian Gulf in conjunction with Operation Desert Shield. Bob saw ports of call in Saudi Arabia, Bahrain, Oman, Yemen, Kuwait, and the United Arab Emirates (UAE).

Bob retired from the USN on December 31, 1991, after twenty years of service. He currently resides in Meridian, Mississippi.

STANLEY RAY MERRELL, SERGEANT, E-4

United States Air Force
September 16, 1971–September 15, 1975

Stan was one of five kids who grew up on a farm just a couple of miles south of Milo. The farm was known by local residences as the one with the big round red barn. As a youngster and into my adult years, I drove past that barn what seemed like a million times and always remembered the comment about the barn made by my dad some fifty years prior. He said, "You know, son, a guy killed himself in that old barn years ago."

Astonished, I replied, "He did? What happened?"

My dad chuckled and continued, "He ran himself to death looking for a corner to corral a cow." I chuckled, too, and must admit that I passed that same joke onto my own children when pointing out that old red round barn south of Milo as we drove by.

Stan's older brother, John, joined the USAF a few years after graduating from high school in 1968 as an enlisted airman, and made a career wearing the air force blue. He retired as a junior-grade officer (0-3) after he received a commission several years into his enlistment. Stan's younger brother, Dean, enlisted in the US Army and served three years (June 1974–June 1977). He worked as an intelligence specialist at the Pentagon. Stan's real desire for the military leaned toward the US Navy, but in his own words, "I swam like a rock. I still can't swim even today, so I opted to join the air force in 1971, right out of high school."

Stan left for basic training, headed to Lackland AFB, San Antonio, Texas, in September, the same month in which Frank Lauterbur coached his first game as the University of Iowa head as football coach. Fortunately for Stan, his time in the USAF proved far more productive than Coach Lauterbur's pitiful first year coaching record of 1–10.

Upon completion of basic training in November, the USAF sent Stan to Shephard AFB, located in Wichita Falls, Texas. There he entered training as a C-130 aircraft mechanic with an AFSC of 43151F. In March of 1972, Stan's first duty assignment as a C-130 maintainer took him to Elmendorf AFB, located in Anchorage, Alaska.

Stan became entranced with the natural beauty of Alaska. The wildlife, the mountains, the fresh air, the vast open spaces mesmerized the Iowa farm boy. The landscape differed so much from what Stan knew that he became awestruck with its beauty. In addition to all the hunting and fishing opportunities, Stan also partook in the sport of snow skiing. "I even got to experience a couple of earthquakes while in Alaska," he added. Another unusual experience included the summer months of the midnight sun.

> *Has the rain a father, or who has begotten the drops of dew? From whose womb did the ice come forth, and who has given birth to the frost of heaven? The waters become hard like stone, and the face of the deep is frozen.* ***(Job 38:28–30)***

Stan's deployment at Elmendorf AFB wasn't all play and no work. His mechanical skills kept the C-130 Hercules aircraft airborne as they daily ferried their cargo payloads to smaller bases along the Aleutian chain. On two occasions, Stan deployed in temporary duty status (TDY) to Sondrestom, Greenland, located sixty miles north of the Arctic Circle, in support of the Dutch Air Force radar sites located there. After his time in Greenland, Stan realized the Iowa winters aren't so bad after all.

As the year 1973 came to a close, Stan's time in Alaska drew to an end. He received permanent change of station (PCS) orders to Hill AFB, Utah, where he became a part of the 1550th Consolidated Aircraft Maintenance Squadron (CAMS), Military Airlift Command (MAC). His orders required him to report to Hill AFB by March of 1974.

Back in Iowa, as 1973 came to a close, it wasn't a good year for Coach Lauterbur at the University of Iowa. The Hawkeye football team went 0–11 on the gridiron. The worst record in the history of the school. Coach Lauterbur had his marching orders too.

Just one month after his relocation to Hill AFB, Stan had one of the most surreal experiences imaginable. On April 22, 1974, his dormitory roommate, a guy by the name of Dale Pierre, robbed a stereo store in Ogden, Utah, of $24,000 in stereo equipment and then proceeded to kill multiple occupants inside the store. An anonymous tip led police to Hill AFB where they found some of the stereo equipment in Pierre's possession and personal belongings of the victims in a nearby dumpster.

The Standard-Examiner, the local newspaper for Southern Utah, described the crime as one of the most heinous acts in Ogden's history. Pierre and accomplice, William Andrews, entered the store with the intent to rob it, but when two people entered during the crime, he took them hostage. The store occupants included a twenty-year-old male worker and an eighteen-year-old female worker as well as a sixteen-year-old male shopper. The two who entered the store were the parents of the two employees who came to pick up their children. Pierre panicked. He relocated his captives into the basement where he forced them to drink drain fluid in hopes it would kill them. When they did not immediately die, he resorted to the execution of each individual with gunshots to the head. Pierre shot the mother of the female employee, and she died immediately. Prior to shooting the eighteen-year-old female employee, Pierre raped her, then shot her in the head. The twenty-year-old male employee also was shot and died at the scene. The father of the twenty-year-old was shot in the head but did not die immediately. Out of bullets, Pierre jammed an ink pen into the ear of the father and forcibly kicked it deep into his skull. Unbeknownst to the murderer, the father miraculously survived but suffered extensive brain damage. He was able to relay to the authorities that two black men were the perpetrators of the crime. A third suspect, nineteen-year-old Keith Roberts, was also apprehended and identified as the driver of the getaway car.

The crime not only shocked those stationed at Hill AFB, it reprehensibly changed the psyche for the entire city of Ogden, Utah. The crime complicated race relations within the community for the many, many years that followed. It was a time and situation that is forever etched in Stan's memory. How could someone he knew, his roommate no less, even though oh so casually, commit such brutal acts?

Pierre was executed on August 28, 1987, and Andrews on July 30, 1992, for the murders they committed.

> *If anyone kills a person, the murderer shall be put to death on the evidence of witnesses. But no person shall be put to death on the testimony of one witness. Moreover, you shall accept no ransom for the life of a murderer, who is guilty of death, but he shall be put to death.* **(Numbers 35:30–31)**

Stan discharged from active duty with the USAF on September 15, 1975, and returned to Milo where he engaged in farming. It wasn't long before he realized that the long hours working the fields wasn't exactly his cup of tea. He left Milo and took a job in Des Moines as a network administrator for the Iowa Department of Human Services.

Stan kept his ties with the military, however. He has been a member of the American Legion for thirty-one years and is currently a district commander.

GOODBYE, NEW JERSEY

I received orders to Clark Air Base, Philippines, in October 1972. As much as my two and one-half years of duty in New Jersey opened my eyes to how different things were, in other parts of the country, when compared to growing up in Milo, the journey ahead to South East Asia erased every measuring stick previously known to me.

Once again, Judi and I packed our belongings and headed across country in our little red car. We made a brief stop in Milo to visit relatives, then further on to the state of Washington where my mother lived. The East Coast to West Coast trip took about ten days. My departure to Clark Air Base originated from Travis AFB, California, located just north of San Francisco. I had just two days left before I said goodbye to America. Judi flew back to Iowa and stayed with her mother until I got situated in the Philippines. Neither of us were certain if she would be eligible to join me since my orders distinctly expressed "unaccompanied tour of duty."

I had never been to San Francisco before, but I knew someone that was there. My childhood buddy from Milo, Ed Mosher, had enrolled in mortician school, and I informed him of my impending arrival. He picked me up at the San Francisco airport in a 1957 black Plymouth, a car from his father's fleet of vehicles from Mosher's Funeral Home in Milo. We hadn't seen each other in over two years and much had changed. He no longer drove the burgundy-colored split-window Corvette. He already had been married and divorced from his high school sweetheart. He now was engaged to an attractive gal he met in Switzerland. Her name was Emma, but she went by the nickname of Boya. They resided in an efficiency apartment within the funeral home, where he helped with services between his mortician classes.

We talked about the good old days growing up in Milo. On the Little League team, Ed was the catcher, and I pitched. On the high school football team, he was the fullback, and I was the quarterback. He played center on the basketball team, and I was the shooting guard. He threw the shot put and discus on the track team while I was the middle distance runner. We were connected at the hip in many ways. We reminisced most of the day about various shenanigans that occupied our youth.

I accompanied him to a class at the mortician school that afternoon. That became an unforgettable macabre experience for me as we walked into the morgue with dozens of cadavers in the room that were used to practice facial reconstruction. The distinctive odor of embalming fluid and formaldehyde filled the air. Those few hours freaked me out. I had seen dead bodies before, but the seemingly irreverence of the morgue gripped me like a bad chest cold. I wanted out of there as soon as possible. Ed chuckled at my uneasiness. "What's the matter, Willie, you scared?"

Oh, I told him in no uncertain terms, "I'm not scared but have a bad case of the heebie-jeebies. Let's get the heck out of here. It's time for a drink."

We picked up a bottle of Jack Daniel's whiskey and headed back to the apartment. The rest of that day was a blur. By late evening, the bottle was empty, and we both were snockered. My flight to the Philippines was scheduled to depart the next afternoon. I maintained enough sobriety to know that I better call it quits and give myself enough time the next day to make it to Travis AFB. I asked Ed, "Where do you want me to sleep?"

He pointed to an access door that led to a balcony that overlooked the chapel of the funeral home. I grabbed a pillow and dropped to the floor to sober up and sleep off the bender. I went out like a snuffed candle. It seemed as though only a few hours had passed, and I awoke to an accordion playing some weird polka song. I thought Ed might have turned on a radio to some loud crazy tune just to annoy me. He was a good one for playing pranks like that. I blinked and opened my eyes and realized it was daylight. I glanced at my watch and it was 11:00 a.m. Holy cow! I had to be at the base in four hours to catch my flight. Time to get up and moving. The accordion music continued, and then a violin joined in. I rolled on my shoulder and looked through the railing from the balcony. There directly below me was an open casket with some guy on his back, facing up. Several mourners surrounded the casket as some guy worked the squeeze-box and continued to play. Suddenly they all broke into song. That became my signal to get out of there. Not wanting to disturb the ceremony below and hide my presence, I belly-crawled on the floor to the access door and back into the efficiency apartment. There Ed and Boya were still crashed on the sofa sleeper. "Time to get up, guys, I've got a plane to catch," I shouted to them as the drill instructor voice in me came out. "What's a matter, Ed, can't hold your booze?" I chided him as he appeared much more hungover than I. Then I asked, "What kind of funeral service was going on beneath the balcony? I've never witnessed anything thing quite like that before."

"Oh, it's a Gypsy funeral," Ed answered. "Different isn't it? We're not in Milo, this is San Francisco, Willie. Lots of weird stuff goes on here."

Ed drove me to Travis AFB in time to catch my flight to the Philippines. It was October 21, 1972. I followed news reports about the political unrest in Manila and became somewhat worried when I discovered President Ferdinand Marcos declared martial law for his country a few weeks prior. There were reports of terrorist bombings and a staged assassination attempt against the country's secretary of defense, Juan Ponce Enrile. The first thought that came to mind was the possibility that my wife, Judi, would not be able to join me with all the hubbub that existed in the Philippine archipelago, known as the Pearl of the Orient.

The flight to Clark Air Base took over sixteen hours. Our aircraft, a chartered stretch DC-8, island-hopped from Hawaii to Wake Island then to Guam, and finally the Philippines. When I landed at Clark, I reset my watch as I gained a full day after I crossed the international date line. When I stepped off the plane, I just as well have landed on Mars. I had never been to such a place. The lush green island with bamboo and banana trees all around, the oppressive heat, and the sweltering humidity immediately grabbed me both visually and physically.

WILLIS JAMES VANDER LINDEN, SPECIALIST FOURTH CLASS, E-4

United States Army
October 19, 1972–October 18, 1974

Willis grew up on a farm a few miles south of Milo, one of four children of Dean and Loraine Vander Linden. His father served as a gunnery instructor during WWII for the B-17 bombers. Willis had an older sister, Pat, an older brother, Chuck, and younger sister, Cheryl.

Just like most of the other Milo boys, Willis had fond memories of growing up in Milo. As a farm kid, he became somewhat tethered to the fence post as one of two sons that helped their dad with farm chores. What seemed mundane to some, but not to Willis, were the activities associated with the Boy Scouts. Troop 136 served as a tremendous social outlet for both Willis and Chuck. Their dad, Dean, became actively involved as an adult leader of the Milo Scouts. Willis recalled, "I just loved going to Camp Mitigwa with the scouts located near Woodward, Iowa."

Fond memories surfaced as he visualized the 450-acre scout camp located near the Des Moines River. "On the hills, above the river, in among the trees, flies the flag of Camp Mitigwa, waving in the breeze." There he and a multitude of other Milo boys, over the years, participated in a hodgepodge of activities that big city kids only dreamed about. A military-style regimented rifle range gave youngsters the opportunity to handle a .22 caliber bolt action rifle that tested their marksmanship as well as a skeet range that used bird shot on clay pigeons captivated the young teenagers. Swimming, hiking, axmanship, canoeing, and archery kept them busy from the moment they stepped into the camp. I too attended Camp Mitigwa for several years and vividly recalled the troop formations by the flag-pole each evening when Willis and I stood side by side at attention, as a special detail of Boy Scouts lowered the US flag. The bugler's retreat sounded over the public address system as we wiggled our toes and fidgeted in an attempt—as best we could—to stand still. The retreat ceremony served two purposes: first, it marked the end of the day after our evening meal at the dining facility, and second, it placed before us the desire to pay respect for our flag.

The US military maintains that same protocol on their installations. Whenever revelry or retreat plays within earshot, each and every soldier, when outside, stops immediately any activity and stands at attention. Even kids on the playground at every military base understand the reverence for our country's flag when the call to colors is played. They jump from their swings or stop when on their bicycles and pay homage to the bugler's call. Prior to movies shown at on-base theaters, whether a matinee or evening showing, the national anthem is played on the big screen, and everyone puts down their popcorn and stands at attention. It is the American way, as it should be. A brief moment in time, a mere forty seconds, to show respect for the US flag that so many soldiers from previous conflicts gave their lives to protect and defend.

I often wondered how many National Football League (NFL) players ever wore a military uniform and shouldered a rifle? Instead of playing Pop Warner football during their adolescent years, no doubt, time spent as a Boy Scout might have served them better.

I would assume the number is low based on the behavior of some professional NFL athletes today with their antics of kneeling with blatant disrespect for our country's flag.

In 1962, as Willis stood at attention in his scout uniform and peered upward as the US flag at Camp Mitigwa lowered against the backdrop of a setting sun, little did he know how the call of a bugler's trumpet would impact his future. Was it an omen? Perhaps so. But I am sure as a twelve-year-old kid, Willis had no clue of the opportunity that awaited him. It would dramatically impact the manner in which he served his country in a way that no other Milo boy could imagine.

I best knew Willis during our time together as young kids in Milo Boy Scout Troop 136. Our weekly meetings together, and a few campouts per year, pretty much summed it up. That time only amounted to a few years from ages eleven to fourteen. Our paths crossed again in high school as both he and I participated together on the school's athletic track team. Willis was a distance runner. He had a slight build and the lung capacity to gut out those grueling long-distance races. I had difficulty with anything over an 880-yard race. That wasn't the case for Willis. The longer the race, the better he performed.

Willis also was a member of the school band where he played trumpet. I can still remember him as he blew his horn with a contorted facial expression as a member of the pep band, all the while as I ran up and down the basketball court. Willis certainly had his own style, just like Dizzy Gillespie or Louis Armstrong. He would pucker up, and by the time the tune finished, his face became beet red. If I had only put forth the same effort on the basketball court as Willis did blowing his horn, our team would have won many more games.

After high school graduation in 1968, Willis went to Simpson College and studied music. Coincidentally I was a sophomore at Simpson at the same time, seeking a degree in English. Looking back now, I can attest that Willis was much more serious about getting his degree in music than I was in obtaining mine in English. Very much like the efforts we both put forth during the high school basketball games. I was there just as a participant, casually dribbling down the court, and Willis was there with his ever-present passion, blowing on his trumpet. Needless to say, he graduated in four years with a bachelor of arts degree in music. It would take me another ten years to finish my degree. While both of us were enrolled at Simpson, we held a (2-S) student deferment for the draft. Willis was number 28 with a birthday of June 5. My number was 48. Uncle Sam would soon knock on both of our doors.

Willis graduated from college in May of 1972. He had already interviewed and secured a job as a music teacher with a school in Buffalo Center, Iowa. That was his plan. However, it was not the plan of the US Army. He received his draft notice within a few months of graduation. On October 19, 1972, Willis became a draftee soldier with the US Army. His first stop became Fort Leonard Wood, Missouri.

Basic training became a breeze for Willis. He still retained his physique as a distance runner in high school, he was college-educated, and knew what a hard day's work meant with his time on the farm. From his days at the rifle range at Camp Mitigwa, he was also familiar with handling a gun. The eight weeks of marching, push-ups, marksmanship training, and polished boots became a cakewalk for him.

An interesting sidenote surfaced during Willis's time at Fort Leonard Wood. While he participated in live fire training on the range, he requested permission to be excused for a few minutes to visit the latrine. "Permission granted." Barked the range instructor. "Make it quick and don't dribble down your leg."

As Willis stood inside the outhouse and scanned the rafters for an active hornet's nest, he blinked his eyes in bewilderment. There on the inside wall of the outhouse latrine was an inscription that read, "Milo, Iowa." Willis grinned, finished his business, then clicked his heels together and said aloud, "There's no place like home, there's no place like home." He ejected a single M16 cartridge from the magazine of his rifle and, with the tip of the lead bullet, scratched "ditto" below the greeting. There had been other Milo boys before him, and indeed, others would follow.

Like all new recruits, Willis was quizzed about any particular skills he might already have acquired before induction into the military. He quickly stepped forward and raised his hand and told the drill instructor, "I'm a musician."

The crusty sergeant squinted his eyes, then smiled and said in his Southern Texas accent, "We don't get many fellas like you through here, soldier. What do you do, sing pretty songs?"

Private Vander Linden respectfully answered, "No, sir, I play the trumpet." An audition to demonstrate his skills was arranged within a week. Willis made an audio recording for review by the US Army School of Music. That was it, or so Willis thought. Then the military way, as known by those who have ever put on the uniform, played out to its own double treble clef. Unfortunately for Willis, the sheet music was totally wrong.

Once finished with basic training, he received orders to quartermaster school at Fort Lee, Virginia. Willis thought to himself, *Surely the US Army didn't tell me a fib, or did they?* Dutifully Willis reported to Fort Lee and began advanced schooling as a quartermaster. A quartermaster's responsibilities included the storage, supervision, and distribution of supplies. Two weeks into the advanced training, Willis approached the quartermaster's first sergeant regarding his audio audition recorded a month earlier at Fort Leonard Wood and inquired about the audiotape. The first shirt listened to Willis's concerns and told him he would check it out. A few days later, as if taken from the 1964–1969 television series *Gomer Pyle, USMC,* the first shirt told Willis, "Surprise, surprise, Sergeant Carter, there is no audiotape to be found."

Willis was dumbfounded. "What? No audiotape? So where do I go from here, Sergeant?" If divine intervention ever held the possibility of reality, the events that followed left Willis even more dumbfounded than before.

The sergeant asked, "So you're a wannabe musician, huh? I'm guessing you aren't happy with being a quartermaster either?"

"No, sir," Willis replied. "I've got a college degree in music and think my talents would be better served in that field rather than stacking boxes in a warehouse."

Again the sergeant asked, "What kind of musical instrument do you play?"

With all sincerity, Willis quickly responded, "The trumpet, sir."

"Well, Vander Linden, I'll tell you what. If you think you're good enough to attend the US Army School of Music, I might have a way to get your foot in the door." The sergeant continued, "I bowl in a Friday night league. A member of my team is Sergeant Harry Boothe who just happens to be the first sergeant of the army's music school. He's a trombone player. I'll talk to him about you this Friday, and then let's see what happens. I can't guarantee a thing, but I'll give you one shot."

Willis nearly screamed his answer back, "Yes, sir, thank you, sir."

The next week, Willis got his live audition with Sergeant Boothe. They met at the auditorium on base. Sergeant Boothe handed Willis some sheet music and directed him to a room where instruments were stored. "Pick out your horn and show me what you got, kid," the sergeant ordered. "I'll give you fifteen minutes."

Willis quickly looked at the sheet music handed to him. There were thirteen pages of various tunes that ranged from revelry and retreat music to concert band and jazz songs to big band sounds, and even a Sousa march. Willis played his heart out. This was no "Pomp and Circumstance" for a high school graduation ceremony or the "Michigan Fight Song" at a basketball game as a member of the pep band. These fifteen minutes would alter his military experience unlike anything ever imagined. Willis said, "I ended my audition on a high C note (not a $100 bill) that, for musicians, replicated a pole vault to the sun." For Willis, the fifteen minutes seemed like fifteen seconds.

Sergeant Boothe simply nodded his head when Willis finished. "I'll contact you within the next day or two after I talk to my superior. Nice job, soldier, nice job."

Within a week, Willis received new orders. He made the cut! His quartermaster's school ended abruptly. His next assignment took him to Joint Base-Little Creek, located in nearby Virginia Beach, Virginia. There he reported to the US Army/Navy/USMC School of Music. Within days of his arrival, he took a placement test that determined just how qualified he was according to the school's standards. As Willis stated, "I took all the placement tests for the entire school in one day and successfully passed each one."

The normal duration for the army's musical school was 150 classroom days or about thirty weeks. With his background and education, Willis skyrocketed through the course. He was quickly awarded the MOS of 02B20, a trumpet player. Immediately thereafter, he became a music theory instructor at the school. Not bad for a farm kid from Milo. More importantly, it was a world away from the experience most other soldiers endured during the Vietnam era.

In July of 1973, Willis received word of a vacancy for a trumpet player on the US Army jazz band. He elected to toss his hat into the ring and hopefully transition from instructor status at the school to a live performer that played before crowds of thousands. As good fortune continued to follow him, Willis was selected and became a member of the 392nd Army Jazz Band stationed at Fort Lee, Virginia. The band consisted of seventeen members that included a vocalist. Their group traveled up and down the East Coast and performed at various military as well as civilian events. Willis fondly recalled those days with the band. "It was sweet duty, beyond any doubt. When we traveled any distance, we stayed at first-class hotels and were transported in luxurious chartered motor coaches. We were on the road, much like a traveling band, from one to two weeks at a time, all the while receiving per diem, travel pay, and prepaid top-notch hotel accommodations, all the while drawing our military base pay. The lead vocalist, Sgt. Richard Oliver, sounded like David Clayton-Thomas of Blood, Sweat & Tears fame. I aspired to be like an up-and-coming Doc Severinsen and even grew a mustache to mimic his appearance."

The band often traveled to New York City on recruiting tours. It took Willis places that he never ever envisioned he would visit. He performed several times on national television with the band at venues such as the dressage horse-jumping competition held for the United States qualification for the 1972 Munich Olympics. The *Wide World of Sports* broadcast covered that event in which his group provided music for the opening ceremonies. He was one of three trumpet players selected to perform for the US Navy at Norfolk, Virginia, during Easter morning church services for the military that were broadcast live on NBC television. He played at multiple congressional dinner receptions that hosted foreign dignitaries. Willis even performed at the White House for President Richard Nixon.

One of the memorable events of his military experience he most embraced was his introduction into flying. A good friend and fellow trumpet player from the band, Sergeant James Cupps, owned a Cessna 150 and was a certified flight instructor. He took Willis up for a ride. Willis immediately became hooked with the concept of flight. Flying lessons and aircraft rental were a mere $12 per hour. Before long, Willis obtained his pilot's license and has been flying ever since. Today he owns his own Cessna 150 and flies the friendly skies near Knoxville, Iowa.

When reflecting on his military experience, Willis commented, "Oh, I was just like a lot of young soldiers. I complained about everything imaginable during my two years with the US Army. But looking back, now I realize just how blessed I was for the duty I performed, especially contrasted to what others went through. I truly enjoyed my time as a trumpet player, and if I had to do it over again, I probably would have elected the military as a career choice."

In January 1973, the United States signed a peace agreement with North Vietnam that marked the end of direct American involvement in the war and a cease-fire. That agreement provided only a face-saving gesture for the United States as hostilities again arose in early 1974 when Communist forces violated the treaty. Political turmoil bubbled over in America. Nixon went before the country in a nationally televised broadcast. and on November 17, 1973, told America, "I am not a crook." A stagnant war effort dominated the United States that year. On August 9, 1974, President Richard Nixon resigned from office as a result of the Watergate scandal.

Willis had seen enough. Only months before. he personally met President Nixon at one of his performances at the White House. As much as he enjoyed his duty with the US Army band, he pondered, was it time to call the cows home? Willis served two years, two months, and seven days with the US Army and discharged from active duty on October 18, 1974. In that short time, he traversed from the outhouse on the rifle range at Fort Leonard Wood to the White House at 1600 Pennsylvania Avenue; a remarkable journey, indeed.

He returned to Iowa and taught music at the high school in the Bancoft, Iowa. In 2002, he returned to his alma mater, Southeast Warren High School, where he tutored music students until his retirement from teaching in 2008. He ended his teaching career on that high C note and completed his pole vault to the sun. Through his mind's eye, a quick flashback in time took him to that brief moment in the latrine at Fort Leonard Wood, Missouri, where he stood before the inscription "Milo, Iowa." His circle in life was complete. Yes, indeed, there's no place like home, there's no place like home.

> *Sing joyfully to the Lord, you righteous: it is fitting for*
> *the upright to praise him. Parise the Lord with the harp;*
> *make music to him on the ten-stringed lyre. Sing to*
> *him a new song; play skillfully and shout for joy.*
> **—Psalm 33:1–3**

* ⭐ *

CLARK AIR BASE

I arrived at Clark Air Base in late October 1972. Just a few weeks earlier, on September 21, Philippine president Ferdinand Marcos declared martial law due to civil strife within the country and a series of bombings in Manila, less than sixty miles from Clark, that were deemed to be a Communist takeover of his authority. It was a spooky time to arrive, to say the least.

In 1972, Clark Air Base, Philippines, was the largest overseas US military base in existence. The fenced-in area consumed over 14 square miles with another 230 square miles of land called military reservation that consisted of jungle and grassland. The base's permanent party personnel exceeded twenty thousand. With other military personnel assigned there on temporary duty, which included other branches of the service, the population, when coupled with US dependents, approached forty thousand. Clark was an American city within the Philippines.

I was assigned to the 405th Fighter Wing, Civil Engineering Squadron (CES) as a member of its base fire department. Within a day or two, I was working on shift at the flight line crash fire rescue (CFR) station. The entire department consisted of about one hundred Air Force firefighters with about forty each on shift that rotated on a twenty-four-hour duty day, then off for twenty-four hours, and back again for another twenty-four hours. That amounted to a ninety-six-hour workweek. A smaller contingent of firefighters occupied the structural fire station which was augmented by local Filipino nationals.

Within the first week at Clark, Senior Master Sergeant (SMSGT) Smith, the deputy fire chief, called me into his office. I had previously been through a briefing for new troops to the Philippines that

322

gave insight to the customs and courtesies of the country, but what SMSGT Smith threw at me caught me way off guard with his raw point-blank lecture.

"Williams," he said, "have you ever had syphilis or gonorrhea?"

My chin dropped, and my eyes opened wide. "Huh, what did you say?" I mumbled back. "Are you talking about the clap?"

Smith immediately answered, "Yep, Williams, that and many other types of junk you can easily get. We have them all just outside the main gate. Take your pick. It's not a place you want to go. Every street corner and dark alley is standing room only for pickpockets, thieves, hookers, con artists, and drug dealers."

I slowly stuttered and then chimed in. "Well, I'm, I'm, I'm married and hope to get my wife here soon."

In a very matter-of-fact fashion, the deputy chief responded, "Good for you, soldier, good for you. I just don't want to lose any of my troops to sick call when they let their small head do the thinking for their big head. I suggest you stay on base till she shows up. Dismissed."

I left his office as a thousand thoughts raced through my mind. What in the world, what kind of place is this? It would be a full two weeks before I ventured off base due to the lecture given by SMSGT Smith, and I didn't go alone.

> *Let marriage be held in honor among all, and let the marriage bed be undefiled, for God will judge the sexually immoral and adulterous.* (**Hebrews 13:4**)

Within a day or two on shift, I was reunited with my buddy Richard Douglas who had previously been stationed with me at McGuire AFB and departed for the Philippines exactly one month before me. Doug, as everyone called him, was from Riverside, California, a very free-spirited guy. "Willie," he told me, "this place is a single man's paradise. You'll love it here."

Doug introduced me to several guys on shift that first day. One particular fella was Duane Kaltefleighter, a young farm kid from

Donnellson, Iowa. He and I were the only Iowans at the fire department. We hit it off right away and became good friends. Nobody could correctly pronounce his name, let alone spell it, so everyone simply called him Zeke. Zeke and I would have several memorable adventures together in the not-too-distant future.

THE WOLF

eader's Digest has a section entitled "My Most Unforgettable Character." That first week at Clark, I met Wolfgang Kessler, my most unforgettable character. Wolf was a lifer, a career military man. He was a few years older than me and took me under his wing like a big brother. Wolf was a unique individual. He was a full-blooded German who married the daughter of a US citizen who worked as a contractor in Germany a few years prior. His command of the English language was not the best, and his written words were horrible as "Evry wurd speld wuz jist lik it sonded." He spoke with a heavy German accent, and I needed to listen closely when he talked to understand exactly what he was saying. Everyone either called him Wolf or the Kraut. *Kraut* was a derogatory term used to describe German soldiers during World War I and World War II, derived from the word *sauerkraut* which was a common food of Central and Eastern Europeans.

Wolfgang certainly was not deserving of such negative comments. He was one heck of a guy. When he married his wife, Jan, and came to the US, he spoke no English. As Wolf revealed his abbreviated version of his life story to me, he went on to say he got his draft notice from the US Army as a new citizen (by marriage) and was destined for the military. He elected to volunteer for the air force rather than be drafted into the army. For me to tell his entire story would be a lengthy task. Simply to say that he went to military basic training, unable to speak any English, would be a thing of which movies are made. It was troubling yet comical but motivational, all rolled into a good belly laugh as he told of his escapades as a new recruit. He didn't know right face from present arms. The drill instructors were on him constantly like stink on cow dung, but Wolfgang endured.

Gomer Pyle had nothing over Wolfgang. Needless to say, his time in basic training was extended beyond the traditional six-week period. His newly discovered words of the English language, learned among his peers while in basic training, made even the worst of brothel madams blush. When he finally returned home on leave after basic training, his wife, a staunch Mormon, quickly intervened and helped him fine-tune his adjectives, particularly at the dinner table. He told the story of a celebratory occasion with the entire family seated around the dinner table. After a short prayer by his mother-in-law, and proud of his newfound military vocabulary, Wolf blurted out, "Paz me dem fuggin batatas."

Within that first week at Clark, Wolf extended an invitation to go with him and have dinner with his family at their home in the off-base Diamond subdivision of Angeles City. He assured me that the horror stories put forth by SMSGT Smith were far-fetched. I took him up on the offer.

In my lifetime, I've encountered thousands of people through work, school, social activities, and happenstance. Of those large number of people, I can say a great many I categorized as acquaintances. A smaller group I would recognize as friends who I came into contact frequently. Of that group of friends, I would estimate a handful could be considered good friends and very thankful they were in my life. However, just one or two I deemed best of friends. Wolfgang fell into the select circle I called the best of friends. No matter what the circumstance, no matter what the time, no matter what the distance, he was one of a very few I could 100 percent rely on. That intimate friendship lasted well beyond our time in the military. Wolfgang was the older brother I never had. A friend forever, a friend I will never forget.

As we drove through the main gate in his 1970 maroon-and-white Volkswagen bus and turned south on the McArthur Highway,

I couldn't help but notice the armed Philippine Constabulary (PC) troops stationed at each intersection. None carried modern weapons but rather guns that seemed to be issued from a pawnshop. Long-barreled pistols, double-barreled shotguns, and bolt action small caliber rifles were the weapons of choice. The martial law established by Philippine president Marcos was highly visible, front and center. What also caught my eye were the brightly colored jeeps that buzzed up and down the streets and obsessively beeped their horn with no concern for rules of the road. The locals called them jeepneys, and they were, in essence, open-air taxicabs. The jeepney was the symbol of Philippine public transportation that came about after World War II when surplus jeeps of the US military were sold to local Filipinos. They were noisy, with cramped seating, and darted about like bumper cars at a carnival.

Horse-drawn carriages called calesas clopped alongside the roads with a few GIs onboard as well as small motor scooters that zipped in and out of traffic, seeking the quickest route of travel. I even saw a two-wheeled wagon stacked high with freshly cut sugarcane, pulled by a weary-looking carabao as it slowly lumbered on the shoulder of the road. The whole scene was almost too much to absorb. A funny odor hung in the air as if all the funky dirty socks from every barracks on base was piled in front of me. Trash openly burned in barrels along the way, and the smell reminded me of the Milo dump when I took trips there with my grandpa. I wore a T-shirt and shorts, and still, sweat dripped from my armpits and forehead despite the breeze. The heat was stifling. It almost seemed as though Wolfgang had transported me to another planet, one much closer to the sun than Earth.

We finally arrived at the housing area called the Diamond Subdivision, a couple miles off base. There nearly all the houses were occupied by American GIs, either by choice or awaiting the availability of on-base housing. I was thankful to enter his air-conditioned house.

I told Wolf and his wife, Jan, of my desire to bring my wife to the Philippines as soon as possible, despite my status of a first-term airman. It could happen, but unlike Wolf and his family, I needed to pay her transportation expenses, and her presence would not be officially recognized by the USAF unless I were to re-enlist. I didn't want to sign on for another hitch so began looking for options. Wolf gave me the lowdown on off-base housing, and I thought it was doable even on my meager buck sergeant salary. That day, with his encouragement, I began the process of getting my wife to join me. He took me on a windshield tour of various off-base housing areas, and I began to get excited. Things were so, so cheap. It took about a week of house shopping, but things fell into place quickly.

I picked out a cinder block three-bedroom ranch-style home with a corrugated tin roof and attached carport on Don Juan Street, located just a couple blocks away from where Wolf and Jan lived. Another fireman and his wife, Mike and Dale Flarida, lived just a few houses down the street from the home I decided to lease. The monthly rent was a meager $45 per month which included utilities. What a deal! Now the wait began for my wife's arrival. It would be nearly five weeks before that would happen. I had no furniture, no bed or linen, no dishes, no car, and not a whole lot of money either. We previously sold our car, a red 1968 Opal Kadet, while visiting my mother in Hoquiam, Washington, before my departure overseas. That would pay for Judi's plane ticket to Manila with a few bucks left over. Life seemed good.

And we know that for those who love God all things work together for good, for those who are called according to his purpose. **(Romans 8:28)**

On my days off from work, I regularly ventured off base and rode in a jeepney to my house in the Diamond Subdivision to make it ready for Judi's arrival with locally purchased furniture. I bought a rattan dining room table and chairs, along with a complete bedroom set to include dresser and mattress for just $100. The base housing office had an excess amount of rattan living room furniture which they loaned out for free to first-term airman like me whose wife joined them on what was termed an *unaccompanied tour*. I was just about set for the big day of her arrival, just a few days beyond Thanksgiving in 1972.

The following week, my Iowa buddy Zeke asked me if I'd like to go to Manila with him for the day. I asked, "What in the world for?"

He informed me that his in-laws back in Donnellson, Iowa, were currently hosting a foreign exchange student from the Philippines. When the parents of that student became aware that Zeke was in the Philippines, they insisted he go for a visit so they might reciprocate the hospitality. My next question became, "How we going to get there, take the bus?"

He laughed and said, "No, they are sending their chauffeured car with driver to pick us up."

My immediate response was, "Sure they are. You're pulling my leg, right?"

Zeke went on to explain that the father of the exchange student was president of Philippine Airlines and a good friend of President Ferdinand Marcos of the Philippines. They had fought together as foxhole buddies during World War II, and under martial law, Marcos appointed him as the Philippine Secretary of Transportation. His name was Dido Adriano. I again asked Zeke, "You're kidding me, there is no way this is true, you're making this up?"

Zeke chuckled. "Well, you want to go or not?"

A couple days later, a brand-new 1972 white Ford Crown Victoria, with driver, picked us up at the main gate of Clark Air Base. When we began the sixty-mile ride south to Manila, I just shook my head and looked out the window from the back seat. I saw Mount Arayat in the distance as we passed the rice paddies and sugarcane fields. I saw Filipinos scattered about the farm ground. They toiled as they waded knee-deep between the flooded rice field dikes. Zeke and I glanced at each other occasionally and just giggled. I thought to myself, *This isn't real, is it?* I felt like a junior high student on some exotic field trip. I had never seen anything like this and was mesmerized at the sight. I certainly wasn't in Iowa anymore.

When we arrived at the Adriano home, somewhere in Manila, as I had lost all concept of direction and distance on the ride, the driver honked his horn, and an ornately decorated iron gate to the driveway swung open. Dido and his wife, Letty, greeted us as we stepped out of the car. "Mabuhay, welcome to our home," they greeted us. "Please come inside."

We visited cordially and spoke of each other's family. The Adrianos expressed their gratitude to Zeke and his in-laws where their son, who they called Boy-Boy, seemed so happy to enjoy his American experience. I had never heard a name like that before, so I wasn't sure if it was a nickname or his real name. In my short time in the Philippines, I had already learned not to take anything at face value.

I told them of my wife's pending arrival in a few weeks, and both Dido and Letty seemed as excited as me about her coming to the Philippines. "We would like to meet her when she gets here," they told me.

"That would be great," I replied.

Mr. Adriano then asked if we would like a drink. Zeke and I both nodded yes. He clapped his hands together, and as if she had dropped from the ceiling, a housemaid appeared. He said something to her in Tagalog (the Philippine native language), and then pointed to the door that led to the outdoor patio. We walked outside, and within seconds, the maid appeared with a tray that carried a bucket of ice, three tall glasses, and a bottle of Johnnie Walker Red and a bottle of Aristocrat brandy. No mixer, mind you, just straight hard liquor. Zeke and I looked at each other, not knowing what to do. We both thought perhaps a cold San Miguel beer on a hot day to quench our thirst but questioned the choices of booze. Dido grabbed a glass, took the tongs, and filled it with ice. He then took the bottle of Johnnie Walker scotch and poured the glass full. Its light-brown color made it look like a glass of freshly brewed iced tea, but I knew better. There was no lemon that garnished the drink. He handed the glass to Zeke. "Well, thanks, Dido," Zeke belted out as he took a sip. "Oh boy," he whispered under his breath as he winced upon swallowing that first gulp.

I was no connoisseur of scotch, so before another glass was poured, I spoke up, "I'll take the brandy." The next few hours proceeded with one glass after another. I vaguely remember the patio.

Reflecting now, it wasn't a patio but more of an outdoor garden with smooth granite stone as flooring and exotic flowers spaced perfectly at the outer edges, adorned with coconut and banana trees. A small shallow pool with some weird-looking multicolored fish I had never seen before swam around. They certainly were not the bluegill, bass, or catfish I was familiar with back home in Iowa, at my uncle Jim's farm pond or at Otter Creek just west of Milo. That is about as much as I remembered of that afternoon in Manila. Both Zeke and I were so snockered we could hardly stand up. I nearly drank the entire bottle of brandy, and Zeke kept pace with the scotch. Somehow late that night, the chauffer dropped us off at the main gate. I don't remember the ride back to Clark. But I remember my stumbled walk from my barracks the next morning to work at the fire station. It was fortunate that Zeke and I did not have to take a breath alcohol test at morning roll call. We both would have failed miserably.

Who has woe? Who has sorrow? Who has strife? Who has complaining? Who has wounds without cause? Who has redness of eyes? Those who tarry long over wine; those who go to try mixed wine. Do not look at wine when it is red, when it sparkles in the cup and goes down smoothly. In the end it bites like a serpent and stings like an adder. Your eyes will see strange things and your heart utter perverse things. You will be like the one who lies down in the midst of the sea, like one who lies on the top of the mast. They struck me, you will say, but I was not hurt; they beat me, but I did not feel it. When shall I awake? I must have another drink.
—**Proverbs 23:29–35**

REUNITED AGAIN

November 27, 1972, was a momentous occasion. My wife arrived in the Philippines as a military dependent on an unaccompanied tour of duty. In a nutshell, she was allowed to join me, but we were not eligible for on-base housing or other perks provided by the military for those that were career soldiers. Heck, I didn't give a hoot or holler about that, I was elated to have her join me.

I leased a car and driver from the base exchange (BX) at Clark Air Base and took off for the Manila International Airport early that Tuesday morning in November. My cost to lease the car for a day amounted to $10, which included the fee for the driver. Gasoline sold for $0.16 per gallon. Just to ensure I had enough cash to get there and back, I borrowed $10 from my station captain from the fire station, Technical Sergeant (TSgt) Norman Reeves.

She arrived in Manila six hours late due to a maintenance issue with her flight while connecting in Honolulu, Hawaii. Needless to say, she was exhausted after the eight-thousand-mile trip, her first overseas airplane trip ever! Hugs and kisses were abundant when I greeted her at the arrival gate. My driver picked us up at the terminal, and we headed north to the house I had rented in the Diamond Subdivision a few weeks earlier. We sat in the back seat and held hands as we retraced our route north. She seemed enchanted by the countryside, much like I had been enchanted a few weeks earlier on my chauffeured ride to the home of the Adrianos in Manila. Our driver never spoke a word the entire trip.

Suddenly traffic on the two-lane McArthur Highway came to a halt. I thought perhaps a car wreck ahead had blocked the traffic as we waited and waited. Finally our driver swerved to the side of the road and into the low ditch and followed others who also took to the same path as if four-wheeling through a field of elephant grass as tall as the car. It soon became apparent why the delay. A red-and-gray bus from the Philippine Rabbit bus service, loaded to maximum capacity with Filipinos, where some even sat atop on the roof, came to a complete stop on the highway. All the passengers made their way to the ditch as we drove past them. To our unbelieving eyes, it was potty break time. Of course, no roadside inn or rest area like we knew along the interstate system in the United States. All the guys unzipped their pants and women squatted and lifted their dresses and did their business right there in the ditch, where they were partially hidden from view, as we drove by just a few feet away. There seemed to be no embarrassment or shame. Judi's nose pressed against the window of the back seat of our air-conditioned car as she watched in disbelief. She turned to me and started to speak, but words didn't come forth. I simply said, "Welcome to the Philippines, babe, we're not in Iowa anymore." She slouched down in the seat and seemed to melt away like a snowman on an unseasonably warm winter day. It would be the first of many eye-openers and unbelievable moments for her while in the Philippines.

I was a little nervous in that I alone had picked the location of our rental house, its style, and all the furnishings hurriedly purchased to make it our home, all without her input. I had not even sent her a photo, so everything was a surprise. I hoped she liked it. As we approached the house, I said, "There it is, the one with the banana tree in the yard."

She was impressed to say the least. "A banana tree?" As we got out of the car, and I grabbed her suitcase and placed it in the

driveway, she immediately walked to the banana tree for a closer look. "Where are the bananas?" she asked.

What little I knew about banana trees came busting out of me like some crazed highly knowledgeable college botany professor. "Well, babe, there are boy and girl banana trees." I began, "Girl trees produce the bananas, but only once in a life span. The boy banana trees begin as flower seeds dropped by the girl tree. The pollen from the flowers are dispersed to the girl tree by birds and sometimes bats, and that's how bananas are made, then the cycle continues to repeat and repeat itself."

Judi squinted, curled her nose, and answered, "What?"

My quick reply was, "Let's go inside, I'll explain in more detail."

Two days later, I was back at work. However, morning roll call that day was different. SMSGT Smith, the deputy fire chief was present. That wasn't normal. We did our usual in-ranks inspection conducted by Staff Sergeant (SSG) Elliott. Elliott was the station captain, and in all my years in the fire service, he was the worst example of a leader I ever met. He went by the nickname Boom-Boom, given to him by the bar girls he frequently patronized. He was a drunkard, a womanizer, and about as worthless foul-mouthed human being that ever walked the earth. How he ever climbed the career ladder to hold any kind of leadership position was beyond me. After inspection, Chief Smith spoke to the group of slightly over forty firefighters. "I need twelve firefighters. You will be going to Da Nang, Vietnam, for a minimum of ninety days and leave here before the week is out. Any volunteers?" Nobody responded. "Okay then," he continued. He began to walk down the back row filled mostly of young guys like myself who were first termers on an unaccompanied tour. He began to poke his finger into the chest of every other man. "You, you, you, you." He barked out. I could see him coming my way. He poked his index finger into my sternum. "You." I gulped and thought to myself, *Oh no!* He paused then and looked me in the eye. "Didn't your wife just get here, Williams?" he asked.

I blurted out, "Yes, sir! Just two days ago." He paused, then said, "All right, you can stay at Clark." Then he continued to fill his twelve-man list. I had dodged a bullet that morning in more ways than one, no pun intended.

THE HOUSE GIRL, FELY

bout a week into our new surroundings at the house in Diamond Subdivision, a young Filipino girl, about my age, knocked at our gate. My wife and I both went outside to see what she wanted. She introduced herself as Felicisima Esconbinas. She wanted to know if we wanted to hire her as a house girl. We shook our heads and both agreed, no, not interested. We didn't need a full-time maid. She continued with a persistence that was undeniable. "I am a good worker, and I do not need much money for pay."

I piped in with the intent to immediately blow her out of the water. "And just how much do you charge to be a full-time maid?" I asked.

The slightly built girl, who maybe stood five feet and two inches tall and weighed less than one hundred pounds, seemed shy to answer. "Only $10 per month, sir."

I raised my eyebrows, then squinted at my wife, then repeated what she said, "Only $10 per month?"

She continued, "Yes, sir, and, ma'am, you will not be sorry if you hire me."

I knew other military families employed house girls or maids since they had young children. Wolfgang and his wife, Jan, had one. It freed up much of the time dedicated to mundane housekeeping. Gee whiz, we even had a houseboy at the fire department by the name of Ernie who took care of the daily duties that included cleaning the latrine, mopping the bay floors, waxing the tile floors in the sleeping area, taking out the trash, and the list went on and on. Judi and I smiled at each other as we both agreed, what a deal. "Yes," I said, "we will hire you as our maid."

That decision turned out to be one of the best we ever made. It began as a novelty but became a cultural exchange between both Fely and ourselves. We learned so much from her about local customs, Tagalog (the Philippine language), directions to the best open markets, and local cuisine. Her English was less than perfect, and we loved helping her understand all the unique phrases we as Americans spoke. I remember the first time we needed to explain to her one such phrase while driving home from the base. I said, "Let's grab something and eat on the road."

Her eyes opened wide as if she became possessed. She looked afraid. I asked her if she was okay. She responded, "I am worried that should we eat on the road, some jeepney might run over us."

I had to laugh. That was just one of many similar exchanges we had. We came to truly love Fely. Within a month, we increased her salary to $15. She lived with us six days per week. She did all the laundry by hand and hung clothes outside to dry, all the interior cleaning, some of the cooking, washed dirty dishes, buffed and waxed our cement living room floors with a coconut husk as she danced a jig sliding the husk side to side beneath her bare foot, served as our personal tour guide and interpreter, and became a lifelong friend who is still in contact with us today.

THE ADRIANOS
CALL AGAIN

Things moved so quickly with my time in the Philippines. Less than a month after Judi's arrival, I received a phone call at work from Letty Adriano, the wife of the Philippine secretary of transportation, Dido Adriano. She inquired if my wife had arrived yet and, in the same breath, asked if we would like to go to Manila again the following weekend for an overnight visit. Without hesitation, I replied, "Why, yes, certainly, let me check with Zeke."

She fired back, "No, no, we don't want him to come, just you and your wife."

I couldn't figure out why she didn't want Zeke to go along. I finally came to the conclusion that Zeke was just an Iowa farm boy through and through and, frankly, a little rough around the edges. He was a good one for blurting out what popped into his mind without regard how it might be interpreted. He certainly was not politically correct, particularly after a couple of beers in his belly.

The following weekend, a chauffeured car, the same one that picked me and Zeke up a few weeks earlier, arrived at the main gate of Clark Air Base. We climbed in and headed south to Manila. I still wondered, why us and only us for the visit. Within the first hour or so of our arrival, I quickly discovered the answer. Dido and Letty just tripped over themselves with adoration for my wife. She was a relatively tall Caucasian lady that stood head and shoulders above most Filipinos and quite attractive, as repeatedly mentioned by the Adrianos', and a rarity in Manila. There were plenty of US male soldiers who walked down Roxas Boulevard in Manila, but a tall white American girl, who looked like a movie star, stuck out like a sore thumb. Some people refer to their spouse as a trophy wife. The Adrianos viewed both of us—especially my wife—as trophy guests.

Dido had business at his office that afternoon, so their chauffeur drove Letty, Judi, and me to lunch at an exclusive private Pelota Club somewhere in downtown Manila. I had never in my life seen anything quite like that place. Perfectly manicured lawns with what appeared like real granite pillars and statues of Greek gods spaced near the entrance. We dined inside and were the only ones eating. I had my first taste of Butterfly iced tea. Two patrons played the game of jai alai in an open court within our viewing distance. Their play mesmerized me. Never before had I witnessed such a game. Clearly Letty attempted to impress us with the wonders of Manila. She did, indeed. We left the Pelota Club and took a quick windshield tour of Manila and Quezon City, the capital city of the Philippines. As we drove down Roxas Boulevard, we could see Corregidor Island in the distance of Manila Bay where General Wainwright surrendered eleven thousand US troops to the invading Japanese Army on May 6, 1942. She pointed to a restaurant along the boulevard. "That's where we are going to dinner tonight. It's a great place to eat."

When we arrived back at the Adriano home, Letty gave us a quick tour of the layout of the house. It was a nice place but not anything overly fancy compared to upscale homes back in the States. But compared to the typical home in the Philippines, it was a mansion. She took us upstairs via a twisting and winding staircase, similar to what one could expect in a submarine. I was almost too big to squeeze up the steps. Surely, I thought, there had to be another entrance because there was no way any furniture could be carried up this entrance. We arrived at the master bedroom, and she reached for a Brach's candy box atop her dresser. "Let me show you some of my jewelry," she said as she dumped it all on the bed. There were diamonds, pearls, rubies, sapphires, gold rings and necklaces, and emeralds galore. Judi's jaw dropped to her chest.

I chimed in, "Holy cow, how much is this worth?"

Letty replied, "Oh, I guess in American money, maybe $20,000."

I blurted out, "And you keep this kind of expensive stuff stored in a candy box atop your dresser? Aren't you worried someone might steal it?"

As nonchalant as I could ever imagine, she answered, "Oh, this is my everyday jewelry, Dido makes me keep my expensive stuff in the vault at the bank." I just shook my head. Unbelievable, simply unbelievable what we had witnessed that day.

She went on to say that since her husband is president of Philippine Airlines, she did her weekly grocery shopping in Taiwan. Again Judi and I were flabbergasted. We were out of our league—way out of our league—but relished the moment. I began to figure out Letty made every effort to brag about her wealth and impress us on her status as the wife of an airline executive and whose husband was a member of the president's cabinet. We got the point. Very clearly, we got the point.

> *And he said to them, "Take care, and be on your guard against all covetousness, for one's life does not consist in the abundance of his possessions."*
> **(Luke 12:15)**

Dido came home from his office early that afternoon. He immediately apologized to us for the need to cancel our dinner reservations on Roxas Boulevard that evening. He went on to explain that he had received a phone call earlier in the day from President Ferdinand Marcos. Dido had been tasked to make a promotion within the Philippine government that evening. He was to present an ambassadorship to the country of Taiwan. Of course, my first response was, "No problem, Dido, no problem with the dinner engagement."

Suddenly things began to sink in as to the enormity of this situation. There I was, a young kid from Milo, Iowa, halfway around the world, with my wife, and about to have dinner in the private home of the Secretary of Transportation of the Philippines and be in the company of the Philippine Ambassador to Taiwan. I just couldn't imagine making up such a story, but it happened.

The ambassador-to-be arrived, and Dido introduced him to Judi and me as his American friends and house guests. The ambassador spoke perfect English. Dinner that evening in their home could not have been more elaborate than if we had been to the most elaborate Gloria Maris restaurant on Roxas Boulevard. Just six of us sat at the table. Dido, Letty, their oldest daughter, the ambassador, and Judi and I. Two housemaids were present and took care of every need as if a professional waitress. A houseboy stood at attention against the wall, and with nearly every drink of water—even the tiniest sip—he immediately refilled the glass. It was an amazing evening and unforgettable moment, but soon it would became even more incredible.

After dinner, Dido stood up from the table and spoke, "Gentleman, let's go outside to the patio for a drink." Judi, Letty, and the daughter stayed inside. As I stepped into the paradise garden, the maid magically appeared just as she did when Zeke and I were there, just a few weeks earlier. She carried that same bucket of ice, three glasses, and yes, another full bottle of Johnnie Walker Red scotch whiskey and a full bottle of Aristocrat brandy. Once again, I chose the brandy but made a strong effort to pace myself with the booze. A few drinks later, all three of us were telling stories and slapping one another on the back as if lifelong friends. The ambassador placed his glass on the table and began to pour another scotch for himself. I placed my empty glass beside his and blurted out, "Just as well fill me up too." I glanced down at his hand. On his finger, he had a large ring with the raised initials "BV" on it. I leaned over for a closer look. I couldn't believe my eyes. It was a college ring from Buena Vista College, located in Storm Lake, Iowa. I shouted out, "Are you a Beaver from BV?"

"I am," he said. "I am."

I couldn't wait to tell him I attended Simpson College where I played baseball. Small world, I thought, small world. We immediately made a new connection, and as the night drew on and the bottles of booze were no longer full, he told me, "If you ever come to Taiwan, you will be my guest at the embassy. You can have full access to any transportation, to include a driver, that you might need. Just give me a call."

Early the next afternoon, the Adrianos' chauffer drove us back to our house near Clark Air Base. Judi and I just giggled in our conversations on the return trip. We absolutely could not believe the weekend we just experienced. It was beyond surreal.

* ⭐ *

FLIGHT LINE DUTY

As much as the Philippines intrigued me, I still had a job in the air force that required my presence for twenty-four hours straight, every other day. The flight line crash crew kept busy all day long and into the night. The department performed standby operations for the constant stream of medical aero evacuations (airvacs) on either the C-141 Starlifter or the C-9 Nightingale. These aircraft arrived daily at Clark Air Base laden with wounded soldiers, straight from the battlefield to the two-hundred-bed hospital at Clark, newly remodeled in 1964 at a cost of $4.5 million. The flight from Da Nang, Vietnam, to Clark Air Base was a mere 826 miles and routinely became the first stop for advanced medical care for soldiers injured in the Vietnam War. I would hate to estimate how many of those medical aircraft passed through Clark during the fifteen months I was stationed there, but no doubt in the hundreds. Upon notification of a medi-vac that approached the base, a crew immediately dispatched to the taxiway parallel to the active runway and escorted the aircraft and its fragile cargo, from the time it touched down till all ambulatory and liter patients were removed. Likewise when a departing aircraft with injured soldiers headed back to the US, loaded on the tarmac, a fire crew maintained a steady guard until the aircraft were airborne.

It was indeed a sad sight to watch the soldiers disembark with crutches, some limped, and others carried out on stretchers. I knew each had their own harrowing story and never interacted with any of them. A list of liter and ambulatory patients was presented to the fire crew on each flight. No names, mind you, just the fact that they could either walk on their own or needed to be carried out if any type of fire emergency should occur. They were a helpless bunch and a reminder just how fortunate I was.

> *If one member suffers, all suffer together, if one member is honored, all rejoice. (**1 Corinthians 12:26**)*

In addition to standby operations, the fire department ran a 24-7 ramp patrol that slowly roamed the airfield that checked static ground lines to aircraft, location of fire bottles, fuel leaks, as well as security of the tarmac. In a nutshell, ramp patrol was, beyond a shadow of doubt, the most mundane boring job on the entire base, particularly when a two-hour shift fell in the wee hours of morning. I recall on two occasions at Clark Air Base where the driver of the P-6 ramp vehicle fell asleep while it creeped down the tarmac. On those two incidents, the P-6 (nothing more than a pickup truck with a skid load fire suppression kit in the truck bed) drove into a T-33 aircraft and did significant damage to the aircraft's wing. The first incident prompted a visit to the fire department by the squadron commander for a real butt-chewing to all the troops. The second incident, which happened within thirty days of the first, prompted the base commander to make an appearance at morning roll call. Another more rigorous butt-chewing followed. After that, many of the guys who pulled that dreaded two o'clock-to-four o'clock morning duty simply parked somewhere out of sight and slept until awakened by a radio call to return to the station. It was a job a monkey could do, and the department had its share of monkeys.

LETTY ADRIANO
CALLS AGAIN

Nearly a month had passed since my wife and I made the trip to Manila to visit the Adrianos. I just happened to be at home that particular day when a car pulled up in front of our house. It was the same chauffer, the same white Ford Crown Victoria who picked up me and Zeke months earlier. I walked outside to greet him and find out why he made the trip from Manila to our humble house. To my surprise, Letty Adriano climbed out of the back seat and approached me with open arms. "Oh, I so missed you and your wife's company," she said. "I just had to come and visit you. I've brought some gifts."

The chauffer opened the trunk, and I saw it was loaded with all kinds of local fruits. A full rack of bananas, the little tiny ones about six inches long, native to the Philippines, several watermelons, and a box of mangoes. The driver brought them all into the house and placed them on our rattan dining room table. Frankly I had never paid that much attention to the bananas I saw hanging from trees. Up close, they looked so, so small. Letty insisted we try one. We did, and before I could eat it, she asked for a knife to cut the watermelon. When she cut the melon in half, I had to blink and refocus my eyes. The inside was orange! I had eaten plenty of watermelon back in Iowa but wasn't aware that orange watermelons even existed. Of course, I had to try it too. My eyes turned toward the mangos. I had never tasted a mango before, so I just had to do the trifecta and taste all of the three fruits she brought. I liked them all.

In the back of my mind, I wondered why she had driven all this way to bring us fruit. I guess I was a little naive, in a way, and took everything for face value. She was a very nice lady. We chitchatted for a while and then came the bombshell. She asked, "I was wondering if you could buy some American chocolate for my daughter, she just loves chocolate."

I shrugged my shoulders and answered, "I guess so. What kind of chocolate?"

Letty answered quickly, "I want Hershey's Chocolate, can you do that for me?"

With that, she reached for her purse and handed me a hundred-dollar bill in US currency. I was dumbfounded. I couldn't remember the last time I held a hundred-dollar bill in my hand. That was almost two week's wages at my military pay grade. I took the money and told her to give me a few days to get the chocolate.

Clark Air Base had a strict policy on the black market sale of items purchased from the BX. Those soldiers who resided in on-base housing or in the barracks were limited to what items they could take off base as well as the quantity of items. Those of us who resided off base had unlimited purchase ability, but an inventory of specific items were kept by the base, and those items had to be accounted for when returning Stateside. Off-base personnel carried ration cards, much like those used during World War II that limited the number of cartons of cigarettes or bottles of booze that could be purchased during the month along with a long list of other items. My neighbor in the Diamond Subdivision paid his rent with several cartons of Marlboro cigarettes in lieu of the Philippine peso. I wasn't aware that chocolate was on the restricted purchase list, so the following day, I went on a candy shopping spree. I made stops at the BX, the commissary, the package store, the bowling alley, the base gas station, and pretty much bought every Hershey candy bar on base. I came home with boxes and boxes of Hershey's candy bars. I had to place them in the refrigerator because with temperatures that reached 90 degrees daily, they would have melted. My refrigerator was stuffed with Hershey's candy bars—a hundred dollars' worth of candy bars!

As promised, Letty Adriano returned in two days. I gave her the year's supply of candy bars she asked me to purchase. She was overjoyed. Still I couldn't quite understand why she wanted so many.

However, it all came into sharp focus before she left. Again she reached into her purse and handed me several hundred dollar bills. She asked, "Here is a list of things I'd like for you to get for me."

First on that list was an air conditioner. Suddenly my relationship with her came into focus. I had been a chump. She only wanted to use me as a source to get exclusive American items unavailable to the general Filipino population. What I thought had been an honest friendship became a doorway to the black market so prevalent outside the main gate of Clark Air Base. I told her I would not purchase the items she requested. She left shortly thereafter and returned to Manila. I never heard from her again.

PEANUT BUTTER SANDWICHES

I can truly say that my time in the Philippines was a delight in many ways. I experienced so many things I never dreamed possible. I saw so many things never before imagined. Each day became an adventure unto itself. One such event took place on a Sunday morning after arriving home from work at the fire station. My wife had made a wonderful breakfast of pancakes and bacon. I remembered as a youngster growing up in Milo, the pancake-eating contest on Sunday mornings between my dad and myself. Who could eat the most? It seemed he always let me win, and maybe for good reason, if only to appreciate the goodness of something as simple as a pancake and a full stomach. That morning in the Philippines, I ate till my belly was full and had no competition. I helped clean the kitchen after breakfast and then dumped a partially eaten pancake into the trash. I poured the unused batter and still-warm bacon grease into the trash that made a pile of mushy goo. I knew that the next day was trash-pickup day, so I took the garbage outside and set it on the curb next to our impotent banana tree.

Within the hour, I noticed four little Filipino kids, maybe eight to ten years old, pushing a wheelbarrow and rummaging through my garbage. I yelled at them out the window, and they took off running down the street. I assumed they were scavengers

looking for discarded items to feed to their pigs. We lived perhaps two blocks away from a cluster of nipa huts where chickens and pigs ran freely in their front yard. I had driven by that location many times and knew their source of water was a hand-pumped well in the front yard. I never saw any lights at night, so I also knew they had no electricity. It was a stark difference between what little we had and the nothingness they had.

The following week, the same kids came back and began to rummage through my trash. I asked our house girl, Fely, "Go tell them to leave and not come back." Maybe they didn't understand English, so I told her, "Talk to them in Filipino and tell them I don't want them doing that."

She did as I requested and they proceeded on. I engaged Fely in conversation afterward and asked her if they were taking our garbage as well as our neighbors and feeding it to the pigs at their home. She said, "No, sir, they are eating it."

My immediate response was, "What? They are eating garbage?" I just couldn't believe it.

I asked Fely to go with me, and together we went outside. The four kids were about a block down the road, poking through someone else's trash. I loudly yelled at them and motioned with my arm to come my way. Fely shouted something in Filipino, and they slowly walked toward us. I began to question them about what they were doing, and it became apparent that their command of the English language was about the same as mine of the Filipino native tongue of Tagalog—zilch! Fely became my translator. It was a short conversation. I asked them, "Why are you taking my trash?"

They answered in Tagalog, and Fely translated, saying, "They want to eat something."

I shook my head and said to myself, "Let's stop right here."

I asked them to step into the carport of the driveway, out of the sun. I went inside and told my wife of what had just happened. I headed to our kitchen cupboard and grabbed a loaf of bread and a jar of peanut butter. Quickly I made some peanut butter sandwiches with extra peanut butter spread heavily on each slice. I grabbed four sodas from the refrigerator and took them outside to the boys. They smiled and took the drinks and sandwiches, then walked out the gate down the street. After they left, we talked about how horrible it must be to eat from the garbage others discard. I couldn't comprehend the events of the past thirty minutes.

Two days later, when I returned home that morning from work, the boys were waiting at the gate. They must have known my work schedule as they were not there according to my wife the day before. However, this time, there were six boys, not four. Again I made peanut butter sandwiches and served the kids.

Again two days later when I returned from work, the boys sat on the curb by the banana tree, waiting for my arrival. However, this time, there were a dozen kids. I knew what they wanted, and as soon as I opened the gate to the carport, they entered the driveway and crouched down in a squat, like a baseball catcher. All the Filipinos sat like that when resting. I wasn't limber enough to sit like that very long. If I did get in that positon, it was tough to get up. All the kids had the look on their faces, like a nest of baby robins waiting to be fed a worm. I used an entire loaf of bread and full jar of peanut butter and fed them all.

Not to my surprise, two days passed, and the kids showed up at my front gate again. This time, I guessed maybe twenty kids waited in anticipation. I was unsure how to respond. I had empathy for the kids. I had frustration for their situation. Their numbers at my front gate increased exponentially every other day. I simply could not continue with the peanut butter sandwiches. In fact, I had no more peanut butter or bread in the house. I asked our house girl, Fely, to go and talk to them in their native language and tell them I would like to help, but I can no longer do this. I sent her outside to the carport as I watched from the doorway. She spoke with them for maybe five minutes in a soft voice. I couldn't hear what she said, and it really didn't make any difference because I didn't understand the language anyway. They quietly walked away, never to return again, not for the peanut butter sandwiches, not even to rummage through my garbage.

All you need to say is simply "Yes" or "No";
anything beyond this comes from the evil one.
(Matthew 5:37)

Later that morning, as I sat in my swiveled papasan chair in the living room, I pondered what the last few months in the Philippines revealed to me. I felt as if I had been singled out for a spiritual lesson in humanity, and it bothered me. As a kid growing up in Milo, I never rummaged for something to eat in other people's trash. I never had the luxury of being driven in an expensive chauffeured car or had my parents fly to another country to buy groceries or had a maid serve me meals or a houseboy that daily shined my shoes. It made me stop and think, just who am I? Why am I here? I witnessed both ends of the cultural and economic spectrum in the Philippines, and I didn't like it. The Philippines was a country sharply divided between those who have and those who have not. I told the Adrianos no, I could no longer help them. I did so because I recognized their greed. I also told the hungry kids no, I could no longer help them. It wasn't because I didn't want to help, but their needs were well beyond my financial capability.

> *Behold, I am sending you out as sheep in the midst of*
> *wolves, so be wise as serpents and innocent as doves.*
> **—Matthew 10:16**

OPERATION LINEBACKER

From May 9, 1972, through October 23, 1972, air operations at Clark Air Base took a huge jump in activity due to an aggressive military action called Operation Linebacker. President Nixon took the fight to North Vietnam in an air assault against Hanoi. I simply went to work one day, and the ramp was jam-packed with aircraft parked wing tip to wing tip. We had no pre-briefing as to the reason for all the airplanes or what they would do while at Clark. I certainly wasn't privy to all the minute details, but I saw firsthand aircraft movements the likes I had never witnessed before. Virtually every parking spot on the Clark tarmac had one of the KC-135 Stratotankers. The USAF deployed 195 of them to the Western Pacific in support of Operation Linebacker and positioned them in Okinawa, Taiwan, and the Philippines. I didn't carry a stopwatch, but I guessed that every ten minutes, one of the tankers either returned from a refueling mission or departed Clark with a full load of 30,758 gallons of JP-4 jet fuel for an inflight refueling with B-52 bombers, F-4 Phantoms, F-104 Wild Weasels, F-111 Aardvarks, A-4 Skyhawks, A-6 Intruders, and A-7 Corsairs. These departures and arrivals went on around the clock for days and days on end. I had a front-row seat to a spectacular air show.

When on ramp patrol positioned on the taxiway adjacent to the runway, the deafening noise on takeoff generated by the Stratotanker's four jet engines, each with twenty-one-thousand pounds' thrust, was so loud I couldn't hear the transmission of radio traffic within my vehicle, even with the windows rolled up. My chest shook as they passed by my position then lifted off. Sooty black jet exhaust from the four engines left a trail behind them that eventually dissipated in the wind, much like contrails at high altitude. In 1972, there were no concerns for either air pollution or noise pollution, particularly in the Philippines. The tankers had both and plenty of it. The jet engine of the KC-135 tanker produced noise levels as high as 140 decibels to the human ear at a distance one hundred feet. That equated to a chain saw running at high speed just three feet from my ear. The KC-135 had four engines that cranked out a thunderous roar. Even with the windows on my vehicle rolled up, I should have worn hearing protection, but I didn't. As a result, today I find myself saying, "Huh? What did you say? I didn't hear you."

That first day of Operation Linebacker, US forces flew a total of 414 sorties. The US Navy accounted for 294 while the air force flew 120. The bombing campaign saw a dramatic increase in the number of strike and support sorties flown in all of Southeast Asia as a whole. The month prior, 4,237 sorties were flown for all branches of the services and that included South Vietnamese aircraft. That number jumped to 27,745 the following month. In total, Operation Linebacker missions amounted to 41,653 sorties, and our aircraft dropped 155,548 tons of bombs.

Combat, particularly air combat, was a treacherous business. The bulk of aircraft used during Operation Linebacker were the F-4 Phantom and the A-7 Corsair. Other aircraft included the F-111, the A-6, the RF-8, and the A-4. Twisting and turning in dogfights, dodging antiaircraft fire, and avoiding SAMs became a high-risk occupation for the pilots. At times, it did not go well. The United States forces lost 134 aircraft during Operation Linebacker. The air force lost 70 aircraft, of which 51 were direct combat losses. North Vietnamese MiGs (Russian-built jet aircraft *Mikoyan-i-Gurevich*) shot down 22 of our aircraft, another 20 were lost to antiaircraft fire, 4 were lost to surface-to-air-missiles (SAMs), and 5 were categorized as induced losses. Induced losses simply meant that one of three things happened to the aircraft. It was lost because of pilot error, environmental weather issues, or a system malfunction.

The US Navy lost 43 aircraft. Russian MiGs shot down 4, another 13 were lost to SAMs, 27 lost to anti-aircraft fire, and 2 categorized as induced losses.

The US Marines lost 10 aircraft. One to a MiG, one to a SAM, and 8 to antiaircraft fire.

Operation Linebacker brought forth the first aces of the Vietnam War on the very first day. Navy Lieutenant Duke Cunningham and his radar intercept officer, Lieutenant William Driscoll, downed their fifth MiG in air combat. Several weeks later, Air Force captain Richard Ritchie gained his ace status when he downed his fifth enemy aircraft.

Operation Linebacker proved to be a watershed for aerial warfare as later reported by air force historian Earl Tilford. It became the first modern aerial campaign that used precision-guided munitions and changed the manner in which US forces used their airpower.

On October 23, President Nixon announced a halt to the bombing of North Vietnam and announced that peace was at hand. The massive destruction caused by the bombing of North Vietnam helped convince the Viet Cong to come to the bargaining table. Serious peace discussions began but stalled when the parties concerned could not agree on the issues of American withdrawal of troops, the recognition by North Vietnam of the South Vietnam government, and the release of prisoners of war (POWs). Additionally Nixon proposed forty-four additional changes in the initial bargaining agreement, the most significant being the recognition of the 17th parallel, the demilitarized zone (DMZ), as an international border. By mid-November, the North Vietnamese balked at the revised initial peace proposal and withdrew some of their earlier concessions and stonewalled the entire negotiations from the get-go.

The US response became a renewed bombing effort called Linebacker II which began on December 20, and lasted nine days. The bombings of North Vietnam resumed. However, the US military learned from the initial Operation Linebacker that the air assault by tactical aircraft (F-4s and A-7s) exposed aircrews to higher losses. Because of lessons learned, the B-52 bomber became the weapon of choice. There were 207 B-52 bombers available in Southeast Asia (SEA). One hundred fifty three bombers were stationed at Anderson AFB, Guam, and another 54 were stationed at U-Tapao, Thailand.

The first night bombings on December 18, in Operation Linebacker II, 129 B-52s launched, each loaded with seventy thousand pounds of munitions destined for Hanoi. Fifty-four of those bombers came from U-Tapao while another 75 flew from Anderson AFB. Thirty-nine support aircraft flew escort for the B-52s. Clark Air Base once again supplied the KC-135 tankers for refueling. My air show continued, with a vantage point of slightly over one thousand miles from the drop sight in Hanoi. But it was awesome!

That first night, three aircraft were lost. Two B-52s were shot down and an F-111. Two other B-52s received heavy battle damage but managed to limp back to U-Tapao. Of the three downed aircraft, only one was rescued.

On the second night, December 19, ninety-three bombers launched against the North Vietnamese targets. None were lost, despite twenty SAMs launched against them, but several received significant battle damage.

On the third night, December 20, ninety-nine bombers launched. This time, however, the North Vietnamese shot down seven B-52s over Hanoi, and an eighth bomber crashed in Laos before it reached U-Tapao. The repetitive nature of the attack that used the same approach patterns, same aircraft formation, and same altitude of the two previous missions proved fatal. The Vietcong predicted the same matrix and launched thirty-four missiles to those coordinates. Of the eight aircraft lost that night, only one aircrew was rescued. In the words of air force historian Earl Tilford, "Years of dropping bombs on undefended jungles, poor tactics, and a good dose of overconfidence by Strategic Air Command (SAC) commanders, that night became a nightmare for B-52 crews."

The bombing continued on a daily basis up until December 29, for Operation Linebacker II. In total, B-52s flew 795 sorties to North Vietnam and dropped 15,237 tons of ordnance. Fighter aircraft added another 5,000 tons of dropped ordnance to the final count. The USAF flew 769 sorties in support roles, and the USN/USMC flew 505 sorties in support of the B-52s.

During Operation Linebacker II, the USAF lost fifteen B-52s, two F-4s, two F-111s, one EB-66, and one HH-53 rescue helicopter.

The USN lost two A-7s, two A-6s, and one F-4. Thirty-three B-52 aircrew members were killed or missing in action (MIA), another thirty-three became prisoners of war, and twenty-six were rescued. Hanoi claimed 1,624 civilians were killed during the air attacks.

The carpet bombing of North Vietnam during Operation Linebacker and Operation Linebacker II served its purpose. It brought Hanoi back to the negotiating table in Paris. Neither side willingly admitted to the strife it caused for both. However, on January 27, 1973, the Paris Peace Accord was signed. The agreement included only the United States and North Vietnam. North Vietnam refused to recognize its neighbor to the south. The United States agreed to withdraw all of its troops and dismantle its bases within sixty days. North Vietnam agreed to release POWs held in captivity, recognize the provisional division between North and South Vietnam at the 17th parallel, with the promise not to initiate military movement across the DMZ in a forceful reunification of the country. It would be a promise the North Vietnamese later broke.

OPERATION HOMECOMING VIETNAM PRISONERS OF WAR ARRIVE AT CLARK AIR BASE

Operation Linebacker and Linebacker II, coupled with the signing of the Paris Peace Accord, ushered in the release of American POWs held in captivity. Their return was coined Operation Homecoming.

I was on duty at the fire station at Clark Air Base on February 12, 1973. It was a day that I will remember forever. Hanoi released the American POWs. The first freedom flight on a C-141 Starlifter, tail number 66-1077, marked with a huge medical Red Cross on its tail section, landed at Clark Air Base and parked on the tarmac adjacent to the flight line fire station. By coincidence that day, I happened to be on ramp patrol and followed the first aircraft in my P-6 ramp vehicle as it taxied to a stop. I parked my escort fire truck under the wing of the aircraft, got out, and stood at the parade rest position as the first two POWs, Everett Alvarez and Jeramiah Denton, exited from the rear side door to the cheers of about five hundred base personnel and news media. Both had been held as a

POW for over eight years. A red carpet stretched on the tarmac from the aircraft to the awaiting medical buses that transported the first group of forty POWs to the base hospital for an initial medical evaluation. It was a solemn moment. There were cheers, there were tears. I stood in silence, mesmerized by the magnitude of the moment.

One by one, the POWs stepped off the plane and still wore the bland garb given them by their captors. Admiral Noel Gayler, USN commander of American forces in the Pacific greeted them as well as an entourage of dignitaries. Each POW saluted Admiral Gayler, who wore his white service dress uniform, then shook his hand and turned to the US flag positioned near the red carpet and again saluted the Stars and Stripes. Some had visible injuries. I noticed one POW saluted the admiral with his left hand. A left handed salute within the military indicates the disdain of a soldier toward an individual or situation. I found it hard to believe he would do such a thing. As he turned to walk away, I saw that his right arm hung limp and swung uncontrolled at his side as he walked to the bus. He couldn't do a right-handed salute. As he passed the American flag, he stopped on the red carpet. The soldier did a sharp left face and, with his good left arm, saluted Old Glory. Others had noticeable altered gaits in their step as they walked, obviously from untreated injuries. Some walked with crutches, and a few were carried off on stretchers out the rear of the aircraft.

Once again, I had a front-row seat to another historical event a mere twenty paces away. A lump developed in my throat as the emotional moment got the best of me. I noticed that one of the POWs had a young puppy with him. It appeared to be a German shepherd. I thought it strange to bring a dog along, but no doubt it was an escape for the pup as well. I walked over to the bus and stepped inside the door. I intended to say, "Welcome back, guys," but I was so choked up, words didn't come out. I just waved, gave them a thumbs-up, then stepped back onto the tarmac.

As the last of the POWs exited the aircraft and made their way to the blue shuttle buses for transport to the Clark hospital, I returned to my vehicle. Once inside, I cranked the air-conditioning to high and reflected on the moment. I was so, so much like many of the other GIs I knew. I wouldn't have called myself a whiner, but I readily expressed my discontent. I was the first to complain about the long duty hours of work at the fire station and the mundane ramp patrols up and down the flight line at 0300. I worked a crazy scheduled that rotated from seventy-two hours a week, then ninety-six hours the next week. I complained about the food served at the chow hall. I mumbled under my breath about some of the low-quality leadership at my duty station. I complained about the sweltering heat. I complained about my paltry paycheck from Uncle Sam. I complained about some of the extra work details assigned to me. I complained about my relatively low rank as a buck sergeant. I was unsettled for being so far away from my extended family back in Iowa. There was a sourness in my thought process I just couldn't shake.

That moment became an epiphany for me. I thought, *Who am I to complain? These POWs endured suffering and torture a thousand times my own misery. Some died. How shallow of me to even think, "Woe is me." My military service would be considered a walk in the park by those who served in Vietnam and trudged through the jungles and rice paddies with rifle in hand or soared through the sky as they dodged antiaircraft fire. I wasn't unfortunate, I was pretty darn lucky.* That instance, as I sat in my air-conditioned ramp vehicle, one might say the light came on for me. The comments of President John Kennedy from his inaugural speech on January 20, 1961, blipped on the radar in the back of my mind, *Ask not what your country can do for you, but what you can do for your country.* There it was, right in front of me. I was an airman in the United States Air Force. I was a member of the greatest military in the world. My job was to serve in whatever small way I could.

> *Do everything without complaining or arguing. So that you may become blameless and pure, children of God without fault in a crooked or depraved generation, in which you shine like stars in the universe. (**Philippians 2, 14–15**)*

Other aircraft followed that same day as well as the days that followed. By April 4, 1973, 591 POWs passed through Clark Air Base on fifty-four evacuation aircraft. North Vietnam released 457

POWs with the remainder freed from South Vietnam POW camps. I witnessed the bulk of their arrivals as well as the ceremonial departure back to the United States. On the final leg of their trip home, I saw them dressed in crisply pressed uniforms of each respective branch of service, not the drab pajama-like attire they wore upon arrival. Thereafter, when I heard reveille or colors played on the base public address system at the beginning or end of each day, I stood at attention straighter, taller, and more proud than ever before.

It was an honor to have witnessed firsthand the return of the POWs and grateful to have played a small part in their return. Their misfortune became one of the most unforgettable moments in my military career. Their courage and perseverance became a standard for all to admire. I again asked the question, why them? Why not me? I didn't really consider my job as a fire protection specialist a life-threatening position. In fact, much of my work was mundane and downright boring. Even my fellow firefighters joked about all the downtime we enjoyed and how slow the hands on the clock moved as we played cards or checkers or watched television while we waited for the bell to ring. Yet a few spoke of the extreme dangers of firefighting. I considered my situation like the luck of the draw in a card game. I just had to play the hand dealt to me and make the best of it. Other firefighters who performed exactly the same tasks as I, each and every day, were dealt lousy hands.

One such lousy hand was dealt to USAF firefighters on July 15, 1967, at Da Nang Air Base in Vietnam. That day the base came under attack by the Viet Cong and suffered its worst single day of devastation for the entire war. A rocket attack centered on the aircraft located on the flight line ignited fires that destroyed ten aircraft. A rocket hit a F-4 Phantom loaded with five-hundred-pound bombs and set it on fire. Firefighters rushed to the scene and made valiant efforts to extinguish the flames. One of the five-hundred-pound bombs exploded and killed 8 firefighters. That day resulted in 160 casualties and killed a total of 9 soldiers. The luck of the draw.

> *And they cast lots for their duties, small and*
> *great, teacher and pupil alike.*
> **—1 Chronicles 25:8**

* ⭐ *

MIKE, IS THAT YOU?

I had been at Clark Air Base several months and felt I finally had my feet on the ground. I knew my way around the base and somewhat able to maneuver off base beyond our housing area. Just outside the main gate, beggars sat along the roadside and relentlessly stuck their hands out asking for money. It was a pathetic sight. The two-mile jeepney ride to my house took me past the red-light district with dozens and dozens of strip clubs, bars, and off-the-wall businesses that, no doubt, were a front for illegal activities. The alleyways and backdoors along McArthur Highway offered a glimpse at the underbelly of the illicit activities conducted on a daily basis within a few hundred yards of the base. Someone told me, the first few days upon my arrival, that anything could be bought off base for five dollars. Then without hesitation, they said it again, emphasizing the word *anything*! How true that statement was. I can tell you that I witnessed more than one GI who made a terrible decision and ended up in serious trouble. Some were mugged and robbed, others drank too much and, in their impaired state of mind, were fleeced by bar girls or drug dealers. Many were regular customers not just to the bars but to the base hospital for penicillin injections from the sexually transmitted diseases (STDs) they contracted.

I recall one morning, when I left for work, a huge pile of banana tree leaves covered the road in front of my house. I questioned my buddy Wolfgang about it, who lived just a block away, when he picked me up for a ride to the fire station. In his heavy German accent, he responded, "A Pilipino was kilt lus nite and had der troat kut."

I kicked some of the leaves aside to discover a huge pool of blood still fresh on the road. That murder happened right in front of my house, and I never heard a thing. I had new concerns about

360

my own safety after that incident as well as that of my wife who was home with our maid, Fely, when I was gone for twenty-four hours at a time when on duty.

However, once on base, a different world existed. Clark had all the amenities Americans enjoyed back home. My wife joined a bowling league. She took piano lessons twice a week at the service club. The base had an excellent golf course with dirt-cheap green fees. A number of recreational activities that included a softball league and flag football league kept many entertained. The base also had an outdoor theater called the Bamboo Bowl, much like the drive-in theaters back in the States but rather than drive a car and park, moviegoers brought blankets and lawn chairs. Clark also had the indoor movie theater, The Kelly Theater. Like all military theaters, prior to the movie, "The Star-Spangled Banner" played on-screen and everyone, to include children, rose from their seats and stood at attention while the national anthem played. Clark also had a gymnasium with basketball courts and racquetball courts for those who wanted to work up a sweat. With the sweltering heat, no matter day or night, players were soaked in perspiration in about thirty seconds.

The base had three clubs that provided fine dining and local entertainment weekly: the Clark Air Base Officer's Open Mess (CABOOM), the NCO club (The Top Hat), and the airman's club (The Coconut Grove). A hobby shop, a service station, a swimming pool, the elementary, middle and high school, the commissary and package store for alcohol purchases, as well as the base exchange (BX) provided virtually any and everything needed. For the adventure seekers, the base had a riding stable, an aero club for flying lessons, and a parachute club. I never had a desire to jump from a plane, but several guys from the fire station were members. Overall Clark was an ideal duty location.

I did go to the BX quite often. It wasn't Walmart but pretty darn close. I mailed many souvenirs back home to relatives from purchases made there or from woodcarving stores located just outside the main gate. On one such visit to the BX, as I passed through the checkout line dressed in my fatigues, I heard someone shout, "Mike, Mike Williams, is that you?"

I turned around, and to my complete disbelief, there stood Beverly Walk. Beverly and I took high school Spanish class together under the tutelage of Nyno Vargas. She was as shocked as I to see me as I was her. Beverly lived only a couple of blocks from me back in Milo, just off the southeast corner of the city park. Her father, Herb, owned and operated an automotive repair shop adjacent to their home. I gave her a hug and asked, "What in the world are you doing here, halfway around the world? This is beyond crazy to see you."

She went on to explain that she married a guy from Indianola, Iowa, named Ron Wark. He joined the US Navy (USN) and decided to make it a career. Their current assignment sent him to Subic Bay Naval Base, just down the road from Clark. From there, the USN detached him to Clark as his duty assignment. As a dependent spouse, Beverly joined him in the Philippines. We visited for about fifteen minutes. It had been nearly five years since we last saw each other in high school before we went our separate ways. We discovered we both lived off base and just a couple of miles from each other. From then on, we made a point to socialize at least once a month and share what gossip we had received from family and friends back in Milo.

THE UNITED SERVICE ORGANIZATION (USO)

I attended three USO shows while in the Philippines. The USO brought a little of America to soldiers stationed overseas who were starved for a tiny bit of life as they knew it back home. Once such show took me to the Coconut Grove, the airman's club at Clark Air Base. I don't specifically recall why I decided to attend the showing, but the entertainer was none other than Herbert Butros Khaury, better known as Tiny Tim. He made previous guest appearances on the Johnny Carson tonight show, the *Ed Sullivan Show*, and was featured in the *Rowan and Martin Laugh-In* show. I figured with those credentials, he had to be pretty good. I found an up-front seat, perhaps ten feet from the stage where the falsetto-voiced singer performed on his ukulele. Together we "Tiptoe through the Tulips." I was seated so close I could almost reach out and touch him. However, when I saw him that close, I wasn't so sure I wanted to touch him or even tiptoe with him.

Bizarre best described Tiny Tim. What made his performance even more bizarre unfolded about five minutes into his litany of weird songs. The Coconut Grove lost all electrical power. The club became immersed in total darkness. There were no lights, not even battery-operated emergency lights, no electronic accompaniment, nothing. A few people lit candles or clicked their cigarette lighter in order to see. Tiny Tim kept right on singing into his dead microphone as if nothing went wrong. This went on for several minutes until someone reset the circuit breaker. I thought this guy was so wacked out that if he quit singing, he might forget the words to the song. He continued with his high-pitched notes and kept the beat as he tapped his foot on the floor while plucking the strings. For a split second, I thought this miscue was an intentional part of his routine and a gag to hold the audience's attention. His performance fell far short of quality entertainment, but because of its goofy presentation, I vividly remembered it.

Ironically Tiny Tim spent his retirement years in Des Moines, Iowa, where he lived at the Savery Hotel and, later, the Hotel Fort Des Moines. The *Des Moines Register* newspaper reported that he conducted occasional performances at the Holiday Inn South and the Gray's Lake Inn. As noted, many local residents saw him as he shopped at the local Hy-Vee grocery store. Our paths never crossed again despite our close proximity. Tiny Tim died in 1996 after he collapsed while performing at a benefit concert.

Disappointment surrounded my first USO show, but I didn't completely give up on the hope that better things would follow. Yes, things improved greatly a short time later in July 1973; a group of young ladies from the University of Dubuque, located in the far northeastern corner of Iowa along the Mississippi River, performed at the Kelly Theater on base. The great thing about the USO shows were the fact that they were free. With my meager military pay, I could easily afford the free admission. They did an admirable job as they performed in dance and song on stage. They captivated the audience with a rendition of current top hits played on the radio. They also captivated the audience, no doubt, because they were all drop-dead gorgeous women! My memory of that evening remained vivid some forty-seven years later. One of the beauties stepped off-stage and into the crowd. As if following a compass, she walked up the aisle and stopped at my end-row seat and then asked, "Do you mind? What's your name, airman?"

I stuttered, then whispered, "Mike."

She sat on my lap and began to sing the introductory song from the 1972 Michael Jackson movie, *Ben*, the movie about a pet rat. Then she began but substituted my name, "Mike, *the two of us need look no more, we both found what we are looking for, with a friend to call my own, I'll never be alone, and you my friend will see, you've got a friend in me.*"

What a great show, I thought. Later that week, I wrote a letter to the University of Dubuque and thanked them for the group they sent that entertained the soldiers. I found out, some time later, that excerpts of my letter were sent to the *Des Moines Register* newspaper, and they published a short article about the college's tour group with the USO and referenced some of my comments.

In December 1973, the Bob Hope USO show stopped at Subic Bay for a one-day performance. I certainly knew of Bob Hope's fame and USO shows over the years. His first USO show dated back to a 1941 radio broadcast. Frankly I never thought any of his movies I watched as a youngster were that magnificent. I sat through a few of them as a kid, *The Road to Morocco*, *The Road to Bali*, *The Road to Singapore*, and *The Road to Hong Kong*. I rated them ho-hum at best. I didn't think his jokes were that funny either or his vocals that great. Regardless of just the one-star rating I gave him, I decided to take the bus and attend his performance at Subic Bay. Oh boy, I'm glad I made the journey.

Fellow USAF firefighter Tim Lang, who I worked with when stationed at McGuire AFB, New Jersey, back in 1970, told me all about his Woodstock experience in August of 1969, or at least what little he remembered of it as we conversed over a few beers at the airman's club a few years earlier. He commented, "I was whacked out, man. I was there but only vaguely remember it. I walked what seemed like miles through a muddy mess just to get there."

He was from the tiny town of Bordentown, New Jersey, just 163 miles south of the six-hundred-acre site of Woodstock. He told me nearly five hundred thousand hippies gathered at that remote dairy farm near Bethel, New York, and grooved to the music of Janis Joplin, Joan Baez, Jimi Hendrix, and Sly and the Family Stone. Incidentally years later, Tim became the fire chief at Lakehurst Naval Air Station, New Jersey. No doubt he omitted his drug-induced experience at Woodstock from his résumé.

When I arrived at Subic Bay and got off the bus, ready for the outdoor bash that I hoped might compare to Tim's Woodstock experience, what struck me first was the unbearable heat. The temperature topped 100 degrees. I found a seat in some bleachers, maybe thirty to forty yards from the left of the stage. There wasn't a cloud in the sky, not a hint of a breeze in the air, not an awning or a shade tree anywhere. It wasn't a healthy situation by any stretch of the imagination. I don't recall any watering stations or latrine facilities in the immediate area. It appeared little planning went into the comfort for the audience. The majority of the crowd of nearly twelve thousand GIs sat cross-legged, Indian style, on the ground near the stage.

The number of soldiers that came to see the Bob Hope at Subic Bay was miniscule compared to the Woodstock gathering, but the hardened soldier's enthusiasm and their feelings toward America outpaced any and all measureable standards previously described to me by Tim Lang. Bob Hope climbed the few stairsteps adjacent to the stage, and the crowd roared as he lifted his infamous golf club in the air. The ovation was tremendous, and despite speakers located nearby, I could not fully hear his words. All that seemed a nonissue with the thousands and thousands of GIs that applauded him. I'll admit, it reminded me of the fervor demonstrated at a college football game when a winning touchdown determined the outcome in the waning seconds. I could see why Bob Hope enjoyed this. It was red, white, and blue in all its glory, and Bob held the entire crowd in the palm of his hands.

Lola Falana, known as the queen of Las Vegas, headlined the Bob Hope show. She sang her signature song, taken from the 1956 Broadway musical, *Damn Yankees,* "Whatever Lola Wants, Lola Gets." Among that crowd, she truly could have gotten whatever she wanted, way more than just a standing ovation, as she pranced and danced on stage. The troops roared and would have readily given her anything she wanted with no questions asked.

The Gold Diggers from *The Dean Martin Show* followed Lola Falana onstage. The dozen scantily clad gals, dressed in blue sequin outfits, gyrated and jumped to the goo-goo-eyed crowd. Just a few short minutes into their routine, one fainted and face planted onstage due to the extreme heat. With the help of two other girls and a stagehand, they carried her offstage. After a short minute, the performance continued as if nothing happened. As those in show business know, the show must go on, and it did.

Miss Universe from Australia, Belinda Green, joined Bob Hope on stage. A tall extremely attractive blond gal played straight man for some of his jokes. The roars continued, not so much because of the deadpan one-liners directed mostly at the senior military leaders of Subic Bay. The roars and whistles were for Miss Universe.

Roman Gabriel, the quarterback for the Los Angeles Rams of the National Football League (NFL), stepped onstage, and the corny jokes continued. He took his turn as the straight man for another round of jokes centered around tough guys and masculinity. Roman Gabriel was the only player of Filipino-American descent that played in the NFL. He tossed a couple of footballs into the crowd, and the GIs went bonkers. Metaphorically the Bob Hope USO tour scored another touchdown, and the roars continued.

As the show came to a close, all the performers appeared onstage together and asked the soldiers to join in as they sang acapella the Christmas song "Silent Night." As the first notes came forth, I noticed a change in the demeanor of the crowd. A soothing calm swept over the twelve thousand soldiers, and in softly voiced words, they sang, "Silent night, holy night, all is calm all is bright, round yon virgin mother and child, holy infant so tender and mild, sleep in heavenly peace, sleep in heavenly peace." Despite the sweltering heat from the tropical midday sun, for a brief second, I was transported home as I sang. I felt the cold air on my cheeks from a snowy winter day. I envisioned packages under the Christmas tree and the wonderful smell of a Christmas turkey as it baked in the oven. Just like Dorothy in *The Wizard of Oz*, I wanted to click my heels together with the thought, *There's no place like home, there's no place like home.*

I left Subic Bay with a new appreciation for Bob Hope and another lump in my throat. He brought more than laughter and entertainment to the military troops stationed far from home. He brought what his name implied—*hope*. Hope that things will be better, hope that peace will prevail, hope that America will remain strong. Thanks for the memories.

* ⭐ *

RETURNING HOME

As the days of December ticked off the calendar, the date of January 16, my date of return from overseas (DEROS) inched ever so close. The phrase being short fit me perfectly. I wasn't short in stature or short of things to say or do, or even short-tempered. I was very close to discharge from the USAF and a trip back home. In the final few weeks at Clark Air Base, I made arrangements to fly my wife back to the United States, sell my old clunker, a 1955 Oldsmobile I had purchased for $300 several months earlier, and packed what hold baggage the military allowed me to ship home. The pace quickened after Christmas.

A few weeks earlier, I mailed some Christmas cards to family and friends back home. The day before we headed to Manila for my wife's return to the United States, I received a letter from Joe Graham who responded. Joe lived just down the street from me in Milo and was the veterinarian (DVM) for the community. In the letter, Joe told me he was stationed in the Philippines during WWII. There he fought with and befriended a Filipino with the last name of Francisco who now lived in Manila. He asked me, "If you ever go to Manila, can you look up Mr. Francisco?"

Once in Manila, we checked in at the Ambassador Hotel the night before my wife's return flight to America, with connections through Tokyo, Japan, and a final destination of Seattle, Washington. I had a few memories of that trip. The first included our good friends Randy and Mary Dombaugh of Wichita, Kansas, who were our neighbors back at our off-base housing subdivision near Clark Air Base. They joined us for the trip to Manila in a send-off celebration for Judi. After we checked in to our rooms, Randy and I explored the area. We ended up at the swimming pool on the top floor of the hotel. There wasn't much happening as we only saw one swimmer in the pool. As we surveyed the area, the swimmer climbed out of the pool and headed to a nearby table. Randy and I both looked at each other in disbelief. The swimmer, a very attractive dark-haired lady, climbed out of the pool completely nude! She casually walked past us to a nearby table and began to towel herself off as Randy and I stared with our jaws wide open. From around the corner, a gentleman arrived. They spoke to each other in what sounded like German. Randy spoke, "Well, I guess we're not in Kansas anymore, Toto?"

I nodded and said, "*Achtung*, we better head back to the room." Of course, neither Mary nor Judi believed our story, and neither did they entertain the idea of themselves skinny-dipping.

Before we headed out for dinner, I decided to honor Doc Graham's request and tried to locate his Philippine war buddy, Mr. Francisco. I grabbed the phone book in the room and looked for the name. The phone book was huge. I thumbed through its pages and finally found the name Francisco. In 1973, Manila's population exceeded four million, not to mention Quezon City. I wondered how many of those people even had a phone in their home let alone be home or even spoke fluent English? Upon further examination, I discovered pages and pages of the name Francisco, hundreds and hundreds all with the name Francisco. I dialed the first name on the list of numbers, no luck. Next I tried the subsequent name, no luck. I thought this would be an exercise in futility. I tried a third number. I began by telling them I was an American in Manila and hoped to find a friend of Dr. Joe Graham. The voice on the other end exploded in excitement and rattled off something in the native language of Tagalog that I didn't understand. Someone else came on the line and said, "Joe Graham, Joe Graham, you know Joe Graham?"

Surprisingly I made the connection Doc Graham asked about. The party on the line insisted that I come to their residence that day. Unfortunately I could not because of the tight schedule already on the docket that day. I told the Franciscos I could visit them the following week, just days before my DEROS. They were elated. The following day, my wife left the Philippines, and I headed back to Clark with the neighbors Randy and Mary.

The following weekend, I bought a ticket on the bus that made stops at the US Embassy in Manila. It was a much nicer bus than the Rabbit Bus line so familiar to McArthur Highway on which the bulk of the Filipinos crowded into and made the similar trip to Manila. It had nice roomy seats, and the air-conditioning was great. When I arrived at the embassy, I called the Francisco residence and let them know I had arrived. Their son drove to the embassy and picked me up. We drove for about half an hour, up and down crowded streets. I had absolutely no idea where I was or how to get back to the embassy.

When we arrived at the Francisco residence, I saw it to be a very, very modest unpainted wooden-structure house, raised above the ground perhaps six feet and supported by four-by-four pilings. It reminded me of a cabin from my Boy Scout days, except raised on stilts.

Once inside, I met the Francisco family. His wife spoke very little English. Two of his adult children were there as well, the son who picked me up and a daughter. Their English was perfect. They treated me like a king. It was then I heard the story about how he knew Doc Graham. As his story unfolded, he occasionally struggled to find the right words and then deferred to his son for translation. I listened intently. He and Joe met during WWII when US troops fought in the Philippines against the Japanese. He went on to tell how they concocted an alcoholic drink made from sugarcane juice. I didn't know Joe was a drinker. I knew him as perhaps the most straitlaced, down to earth, honest, churchgoing person in all of Milo. War does strange things to people, as any soldier will attest.

Then he continued with his reverence for Joe Graham. Well, after the war, Mr. Francisco became very ill. In fact, as he relayed his story, he was on his deathbed at home. He had no insurance coverage for hospitalization. Medicine was scarce, and he had little or no money to buy any. It was then that he reached out in the form of a letter to his foxhole buddy, Doc Graham, back in the USA. Joe had recently completed his doctor of veterinary medicine (DVM) degree from Iowa State University. Doc Graham sent penicillin to his friend in need. It saved his life. Mr. Francisco was virtually in tears as he told me of his gratitude for his GI friend from years past.

Mr. Francisco was an old wrinkled man that weighed no more than 120 pounds. He walked bent over with the use of a cane. He stood up and, as if partially hobbled, made his way toward me, then reached out with his cane in hand. "Please give this to Joe as a symbol of my gratitude for saving my life." I was speechless. The cane carried so much meaning. It was ornately hand-carved from Philippine mahogany with mother-of-pearl inlay. I told him I would deliver it in person to Joe. Again he gave thanks.

He insisted that I stay for dinner. That was not what I planned. I was on a tight schedule to catch the bus from the US Embassy back to Clark. However, I agreed. That gathering at the dinner table in their humble home became a very memorable occasion. Just Mr. and Mrs. Francisco and I sat at the table. Their two adult children stood around us and served the food. When a plate was put before me, I was dumbfounded. I recognized it as a cow's hoof, about six inches tall. The cooked bone remained intact with the hoof! I had no idea how to go about eating it or if I wanted to. It stood on end and was garnished with rice. I wasn't sure if I should pick it up and eat it like a huge turkey drumstick or cut through the skin with a knife and look for some meat. I did the smart thing. I continued to talk and observed how the Franciscos went about eating their cow hoof. The afternoon ended after dinner. I can attest it wasn't like a meal at the Iowa Beef Steakhouse but an experience I will never forget. I will just say that the rice was good.

Mr. Francisco's adult son drove me in his car back to the US Embassy for the bus ride back to the base. I was less than a week away from discharge from the USAF and happy as a lark about that fact.

On January 15, 1974, I left Clark Air Base, headed to Travis AFB, California. My good friend Wolfgang Kessler picked me up at the barracks for the ride to the Clark passenger terminal. Once again, I island-hopped back to the States and almost arrived before I left as I crossed the international date line headed east. It was sunset when I arrived. I was dog-tired from the fifteen-hour flight. As elated as I felt, I reflected on the POWs flight to the United States nearly a year earlier and could only imagine their euphoria. *God bless, America,* I thought. *God bless, America.* I wanted to bend down on my knees and kiss the ground.

The military always found a way to put a soldier in their place. They gave me one parting shot the next morning. I overslept in the barracks and rushed to the personnel office several blocks away to out process from the military. As I started my walk, a light rain fell. I quickened my pace. The faster I walked, the harder it rained. I upped my pace to a full run in the hopes that I wouldn't be totally drenched by the downpour. Suddenly a car pulled up beside me, and the passenger window rolled down. I thought to myself, *What a pleasant gesture, someone is about to offer me a ride.*

Instead a master sergeant leaned to the window as I reached for the door handle. In a growling voice, he barked out. "Get a hat on the head, soldier!" I heard him loud and clear and was about to unload on him and tell him in no uncertain terms and not in a very polite manner either, "Go take a long walk off a short pier." However, I didn't. From there on, I took a slow casual walk the final block. I arrived at the personnel office soaked wet, through and through, even my socks and underwear. Through it all, I had the biggest smile on my face. Metaphorically speaking, I became drenched in the joy of the moment. I once again became a civilian on January 16, 1974. My time as a soldier ended.

On the airplane ride from Travis AFB to Seattle, I thought about my last four years in the USAF and the many things it taught me. One of first things that popped into my mind were some scribbled rambling thoughts I put on the blank backside of a military form I used for scratch paper. I wrote it during some of the hours and hours of boredom I spent at the fire station. I pulled it out of my folder with all my discharge papers and read it again in a whispered voice.

Humdrum Hero

The Battle of Coral Sea, The Longest Day, The Sands of Iwo Jima, To Hell and Back.
How many times I watched those movies and wondered how the American soldier endured.

I've been called too, but combat is still a Saturday
    night thriller.
Love for those who died,
Praise for the distinguished hero,
But what of me?
I was there, and there, and there, but where?
Yes, I'll tell my grandson of the role I played.
Of my bodily wounds, an important part.
Certainly not worthy of a Purple Heart
For having lost blood to the blade.
Perhaps a more savor prize for those like me
Whose saber I keep for colonels so neat.
No wicked scars from hand to hand encounter
But my humility might heal faster,
Had those wounds been inflicted by the enemy
Instead of the master.
Now a new front, new ambitions,
But an old wound.
Where does this great American liberator loom?
Turned in his guns before his boots, to walk away
    clean.
What a dream!
Hail! Home returns the humdrum hero.

MUM IS THE WORD

Brothers I do not consider that I have made it my
own. But one thing I do: Forgetting what lies behind
and straining forward to what lies ahead.

—Philippians 3:13

There has never been a soldier whose life has not been altered one way or another by their military experience. A walk in a soldier's boots changed the course of direction for many a wayward young man. A soldier buddy of mine, Mike Hanni, from Mackay, Idaho, once revealed to me that before he joined the air force, he had been arrested for selling alcohol to minors at a huge profit. A cash profit so huge, in fact, that over time, he bought a Corvette. When he appeared in court, the judge offered him two choices. The first was a lengthy jail sentence for his crime. The second choice was to join the military. Mike joined the air force.

The military offered discipline, orderliness, neatness, camaraderie, esprit de corps, teamwork, and a sense of purpose for those that adhered to the military way of life. It was a good life and gave a sense of direction and path to follow for many.

There were others, however, unlike my friend Mike Hanni, who already walked the straight and narrow as youngsters before the military called them to duty. They laced up those same boots, but the military sent them in another direction. They did things, saw things, and heard things that ripped at their moral character and made them question their own inner strength. Because of the emotional trauma experienced, they chose to simply not talk about it. While some felt pride in their service to their country, others felt guilt and only wished they could have done more to serve while in uniform or, in

374

some cases, remorse because they had done too much. Neither can be categorized as winners or losers but only as mortal men who felt pain, loneliness, and regret for their wartime actions. A few of the boys of Milo fall into that category and chose to remain silent, not just telling their story for inclusion in this book but remained silent to their spouses and children. Their stories, their heroics, their memories are partially lost. Some have already died, and those who knew them can only guess what they saw, where they went, or who they befriended. Here are just a few of those who elected to remain mum with scant information about their time gathered from public records or fading memories of family.

ROBERT DENNIS NUTTING, WARRANT OFFICER 2

United States Army
United States Army Reserve
May 12, 1969–November 14, 1974

A s a youngster, Bob Nutting lived about a mile south of Milo on the family farm. He graduated from high school in 1965, then went to college at Iowa State University. When doing research for this book, I talked to him on the phone twice and once in person when, by chance, we happened to meet at a Barnes and Noble bookstore. I quizzed him about his time in the military. He didn't say much other than, "What I can tell you about my time in the military and my tour of duty during the Vietnam War, you don't want to hear. I saw too much death and destruction and have nothing good to say." I thanked him and told him I certainly understood and respected his reluctance to speak of his time in the military.

Through public records, I gained a tiny bit of information about Bob. After college, he joined the US Army and became a rotary wing aviator. He took the twenty-week primary warrant officer rotary wing aviator course (WORWAC) at Fort Wolters, Texas, then followed up with an advanced sixteen-week WORWAC at Hunter Army Airfield, Savannah, Georgia.

Upon completion of flight school, Bob headed to Vietnam where he flew helicopters from May 31, 1970, until May 30, 1971.

He received an early out from the army and served just two years and two months of active duty. Upon discharge from active duty, he flew helicopters with the army reserve unit located at the Des Moines Airport until November 1974.

His military awards include the National Defense Service Medal, the Vietnam Campaign Medal, the Vietnam Service Medal, the Army Commendation Medal, the Bronze Star Medal, the Army of Occupation Medal, and the Army Aviator Badge.

Today Bob still farms the homestead a mile south of Milo. He is well respected in the community where he always kept a low profile. I often honk when I drive by and see him outside the barn. He always waves back. God bless Milo guys like Bob.

KENNETH S. NUTTING, SPECIALIST FIFTH CLASS, E-5

United States Army
June 17, 1967–May 21, 1969
March 19, 1970–March 16, 1973

K en Nutting was just enough older than me that I never really knew him personally. The five-year difference in our ages placed us in different social circles. I saw him around town but never had any social interaction with him. I remember him as a stocky built down-to-earth guy. I knew his younger brother, David, much better and his older brother, Henry. David was a year ahead of me in school, and I saw him all the time. Henry was a little older than Ken, but since he was the telephone maintenance guy in Milo, everyone knew Henry.

My first occasion to meet Ken came when I was about thirteen years old. My dad and I were road hunting, along with my uncle Verle Cotter, after a fresh snowfall on a Sunday morning. I remembered road hunting as a fun event as we slowly cruised his green 1956 Buick down old country roads, as we scanned the ditches for pheasants, quail, and rabbits. We slowly crept along an old dirt road that ran north of the Brown's Chapel Church off Highway 65. The road was lined with hedge trees on both sides and thick overgrown brush pushed right up to the road's edge, an ideal spot for wild game to flourish. That same patch of road had a nickname. Those who had a driver's license called it the "thrill hills." For a stretch of about three miles, the narrow road was up and down and up and down. At speeds of 60 to 70 mph, a car could easily go airborne for a few feet and gave the effect of a roller-coaster ride. I dare say every Milo youngster, and even some adults too, took that thrill ride at one time or another.

We had stopped alongside the road because we spotted two rabbits hunched up against a hedge tree. I got out and quietly walked back with my .22 rifle to get a good shot. I looked up and noticed a car just crested the hill and was headed my way. The dirt road was snow-packed and just wide enough for two cars to safely pass. The oncoming car tried to hit the brakes, but the slick road sent him partially sideways. He overcorrected, then spun to the right. I jumped down into the ditch to avoid getting hit. The driver somewhat gained control and avoided a 180-degree spin, but the speed and stopping distance was not in his favor. The car slammed into the rear of my uncle's parked Buick. *Holy cow*, I thought to myself. I was certainly glad I was in the ditch and out of harm's way! I hurried back to the car to see if my dad and uncle were okay. Fortunately they were but shaken and surprised. They never saw the impact coming.

The driver of the car got out. It was Ken Nutting. He apologized for his reckless driving, but we all knew what he was doing. He was joyriding on the thrill hills, hoping to get that weightless feeling in his gut for a few seconds. No doubt he had a gut feeling after the crash, but it wasn't a feeling of weightlessness. It was a sickening feeling of remorse. Neither car had significant damage, as I remembered, and I let the adults settle how the insurance would pay for this incident. As a thirteen-year-old, my big concern at that moment became the two rabbits that escaped during all the confusion. I shot many more rabbits in the future, and forget exactly how many, but I would never forget that first meeting with Ken Nutting.

Ken's military story began on June 17, 1967, when he was drafted into the US Army at age twenty-one. Information about the bulk of his time with the military came from military records and unit historical reports. According to his older brother, Henry, Ken spoke very little about his time with the US Army. What came to surface, however, was the fact that Ken served two separate and distinct hitches in the army. Upon his first enlistment, he quickly ended up in Vietnam with a MOS of 62E20, a heavy equipment operator.

When deployed to Vietnam on his first trip, he was assigned to Company E, 4th Engineering Battalion, 6th US Army, located south of Pleiku at Camp Enari, at the foot of Dragon Mountain. Camp Enari was named in honor of the first posthumously awarded Silver Star recipient, Lieutenant Mark Enari.

While at Camp Enari, Ken performed mine clearing and "jungle busting" tasks. He ferreted out enemy tunnels and cleared a pathway for troop advancement as he built roads, cleared landing zones (LZ), and plowed new runways with his HD-16 Allis-Chalmers  bulldozer. Ken and those who drove the bulldozers were described by one junior-ranking officer as "the grubbiest bunch I've ever seen." They often worked ten-to-sixteen-hour days with temperatures atop their iron beasts that reached 130 degrees. They fought bugs that nested in the trees above, and red ants fell on them, and their stinging bites made the task almost unbearable. In a brief confession by Ken to his older brother, Henry, upon his return from Vietnam, he said, "Bullets from small-arms fire often pinged, then ricocheted off my bulldozer as I made my way through the dense underbrush. I was lucky, I don't know how I wasn't hit."

The worst job of a bulldozer operator was being the lead plow that knocked brush and trees to the side. Operators had little forward visibility and often relied on directional guidance from helicopters that hovered above as they drove blindly forward.

Ken returned to Iowa unscathed after his tour of duty in Vietnam and discharged from active duty at Fort Lewis, Washington, on May 21, 1969. For some unknown reason, after nearly a year in civilian life, Ken volunteered for re-entry into the US Army. He signed up for another hitch after a break in service, and on March 19, 1970, once again put on the army green uniform.

It didn't take long before Ken, the hardened veteran, found himself back in Vietnam, once again with the 4th Engineering Battalion. He knew the routine, he knew the dangers, and he was good at his job. Ken served his second tour in Vietnam from April 3, 1970, until January 28, 1972. He honorably discharged from active duty for a second time on March 16, 1973. His combined time in Vietnam for both tours totaled, three years, nine months, and twenty-six days.

Ken's military awards speak for themselves. He received the Meritorious Unit Commendation Medal, the US Army Commendation Medal, the Vietnam Service Medal, the Bronze Star with two devices, the Vietnam Campaign Medal with six devices, and five Overseas Bars.

Unfortunately Ken died five years after his discharge in a tragic auto accident within the city limits of Milo on April 22, 1978, at age thirty-three. At the time, he worked for the city of Milo as a maintenance man.

Sometimes there are things that cannot be explained. Ken stood at the doorway of death for nearly four years while in Vietnam, yet when he returned to the tranquil community of Milo, he fell victim of a premature and tragic death. There is no worldly answer to the question: Why?

A quote from Don Juan's 1833 publication, *Life of a Sailor*, perhaps best touched on the life of Ken Nutting. Despite the fact that he was an army soldier rather than a sailor, the words ring true.

> *I know many a men in the Navy, who have served their years afloat, untouched by the enemy, and unhurt by misfortune. How true it is, "that in the midst of life we are in death!" That the very moment of intoxicating joy may be our last of existence; and the instant of the greatest security, the date of our death;—How vain are all our precautions against the unerring hand of fate?*

DANIEL JOSEPH NASH, SERGEANT E-5

United States Marine Corps
September 2, 1973–September 20, 1975

I first met Dan as a Little Leaguer. If ever a person warranted a description as an eager beaver, Dan Nash would be the first person that came to mind. He didn't care where he played, he just wanted to play regardless of the position. Dan seemed easily pleased with whatever came his way, and that characteristic carried forward to his relationship with others. He made every effort to accommodate people in any way possible.

Our paths crossed again in the Milo Boy Scouts Troop 136. I was a Life Scout about to outgrow my time as a Boy Scout, so I helped the adult leadership as a junior assistant scoutmaster. Dan had just joined and earned his Tenderfoot badge. One particular Saturday morning, the scouts gathered for a cleanup day to polish up the troops' camping equipment. I specifically remember giving Dan a campfire coffeepot that needed cleaning. It was perhaps the most menial task of the day. It was grubby and so covered with soot that I contemplated throwing it away, but Dan insisted he could make it look like new. He took a Brillo pad and polished that pot until it had a mirror-like finish. He scrubbed and scrubbed on it for over half an hour despite the fact that he would never use it to percolate any coffee at his tender age as an eleven-year-old. That became a good indicator of the type of person Dan would become as an adult. As I saw it, there were basically three types of people in the world. Those who get paid for what they know. Those who get paid for what they do, and those who get paid for what they can get other people to do. Dan was a doer with a heart of gold, as everyone who knew him would readily agree.

At the tender age of nineteen, Uncle Sam called Dan to duty. He was drafted into service on September 21, 1973, and ended up in the USMC. He served two years as an administrative clerk and spent his entire time with the corps on Stateside duty.

Years later, I telephoned Dan on several occasions only to get a recorded message on his answering machine. I told him I'd like to hear about his time in the military, but he never returned my call. I knew he had an ongoing battle with cancer, and if he wasn't feeling up to par, I didn't want to impose with less important things. Dan died on June 5, 2018, at age sixty-three. I attended his funeral, as did a number of other boys of Milo. During the memorial service, I sat next to one of my high school classmates, Greg Weaklend, himself a former marine reservist and Milo boy.

On my drive home, I reflected how virtually every funeral I've attended when the deceased previously served in the military, there is always, always mention of their time in uniform. The words written in an obituary at times seem so small to the contributions made to this country. "He proudly served. He honorably served. He earned medals for heroic acts. His interment will be in a military cemetery." The grave marker often carries an image of the US flag or military insignia. Just two years as a marine, from the sixty-three years of Dan's time on earth, so impacted his life and the lives of those who knew him is such a remarkable thing. The corps set Dan's compass for years to come, as it has for many, many others who have served.

I talked to his wife, Carol, sometime later as well as his children. They knew very little of Dan's time in the USMC, other than he served. In 1779, USMC Captain William Jones let it be known that he was looking for "a few good men" to serve aboard his ship. That slogan of the USMC has survived for 241 years. Dan Nash met that standard as one of a few good men. I stand at attention and salute Sergeant Nash, *semper fi*, always faithful, always strong.

THOMAS MAX LONG, SPECIALIST FOURTH CLASS, E-4

United States Army
January 10, 1966–January 9, 1968

Tom graduated from high school in the spring of 1964. Just over a year later, he received the worst Christmas gift ever imagined. In the mail on Christmas Eve, he received his draft notice. Things moved quickly, and Tom enlisted on January 10, 1966, as a draftee in the US Army. Tom's younger brother, Henry, would also be drafted into the US Army just three years later.

Tom had a very interesting and unique experience while in the army, unlike any of the other boys of Milo. However, he requested that none of that information be revealed. He performed the entire two years of duty Stateside. He received an honorable discharge on January 9, 1968.

STERLING R. GREUFE, PETTY OFFICER THIRD CLASS, E-4

United States Navy
May 31, 1962–August 20, 1965

S terling joined the US Navy at age eighteen, a skinny kid who stood just five feet and eight inches and weighed a mere 135 pounds. He was another Milo boy who cherished his privacy and preferred to offer very limited information about his time in the military. What information revealed here came from public military records and historical reports.

He enlisted on May 13, 1962. After basic training, he attended advanced schooling from October 8, 1962 to May 31, 1963, and earned the classification as a sonar technician, designated as a STG 3. As a STG 3, his duties included underwater surveillance as well as navigation and search-and-rescue operations.

His first ship assignment was the USS *Shelton* (DD-790), a Gearing-class destroyer, 390-foot long battleship that carried six five-inch 38/AA guns, twelve 40 mm/AA guns, and eleven 20 mm/AA guns, and ten twenty-one-inch torpedo tubes. The USS *Shelton* had a crew of 336 sailors and was based out of Yokosuka, Japan, when Sterling arrived in June of 1963.

As conditions in Vietnam continued to deteriorate, the US Navy sent the USS *Shelton* to join other vessels in the Gulf of Tonkin on June 2, 1964. It remained there until July 18, then via Pearl Harbor, headed back to its port in San Diego where it arrived on August 31, 1964.

Sterling spent three years, two months, and twenty days in the US Navy. Of that time, two years, one month, and fourteen days were aboard ship overseas. He received his honorable discharge on August 20, 1965. Four days later, on August 24, the USS *Shelton* sailed back to the Gulf of Tonkin and joined the 7th Fleet off the shores of Vietnam. By then, Sterling was back home in Milo.

TRY IT, YOU'LL LIKE IT

I relished the life of a civilian for a few years without the morning reveille call. At last, I had my feet on the ground and carved out the beginning of a professional career in civilian life in the insurance business. I wore a suit and tie to work, not jungle fatigues. I sat in an office rather than behind the wheel of a fire truck that rushed to the scene of an emergency. My afternoon workouts were conducted at the YMCA where I played racquetball instead of dragging a fire hose or climbing a ladder. I quickly shared with anyone interested, my impression of the military. "Hurry up and wait" was a favorite quote. Another was "If you like standing in line for anything and everything, join the military."

In July 1977, the 132nd Fighter Wing, Iowa Air National Guard (ANG) held an open house for the general public with static displays of various aircraft, all of which I was quite familiar with from my active duty days in the USAF, as well as equipment used by the military in support of their aircraft, the A-7 Corsair. I decided to go and check out the airplanes. Upon arrival, to my surprise, they had an intact fire department that provided protection not for just the ANG base but crash rescue services for the entire Des Moines Airport. It was exactly the same equipment I used when I served on active duty. My heart fluttered and brought back old memories. I loved the job, I loved the camaraderie of fellow soldiers and fellow firefighters, but I hated the pay and all the malarkey that accompanied the military. I kicked a few tires when on base and talked shop to some of the firefighters. They introduced me to the fire chief, Senior Master Sergeant Leland Kenney, and he in turn introduced me to the ANG recruiter, Master Sergeant Bud Erickson.

Bud called me the following week and encouraged me to come to the base again for another visit. He thought I would make a great addition to the 132nd Fighter Wing. I wasn't so sure. I expressed, in no uncertain terms, my concerns to once again sign on the dotted line and be at the whim of Uncle Sam. He replied, "Soldier, have I ever got a deal for you. The ANG just implemented a program called Try One. Since your initial obligation on active duty is complete, the ANG will give you the opportunity to walk away at any time should you become unhappy with the ANG enlistment."

I asked him, "Any time?"

He answered back, "Any time. Even after the first weekend drill, if you're not happy, you are free to walk away."

I thought about it for a week, then called him back. "Sign me up," I told him. "I'll try one." I tried one for another twenty-one years.

My first duty day with the Iowa ANG began on August 3, 1977. A general assembly of members formed beneath the flagpole for an awards ceremony. To my amazement, I knew many within the squadron. Some were Milo boys!

THE WEEKEND
WARRIORS

T here were many who held the view that membership in the national guard carried with it a stigma of second-class citizenship. The general perception arose that active duty air force personnel pooh-poohed those who joined the ANG. This condescending viewpoint held true for all guard and reserve branches of the military which included the army reserves, the naval reserves, and the marine corps reserves. I witnessed firsthand during my own active duty time, when stationed in New Jersey, when those on active duty looked down their noses at their counterparts when drill weekend arrived. Rarely did the guard troops intermingle with those on active duty. That included specific tasks for their trained AFSC, or something as simple as a shared cigarette or a cold soda during downtime. In fact, during basic training, ANG troops trained apart and separate from those who signed up for active duty. I dared to speculate which made the right decision, those who joined the guard during the Vietnam conflict or those who signed up for active duty.

A recruiting motto, "One weekend per month, two weeks per year," attracted many young men and a few women. So many, in fact, that a waiting list existed to join the air national guard in the late 1960s. To understand the meaning of that motto, a historical look at guard units from years past should be examined. Back during World War II, our country came under attack, and those who joined the guard expected to see overseas duty. That same concept held true during the Korean War. However, during the Vietnam War, President Lyndon Johnson made it clear that the national guard would not be involved in overseas deployments. They would be deployed for

Stateside duty only. In a nutshell, that meant those who were lucky enough to be inducted in to the guard could be assured they would not see any action in the Vietnam War. Thus the phrase "weekend warriors or guard pukes" became prominent. That viewpoint, held not only by active duty members but the general public became reinforced when national guard troops were called to duty during the Detroit riots of 1967. That riot lasted five days with 43 people killed, 342 injured, and 1,400 buildings burned. Over seven thousand national guard members were sent to quell the riots, and their dismal performance to bring things under control underscored their abysmal ability to perform under pressure. A few years later in 1970, the governor of Ohio sent the national guard to thwart a college campus protest at Kent State University. That resulted in the death of four students shot by national guard troops! Their weapon of choice: an M1 Garand rifle, an M1911 pistol, and a twelve-gauge shotgun. Added to the mix, in 1968, was the My Lia massacre in which US soldiers brutally killed women, children, and old men in the small Vietnamese village. The image by the general public of the military and the national guard took a nosedive, and it headed straight to the toilet.

The national guard versus active duty controversy carried with it a myriad of complex issues, mostly political at the time, and much to do about funding by the federal government to properly train the guard as well as provide needed equipment. Too many times, the ANG became an afterthought and subsequently supplied with hand-me-down equipment and aircraft. To emphasize that point, in 1968, the 132nd flew the F-89 Scorpion, an aircraft first brought into service with the USAF in 1950. Its straight-wing configuration limited its performance, but it became the first jet that carried air-to-air missiles. An F-89 assigned to the 132nd crashed in December of 1968 on a local training mission. The cause of that crash was never determined.

In 1969, the unit converted to the F-84 Thunderjet. That aircraft was plagued by so many structural and engine problems, the USAF deemed it unable to execute the mission for which it was designed. The Air National Guard Bureau (ANGB) subsequently sent the F-84 to the Iowa ANG rather than the boneyard located at Davis Monthan AFB, Arizona. The ANG made do with what they had. They always strived in their attempt to be as good as the active duty but worked with inferior outdated equipment and a constantly underfunded budget.

Added to that complex dilemma, President Johnson altered his stance on the use of ANG members serving overseas. The war began to spin out of control. The 174th Tactical Fighter Squadron (TFS) located in Sioux City, Iowa (the sister unit to the Des Moines ANG), deployed to Vietnam on May 11, 1968. While stationed at Phu Cat, Vietnam, the 174th TFS more than carried its weight. They flew 11,359 hours in combat with a total of 653 sorties in the F-100 Super Sabre. Other ANG flying units that deployed to Vietnam in 1968 were the 120th TFS from Colorado, the 188th TFS from New Mexico, and the 136th TFS from New York. The guard stood shoulder to shoulder with the active duty air force and never blinked and never flinched.

Fortunately things changed over time with the ANG, but it took a while to overcome the weekend warrior mentality. The ANG seemingly turned the corner with their wartime tasking in the mid to late 1970s. It was then the Iowa unit received the A-7 Corsair aircraft, not as a hand-me-down from the active duty air force but directly from the factory. They flew the Corsair until 1989. During that time, the pace quickened. Pilots participated in the Red Flag combat training held at Nellis AFB, Nevada, and flew alongside active duty counterparts. The 132nd sent aircraft and support personnel all over the world. Deployments included trips to Panama, England, Canada, Puerto Rico, and Japan. The ANG became embraced by the Pentagon as an integral part of the Total Force Concept and carried a heavy load as part of the air defense of the country.

Again in 1990, the 132nd Fighter Wing upgraded its aircraft with the introduction of the F-16 to its inventory. These were front-line aircraft that the unit deployed along with support personnel to the Middle East during the Gulf War. The term *weekend warriors* no longer applied. The phrase "two days per month and two weeks per year" no longer applied. Personnel often deployed to godforsaken parts of the world such as Djibuti, Africa, Balad, Kazakhstan, Baghdad, Iraq, and Kabul, Afghanistan, where they came under hostile fire. Tours of duty for some lasted up to six months under harsh conditions. Some asked, "Who were these warriors?" The answer became simple. They were not just young college kids who sought to avoid active duty. They were not just guys between jobs who looked to the guard for extra money.

The guard pilots who deployed took a leave of absence from their position as commercial airline pilots. The security forces took a leave of absence from their position as city police officers. The firefighters left their position as paramedics and emergency medical technicians (EMTs) for their hometown cities. United Parcel Service (UPS) drivers took a leave of absence from their routes and drove supply trucks and Humvees through roads laden with improvised explosive devices (IEDs). School teachers left the confines of their classrooms in exchange for a tent with a cot and laptop computer that rested atop stacked wooden pallets that sufficed for an office desk where they coordinated logistics for equipment and supplies. They brought with them a wealth of knowledge, not just from their military training but from their day-to-day knowledge from nearly identical civilian jobs. Just as important, however, they brought a degree of maturity with their life experiences. Those skills equaled those of their active duty counterparts and, in many cases, surpassed them. No longer were members of the guard looked down upon— they were looked up to.

The Iowa ANG leaned forward for a number of years as they flew the F-16, but due to the Obama administration's desire to reduce defense spending, the F-16 squadron in Des Moines saw its final flight in 2012. Not to be disheartened, particularly since the unit frequently outperformed active duty units, they picked up a new highly technical mission. In 2013 the ANG unit began to fly the MQ-9 Reaper, a remote-piloted aircraft (RPA), described as the most feared RPA in the world. The MQ-9 was the aircraft that eliminated Iranian terrorist Quassim Soleimani in January 2020.

The new mission of the 132nd Iowa ANG became threefold: (1) remote flight operations of the RPA, (2) the establishment of a Cyber

Defense Squadron that provided vital classified information to state, Department of Defense (DOD), and friendly foreign entities, and (3) the establishment of an Intelligence Surveillance Reconnaissance Group (ISRG) that provides lethal reach back capabilities to military commanders around the world. The guard's operational tempo today puts to rest any Beavis and Butt-head argument that "we're not worthy."

ROGER MICHAEL UTTLEY, MASTER SERGEANT, E-7

132ⁿᵈ Tactical Fighter Wing
Iowa Air National Guard
January 19, 1970–July 7, 1980

During unit formation of my very first weekend drill with the Iowa Air National Guard, Mike Uttley was called front and center for an award. I hadn't seen Mike since high school. *Holy cow*, I thought, *Mike is a master sergeant?* Even though he joined the air guard in January, Mike didn't go to basic training until February 22. That was the same month that I joined the air force. In fact, we were both at basic training at Lackland AFB, Texas, at the very same time but never saw each other. Even though I retained my active duty rank as a staff sergeant when I joined the ANG, he far outdistanced me in stripes. In our younger days, back in Milo, Mike lived across the street from the baseball field. I knew him and his family pretty well. His dad, Keith, worked for the city of Milo, and his mom, Dorothy, worked at the Milo branch of People's Trust and Savings Bank.

After basic training, Mike went to Sheppard AFB, Texas, for advanced schooling. There he earned the AFSC (air force specialty code) as a 36370, a communications relay repairman. Mike was a sharp cookie and parlayed his education from the military into a civilian job with the Northwestern Bell telephone company. He later enhanced his positon with the phone company while a member of the ANG when he earned the AFSC of 30670, crypto repairman yet again another educational jump to the AFSC of 29190, tele-communications operations supervisor. He went on to complete the Non-Commissioned Officer (NCO) Academy located at McGhee Tyson AFB, Tennessee. There he earned the Distinguished Graduate recognition.

As told by Mike, most of his military deployments included two-week trips to Volk Field, Wisconsin, and Gulfport, Mississippi. The highlight of his time with the ANG was marked by an over-seas deployment to Waddington RAF (Royal Air Force), located near Lincolnshire, England.

Mike's civilian job with the telephone company relocated him to Illinois. It made it extremely difficult to maintain his status as a member of the ANG. After slightly over ten years as a member of the ANG, Mike took off his uniform for the last time on July 7, 1980, and was honorably discharged.

Mike retired from American Telephone and Telegraph (AT&T) in 1998 and then took another position with CenturyLink located in Dallas, Texas. He now lives in Kauffman, Texas, located a few short miles southeast of Dallas, where he and his wife operate a shelter for abandoned dogs.

BENNY P. HAMILTON, STAFF SERGEANT, E-5

132ⁿᵈ Tactical Fighter Wing
Iowa Air National Guard
April 15, 1968–April 14, 1974

Less than a year out of high school, Ben joined the Iowa ANG, located in Des Moines, in April of 1968 and within a week found himself at Lackland AFB, Texas. After six weeks of boot camp, Ben returned to the Des Moines unit and began OJT for the AFSC of 242×0, a disaster preparedness technician. During his six-year enlistment, Ben spent three separate two-week deployments to Lowry AFB, Colorado, for disaster preparedness training.

Military disaster preparedness encompassed a number of areas that included natural disasters such as floods, tornadoes, and earthquakes. The Cold War with the Soviet Union of the 1950s gradually intensified through the years. However, in the time frame of the late 1960s through the 1990s, the focus for the USAF disaster preparation at the Iowa ANG base geared itself for attacks in the form of chemical, biological, and radiological agents or a nuclear attack. The Mission Oriented Protective Posture (MOPP) gear provided protection for such attacks. The charcoal-lined suits with respirator, hood, rubber gloves, and boots became a ritual remembered by those who served. The suits were hot, cumbersome, and extremely uncomfortable to wear, particularly for hours on end. The suits were difficult to put on by oneself and best done with a buddy that helped with straps, booties, and hood. With the MOPP 4 gear donned, all normal duty tasks were expected to be performed with a degree of proficiency. It became a tough job to keep the troops enthused about wearing the MOPP gear and convincing them of the practicality of ever using it in a life-threatening situation. More than one soldier succumbed to heat exhaustion and passed out during extended training exercises. If anyone had issues with claustrophobia, MOPP gear became a real nightmare. Ben had a tough job keeping the guard troops excited about wearing the protective suits.

Fortunately not only for Ben, but the entire world, President Richard Nixon engaged in the Strategic Arms Limitation Talks (SALT), and on May 26, 1972, he signed an agreement with Russian general secretary Leonid Brezhnev that limited the use of antiballistic missiles (ABM) for both the United States and the Soviet Union. The US Senate ratified the agreement on August 3, 1972. Because of that agreement, the tension level between both countries dropped significantly. Ben continued to train up members of the unit, but quite frankly, the enthusiasm to wear the MOPP gear waned significantly as the Cold War wound down and eventually ended in 1991. The disaster preparedness training certainly didn't have the same appeal as a trip to the firing range. Coincidentally Ben also conducted the annual firing range qualifications for unit members in addition to his regular duties as a disaster preparedness instructor.

An interesting story told by Ben involved a particular incident he witnessed at the firing range located at Volk Field, Wisconsin. One of his peers, TSgt Henderson, had an attitude as perceived by more than a few troops he instructed. His arrogance was boldly displayed with an ever-present chip on his shoulder. One particular weekend, TSgt Henderson began instruction with a group of pilots for pistol qualification. Henderson wore a flight suit. The flight suit, in a way, represented a status symbol for those who flew aircraft, and the fact that this outsider wore one did not impress the aircrews. Unbeknownst to Henderson, one of the pilots placed a lit cigarette into the pocket of the flight suit. As Henderson began the demonstration, he assumed the prone position, with the pilots standing behind as they smirked and awaited with great anticipation. About the time he fired the first round from the .45 caliber pistol, the burning cigarette found its way to his bare skin. He immediately jumped up to his feet and frantically flailed in his attempt to dislodge the burning cigarette. With each jerk of his free hand and the .45 pistol in the other, his reflex action continued to trigger the weapon. The pilots scrambled in all directions as they dodged the bullets. It was funny, but it wasn't funny. An official investigation ensued. A bad attitude, disrespect for the weapon, and a dramatic violation of firing rage protocol, coupled with a prank, nearly resulted in serious injury. Needless to say, TSgt Henderson never again conducted firearms training, nor did he ever again put on a flight suit. Who was it that said weekend warriors would never walk in harm's way?

After his six-year obligation with the air national guard, Ben received an honorable discharge and returned to civilian life on April 14, 1974. Today Ben lives in the southwestern part of the United States.

ARNOLD KEITH GREUBEL, SERGEANT, E-4

132nd Tactical Fighter Wing
Iowa Air National Guard
August 8, 1968–August 7, 1974

Arnie joined the Iowa Air National Guard in August of 1968, just three months out of high school. He didn't leave for basic training at Lackland AFB, Texas, until September 8, 1968. His arrival in San Antonio didn't go without a hitch. Arnie boarded the wrong bus at the airport and found himself headed to the officer candidate school (OCS) rather than basic training for new recruits. Once the error was discovered, the TIs graciously welcomed him with a smile and handshakes at his proper place and humbly apologized for the mistake. Upon completion of boot camp, the USAF sent him to Lowry AFB, Colorado, where he earned the AFSC of 70230, an administrative clerk. Arnie worked in the clothing issue section of the base supply warehouse. If any guard troops needed new boots, a field jacket, or a set of fatigues, Arnie became the guy who took care of the need.

Early Sunday morning, March 30, 1969, the base supply warehouse where Arnie worked during drill weekends caught fire. Severe damage to the south end of the building required a temporary relocation to conduct normal business. Fortunately the loss of inventory was limited.

During his six-year obligation, Arnie deployed to Offutt AFB, Nebraska, as well as Volk Field, Wisconsin, and Gulfport, Mississippi. Arnie best enjoyed the Gulfport deployments, and on his last trip there, in 1974, drove his Volkswagen Beetle the one thousand miles south to the Gulf Coast. As most every guardsman would attest, deployed with no transportation proved to be a poor decision. Arnie not only managed several trips to the beach but squeezed in a weekend trip to New Orleans for the Mardi Gras celebration. As the saying went in New Orleans, "*laissez les bon temps rouler*" (let the good times roll).

Arnie completed his six-year obligation with the Iowa ANG, and despite the offer of a promotion to staff sergeant if he would only reenlist, he elected to call it quits. He received an honorable discharge on August 7, 1974.

LEROY CHARLES RODGERS, SPECIALIST FOURTH CLASS, E-4

United States Army Reserves
March 30, 1967–January 9, 1972

eroy grew up on a farm east of Milo and graduated from high school in 1965. Like most other fellas during those days, he knew it would be just a matter of time before Uncle Sam called him to duty. The choices back then were limited. Either enroll in college and obtain a student deferment from the draft selection board, volunteer for one of the armed services, wait and likely get drafted into the army, or try to get a job in town. Virtually every employer pushed job applications to the bottom of the pile when they discovered the potential hire was classified 1A. Leroy wanted to farm. The other choices didn't appeal to him.

Through a connection with the family attorney, Darrell Goodhue, the conversation arose that no doubt Leroy would soon be in uniform. Darrell himself was a member of the US Army Reserves located at Fort Des Moines. He suggested Leroy sign up. Darrell told him he would do what he could to grease the wheels and make that happen. As the saying went, "It's not what you know, it's who you know." With some inside pull, Leroy became a reservist and headed to basic training at Fort Leonard Wood, Missouri, on March 30, 1967.

Leroy never participated in any school sports. He was a farmer and got his exercise working on the farm. His time at basic training became a challenge due to his portly build and, in his own words, began to wonder if he could endure all the rigors of fitness training demanded of recruits. When it came time to complete the final phase of basic training with the completion of the confidence course, Leroy had his doubts, and the doubts were justified. He endured previous trial runs where he ran, crawled, climbed tall fences, walked on a beam, and swung on a rope across a ravine. He didn't do so well on those physical challenges. His day of reckoning arrived, and he became extremely nervous. As luck would have it, a torrential downpour of rain fell as his group marched to the confidence course. It rained so hard, and for so long, the drill instructors deemed the confidence course unsafe to use. The final phase of training was scratched, and Leroy breathed a sigh of relief.

He stayed at Fort Leonard Wood for advanced training with a MOS of 92A, an automated logistics specialist. His duty was simple, Leroy maintained records for the management of warehouse functions for the storage of equipment and parts. Upon his return to Fort Des Moines, he was assigned to the 312th Quartermasters.

Leroy missed a weekend training session when he decided that deer hunting should take precedence. Upon his return to Fort Des Moines the following month, he found he had been transferred from his quartermaster position into the 974th Personal Records Company as a clerk typist. That seemed fine with him. As a member of the 974th, he recalled a deployment to the supply depot located in Columbus, Ohio. There he spent two weeks and shuffled papers.

On his last deployment, cited as his most memorable, his company deployed to Fort Carson, Colorado. Leroy commented, "Was it ever a trip getting there! In a convoy, I drove a manual shift 1952 Studebaker two-and-a-half-ton truck the entire seven hundred miles. The ride couldn't have been worse if I had ridden on the back of a hay wagon the entire journey."

On the free weekend, Leroy and a friend decided to take a tour of the Cheyenne Mountain military complex. Cheyenne Mountain is the underground operations center for the North American Aerospace Defense Command (NORAD) built 2,000 feet beneath the triple-peaked granite mountain, formerly called Mount Albrecht. The complex consumed five acres of facilities buried deep inside the mountain. The elevation of Cheyenne Mountain is 9,564 feet. In order to get there, Leroy drove the 1952 two-and-a-half-ton olive-green truck the sixteen miles that wound up the mountain from Fort Carson. Upon arrival, he soon discovered that no tours were scheduled that day. He headed back to the parking lot for the ride down the mountain.

To his dismay, the old Studebaker would not start. After several attempts, he looked under the hood for any obvious mechanical problems. He determined that with the nearly ten-thousand-foot high altitude, the air pressure prevented the carburetor from getting enough oxygen to properly fire up the engine. With some old-fashioned farmer's ingenuity, Leroy disengaged the clutch and used the starter motor and cranked the engine enough to turn the truck around where it faced the downhill road. With fingers crossed, he shifted the drab olive-green monster into neutral and began to coast down the hillside as he carefully rode the brakes. Occasionally he shifted into gear and popped the clutch to see if the old girl would pop off. Not right away, however. Nearly halfway down, the mountain air finally provided enough oxygen, and to Leroy and his partner's delight, the behemoth coughed and sputtered, then fired off. That trip was one that Leroy would never forget and one he never repeated.

Upon the completion of his six-year obligation with the US Army Reserves, Leroy discharged on January 9, 1972.

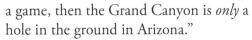

RICHARD ALLEN UTTLEY, CHIEF MASTER SERGEANT, E-9, RETIRED

132ⁿᵈ Fighter Wing
Iowa Air National Guard
April 23, 1971–October 1, 2002

I first met Rick Uttley as a Little Leaguer in 1961. It was my last year of eligibility as a twelve-year-old and Rick's first year as an eight-year-old. We both loved the game of baseball, particularly so since it was the only game in the town of Milo. There were no Peewee or Pop Warner football teams, no soccer, or Junior Golfers League. Baseball was king. In the words of George Frederick Will, a syndicated columnist and television commentator, "If baseball is *only*

a game, then the Grand Canyon is *only* a hole in the ground in Arizona."

Rick had a great sense of direction and knew exactly what he wanted to do. He wanted to be a diesel mechanic. His older brother, Mike, previously joined the Iowa Air National Guard in 1970 and whispered in his ear, "The ANG is a pretty good deal for you if you want to be a mechanic." Rick took his advice and joined the 132nd FW, Iowa Air National Guard on April 23, 1971, a month before his high school graduation. He left for basic training at Lackland AFB, Texas, a week after he received his diploma.

After six weeks of indoctrination to the air force way, Rick headed to Sheppard AFB, located in Wichita Falls, Texas, where he learned the skills as an aircraft maintenance repairman for reciprocating engines, sometimes called piston poppers. While at Sheppard, to his surprise, he crossed paths with fellow Milo guy Stan Merrell, who also was enrolled in school there on active duty with the USAF.

In 1974, Rick accepted a full-time position with the Iowa Air National Guard as an air technician. Air technicians were civilian employees of the military yet a prerequisite of the position mandated membership in the ANG. He wore the uniform, not just on guard weekends but throughout the week as a civilian employee. With that new status, Rick switched to the Consolidated Aircraft Maintenance Squadron (CAMS) and worked on the newly acquired F-100 Super Sabre jets.

In 1976, the unit transitioned to the A-7 Corsair aircraft, and Rick again transferred, this time, to the avionics section where he conducted maintenance on the jet's electronic navigation and communications systems. That required additional schooling. Rick spent six months at Lowry AFB, Colorado, and returned to the unit with a new set of skills.

In 1989, he transferred to the A-7 flight simulator. The flight simulator located at the Des Moines unit was just one of a handful within the entire country. It provided realistic flight training for pilots without ever leaving the ground. In simple terms, it was the ultimate video game with all the sounds, cockpit movements, and visual displays imaginable that included all weather fight options, and even aircraft carrier landings.

Less than two years later, the unit lost the simulator due to the arrival of the F-16 Falcon aircraft. Once again, Rick switched occupations with the ANG. In 1991, he returned to Lowry AFB for another six-month advanced school for maintenance on the F-16. His new title became avionics intermediate shop technician.

In October 1995, Rick deployed to Incirlk, Turkey, as part of Operation Provide Comfort II. Provide Comfort II served as a continued effort by US and coalition forces that protected the Kurdish population of Northern Iraq from attacks after the Persian Gulf War and provided them not only security but humanitarian support. ANG units rotated personnel and aircraft from 1991–1996 in that capacity. On that deployment, unit members slept in a tent city on the perimeter of the 3,320-acre installation.

Rick returned to Turkey in May of 1997 as a senior master sergeant, along with F-16s from the 132nd FW and a contingent of support personnel, as part of Operation Northern Watch, the successor to Operation Provide Comfort. Operation Northern Watch enforced the no-fly zone above the 36th parallel in Iraq. Never before had Rick experienced any fear, but those two deployments shed new light on his own anxieties, not just for his own safety but the entire guard unit. The Middle East presented a different perspective on many things for Rick and gave him the opportunity to reflect on the kind of life he knew back in Iowa. He admitted he had several sleepless nights as he thought of his family back in Milo and of the potential danger he faced by his mere presence in a foreign land. It became a real eye-opener for him.

> *Then you will walk on your way securely, and your foot will not stumble. If you lie down you will not be afraid; when you lie down, your sleep will be sweet. Do not be afraid of sudden terror or of the ruin of the wicked, when it comes, for the Lord will be your confidence and keep your foot from being caught.* (**Proverbs 3:23–26**)

One of the events Rick cherished most during his time in the military was an F-16 flyover during the Milo Fourth of July celebration parade in the early 1990s. Rick coordinated that special event in conjunction with Milo mayor, Tom Stoutner, and the Iowa adjutant general.

Rick retired after thirty-one years with the air national guard. As a professional soldier, he climbed the career ladder in the military to its highest point and, upon discharge, held the highest enlisted rank of any of the boys of Milo, a chief master sergeant. Today Rick lives in Bella Vista, Arkansas, where you can often find him on the golf course.

LARRY J. HELLER, STAFF SERGEANT, E-5

US Army Reserves, Aurora, Colorado, First Lieutenant,
0-2
1979–1982
Iowa Air National Guard
April 27, 1963–April 26, 1969

As a youngster, I best remember Larry when I became a pickup player on an ad hoc basketball game frequently played at the Milo park in the late 1950s into the early 1960s. He was seven years older than me, and my role on the team became simple. I played and balanced out an even number of kids on each team. Larry had some great basketball skills, as I remember, and his on-court skills reminded me of Bob Cousey who played professionally with the Boston Celtics from 1950 to 1963. His no-look passes became his trademark, and for me, it became a chore to avoid taking one of those passes in the nose. That outdoor cement court entertained dozens of Milo kids during those years. A group of us would meet after a fresh snow with shovels in hand and clear off the court for a game before we shoveled our own sidewalks at home. As soon as the sun came out and temperatures reached 40 degrees or more, it became game on. Oftentimes our fingers were so cold, we couldn't get a firm feel for the basketball, but we dribbled on. A single overhead light dimly lit the court and allowed games for the boys of Milo to be played well into the night. The court is still in the park, over fifty years since we honed our basketball skills, but I can attest I haven't seen a group of kids shooting hoops there for many years.

Larry joined the 132nd Tactical Fighter Wing in May 1963, three years out of high school. He said he joined for no particular reason or outside pressures. It became a quick source for some easy money during his college years.

He attended basic training at Lackland AFB, Texas. Upon completion of boot camp, he returned to his guard unit in Des Moines where he enrolled in OJT with an AFSC of 2S0X1, a material supply control technician. In Larry's own words, it was a pretty straightforward job. "I maintained an inventory of supplies and equipment and issued them as requested."

During his time with the unit, the 132nd flew the F-89 Scorpion. Larry recalled that each month, during weekend drills, the rumor became the activation of the entire unit for duty in Vietnam. He couldn't worry about that day in and day out, but it almost came to pass. The F-89 was an outdated aircraft, so when the call came for activation, the sister unit in Iowa, the 174th Fighter Squadron from Sioux City who flew the F-100, took the mission in May 1968. Larry remained in Des Moines.

With the sour taste of antiwar protests in America during that time frame, Larry recalled a whole bunch of riot training during his weekend drills. There were protests along McKinley Avenue, near the entrance of the guard base as well as the Iowa State fairgrounds, but Larry himself was never called upon to forcibly counter the protesters. In a nutshell, Larry described his time with the air national guard as uneventful; in fact, nearly all his two-week long summer camps were spent in Des Moines. He honorably discharged in May 1969, with his six-year commitment completed. He had fond memories of those he worked with during those six years and mentioned how great a group of people unit members were to work with. "They could do and fix just about anything, regardless how small or large the task."

In Larry's own words, "I had a decent job in civilian life, but I had my eyes set on bigger things." He enrolled in medical school at the University of Iowa after he completed his undergraduate degree at Iowa State University. He earned his doctor of medicine (MD) degree in 1978. His residency took him to St. Luke Hospital in Denver, Colorado, from 1978–1982. While in Colorado, he met and worked with a doctor by the last name of Holloman. Holloman held the rank as a colonel in the US Army Reserves. At the colonel's urging, Larry joined the Colorado Reserve unit in 1979 and was commissioned as second lieutenant. His army reserve status sent him to Fitzsimons Army Hospital, located in Aurora, Colorado, where he became a member of the Mobile Army Surgical Hospital (Mash).

Larry completed his doctoral residency at St. Luke Hospital in 1982. In just a few short years with the army reserves, he advanced to the rank of first lieutenant. However, since he previously fulfilled his military obligation, he opted to once again discharge from the military. He hung up his uniform, both the blue and the green, long ago. Today Larry J. Heller, MD is a pathology specialist at Methodist Hospital in Des Moines, Iowa.

Keep the charge of the Lord your God, walking in his ways
and keeping his statutes, his commandments, his rules, and
his testimonies, as it is written in the Laws of Moses, that you
may prosper in all that you do and wherever you turn.

—1 Kings 2:3

RICHARD JOHN GREUBEL, PRIVATE FIRST CLASS, E-3

United States Army Reserves
December 4, 1967–November 30, 1973

I best knew Rich in high school when we both were in the same Spanish class. I'm not so sure how much of the language either of us retained over the years, but I do remember the requirement to call each other by our Spanish names while in class. Rich went by the name Carlos, he called me Miguel. *"Buenos dias, Carlos. Cómo estás?"*

Rich Greubel joined the army reserves in December 1967, and performed weekend drills for six months at Fort Des Moines before being sent to basic training on July 22, 1968, just a month prior to his brother, Arnie's, enlistment in the air national guard.

He completed his basic training at Fort Jackson, South Carolina. During firing range exercises, the army recognized Rich as the top firer for the entire Sixth Battalion, comprised of nearly eight hundred recruits. He was awarded a trophy for his expertise with the rifle. He remained at Fort Jackson after basic training for his advanced schooling and received a MOS of 76A10, as a supply clerk, on November 18, 1968.

Once back in Iowa, Rich returned to the 312th Quartermasters unit, located at Fort Des Moines. The majority of his summer training camps were held at Fort McCoy, Wisconsin. While a member of the army reserves, Rich continued with college and graduated from Simpson College with a degree in political science. He received an honorable discharge on November 30, 1973.

A noted point for both Rich and his brother, Arnie: their father, Albert "Bert" Greubel, served in the US Army during World War II and fought in the Battle of the Bulge from December 16, 1944–January 24, 1945. Bert never spoke to his sons about his experiences during the war, but they heard bits and pieces from their mother. It was ugly. The Battle of the Bulge was one of the largest and bloodiest battle of World War II. The German's last offensive battle sent 450,000 troops into the Ardennes Forest. Though the numbers for German forces are estimated, historians calculated as many as 98,000 were killed, wounded, or captured. The US forces reached 610,000. Of those, 19,000 were killed and another 89,000 injured in combat. Needless to say, Bert was overjoyed his two sons chose to serve with the US Army Reserves and the air national guard with some degree of assurances they would not face the same combat as he.

The father of a righteous child has great joy;
a man who fathers a wise son rejoices in him.
(Proverbs 23:24)

Rich retired a project manager for Pioneer Hi-Bred International located in Johnston, Iowa. He now lives in Papillion, Nebraska, and on warm summer days, he can be found riding his Honda Goldwing motorcycle.

DALE FREDERICK SCHRADER, TECHNICAL SERGEANT, E-6, RETIRED

132nd Fighter Wing
Iowa Air National Guard
September 16, 1969–January 29, 1990

D ale lived in the country east of Milo in Belmont Township, near the unincorporated hamlet of Motor, just a stone's throw away from the Marion County line. As a youngster, he rode the same school bus as other Milo boys who would, years later, join him and wear the uniform as a member of the United States military. Brothers Rich and Arnie Greubel, Leroy Rodgers, brothers Albert and Rudy Wadle, Larry Kubli, Dan Dykstra, Jim Heller, and Rick Rodgers bounced on their seats of the school bus with each chuckhole as it made frequent stops on the dusty gravel roads east of Milo. A whole passel of blond-headed girls joined them along the way. The Wright sisters Karen, Cheryl, Polly and Pam and the Rodgers girls, Vivian, Debbie, and Tammy crowded the front seats. None of those girls either confirmed or denied that Dale was the best-behaved kid that ever rode the bus, but there was a reason none of them wore pigtails.

Dale pretty much knew where he wanted to go and what he wanted to do, even as a teenager. He decided that the air national guard would be his path of the future. A waiting list existed for entrance into the air national guard, and Dale tossed his hat into the ring as a junior in high school in November 1968. It wasn't until September 1969, that an available slot opened. Dale readily signed on the dotted line with the guard and awaited basic training. He attended weekend drills for the next three months in Des Moines, and on November 16, 1969, headed to San Antonio, Texas for basic training. While at Lackland AFB, he received his draft notice from the US Army in the mail. His preplanning paid big dividends. Dale graduated from basic training a day after Christmas, on December 26, 1969.

Once back at the guard base in Des Moines, Dale entered on the job training (OJT) with an AFSC of 445X0, warehouse supply technician. There he worked with War Readiness Spares Kit (WRSK) that maintained a ready supply of spare parts for the wartime tasking of aircraft assigned to the unit. He worked in that capacity until March 15, 1970, when he accepted a full-time position as an air technician. He just didn't accept the position, he jumped all over it with joy. However, the new position sent him to an advanced technical school for air ground equipment (AGE). His next stop became Rantoul, Illinois, home of Chanute AFB. When he returned to the 132nd Fighter Wing, he became a member of the Consolidated Aircraft Maintenance Squadron (CAMS) and worked on repair and maintenance of power carts used for startup of aircraft.

Dale kept on the move over the years and sought out opportunities within the organization. In 1974, he transferred to the publications and distribution office (PDO) and worked with Milo boy Rusty Burson. Again in 1977, he transferred back to CAMS as an orderly room administrator and served as the noncommissioned officer in charge (NCOIC).

During Dale's twenty years with the unit, he witnessed three aircraft conversions. The first was from the F-84 to the F-100, and then the A-7 and finally the F-16. If asked, "Where have you been?" Dale's quick reply would be the 1963 Hank Snow rendition of "I've Been Everywhere Man, I've Been Everywhere." He's been to Offutt AFB, Whiteman AFB, Nellis AFB, Kirtland AFB, Howard AFB, Panama,

Chanute AFB, Lackland AFB, Mountain Home AFB, Gulfport, Volk Field, Cold Lake Canadian Forces (CF), Waddington Royal Air Force (RAF), Chitose JASDF (Japan Air Self-Defense Force), and Wendover.

Dale retired on January 29, 1990, just eight months before the Gulf War. Had he stayed longer, his list of stops would have expanded to include a trip to the sandbox.

ROGER MARTIN KEENEY, SPECIALIST FIFTH CLASS, E-5

United States Army Reserve
November 1, 1972–April 1 1978

As a kid, Martin lived across the street from the big swing at the Milo City Park. I often joined him as we both took the simple pleasure of what playground equipment was available. Countless times, we climbed the ladder to the huge slide and placed a sheet of wax paper under our rump as we slid down the biggest entertainment venue in all of Milo. Oh, if only life could have remained that simple and carefree. We often saw each other at high school sporting events several times per week since his older sister, Kayla, played on the basketball and softball teams and regularly contended for state championships.

Martin finished high school in 1970 as he kept abreast of world events. That year, President Nixon approved an invasion of Cambodia, and the antiwar movement continued to grow. Over one hundred thousand protesters marched on Washington DC, and protested the Vietnam War. Even though the Vietnam War seemed to slow down from its peak of 536,000-deployed US soldiers in 1968, over 334,000 US troops remained there in 1970. It was not a good time to be draft-eligible. Martin decided, at the encouragement of his father, Bill, who fought in the Philippines during World War II, that the national guard might be something to consider. A year and a half out of high school, Martin joined the US Army Reserves, located at Fort Des Moines, on November 1, 1972.

Martin headed to basic training at Fort Jackson, South Carolina, and followed that up with another six weeks of advanced infantry training, also held at Fort Jackson. When completed, Martin held the MOS of 63B20, a light vehicle mechanic. Once back at Fort Des Moines, he performed duties as a supply sergeant in the mechanical part warehouse.

During his time in the army reserves, Martin deployed for his two-week summer camp on four occasions to Fort McCoy, Wisconsin. On another occasion, he deployed to Fort Sam Houston, Texas.

Martin easily parlayed his military training into the civilian sector. He worked in the parts department of the local Chevrolet dealership. I often saw him there when I made repairs on my own vehicles. What caught me off guard, however, was the name on his shirt. Everyone at the dealership called him Roger. To me, he was still Martin. Today Martin is retired and still lives in Milo.

OH MY GUARD

I spent twenty-one years in the air national guard. The time quickly sped by. I traveled with the guard to Europe, Japan, Canada, and Puerto Rico. I spent time in all four corners of the United States and multiple stops in between. Most deployments were enjoyable, but a few tested my patience. I stayed at some of the most luxurious hotels imaginable, such as the Embassy Suites in Seattle, or the Scottsdale Plaza resort in Arizona. There the ANG hosted a wine-and-cheese meet and greet for attendees. I deployed to Andrews AFB, Washington DC, where I received a VIP behind-the-scenes tour of the Smithsonian Institute's Air and Space Museum. With my top secret security clearance, I received a private tour of the restricted area called the boneyard, at Davis Monthan AFB, where thousands of aircraft are kept in the dry Arizona desert.

On the flip side, when our unit played war games, I huddled in an open bunker adjacent to the flight line in the predawn darkness of a cold Wisconsin morning while a steady rain fell and only hoped my poncho wouldn't leak. I took ice-cold showers as I stood on wooden pallets in rundown latrine facilities. I dined on cold spaghetti from prepackaged Meals, Ready to Eat (MREs) yet had the good fortune to eat ribeye steak and shrimp cooked on an open grill near the gulf shores. As good friend, coworker, and fellow guardsman Johnny Parkin often told me, "It's all good, brother, it's all good."

Fred Astaire sang in his 1936 musical, *Follow the Fleet:*

> *We joined the Navy to see the world, and what did we see? We saw the sea. We saw the Pacific and Atlantic, but the Atlantic isn't as romantic as it's cracked up to be. We joined the Navy to do or die, but we didn't do and we didn't die. We were much too busy looking at the ocean and the sky. And what did we see? We saw the sea.*

The air national guard, not the US Navy, let me see the world, and what did I see? Unlike Fred Astaire, I didn't see the sea—I saw opportunity. Under the GI Bill, I bought a home with guaranteed GI financing, then later completed my college degree in English back in 1983, as Uncle Sam picked up the tab for my education. The air national guard opened the door for employment in 1981 when I accepted a position as a civilian firefighter with the 132nd Fire and Emergency Services at the Des Moines Airport. Our department provided aerospace fire protection, not only for the squadron of aircraft assigned to military base but the entire airport for commercial passenger travel, cargo aircraft, as well as small corporate aircraft. I retired from that position as an assistant fire chief in 2007 after twenty-six years of service.

In 1987, I transferred out of the fire department in my role as a guardsman and accepted a position as the wing historian for the unit. As much as I loved the fire department, I truly embraced the historian's position. I attended a three-week historian school at Maxwell AFB, Alabama, and became indoctrinated into a fast-paced career that absolutely fascinated me. When I returned, I was the guy—the only guy— responsible for documentation of the unit's activities. I reported to no one other than the base commander. I carried a top secret security clearance and was afforded the opportunity to come and go as I pleased. I sat in on pilot debriefings, looked through logistics and after-action reports, interviewed retirees, made comparisons and contrasts of maintenance records from previous years and documented trends. I reviewed the unit's hours of flight, the mission-capable status of aircraft, analyzed accident reports, examined promotion percentages, and training reports. I asked questions to squadron commanders as to what went right and what were the shortcomings. I gained valuable insight to the inner workings of the unit. Once collected, each year, I submitted a lengthy report to the Air Force Historical Research Center located at Maxwell AFB, as well as the Air National Guard Bureau (ANGB) at Andrews AFB. That position immersed me not just knee-deep but neck-deep to events that shaped the Iowa Air National Guard. In 1993, the military selected my report as the best for all ANG units throughout the entire nation and honored me with the Beckwith Haven's Outstanding Historian Award. As the saying went, with that award plus a dime, I could get a cup of coffee.

Through all those years, my family closely supported me on the deployments away from home. They often joined me at social events sponsored by the guard base. Some of those events included Christmas parties where Santa arrived in the cockpit of either an A-7 or F-16 aircraft and handed out gifts to my kids. There were open houses, air shows, picnics and barbecues, family day at the local Adventureland amusement park, or ANG guard night at the Chicago Cubs AAA affiliate baseball park. I marched in the Milo Fourth of July parade and proudly wore my uniform, along with other military members of American Legion Post 263. I strongly encouraged my two sons, Curt and Ben, to consider joining the military to reap some of the same benefits as I. I didn't pressure them but took every opportunity and pointed out all the good things the military brought my way. One took my advice, one didn't.

On February 17, 2000, thirty years and one week after I enlisted in the USAF, my oldest son Curt, with my nod of approval, joined the Iowa Air National Guard. His mother and I made the pilgrimage at exactly the same time of the year that I completed basic training, thirty years prior, and watched his graduation and parade ceremony. As the TIs barked out marching orders, I looked over my shoulder to see if my old TI was still there. The voiced sounded oh so familiar.

Yes, we visited the Alamo. It did not look the same. It seemed so, so small. But yes, indeed, I did "remember the Alamo." Furthermore, Lackland AFB seemed so, so large! I had great pride that day in 2000 when my son graduated from basic training, and he too became a firefighter. My feelings in 1970 didn't hold a candle to the emotions that welled up in me that day. Old codgers aren't supposed to tear up. Neither are hardened soldiers or tested fireman. But it happened.

However, Curt did not get a DDA assignment. He went to Goodfellow AFB, San Angelo, Texas, for his advanced fire training.

What also caught my attention that day in San Antonio, in the spring of 2000, was a young mother I noticed as she poked around the souvenir section of the base exchange (BX). We glanced at each other, and I detected a tear in her eye. I asked her, "Are you okay?"

Her response was, "I don't know what they did to my son in just six short weeks here that I was not able to do in eighteen years, but I am so thankful for the USAF. God bless them, and God bless the USA."

THE FIRE IS OUT

In an effort to save grain for the war effort during the presidency of Woodrow Wilson (1913–1921), the US Congress passed the temporary Wartime Prohibition Act that prohibited the sale of alcohol above 1.28 percent. The Secretary of the Navy, Josephus Daniels, strictly implemented the act and prohibited alcohol consumption for his navy sailors. He hoped that those restrictions, coupled with an increased number of chaplains within the military ranks, might improve the moral fiber of the sailors. Stewards ordered extra quantities of coffee as a replacement beverage. Thus the name for a cup of coffee among the military became known as a cup of Joe as associated with Joe Daniels, the Secretary of the Navy.

Time has passed. The fire has long been out, and the pot of campfire coffee that sat atop the burned-out bed of coals no longer offers up a sip of Joe. The pot is empty. Those who drank the brew as boys of Milo are now old gray-haired men. The lives of some are gone, like the black mud that once filled the pot. Medical professionals insist that regular consumption of a cup of Joe improves the memory, lowers the risk of diabetes, and boosts our metabolism. Many of the boys of Milo—now the old men of Milo—might disagree.

The unanswered question still remains. Who were these ordinary farm kids, Little Leaguers, Boy Scouts, and high school athletes? These ordinary boys of Milo did extraordinary things when their country called upon them. Once their duty for their country was finished, they went on to become teachers, successful businessman, key employees, doctors, farmers, lawyers, and firemen. I personally knew each and every one. Each different from one another in so many ways, yet each the same as if their inner character shared a common deoxyribonucleic acid (DNA). In the words of Charles Spurgeon, an influential Baptist preacher (1834–1892), "High character might be produced, I suppose, by continued prosperity, but that is very seldom the case. Adversity, however it may appear to be our foe, is our true friend; and after a little acquaintance with it, we receive it as a precious thing—the prophecy of coming joy. It should be no ambition of ours to traverse a path without a thorn or stone."

The character of the boys of Milo cannot be challenged. They walked a rough and rocky path during the Vietnam era. Their legacy will be remembered in the hearts and minds of those who knew them. Their stories will be etched not on gravestones but on the lips of those who say, "Oh, I remember him. He was one of the boys of Milo."

A LOST FARM BOY OR A MISPLACED SOLDIER

I gasp with thought the beautiful land,
Which is intimate yet, but so far from hand.
Years of sweat, with goals unmet,
Things though carefully planned.
My presence here I do regret.
How much longer must I set?
Who but me will plow the field
And plant the corn to later yield?
Winter's scorn, with hearts forlorn.
Who will be their shield?
Let me go, for here I'm foreign.
Why pick me to blow your horn?
Never before have I been away
When time to break the sod or pitch the hay.
I crouch and nod, and feel quite awed.
Is now the time to pray?
Who needs me in fields to plod?
They've always got it, the hand of God.

ABOUT THE AUTHOR

As a youngster, Michael Williams lived in the small Southern Iowa town of Milo during the 1950s and early 1960s where he enjoyed a utopian existence, along with the five hundred residents of the community and a cluster of young boys who shared his passion for life.

He served in the United States Air Force for four years where he spent fifteen months in Southeast Asia, then later joined the air national guard and served another twenty-one years.

He is a graduate of Simpson College with a bachelor's degree in English. For two years, he worked on the editorial staff of the military publication *The Intake*. The last ten years in the military, he served as the historian for the 132nd Fighter Wing. In 1993, he was recognized as the top historian by the National Guard Bureau and again in 1997 recognized as the runner-up.

He is a retired assistant fire chief and lives in Carlisle, Iowa with his wife of fifty years.

9 781638 144328

CPSIA information can be obtained
at www.ICGtesting.com
Printed in the USA
LVHW092152301021
702010LV00001B/1

9 781638 144328